# THE BUILDING OF ETERNAL ROME

LONDON : HUMPHREY MILFORD
OXFORD UNIVERSITY PRESS

TROPAEA AUGUSTI

(*See p. 217*)

# THE BUILDING OF ETERNAL ROME

BY

## EDWARD KENNARD RAND

POPE PROFESSOR OF LATIN EMERITVS
IN HARVARD UNIVERSITY

CAMBRIDGE
HARVARD UNIVERSITY PRESS
1943

PRINTED AT THE HARVARD UNIVERSITY PRINTING OFFICE
CAMBRIDGE, MASSACHUSETTS, U. S. A.

PATRI · MATRIQVE
ET · NVNC · ET · OLIM
AETERNAE · VRBIS · CONCIVIBVS

# PREFACE

ROME was not built in a day; still less can the story of an eternal city be told in the eight hours of a course of lectures. But happily it is also proverbial that all roads lead to Rome; and swift is the journey to it. Swift also is the journey from Rome to many another region in time and space. Any traveller knows the peculiar call that comes from the monuments of every age in Rome.

In Athens the modern city has little to say; and almost as silent, though they can tell a tale worth hearing, are the churches of Byzantine structure and the Tower of Hadrian. They keep discreetly in the background while we pass before the unrivalled relics of Greek archaic art in the Museum, or turning from their place of detention look gratefully at the Parthenon, standing freely among the other wonders of the Acropolis and, with its fallen columns now restored, shining with some of its ancient brightness. In London, history is built into monuments that with a single voice testify to the past; London is established on a solid rock of antiquity in which chronology seems relatively unessential. Paris gleams in the radiance of the present. It is full of history, and opens its secrets to those who will make the quest. But all is caught up into the joyous art of life that only the French understand — yes, even at the present moment, I venture to assert, no brutal tyranny from without can crush that spirit; the boot may stamp, but from underneath, on wings of laughter, the spirit has taken flight.

But in Rome, all moments of history confront us; past and present cry aloud together. If a fortunate youth from our country becomes a student at the American Academy high up on the Janiculum, he finds himself now by the site of the ancient bridge where Horatius and his two companions blocked the Etruscan host, and now by the trenches thrown

up by Garibaldi before the attack on Rome that established
the united kingdom of modern Italy. In the Roman Forum
relics of all periods of the ancient world, Pagan and Christian, clamor for attention, asking not like beggars for our
coins, but like the Ancient Mariner offering us a rich reward
if we listen to their story. So at San Clemente the student of
Roman topography who would inspect the ancient foundations of the church must linger with the verses of Pope
Damasus, set in a glittering mosaic of his time; for the moment, this Classical scholar is living perforce in that great
Fourth Century of the Christian Church. Such experiences
for one whose eyes know what to see are inexhaustible. Inexhaustible is the pleasure of reading Horace or Cicero or
Ovid or any of the Romans in the very City whose streets and
squares and palaces and corners are pictured in their works:

> Nunc et campus et areae . . .
> Composita repetantur hora.

The sense of the might and majesty of the Eternal Rome
was felt at least as far back as the remains of Roman literature
extend, that is, to the age of Ennius at the end of the third
and the beginning of the second century B.C. We will follow
together the history of this sentiment from the days of the
Republic to the establishment of the Ideal Empire under
Augustus and to that of the City of God into which Rome
was transformed, not only by Christian writers, St. Augustine
above all, but almost imperceptibly by such pagan authors as
Cicero and Virgil and even Ovid. With the founding of a
New Rome at Constantinople, the ancient city moved, in a
sense, to new quarters; and from Constantinople it proceeded
to Moscow. And yet it remained on the banks of the Tiber
and is there today, with a world-empire as before; and today
its gates are open to any citizen of whatever country, to any
mind of whatever creed.

In tracing the course of this development, some attention
is paid to the historical background and even to some minor
affairs. At times the treatment might seem purely historical.

But only literature, prose and poetry, gives the full flowering
of history, of science and of art. Sometimes the historian has
examined everything in the garden but the flowers, or treated
them as *epiphenomena*, good enough in their way, as pretty
decorations. I shall endeavor to consider poetry as solid
material for the building of the City, and even, particularly
in the poetry of Virgil and Horace, as part of the foundation
of their sovereign's great design. Moreover, certain monuments of both poetry and prose will be analyzed in such a
way as to present, with many gaps, a series of brief essays, or
remarks, on Latin literature. I hope that this amorphous
feature of my undertaking will not utterly obscure the reader's vision of the one through the many. Now and then the
opinions expressed may well prove unacceptable to other
students of the ancients' works. No one can compass the vast
scope of Rome, but each may travel by the ways that suit his
fancy. It is better to rush in like fools without fear and blaze
a trail, leaving it for angels to broaden and extend the path,
or to show that the end is an *impasse*. Whether exploration
leads to discovery or not, the danger's self is lure alone.

A book like this should be supplemented with the reading
of similar treatises dealing with other aspects of the same
theme. Recent standard works in English on Roman history, like those of Tenney Frank and Rostovtzeff, and on
Roman literature, like those of Duff and Mackail, should be
at the reader's side. Still more closely related are William
Chase Greene's *The Achievement of Rome*, and, for the
daily and the public life of the Romans, Frank Gardner
Moore's *The Roman's World*.

Of prime importance is Grant Showerman's *Eternal Rome*,
in which art is fused with literature and history, all conjured
from the soil itself by one to whom for many years the City had
become a second home. Another of the citizens of the local
and the ideal Rome is Albert William Van Buren, Professor
of Archaeology, editor and librarian at the American Academy in Rome, who keeps us up to date — even up to last May
— with his "News from Rome" in the *American Journal of*

*Archaeology*, and who in his many writings has made one of the most substantial contributions coming from this country to our knowledge of the art, the letters, and the life of Rome.

Our main concern will be with ideals. For only there is firmness found — never in the shifting world of things, events and material inventions. Nor can these form the basis for large surveys of human progress, or regress, or cyclic permutations, with diagrams and terminologies. Progress there has been when some thinker, like Plato, has arisen, to show in myth and poetry new visions of the ideal, or when some watcher of the skies or earth, with telescope or microscope, has found new laws of nature. There was progress when at Christ's coming the principles of a good and happy life set forth by ancient thinkers attained a new fruition, with promise that the Spirit should lead us to new truth. Since then little progress in society has been observed; for governments and men of high estate have been only too swift to lose what once was gained. The present moment seems particularly black; and yet, if one examines minutely any of the periods of human history, the same high villainy, the same petty selfishness, the same disheartening frustration will be discovered.

The remedy does not consist in some political or economic panacea. No flourishing of banners inscribed with watchwords like "Democracy," or "Classless Society," admirable though these terms may be, will guide our feet into the way of peace. The only progress that is sure and measurable is that of the individual, who, like Augustine, in Dante's words, may go from bad to good and from good to better and from better to best, achieving at each step a sense of progress and an abiding calm. One success amid an age of failures saves that age. No law of Utopian attainment may be predicted for the age to follow, nor a law of utter collapse; for the vision of the Eternal City abides above the turmoil as before, ready for human eyes to see.

I wish to express here the gratitude I shall ever feel to the late President Lowell, true friend of the humanities, and to

Mr. Ralph Lowell, his nephew and worthy successor as Director of the Lowell Institute, for their kindness in inviting me to present this series of lectures during February and March of the past year, and to Professor W. H. Lawrence, Curator of the Institute, for many courtesies both before and during the course. Not all of what I had written was given in the lectures; notes have been added, and some slight changes have been made. I have paid little attention, perforce, to certain important works that have appeared since the lectures were delivered. It would have taken, for instance, too intricate an operation to defend or to modify or to abandon certain of my views on Virgil as a result of the vigorous and scholarly Sather Classical Lectures on *The Eclogues of Vergil* which were delivered at the University of California by Professor H. J. Rose of the University of St. Andrews and published in 1942, but too late for my consideration.

Several of my colleagues, in particular Robert Pierpont Blake, Mason Hammond, and Arthur Darby Nock, have been good enough to satisfy some of my inquiries and to refer me to recent literature — but they are not responsible for any indiscretion that I may have committed against their advice. The Harvard Press has exercised the same skillful surveillance that it bestowed on my Lowell Lectures on "Founders of the Middle Ages" in 1929. I am also indebted to Mr. Harold Ferdinand Van Ummersen, Jr., Harvard '44, for help in preparing the Index and for other welcome services.

But the Press could not have proceeded so expeditiously had it not been for the patience, good cheer and expertness with which Mrs. Sylvia Linscott Reynolds, assisted by Mrs. Beatrice Saxesmythe Smith, transformed hieroglyphical first drafts into swift and flawless typing.

EDWARD KENNARD RAND

CAMBRIDGE, MASSACHUSETTS
March 1, 1943.

# CONTENTS

I. FOUNDATIONS: THE REPUBLIC . . . . 3

II. THE IDEAL EMPIRE AND ITS FULFILMENT . . 36

III. ROMAN HIGH SERIOUSNESS AND ROMAN
    LAUGHTER . . . . . . . . 81

IV. THE IVORY GATE . . . . . . . . 115

V. DECLINE AND FALL . . . . . . . 145

VI. THE ROMAN CITY OF GOD . . . . . 180

VII. NEW ROME: EAST AND WEST . . . . . 210

VIII. THE ETERNAL CITY . . . . . . . 253

LIST OF BOOKS . . . . . . . . 287

INDEX . . . . . . . . . . 299

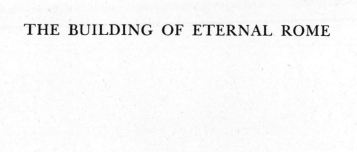

# THE BUILDING OF ETERNAL ROME

# CHAPTER I

## FOUNDATIONS: THE REPUBLIC

Arma virumque cano Troiae qui primus ab oris
Italiam fato profugus Laviniaque venit
Litora   \*   \*   \*   \*   \*   \*   \*   \*   \*
Multa quoque et bello passus, dum conderet urbem
Inferretque deos Latio — genus unde Latinum
Albanique patres atque altae moenia Romae.

Arms, and the man I sing, who forc'd by fate,
And haughty Juno's unrelenting hate,
Expell'd and exiled, left the Trojan shore,
Long labours, both by sea and land, he bore,
And in the doubtful war, before he won
The Latian realm, and built the destin'd town;
His banish'd gods restor'd to rites divine,
And settled sure succession in his line,
From whence the race of Alban fathers come,
And the long glories of majestic Rome.

SUCH is Dryden's stately and resonant translation of Virgil's familiar lines, with a nearer approach to the rich music of Virgil's hexameters than in any rendering that I know. The passage brings back memories of our schooldays, when we, too, suffered many things with Aeneas on land and sea. We were dimly aware that what we dissected and pieced together again was great poetry. I doubt if we caught much of the poet's meaning. His verse flows so smoothly that he seems merely to be telling again a thrice-told tale. We were not aware that he told it for the first time, or that from a tangled mass of tradition preserved for us in various ways by the historians of Rome and the long line of commentators on his poems he selected what suited his purpose, moulded it into a new form with Homer ever in view, brought his gods like Aeneas to Latium, and founded his Rome.

In the long story of which I would present certain episodes, I mean to walk humbly in Virgil's footsteps — *longo nec proximus intervallo* — invite you to see the Rome that he and his predecessors built, and then to contemplate its course down the centuries, ever changing, ever the same, *urbs nova et aeterna*, and finally consider in what sense it exists today. Our concern is not primarily with the external facts of history, though these must form the background: it is rather with the spirit and the genius of Rome, and it is expressed in political institutions, in art and literature, in philosophic thought and in religion. With none of these matters — particularly with Roman art — can our treatment be historically exhaustive, or even adequate. I take refuge in the definition of history given by Mr. Santayana in his latest, and we hope not his last, work, *The Realm of Spirit*:

> History extends a man's dramatic view of his own life and of contemporary society and the past by the aid of documents and monuments. History is true or plausible fiction, such as we compose instinctively concerning one another's motives and mind and even concerning our own.[1]

On this understanding we may fly about in the upper regions of thought and interpretation, safe from the antiaircraft fire of thoroughgoing historians. For even if their bullets hit our diaphanous and autobiographic texture, they merely pass through it without leaving a rent.

The Roman spirit is not primarily creative, like the Greek. It is a spirit that receives, adapts, and conserves. It is more pliant, more urbane, and more human than it is sometimes conceived to be. And it knows how to build. Says Cicero in a work that will much concern us later, his *De Re Publica*: "There is no act in which human virtue approaches more nearly the power of the gods than either to found new states

[1] New York: Scribners, 1940, p. 276, or in the one-volume edition of *Realms of Being*, 1942, p. 830.

or to preserve them when founded." [2] These are the words of a builder.

## I

In watching the laying of the foundation of Rome in the times of the Republic, it is somewhat disconcerting to discover that in the long stretch of years from the traditional date of the beginning of the Republic in 509 B.C. down to the days of Cicero and Caesar, let us say roughly 75 B.C., no complete literary work in Latin prose or poetry, except the comedies of Plautus and Terence, has been preserved to us. For the period in which Plautus and Terence wrote, when Latin literature really began, in the last half of the third century B.C., we have an abundance of other authors' names, but only fragments of their works, cited by later writers. Above this wreckage the comedy of Plautus and Terence smiles, thankful that it alone has brought more than *disiecta membra* to the shore. When, further, we consider the legendary character attributed to much of the Roman history before the Punic Wars, how can we hope from the literary remains to build anything but a mosaic in laying the foundations of ancient Rome? Here, however, a Greek writer, and one of the best, comes suddenly to our aid — one of the Greeks whom Romans had no need to fear when bringing gifts.

## II

In the year 168 B.C. Lucius Aemilius Paulus, the hero of the day, defeated King Philip of Macedon and thereby made Rome Queen of the Mediterranean countries, that is, in effect, sovereign of the western world. In the following year a thousand men of high station, members of the Achaean League, were sent to Rome for trial.

This Achaean League, a revival of an earlier League, was a confederation of most of the Greek states, or rather cities,

[2] I 7. 12: Neque enim est ulla res in qua propius ad deorum numen virtus accedat humana quam civitates aut condere novas aut conservare iam conditas. The text followed is that of C. W. Keyes, with an English translation, in The Loeb Classical Library, 1928.

south of the Gulf of Corinth. North of that Gulf there was a somewhat similar, and hostile, confederation known as the Aetolian League. For something over a hundred years this twofold experiment in confederation had operated, with ups and downs. The Achaean League was at its height from 250 B.C. on. Athens played with it warily, while Sparta, with some of the neighboring cities, stood aloof, in splendid isolation. In the northeast loomed Macedon, the Grecian remnant of the empire of Alexander, still technically, it would seem, the sovereign of all the states of Greece, yet finding them all most refractory participants in the blessings of its New Order.

Some will look back with amusement from our age of boundless terrestrial spaces and teeming populations at these operations of Lilliput, these miniature battles, like those of Virgil's bees. But if we focus our microscopes more sharply or, better, if we do not blur our mental vision by always seeing big, we shall find in the story of this tiny Achaean League principles that govern, or ought to govern, our own democracies. These principles are stated by Polybius.[3] Freedom of speech is one; equality and humanity, the love of one's fellow beings, are the others. And what are these — παρρησία, ἰσότης, φιλανθρωπία — but the only temporarily abandoned motto of liberté, égalité, fraternité? Polybius adds that, when persuasion failed, force won over new adherents, who quickly became reconciled to their new positions. This was a League with teeth.

Now the Achaean League, when hard pressed by the Aeotolian League and by Sparta, had appealed to Macedon. That is why Rome, after absorbing all the contending parties, viewed the recent ally of Macedon with some suspicion and exacted a thousand hostages from the Achaean League.

The new arrivals were distributed among several Italian cities and seem to have made a good impression; at any rate they were never brought to trial. At the end of sixteen years, those who survived were allowed to go home. One of them,

[3] The Histories, with an English translation by W. R. Paton (Loeb Classical Library, 1922), II 38. 6–9.

after a brief visit home, remained for a longer period. He was Polybius, whom I have just quoted, an important officer in the Achaean League, a most informing witness to the building of Rome, and himself, as we shall see, one of the builders. He had been pro-Roman from the start, and may have served with the Romans in their war with the Gauls in Asia Minor in 189 B.C. Besides being a well-educated Greek gentleman, he knew war and politics at first hand. As a student of the philosophy of the state, a philosophy drawn from facts and not imposed upon them, he has few equals, if any, in ancient or in modern times. So thought that man of exceeding wisdom, John Dryden.[4]

Polybius at once became associated with the leading families of Rome, and in fact was taken into the household of the great Aemilius Paulus as the tutor of his two sons, who later were adopted by two Romans no less eminent, the one by Quintus Fabius Maximus Cunctator and the other by Publius Cornelius Scipio Major. Polybius had met them with their father during the war with Philip. The invitation to join their household came about, Polybius tells us,[5] in the following way. He was walking along with Scipio one day when the lad, blushing modestly, asked him why he addressed all his questions at the dinner-table to his brother and none to himself. He was afraid, he said, that Polybius took him to be the weak and un-Roman sort of person that everybody else did. "Not at all," said Polybius. "Your brother is your elder. I took it for granted that you would share his opinions. On the contrary, you are a lad of high spirit. Nothing would please me more than to let you see that you are altogether worthy of your ancestors. In your regular studies, which you and your brother are pursuing with commendable energy and

[4] "The Character of Polybius," a preface to the translation by Sir H. S. (i.e. Sheeres), London, Birscoe, 1793. Sheeres, Dryden remarks, was an admirable man for the task. He was no mere scholar, but, like his author, a great traveller and a master of mathematics, navigation, and military tactics. Dryden's estimate was shared by the late Lawrence Joseph Henderson, who, after his deep reading of Machiavelli and Pareto, could have placed the excellence of Polybius in a new and modern light. *Dis aliter visum est.*

[5] XXXI 23–25. 1. This, says T. R. Glover (*Cambridge Ancient History*, VIII,

emulation, I am sure that you will find plenty of competent teachers, especially since there is nowadays such an influx of learned men from Greece. But in the matter that seems to be your special worry, I think I may be better fitted to be a fellow-contestant and fellow-workman with you (συναγωνιστὴς καὶ συνεργός) than anybody else."

The youth grasped his hand. "Come to me, and live with me, and I shall become worthy of my ancestors," he said. So they did live together, and work together, each striving to prove himself worthy of his task, and, adds Polybius, showing for each other the affection that binds a father to a son.

What volumes of educational theory are written in this brief passage in Polybius, of which I have given the essence! Such a teacher sets before his pupil not a royal road to learning but a hard fight. He is not versed in child psychology. He does not discover that his pupil has a non-Greek or a non-mathematical mind, though he is quite convinced of his intellectual aptitude. He tells him what he has to learn in order to be worthy of his forebears; and he loves him as a son. In the act of contesting and working with his pupil, he learns from him. He makes his pupil mature and his pupil keeps him young.

The Romans were good teachers. They formed character as well as trained the intellect. They justified an educational program by the fact that it did train the character and prepare young men to serve the state. All down the course of Roman history we find teachers of this sort, whether professional teachers or not. So the mind of the young orator Cicero was formed by Crassus and Antonius; so the boys of Piso were instructed by Horace in the art of poetry as Horace himself had been given by his father lessons in the art of life; so Persius learned a noble Stoicism from Cornutus; and so the mind of young Marcus Aurelius, as we shall see,[6] was trained by his master Fronto to live again in that ancient Republican

---

8), quoting Ward Fowler, is "one of the most delightful passages in all ancient literature."

[6] See Chapter V.

Rome which Polybius had come to describe. Thus Rome was built by well-built men. The Romans liked to hand things down, not only worldly goods, but educated character.

## III

Polybius was, as we have seen, pro-Roman from the start. He scented from afar the inevitable destiny of Rome, the *fatum Romanum*, and warned his fellow members of the Achaean League to submit to it. While he insists in his book that no episode in history can be understood without its general context, and hence presents the complete course of current events in every important country, he centres his attention on the history of Rome in the fifty-three years that preceded the Battle of Pydna in 168. His subject was the rise and triumph of the Roman state. He began his work in Rome, at the moment of high tide. He was a foreigner, but sometimes a foreigner can better interpret a nation to itself than can one of its own number. Natives may take as matters of course what foreigners discover are national characteristics. Thus we saw ourselves in Lord Bryce's *The American Commonwealth*; thus the English better knew how they were governed from Lowell's *The Government of England*; and thus for the ancient Romans and for readers in every age Republican Rome is writ large in the *Histories* of Polybius.

If I have implied that we have this work intact, that is unhappily not the case. Fate has been as unkind to his masterpiece as to that of Livy. Were the gods enraged at Greece and Rome that they should conduct a *Blitzkrieg* — if my reader will pardon the word — on so many of their literary monuments? Of the forty books that the *Histories* of Polybius comprised, only the first five have been preserved intact. Yet significant portions of the rest have come down to us, mainly in a series of excerpts, which we shall consider later,[7] prepared for that enlightened Emperor of the East, Constantine VII Porphyrogenitus, who ruled from A.D. 912 to 959. All in all, there are sufficient portions of the *Histories* of Polybius extant

[7] See Chapter VII, note 48.

to give us a tolerably satisfactory idea of its scope, with its priceless information on the Roman army of his days, on Roman tactics and strategy, on the Roman government, and on Roman character.

The critical historian of today values Polybius chiefly because of his objectivity, his impassioned search for historical truth without fear or favor, his researches in the Roman archives, his travels to examine events in the spot where they occurred — his attempt,[8] for instance, to ascertain by wandering in the Alps just where Hannibal crossed those summits on his way to Italy — his elimination of miracles and his quest of natural causes. Such an historian, if he did not know the real Polybius, might place him in the school of Aristotle rather than that of Plato, who is anathema to many men of science today. For is not Aristotle the critical examiner of numerous city governments, which he dissected as scientifically as he dissected fishes? And is not Plato a dreamer, a poet, who though he excluded all other poets from his *Republic* remained there himself?

None the less, the political science of Polybius is drawn straight from Plato, as he tells us. He gives Aristotle due praise for his cool-headed accuracy[9] and rules out Plato's *Republic* from his own discussion, which is concerned with actual governments and not ideal.[10] But his classification and his estimate of governments[11] are taken from a passage in Plato's *Statesman;*[12] for Plato can sober down. Aristotle reproduced Plato's ideas in his *Politics,*[13] a work, at least in modern times, of greater fame. Polybius, in any case, as a scientific historian, quotes the primary and not a secondary source.[14]

---

[8] III 47–48.

[9] XII 5–9. He is here defending Aristotle from the attacks of Timaeus, a mendacious historian who professed a scrupulous attachment to the truth.

[10] VI 45, 47. 7–8.                                                    [11] VI 3–5.

[12] *Politicus* (302 c) gives the gist of the matter, but one should begin with 291 d, or rather at the beginning of the treatise, to understand the subtlety and playful irony with which Plato, using fact and reason and myth, discusses the question. Santayana may have learned his art of history from Plato.

[13] IV 2.

[14] Of course Plato was not the first to analyze the nature of governments. See J. H. Finley, *Thucydides* (Harvard University Press, 1942), pp. 45–48.

There are six forms of government in all, according to Polybius, three good and three bad; the latter are travesties or corruptions of the former. There is, first, kingship (βασιλεία), which degenerates into monarchy (μοναρχία). The second is aristocracy (ἀριστοκρατία), the perversion of which is oligarchy (ὀλιγαρχία). The third is democracy (δημοκρατία); sinking into its corruption it becomes something for which Plato had no exact name but for which Polybius invents a splendid one, "ochlocracy" (ὀχλοκρατία), a more elegant equivalent of that hybrid form "mobocracy" which we sometimes hear.

The historical process, according to Polybius, is this. Mankind starts off in a blissful anarchy, which theoretically, anybody but a politician will admit, is the best of all governments, even as Tacitus describes it.[15] But a ruler arises to quell the inevitable confusion, and if the ruler is benevolent the rule is true kingship. But if he is bad and lustful for power, his rule becomes not kingship but monarchy. One thinks not of a person, a kindly king, but of a one-man (μόνος) government, that is, a tyranny, as Plato and Aristotle would say, or an autocracy.

Monarchy, in Polybius's sense, cannot be endured forever; the best of the citizens (οἱ ἄριστοι) rebel, and drive the tyrant from his throne. They rule, and when they rule benevolently their rule is good. But squeeze personality from their administration, they are no longer "the best," but "the few" — another merely numerical term. Those beneath them, the people (ὁ δῆμος), arise in wrath, and so long as their government is based on law and order it abides. But that, too, does not last forever. Its officials lose the virtues that gave them the right to rule. They in turn become mere numbers, and constitute a mob. Ochlocracy has its day; we thus go back to the original anarchy, and the ancient process starts once more. No wonder that, with this sequence in mind, this governmental cycle (πολιτείων ἀνακύκλωσις),[16] Polybius is keen to examine the condition of any particular government and to prophesy about how long it will last before the next stage

---

[15] *Annales* III 26.                    [16] VI 9. 10.

comes on. This art of political prophecy he might have taken
from Thucydides.[17] Polybius, like Thucydides, is no less
intent on causal sequence than are modern students of human
society. He differs both from the cheerful optimists of the
nineteenth century, the "heirs of all the ages in the foremost
files of time," and from the deep-browed pessimists of any
age, and from the determinists of the Spenglerian school, who
set their cycles going and watch them run. For Polybius is
aware of the human and unpredictable factors in the process.
He therefore finds no place for permanent hope or permanent
despair. A solid structure is possible only if it is founded on
Platonic ideas, on freedom and justice, on the *liberté, égalité,
fraternité* of the Achaean League. But men are not angels.
They begin well, misbehave, and down they go — it all is as
simple as that.

The task of the philosophical statesman, therefore, is to
choose the best and most durable of the possible forms of
government. Polybius will not, however, prescribe any one
of the three. Do not think, because he sounds so often a note
that we should call democratic today, that he would favor our
modern democracy as a form of government. Far from it.
The ideal government, to his mind, is composed of all the
three forms. Waiving his precise terms, we may recognize
here a tripartite society with a top, a middle, and a bottom.
We see that each of the three classes for its own well-being
must consider the welfare of the other two. This is a system
of checks and balances. It is the *concordia ordinum* of Cicero
and Livy; it is the *suum cuique* of Cicero; [18] the idea is implicit in the systems of Plato and Aristotle. The car of government, if constituted on such principles, ought to run
on forever — provided that the drivers are as mechanically
perfect.

The credit for putting this political theory into effect is
given by Polybius to Lycurgus. Like Plato and others before
him, he seems surer of the historicity of that personage than

[17] Finley *op. cit.*, Index, *s.v.* History.
[18] *De Re Publica* III 15. 24.

are some of our historians today. His date has been variously
assigned. If we say round about 800 B.C., that will at least
indicate a period before the traditional date, 754–752, of the
founding of the city of Rome.

Now Polybius finds [19] that exactly what Lycurgus had
thought out the Romans discovered by dint of experience, of
many struggles and hardships.[20] This is his tribute to the
genius of Rome. He also praises Roman character, in various
passages of his work. He admires the Romans' sense of organization and the gallantry of the individual soldier,[21] their
energy and their extraordinary audacity in building a navy
when they knew nothing of naval warfare,[22] their pushing
ahead in campaigns far afield when plentifully occupied with
the war against Carthage.[23] The invincible Roman soul is
undaunted by defeat; their fleet is destroyed and they build
another.[24] Says Horace of this disaster:

You may sink her in the depths; more beautiful she rises.[25]

She fights fairly, Polybius goes on to say. Some have ac-
cused her of cruelty to Carthage when that city was razed to
the ground,[26] but in general the Romans waged war simply
and nobly, ἁπλῶς καὶ γενναίως, abstaining from night attacks
and ambuscades and from any kind of deceit or trickery.[27]

The ancients, both in the Roman state and elsewhere, Polybius declares,[28] went even farther in decorum. They did not
approve the use of secret weapons, or those flung from afar.
Nothing but the good old hand-to-hand attack was quite
honest — what they would have thought of poison gas we can

[19] VI 10. 12–14.
[20] So Virgil's hero (*Aen.* I 204):

> per varios casus, per tot discrimina rerum
> tendimus in Latium.

[21] I 64.
[22] I 20.
[23] VII 1. This is the spirit that Lucan, *malgré lui*, recognized in Julius
Caesar (*De Bello Civili* II 657): nil actum credens cum quid superesset agen-
dum ("Thinking naught done when aught remained to do").
[24] I 55, 59.
[25] *Odes* IV 4. 65: Merses profundo, pulchrior evenit.          [26] XXXVI 9.
[27] XXXVI 9. 9.          [28] XIII 3.

readily guess. Further, they declared wars decently and in order, by a liturgical rite. They informed the enemy just when and just where they were going to attack. On one occasion, as Livy tells us,[29] there was even a referee. At the end of the bloody battle fought between the Romans of the new republic and the exiled Tarquins with their Tuscan allies, the result was uncertain. Then in the silence of the answering night a mighty voice was heard from the Arsian wood — the voice of the woodland god Silvanus, so the story ran — and thus it spake: "One more of the Tuscans has fallen in the fray: the Romans are victors in this battle." Of course, then, adds Livy, the Romans left the field as the victors, the Etruscans as the vanquished.[30]

Not only in war, but in private life and in public life, the Romans, Polybius tells us, were conspicuously fair-dealing. "Honest man" and "politician" were for them convertible terms. The virtue of honesty was noticeably rarer, he admits, among both Greeks and Carthaginians.[31] For Romans the acceptance of bribes brought the death penalty. Aemilius Paulus had the chance, if anybody had, to amass a fortune from the spoils of Pydna; and yet he died a poor man.[32]

Nor did Romans fight merely to crush the foe irretrievably. When he was reproached by the Aetolians for not dealing a knockout blow to Philip after the victory at Pydna, Flamininus, who spoke for the Romans at the Peace Conference held at Tempe, declared that it was not the Roman way to exterminate their adversaries.[33] "When in the field of battle," he said, "good men must be rough and wrathful." They must, in Shakespeare's words,

> Disguise fair nature with hard-featur'd rage.

"When they are conquered," Flamininus adds, "they will show themselves noble and high of spirit, and when they con-

---

[29] *Hist.* II 7. 2.

[30] Football has sometimes been compared, not with a complimentary intent, to war. It would be more appropriate to compare primitive warfare to football.

[31] VI 56.

[32] XVIII 35.

[33] XXVIII 37. 6–7.

quer, prove moderate, mild, and humane (φιλανθρώπους)."
When Virgil exhorts the Romans

> To build order upon peace,
> To spare the conquered and subdue the proud,[34]

he is not startling them with novel counsel; he is reminding
them — *memento*, he says — of the virtues of their ancestors;
he appeals to *noblesse oblige*.

The Roman trait that most impressed Polybius as distinctive and admirable was their devotion to religion.[35] What
impressed the *illuminati* among the Greeks and other peoples
as childish superstition was exalted by the Romans into a national virtue and guarded with fit pomp and ceremony. All
this, Polybius infers, was the invention of the wise men of old,
who by stimulating devotion to the gods and the fear of Hell
restrained the base instincts of the fickle mob. Those enlightened moderns, he adds, who throw all that to the winds,
are acting rashly. One sees the result in the dishonesty rampant in Greek politics and the integrity that prevails in
Roman. Polybius has no childlike faith in gods or myths, but
he at least had discovered a use for religion; wherefore by
its fruits shall ye know it.

There must, I think, be something more in it than that.
You can fool some of the people some of the time but none of
them all the time. Awe, not fear or priestcraft, made the first
gods. Livy, who describes the institution of religion in much
the same vein as Polybius,[36] confessed that as he pondered the
records of the past his mind adapted itself to the religious
faith of his ancestors. "My mind becomes ancient," he declares.[37] I feel, as I turn the pages of Polybius, that his was
much the same experience. Polybius is never disrespectful

---

[34] *Aen.* VI 851–853: Tu regere imperio populos, Romane, memento; Hae
tibi erunt artes: pacique imponere morem, Parcere subiectis et debellare
superbos. So Premier Churchill has spoken, more than once.

[35] VI 56. 6–15.                                        [36] *Hist.* I 19. 5.

[37] *Hist.* XLIII 13. 2: ceterum et mihi vetustas res scribenti nescio quo pacto
antiquus fit animus et quaedam religio tenet quae illi prudentissimi viri pu-
blice suscipienda censuerint ea pro indignis habere quae in meos annales
referam.

towards religious rites; there are touches of humor, and even flippancy, in Livy that are absent in him. He has somewhat gone over to Rome.

A deeper reading of the Roman religious sense we find in Horace. He almost might seem to be putting into verse the sentiment of this chapter of Polybius to which I have referred, but with a difference. "Because thou dost order thyself humbly before thy gods, hence thou dost rule," says Horace with an imperial brevity not to be caught in English:

Dis te minorem quod geris imperas.[38]

Perhaps there is a brief rendering after all: "The meek shall inherit the earth." This might not seem a characteristically pre-Christian Roman utterance; but it is precisely what Horace means. He is thinking of the times that Polybius described and he is addressing not only the Roman state but, as is clear in other odes, its ruler.[39]

Such are the stones, some few of them, that Polybius brought for the building of Rome. The later poets back up his observations by their testimony to the heritage of the Roman virtues that had descended to them from the past. He described what he saw in actual operation. He recognized in the government at work the principles that he had himself thought out, with the help of various Greek thinkers besides Plato and of his own study of other states. He taught those principles to his pupil, the younger Scipio Africanus, who appreciated the nobility of his ancestors, but may not have known that the structure they had built by experience had a high philosophical sanction. Thus the services of Polybius both to the Roman State and to the intellectual life of the day are of the highest order.[40]

[38] *Odes* III 6. 5.

[39] The submission of the Ruler of the State to the King of Heaven is described with an equal brevity in *Odes* I 12. 57: Te minor latum reget aequus orbem.

[40] It is strange that Polybius is treated only incidentally in modern histories of Latin literature. He deserves a chapter of his own. Perhaps some bold innovator will translate appropriate selections from Polybius into ante-Ciceronian Latin to accompany the reading of our fragmentary texts of the early Republic.

## IV

Polybius was not the only private tutor who formed the mind and the soul of young Scipio. Another resident in his household was the Stoic philosopher, Panaetius. He was no hard-shelled Stoic. His divine sage, his Homer, among philosophers, Cicero tells us,[41] was Plato. The two masters worked harmoniously to form the character of their young charge. Nor were they alone in their great mission to Rome; think of the other members of that delegation of one thousand, distributed among the various cities of Italy. Nor should we forget another philosophic invasion of Rome in 156–155 B.C., when three philosophers visited the city — Carneades the Academic, Diogenes the Stoic, and Critolaus the Peripatetic. They offered a varied feast of reason, especially Carneades, who represented the sceptical tendency that had invaded Plato's Academy. No greater sceptic ever existed than Plato himself, if we take scepticism in its original sense of unfettered inquiry. But when scepticism had come to mean a doubting of the validity of the quest itself, and when Carneades one day would establish a thesis in an impregnable citadel and the next day knock the citadel over, we can see that the Romans could at least imbibe enough philosophy to turn their heads.

There speedily were established, in consequence, two schools among thoughtful Romans, such as exist in any age: the progressives, or *illuminati,* who welcomed Greek culture with all that it implied, and the conservatives, who resisted the new learning as subversive of the sturdy virtues of the fathers. Foremost among the conservatives was Marcus Porcius Cato the Censor, a one-hundred-per-cent Roman, who

And why should not this translator be the Public Orator of the University of Cambridge? (See Note 5.)

For a discriminating eulogy of Polybius see the lamented Tenney Frank in his great book *Life and Literature in the Roman Republic* (1930), pp. 182–185. He is bold enough to suggest that Polybius's contact with matter-of-fact and legal-minded Roman senators induced him to adopt some of their manners and methods. What heresy! But think it over.

[41] Cicero. *Tusc. Disp.* I 79: quem omnibus locis divinum, quem sapientissimum, quem sanctissimum, quem Homerum philosophorum appellat.

detested Greek luxury and learned the Greek language, it would seem, with something of a protest, yet who was enlightened enough to secure permission for Polybius and his fellow hostages to return to their native land.[42] Polybius, in his turn, was, even before this event, not unkindly disposed towards Cato. He quotes his tart witticisms [43] and shared his detestation of the sham Hellenomaniacs of Rome; [44] for a true Greek then, like a true Britisher today, is not blind to imitations.

A mirror of the circle of the younger Scipio and his friends [45] is given in one of the most remarkable of Roman writings, Cicero's work on the State, his *De Re Publica*. At least we have shattered fragments of that mirror, shattered again by the wrath of the gods. Leaves from a palimpsest manuscript of the famous monastery of Bobbio were found by that *scopritor felice*, as Leopardi calls him, Angelo Cardinal Mai, and were published by him in 1822.[46] Pieced together with numerous quotations by later authors, to whom we shall later pay due respect,[47] and supplemented by the *Dream of Scipio* with which the last book ends, they at least set forth the main argument and, what is more, reveal both the mind of Cicero and the culture attained by Scipio and the élite of Rome in his day.[48]

[42] XXXV 6.

[43] XXXI 25. 5, XXXVI 14. He despaired of prompt action in a certain negotiation, since the envoys, he declared, possessed neither feet nor a head nor a heart.

[44] Such as Aulus Postumius (XXXIX 1) who wrote a history in Greek and apologized to his Roman readers for his insufficient command of the language. So might a boxer, said Cato, before pitching into his opponent, crave the indulgence of the spectators if he were knocked out in the first round. Moral: better not fight (or write) at all. This Aulus Postumius was obviously a cad.

[45] For an excellent brief account of this "Scipionic circle," see H. J. Rose, *A Handbook of Latin Literature* (1936), pp. 98–100.

[46] This work contains not only the *editio princeps* of the text, but a most valuable introduction and useful annotations.

[47] See Chapter VI on Lactantius and St. Augustine.

[48] We owe to a successor and peer of Cardinal Mai, Giovanni Cardinal Mercati, one of the foremost scholars and Christian humanists of our time, a lifelike reproduction of the remaining leaves of the ancient manuscript of this work, with an introduction on the monastery of Bobbio that leaves no gleanings for reapers in this field. See *Codices e Vaticanis selecti quam simillime expressi iussu Pii XI P.M.*, Vol. XXIII, *ex Bibl. Vat.* 1934. The remaining

When Cicero's political career was ended, though at the time he seemed blissfully unaware of its end, he began to record, in a noble series of works, his experience in statecraft, in oratory, and in philosophic thought. He wrote out at white heat, and polished in his impeccable style, the reflections on all these matters that had been mellowing in his mind since the beginning of his career. He is said to have called these works mere copies, ἀπόγραφα, of his Greek originals; they furnish the thought, and he the words, in which, as he says, with a pleasant laugh at himself, he abounded. Many modern scholars, unwilling to credit Cicero with either occasional originality or an occasional modesty, or a relish for banter with his friend Atticus, take him at his word.[49]

The first of these works are the *De Oratore* (55 B.C.) and the *De Re Publica*. However much translation they contain, they both, in different ways, are monuments of the many-faceted humanism of Cicero.

The *De Re Publica* was begun early in 54 B.C., and after interruptions and changes of plan was finished two or three years later. When we note that it was followed by a treatise on *The Laws* (*Leges*), we think at once of the Πολιτεία and the Νόμοι of Plato and expect from Cicero, if we cherish the usual opinion of his originality, nothing more than a harnessing of

gatherings and separate leaves of the old manuscript were probably kept at Bobbio in a collection with other fragments to be cleaned of their script and used for other works. The slender columns on which Cicero's work was written left tempting spaces on the page. The leaves were used again for a Christian work, St. Augustine's commentary on the Psalms, not because Cicero was a contemptible pagan but because parchment was dear. The leaves and gatherings were taken at random and inscribed with Augustine's work. Cardinal Mai attempted with considerable success to plot their original order (see the work cited in note 46, pp. xxvii-xxx), and Cardinal Mercati improved Mai's analysis with his usual *curiosa felicitas*.

[49] *Ad Atticum* XII 52. 3: De lingua Latina securi es animi. Dices, 'Qui talia conscribis?' ἀπόγραφα sunt, minore labore fiunt; verba tantum adfero quibus abundo. This little paragraph comes at the end of a brief letter of miscellaneous contents. No mention is made of the philosophical works at all. As Schwabe in his revision of Teuffel (*Gesch. der römischen Literatur*, 1890, § 132. 2, p. 339 [translation by G. W. C. Warr, London and Cambridge, 1891, I, 301]) well remarks, there is not the same degree of dependence in all these works. Little in Book I of the *Tusculan Disputations*, and little in the present work according to R. Hirzel (*Der Dialog*, p. 469), who gives an exceedingly competent analysis of *De Re Publica*.

Plato's high-ranging thought to the easy elegance of his own periods — to the words in which he abounded. But no guess could be farther from the mark. Cicero, like Panaetius, held Plato to be the prince of philosophers,[50] and gives him due homage in the present work. Plato furnishes many points and the general frame; but this is filled with a new picture.[51]

We should, of course, remembering the nature of the ancient dialogue, and the liberties taken by Plato in using Socrates, sometimes, as a mouthpiece for his own ideas, expect some element of fiction in Cicero's dialogue on the state. In fact he tells us as much in a letter to his friend Atticus.[52] And yet the setting of the dialogue may not have been altogether imaginary. Cicero tells us that such a conversation was actually reported to him by one of those who had taken part in it. This was Publius Rutilius Rufus, with whom he spent several days at Smyrna, where the old gentleman was spending a pleasant sort of exile. There is no reason to deny the actuality of this meeting. It would have taken place during Cicero's early travels in Greece and Asia Minor during the years 79 to 77 B.C.[53] Rutilius was a youth at the time of the gathering at Scipio's house, set by Cicero in the year 129 B.C. He was consul in 105 B.C. He would have been in his seventies when Cicero, aged twenty-eight, met him at Smyrna. Scipio was therefore to young Cicero no legendary figure of the vanished past, but as near as, let us say, Grover Cleveland would

---

[50] *Tusc. Disp.* I 22 (Aristotle is a close second), 49, 55 *et al.*

[51] Cicero had at first intended, so he writes his brother Quintus (III 5. 1), to put forth his views on the best sort of government in the setting of a conversation held by the younger Scipio and some of his friends shortly before Scipio's death. But a friend pointed out that the modern reader would prefer something real and immediate, based on the experience of a great statesman like Cicero. But this tempting design somehow did not succeed. He accordingly returned, with happy results for posterity, to his original idea.

[52] IV 16. 2.

[53] Cicero also had other talks with Rutilius at Smyrna (*Brutus* 85). Obviously not all of the six books of this work could have been delivered in one *conversazione*. Just the *Dream of Scipio* in Book VI would have sufficed. In fact when we find that with the end of Book II the end of one day is marked (II 70: *finis disputandi in eum diem factus est*), it is natural to suppose that each book occupied a day, whether in reality or because Cicero amplified the original one-day talk into six.

be to a young lawyer of today to whom an elderly statesman reported some stirring conversation at the Cosmopolitan Club before Cleveland's second term began. Doubtless Cicero amplified and embellished what he had heard from Rutilius, but he may have heard no brief account. For, before the printing-press was invented, men had better memories than we,[54] and old men always have tongues.

Another and a most important consideration is that, when we listen to Scipio's discourse on the best kind of government, we seem to hear Polybius speaking again.[55] We find that there are three kinds of government, a kingdom (*regnum*), an aristocracy, or government of the *optimates*, and a democracy, or *civitas popularis*, in which the people are the sole source of authority — *in qua in populo sunt omnia*. Any one of these modes which abides by the principle of social equity may not be perfect or the best possible form, but yet it can be endured.[56] This binding principle is the concordant respect for law in the interests of a common utility. The motive is not a feeling of weakness, but an innate desire for a unified life. For no man liveth to himself alone. Man is not naturally individualistic, or in Cicero's more picturesque epithet, "lone-wandering" (*solivagus*). *Concordia* is the key-word in this analysis of human society.[57]

Therefore, any of the three forms of government that remains true to this principle is a good and tolerable government. Cyrus the Persian was a most just and sapient king. Marseilles is governed by its first citizens with complete justice, and Athens, for a time, kept true to the laws and decrees of the people.[58] But corruption and the lust of power creep

---

[54] Cicero himself (*Tusc. Disp.* I 79) cites cases of remarkable memories, including that of Hortensius, his rival in the courts of law. Hortensius could memorize not only his own speech, as any orator had to do, but that of his opponent, and thus possessed a terrific advantage when it came to rebuttal.

[55] Cardinal Mai was more alive to the importance of Polybius in the *De Re Publica* than are most scholars of our day. See *op. cit.* (above, note 46), p. viii: Ergo Polybium praecipue spectans Cicero dialogos suos de rep. in Scipionis Aemiliani et personam et aetatem contulit.

[56] *De Re Publ.* I 42.

[57] I 39.

[58] I 43.

in, and we find a Phalaris, an Athens under the Thirty, and
an Athens given over to the fury and the lawlessness of the
mob.[59] There are seeds of great danger in a democracy; for
the very principle of equality is unjust, since it contains no
grades of dignity.[60] The conception of a "classless society,"
Scipio would argue, is not true to the facts of existence or fair
to those who have an inborn capacity to rise. At the same
time, the worst form of government is that in which the
richest citizens are accounted the best[61] — malefactors of great
wealth, shall we say? The state must be governed by virtue.
The ideal ruler, while governing the other citizens, must not
himself be the slave of greed. He does not impose on the
people laws that he himself does not obey; he must offer them
his own life as a law.[62]

But the ruler needs support. The best government consists
in an equitable combination of all three forms. The king is
the father of his people, the aristocracy furnish him with
varied counsel, the people gladly obey but cannot serve either
one or the other. They must have freedom; for nothing is
sweeter than freedom. A state that combines these three elements is a musical harmony,[63] and it is patterned on the divine
government. Like the astronomer poet Aratus,[64] whom St.
Paul also quotes in his sermon on Mars' Hill,[65] Scipio would
begin with Jove; [66] the state must be founded on religion.

All this in its essence is straight Polybius. In fact, Scipio is
made to declare that he had often talked over these matters
with Polybius, together with Panaetius.[67] His arguments are

---

[59] I 44.

[60] I 43: ipsa aequabilitas est iniqua, cum habet nullos gradus dignitatis (so
I 53).    [61] I 51.

[62] I 52: nec leges inponit populo quibus ipse non pareat sed suam vitam ut
legem praefert suis civibus. So King Numa as Livy describes him (I 21. 2).

[63] II 69.

[64] I 1: Ἐκ Διὸς ἀρχώμεσθα.

[65] Acts 17. 28: ἐκ τοῦ γὰρ γένος ἐσμέν. Since St. Paul says "poets," he probably also had in mind the phrase in the noble hymn, or prayer, of Cleanthes:
ἐκ σοῦ γὰρ γένος ἐσμέν. See Chapter VI, note 22.

[66] I 56: Imitemur ergo Aratum, qui magnis de rebus dicere exordiens a Iove
incipiendum putat. Cf. also Virgil Ecl. III 60, and Horace, Odes I 12. 13–16;
III 1. 5–8. The poets are confirming Cicero's Scipio as they confirmed Polybius.

[67] I 34.

also mingled with drafts direct from Plato, including [68] a passage from the *Republic* on democratic freedom and its abuse.[69] This young Roman had been fed by his tutors with Plato. From his parents and his ancestors he had received the duty of administering the government of the state. The youth whom Polybius instructed has indeed proved worthy of his lineage. He is grateful for the precepts of a liberal education that he has received; yet he speaks not as a philosopher but as a plain Roman citizen, *unus e togatis,* who with the passion for discovery kindled in him has learned from experience and from "household precepts" more than he learned from books.[70]

These principles of political theory we may gather mainly from the fragments of Book I, which is devoted to the theoretical aspects of government. Doubtless there are flavorings of Cicero's own reading, his own reflections, and his own experience,[71] though it were hard to make out just where they come in. Whatever they were, they fit admirably into the political theory propounded by Polybius.

When we turn to Book II, the marks of Polybius are still more in evidence. For here we have a most careful exposition of the theme that the virtues of the tri-formed government had been recognized intuitively by the ancient Romans without the help of Greek philosophy. This, as we have seen,[72] is one of the leading ideas of Polybius. But we are somewhat startled to find Cicero attributing it to none other than old Cato.[73] Cicero is not, with undue patriotism, leaving the foreign historian out of the count. Quite the contrary. He has naught but praise for Polybius. He pictures young Scipio discussing this very question of the pre-eminence of the Roman state with those "experts in political science," Polybius and

[68] I 66–67.
[69] VIII 562 c–563 e. Cicero skillfully gives the gist of the passage without attempting an exact translation.
[70] I 35–37 (36: unum e togatis patris diligentia non inliberaliter institutum studioque discendi a pueritia incensum).
[71] See I 13, and above, note 53.
[72] See above, note 19.
[73] II 2.

Panaetius.[74] But he mentions Cato rather than Polybius in the present passage because he is beginning with Romulus,[75] whereas Polybius's description is confined to the times within his historical grasp. The story is continued in the part of Book II now extant no further than the year 445.[76] Cicero, therefore, presumably following Cato in his famous work called *Origines*,[77] had no reason, for this part of his discourse, to mention Polybius at all. If Polybius borrowed his leading idea from Cato, he amply demonstrated it in his analysis of contemporary history. If Cato caught it up from the courteous foreigner, he intended to show that it applied not only to the present but to the remotest past. No wonder that the historian Niebuhr regarded the loss of Cato's *Origines* as one of the major losses of Latin literature.[78]

Surely Cato was a great man in the eyes of Scipio, at least as Scipio is presented in this dialogue. He had known him since boyhood, he is made to declare, as the admired friend of both his fathers, and never could tire of his talk. For his lengthy experience both in political office and in war was illuminat-

[74] I 34: memineram persaepe te cum Panaetio disserere solitum coram Polybio, duobus Graecis vel peritissimis rerum civilium multaque colligere ac docere optimum longe statum civitatis eum quem maiores nostri reliquissent.

[75] Along with Remus and the wolf. That part of the story, he declares, is involved in myth, but true history begins with the capture of Alba Longa and the assassination of King Amulius (II 4). This is substantially the treatment of the beginnings of Rome given in the preface (6–7) to his *History* by Livy, who perhaps had this passage of Cicero in mind.

[76] II 63. Although there are several lengthy gaps in the text, due to the loss of leaves in the old manuscript, Cicero's historical argument appears to stop not many leaves later (end of 63) with the words: ⟨maio⟩res nostros et probavisse maxime et retinuisse sapientissime iudico. The talk then turns to the nature of the ideal state and the ideal ruler. That leads to a preliminary examination of justice as the base of the true state, and thus a transition is effected to the argument of the following book.

[77] II 3: Quam ob rem, ut ille solebat, ita nunc mea repetet oratio populi Romani originem; libenter enim etiam verbo utor Catonis. In treating Cato's subject, he is glad to use Cato's term.

[78] Niebuhr declared that if he could conjure the spirits to restore just one of the lost works of the Romans, that work would be the *Origines* of Cato (*Röm. Gesch. nach Niebuhrs Vorträgen* von L. Schmitz [Zeiss] I, Jena, 1844, p. 56). See Schanz, *Gesch. der röm. Litteratur*, 68 (I [1907³]), p. 257. Schanz makes it probable that though the latter part was the work of Cato's old age, Books I–III, on the *Origines*, were written by 168 B.C., the year before Polybius came to Rome.

ing, and his oratorical style showed a happy combination of the grave and the gay. In his case the style was the man.[79] It would almost seem, in the present passage, as if Cato were a member of the Scipionic circle; and indeed conservatives do dine with progressives now and then, especially if a goodly dinner, with proper accompaniments, is served. For Cicero, in any case, as he looks back on the culture of the preceding century, the temperament of a Cato forms a notable part of its richness.

We need not linger on Cicero's review of the early centuries of Roman history. We may pause for just two points. One is the relation of the constitution of Romulus to that of Lycurgus of Sparta. The latter had been established, but not long before.[80] We may wonder once more whether Polybius may not have associated Romulus with Lycurgus in the same fashion.

Another point, of all importance, is that religion was firmly built into the constitution of the state. What Romulus began, Numa completed.[81] In fact the golden age appeared to have returned with Numa — an age of justice and peace and religion. He is thus the founder of that *humanitas* that turned the primitives from beasts into human beings. Livy paints a similarly idyllic picture of the reign of good King Numa,[82] and Polybius was at least enough interested in Numa to examine the question of his date and the length of his reign, with his usual exactness in matters of chronology, as Cicero admiringly informs us.[83] Indeed it is quite clear that Polybius, whatever the scope of his Roman history, did not exclude the early part as unworthy of scientific consideration.

The remaining books of the *De Re Publica*, represented by

---

[79] II 1: orationi vita admodum congruens. Cicero has anticipated Buffon's *mot.*

[80] II 15: paulo ante. For similarities between the constitution of Romulus and Lycurgus see II 50, and for the Romans' ability to improve on what they found, II 24, 42–43.

[81] II 17, 26.

[82] *Hist.* I 18–21, especially 21. 1–3.

[83] II 27: sequamur enim potissimum Polybium nostrum, quo nemo fuit in exquirendis temporibus diligentior.

exceedingly meagre fragments, treat successively of justice, moral training,[84] the qualities of the true leader — Numa again being chosen as the great exemplar, since the long peace in his reign was the "mother of law and religion for our state." [85] The good leader had been previously described as a mirror for his citizens in the splendor of his mind and of his life.[86] His reward is the hope of a blessed immortality, pictured with poetic imagination at the end of the sixth and last book of this work.

The dialogue *De Re Publica* does more than set forth Scipio's, and Cicero's, theories about good government and the good governor. It throws a pleasant light on liberal education, humanism, *humanitas*, as it affected the lives of noble Romans in the second century B.C. Here we have a group of nine, who come together for a talk in Scipio's garden one morning,[87] obviously in one of the more clement seasons of the year. Men of different ages make up the party. All of them, with one exception, either had been consuls at the time of the dialogue, or were later going to be — an exceedingly eminent group.[88]

The friends recline comfortably on dinner-couches [89] — at least those couches were comfortable to Romans — but no banquet is being served. They talk in Horatian style, "unfed," *impransi*,[90] and the talk is on a high theme, as in those dinners at the Sabine farm that Horace calls "nights and feasts of

---

[84] Book IV, in which παιδεραστία and Platonic communism are censured. He remarks (IV 3) that Polybius, "our guest," found the Roman way of life defective at only one point, the proper training of young men of good family. Compare Polybius's remarks on the evil influence of Greek habits on the Roman youth and young Scipio's reaction against it (XXXI 25. 2–8).

[85] V 3: illa autem diuturna pax Numae mater huic urbi iuris et religionis fuit.

[86] II 69: ut ad imitationem sui vocet alios, et sese splendore animi et vitae suae sicut speculum praebeat civibus.

[87] I 14.

[88] The one exception was Spurius Mummius, brother of the more noted, or notorious, Lucius Mummius, the Lord Elgin of his day, who rifled Greece of as many works of art as Verres, with similar powers of appreciation, brought back from Sicily.

[89] I 17.

[90] Horace, *Serm.* II 2. 7.

gods." [91] There is an air of leisure, *otium*, in the talk; the dictum of the elder Scipio, reported by Cato to the younger, that he never did more than when he was doing nothing,[92] reveals an urbane mood in these Roman heroes that you might not suspect till you know them. There is pleasant banter,[93] there is a genial despite of wealth and power, there is a Platonic view from on high down upon the affairs of men, possible only for a soul that contemplates the eternal and the divine, a soul refined by the arts proper to a real humanity.[94] The eloquent passage in which these thoughts are expressed [95] might be turned into an Horatian ode; the gist of it is given in Milton's very Horatian sonnet with its precept:

> To measure life learn thou, betimes, and know
> Towards solid good what leads the nearest way.

Perhaps the voice is not Scipio's, but Cicero's, and yet young Scipio might have heard similar words from Polybius and Panaetius, repeating, like Cicero, the wisdom of their master Plato.

The humanism which such a society reveals may not attain the pure Greek form as set forth in his great book by Werner Jaeger; [96] that is because Greek literature, Greek art and everything that the Greek spirit touched shine with a radiance seen in no other human achievements save in the arts and the language of France and its exquisite canons of life. In its essence the humanism of the Romans is true to the standards that they took over from the Greeks.[97] Training in the liberal arts comes first.[98] Religion, as we have amply seen, accompanies education at every step. Some thinkers today would

---

[91] *Serm.* II 6. 65.

[92] *De Re Publ.* I 27.

[93] I 19.

[94] I 28: cui persuasum sit appellari ceteros homines, esse solos eos qui essent politi propriis humanitatis artibus.

[95] I 26–29.

[96] *Paideia: the Ideals of Greek Culture*, translated from the second German edition (*Paideia: die Formung des griechischen Menschen*, Berlin und Leipzig: Walter de Gruyter & Co., 1936; New York: Oxford University Press, 1939).

[97] *Ibid.* pp. xxiii, 298.

[98] See above, note 70.

rule out religion from humanism, thinking that a humanist walks on *terra firma, terra terrestris*, with little interest in nebulous divinity or any other figments. Such a humanism exists today, and by some scholars [99] has been read back into antiquity, but it is not the humanism of Cicero.[100]

Certain modern humanists, moreover, speak as though a stiff fight were on between their side and science. But science in antiquity was one of the liberal disciplines. Astronomy had a lively interest for them all, as well as for such poets as Lucretius and Virgil.[101] The investigation of natural phenomena, their characteristics, their origin, their development, was a normal part of philosophy, however different the answers were to the various questions that the examination of nature raised.[102] Scipio and his guests begin by talking about a scientific phenomenon that had just aroused their curiosity, the appearance of two suns in the Roman sky. The second sun, as a most eminent astronomer informs me, was but a parhelion, a mock-sun, a bright circular spot on a solar halo,[103] though in Cardinal Mai's impressive frontispiece [104] two suns with the equal majesty of two Roman consuls adorn the heavens. The friends talk of eclipses of the sun, with mention of Anaxagoras.[105] They are interested in Archimedes and his orrery, a primitive sort of *planetarium*.[106] Scipio used

[99] E.g. R. Reitzenstein, *Werden und Wesen der Humanität im Altertum* (Strassburg, 1907).

[100] Cf. "The Humanism of Cicero," *Proceedings of the American Philosophical Society*, LXXI (1932), 207–216 (esp. 213).

[101] Cf. "The Ancient Classics and the New Humanism," in *Going to College: A Symposium* (Oxford University Press, 1938), pp. 15–17.

[102] See Paul Shorey, "Platonism and the History of Science," *Proceedings of the American Philosophical Society*, LXVI (1927), 159–182.

[103] Harlow Shapley, who refers me to the *Encyclopaedia Britannica*, 14th edition, vol. XI, p. 110 f.

[104] See above, note 46.

[105] I 25.

[106] I 21. See also *Tusc. Disp.* 63. Harvard College possesses an orrery, or planetarium, made by Joseph Pope of Boston in 1786 and purchased for the College from the proceeds of a lottery in 1789. It was deposited in "the Philosophy Room of the University of Cambridge," later relegated to the loft of the Jefferson Physical Laboratory and then to the basement of the Music Building (a lowly place for the Music of the Spheres), but now has reacquired a position of (historical) dignity in the Astronomical Observatory. See an interesting

to talk of such high matters with Rutilius in the quiet hours of the siege of Numantia in Spain.[107] He wishes that Panaetius, a most eager investigator of astronomical matters, were there to help them out.[108]

But, after all, these gentlemen are statesmen, not men of science; their chief concern is with those broader subjects that may be applied to daily life and the government of the state; [109] for such, Scipio declares, is the most splendid function of philosophy and the greatest test and the greatest duty of virtue.[110]

These, then, to sum up, are the elements in the humanism of the days of Scipio, and the days of Cicero. Reverence for the past; respect for one's ancestors and pride in their achievements; an unbounded resolve to be worthy of the great lineage — *noblesse oblige*; enthusiastic study of the liberal arts — literature, science and philosophy included; religion, on which the state is founded; the practice of the character thus fashioned and refined; and finally the goal of a high career in the service of the state. The reason why Romans governed so well is that every mother's son of them had a liberal education, including Greek literature, studied and practised law, studied and practised oratory, crowned that training with philosophy, and took to the art of war like ducks to water. This program of an abundant life is written clearly not only in Cicero's dialogue on the state but in the history of Polybius and in what we may infer of the teaching of Panaetius. Ultimately young Romans were fitted to be banqueters at the table that Plato had spread, to which Carneades was not invited. Although they had made Platonic humanism voca-

---

article by N. H. Black, "Certain Ancient Physical Apparatus Belonging to Harvard College," in the *Harvard Alumni Bulletin* for March 24, 1933, pp. 660–666, with a picture of Pope's Orrery on p. 662.

[107] I 17. Rutilius might well have given this information to Cicero at Smyrna. See above, note 53.

[108] I 15.

[109] I 30.

[110] I 33. Here is where something of Greek radiance fades from Roman humanism. Science seems somewhat incidental — a wee bit beneath the dignity of the statesman.

tional, Plato at any rate was, invisibly but potently, one of the builders of Rome.

We may add that if Cicero, in his *De Re Publica*, is doing no more than translating and conflating Polybius and Panaetius, as some scholars would have it, his testimony to the intellectual life of the days of Scipio and his friends is all the more reliable.

## V

With the help of Polybius and of Cicero we may reconstruct with tolerable surety the basic ideas on which the early Roman State was built. The evidence is by no means exhausted. Archaeologists and students of linguistics [111] have opened up new and profoundly important information concerning the earliest days of Rome. Livy and other historians can in their way, though a way not regarded nowadays as any too certain, take us back to that distant past. Furthermore, now that we have Polybius's contemporary testimony to guide us, we may explore the fragments of Roman literature of his time and just before it with somewhat more confidence. The student of literature and history becomes an archaeologist, digging precious remnants from some later text, a grammarian's text it may be, and restoring the statute so far as he can — *ex pede Herculem*. He thus is tempted to push farther back into the past, finding, he may surmise, evidence of an earlier acquaintance with Greek than he had thought, and plenty of examples of the character and the training to which young Scipio felt himself lineally bound.

I will not attempt to follow any of these inviting clues, though, with Livy to guide us, we will pay some attention in the next chapter to those dim and distant years in Roman history. Rather, in conclusion, I will devote a few words to Father Ennius. He was born in 239 and died in 169, the year before Polybius came to Rome. He was not only bilingual, but trilingual. He came from Rudiae in Calabria and added

[111] Cf. List of Books; T. Frank, *Literature of the Roman Republic*, pp. 170–171; H. J. Rose, *Latin Literature*, pp. 1–19.

to his native Oscan both Latin and Greek; for Greek was still alive in Magna Graecia. His spirit was utterly Roman; for Rome, like a magnet, drew men of letters to itself — Virgil and Horace under Augustus from the north and from the south of Italy, and Claudian in the late Empire from Alexandria. Ennius was indeed father to poets so diverse as Lucretius and Horace and Virgil and Ovid. Perhaps, as we shall later see,[112] Cicero in certain moods may be placed among the poets. At any rate he cherished the poets of old and Ennius above them all. He owed a debt to Ennius for enlarging the scope and broadening the powers of his mind. And Ennius owes a debt to him, and we to them both; for Cicero has saved more vital bits of Ennius' poetry for us than has any other ancient.[113]

Ennius was the bold inventor who molded the Latin language into the form fit for heroic poetry, for which the short Saturnian ballad line had sufficed before. His workmanship was rough but true; and when the sentiment wrought out in his verse was the majesty of the Roman state or the greatness of Roman virtues, Virgil himself could not hammer out a better line. In the fragments of his tragedies there is at times the gleam of high poetry with a moral strength and a solemnity of imagination that recalls Aeschylus, even when the Roman poet is translating Euripides.[114]

[112] Chapter III, notes 41–43.

[113] A count of the quotations from Ennius, which I owe to Mr. H. F. Van Ummersen, Jr., shows few instances in the Latin grammarians and rhetoricians, more in the commentators, e.g. Servius 12 (17 lines), and, in substantial agreement with the shorter Servius, Serv. Dan. 15 (24); Donatus *in Terent.* has 5 (22). Among men of letters there are few, but made to some purpose, by Apuleius, Horace, Seneca, Quintilian, Lactantius, Augustine. Fronto 3 (5) does just what he ought not to do with Ennius according to the usual estimate of Fronto (see below, Chapter V, notes 5, 23). Virgil uses him with meaning, 10 (20), and he is veritably a part of the literary equipment of Gellius 22 (72) and Varro 34 (66). But to Cicero he makes a particularly deep appeal: 66 (269).

[114] E.g. *Andromache* 94–108 W = E. H. Warmington, *Remains of Old Latin*, vol. I (Loeb 1935). A concordance with the standard edition of Vahlen is given at the end of the volume. This is the passage that moves Cicero (*Tusc.* III 44) to his outburst against the *cantores Euphorionis*, the Roman Neo-Alexandrines of his day. Even more striking is *Iphigeneia* 222–225 W. Mr. J. W. Mackail (*Latin Literature*, p. 8) observes that we find in the fragments of Ennius "ex-

A majestic passage displays the chivalry of Pyrrhus, who thus replied to Fabricius sent to ransom the prisoners taken at Heraclea:

I ask not gold, nor shall ye pay me a price. Not as hucksters of war but as warriors, let both of us fight for our lives with the steel and not with gold. Whether Fortune wills that ye shall reign or I, or whatever she has in store, let us put to the test of valor. And listen herewith to this word of mine. Since Fortune has spared the valor of these men, I am resolved to spare their freedom. I grant them, take them; I give them by the will of the mighty gods.[115]

*Done ducite doque volentibus cum magnis dis.*

It is Cicero, again,[116] who has saved for us these priceless lines; and Dante [117] echoes them once more, through Cicero, as consonant with mediaeval, Christian chivalry.

But Ennius has his lighter moods, and flashes of irony and pungent satire. To descend for a moment from his heights, what genial humor and what a rebuke to our proud humanity there is in the line:

simia quam similis turpissima bestia nobis!

A nasty beast, the simian —
And oh how similar to man!

It is, characteristically, Cicero [118] who has preserved for us this irreproachable pun, one of the few irreproachable specimens of that generally despicable form of wit.

Ennius was a man of liberal culture. As with the friends of the younger Scipio, he was curious about the phenomena of nature.[119] He was versed in philosophy, though it is hard to

amples of almost the whole range of beauty of which the Latin language is capable." Mr. Mackail's little book, with its vividness, insight and charm, remains after nearly half a century the best introduction in any language to the literature of the Romans. The reader of the present work should consult it at every turn.

[115] *Annal.* 186–193, W.
[116] *De off.* I 38.
[117] *Monarchia* II 10.
[118] *De nat. deorum* I 97: (*Sat.* 23, W (I p. 390).
[119] See the fragments of his didactic poem, based on Epicharmus, dealing with nature and the four elements (I pp. 410–414, W.)

determine his school.  One passage has been cited to show that
Ennius had a properly Roman contempt of philosophy:

Philosophize I must, but rarely; to do it all the time, I won't.[120]

But Werner Jaeger [121] neatly points out that the sentiment
comes from Euripides's *Antiope,* who is presenting the oppos-
ing types of the practical man and the philosophic dreamer —
as Ennius might have done after him.

Again, in a famous passage, which was cheered by the
Roman audience, the Epicurean denial of divine providence
is expressed, but the sentiments may merely be those of a
character in the play.[122]  It is Cicero who quotes the passage
and tells us of its reception.[123]  In another, from the same play
and quoted by the same Cicero,[124] he scoffs at the soothsayers,
who promise their clients a fortune and receive a drachma for
the prophecy.  Why don't they take out a drachma from the
fortune, he asks, and hand over the rest of it?

Ennius is free from superstition.  In fact he translated
into Latin that most scientific work of Euhemerus, in which
that rationalist so successfully reduced the myths of the gods
to human history that neither human history nor myths are
left.[125]  At the same time Ennius worships the gods of his

---

[120] Philosophari mihi necesse est, paucis; nam omnino haud placet.
So 400 W, (I p. 368), from Gellius V 15. 9 and V 16. 5.  Cicero (*Tusc. Disp.*
II 1) plays with the phrase, which apparently had become a wingèd word.
[121] *Paideia* (English translation), p. 317.
[122] The *Telamo* (*Trag.* 328–330, W.).  An outburst of this sort would be appropriate enough at the moment when the old man heard of the death of his
son Ajax from his other son Teucer, whom he had told not to come back
home from Troy unless Ajax came with him.
[123] *De div.* II 104: An noster Ennius? Qui magno plausu loquitur adsentiente
populo:
   Ego deum genus esse semper dixi et dicam caelitum,
   Sed eos non curare opinor quid agat humanum genus.
In *De nat. deor.* III 79 he adds the line:
   Nam si curent bene bonis sit, male malis; quod nunc abest,
ascribing this to Telamo: Telamo autem uno versu locum totum conficit cur
di homines neglegant.  Of course this doctrine of divine unconcern is not
exclusively Epicurean.
[124] *De div.* I 132 (*Trag.* 332–6 W.).
[125] See T. Frank, *op cit.* (note 40), p. 138.

country, and Romulus is his hero-god.[126]  Of his theory of government, there are glimpses of the same view that Polybius
and Cato held.  The true king is father of his people, and the
state decays when the bonds of faith and sanctity are dissolved.[127]  Ennius wrote a book, the Third Book of his Satires,
entitled *Scipio* — the elder Scipio, of course.  Of this only a
few insignificant fragments have come down to us.  Elsewhere
we see that he agrees with his friend on the meaning of true
leisure; [128] he has no use for the idle, who with vacant and
unsettled mind are harder worked than those who tend to
their business.[129]  The clue to leisure is the cultivation of the
liberal arts, as Polybius and Cicero would agree.

In a notable passage, which Gellius this time has saved for
us,[130] Ennius describes a man of urbane tastes and sturdy
character to whom the noble Geminus Servilius liked to talk,
even in the spare moments of a strenuous campaign.  Here is
a rude translation of the somewhat rude and difficult verses.

Thus having spoken, he called to him a man with whom he
often courteously shared his table and his talk and his affairs,
when tired of giving his counsel on high concerns of state delivered
in the forum or the sacred senate; one to whom he freely spoke
of matters large and small and bandied jests, and poured forth
anything good or bad, whate'er he liked, and committed it to his
safe keeping; one with whom he had much pleasure in private
and in public; a character whom nobody's advice could persuade
to do a deed lightly or with evil purpose; learned and faithful; a
pleasant fellow, witty, content with his lot and blest; sage, speaking the right words at the right time, genial, sparse of words; retaining much of what old time keeps buried; possessed of the
traits that make our natures old and new; learned in the laws of
the ancient company of gods and men; one who could repeat or

---

[126] *Annal.* 114–121, W, esp. 117–121: Simul inter Sese sic memorant: O
Romule Romule die Qualem te patriae custodem di genuerunt! O pater, o
genitor, o sanguen dis oriundum.  This passage gains meaning from the
context in which it is found — Cic. *De Re Publ.* I 64.

[127] See the preceding note and *Annal.* 258–268 W.

[128] See above, note 92.

[129] *Trag.* 241–248, W.  This is from a chorus in the *Iphigeneia*.  Presumably
Ennius used the choruses of his tragedies for the expression of his views on
many matters.

[130] *Noct. Att.* XII 4. 4. (*Annal.* 210–227 W.).

keep in silence what was said; him in the midst of battle he thus accosts.

It was thought soon after Ennius's day that the poet painted his own picture in these lines.[131] In any event he held up to his age this mirror of a humanist.[132] He spoke to the generation that preceded Polybius. I am convinced that if we had all of Ennius's works, we should find there the full picture painted by Polybius and Cicero of the character and the civic arts that after their perfection in the centuries that followed Romulus made Rome at last the sovereign of the world. It is summed up in one line that Cicero declares an oracle: [133]

In men and ancient character the Roman state stands firm.
moribus antiquis res stat Romana virisque —

Ennius is one of the mighty builders of Rome. And this "oracle" of his pertains not merely to his own day and generation; it tells us that the foundations of the city had been laid back in the ancient past.

[131] *Ibid.* The noted scholar Lucius Aelius Stilo so declared.

[132] On one of the gates to Radcliffe College some of these lines are inscribed in memory of a great lawyer and authority on law and no less fine a humanist, John Chipman Gray. On him see A. Boyden, *Ropes—Gray: 1865–1940* (Boston, privately printed), pp. 145–160.

[133] *De Re Publ.* V 1: quam quidem ille versum vel brevitate vel veritate tamquam ex oraculo mihi quodam esse effatus videtur. Frank, *Lit. Roman Repub.*, p. 38: "His epic was an exposition of the text he himself devised so effectively: Moribus antiquis res stat Romana virisque. And it was Ennius who more than any one else kept Roman society upon that foundation."

# CHAPTER II

## THE IDEAL EMPIRE AND ITS
## FUFILMENT

ONE morning, not long after Scipio had entertained his friends in his garden with that high discourse on the Roman state and Roman character at which we have taken a glance, he was found dead in his chamber. If he was murdered, the murderer was never found, but the motive for the murder is patent. The acme of Scipio's high career was followed suddenly by this tragic downfall. Nor was it Scipio alone that perished. With him was ended that triumph of the Roman state that Polybius had recorded in his history.

If the scene as Cicero records it actually took place, it forms with its disastrous sequel one of those tragic overturns, or περιπέτειαι, like Lincoln's death, that nature herself, with evil men's assistance, can sometimes stage. If, on the contrary, the dialogue is quite imaginary, Cicero is a great dramatic artist, who understands how to place a pleasant episode in a setting potent with horror or with doom. Such a contrast was devised by Ovid for the amorous stories in the Fourth Book of his *Metamorphoses,* by Apuleius for the legend of Cupid and Psyche, by Boccaccio for his *Decameron.* In any case the matter of the *De Re Publica* is in its essence historically true. For even if no such gathering of Scipio and his friends took place, we may be sure that, if it had, their discussion would have followed in the main the lines that Cicero laid down. For that, once more, our witness is Polybius. We may note that Cicero himself was all unconsciously protagonist in a similar tragedy. He had not many years to wait before a convulsion of the state, quite as violent though different in its outcome, swept him away in sudden death. Thus for us readers today Cicero's tragedy of Scipio grimly forbodes his own.

Polybius, who died about 120 B.C., had lived to see his political prognostication unhappily fulfilled. The perfect Roman commonwealth bore within itself the seeds of disintegration. The society of Scipio lived on high ideals and noble ambitions. But life is full of social circles, each with its manners and its intimacies, each with its needs and its hopes. Many of the tragedies of life are due to the separation of these circles, to the tendency to men to keep within their several groups. Hence arise misunderstandings, most potent source of envy, hatred, malice and all uncharitableness. The members of a group, while cherishing within their scope a code of worthy living, may look with suspicion on those whom fortune has placed higher up, or with condescension on those placed lower down. Then, when different forms of pride and greed stiffen the boundaries into rings of steel, there comes the social clash, which generates rebellion and reprisal.

So it was in ancient Rome, even at the moment of its greatness. The pride of the aristocracy led to injustice, to the unhappy metamorphosis of aristocrats into oligarchs. The harmony of the state dissolved. Champions of the people arose in the brothers Gracchi, Tiberius and Gaius, members of the nobility and brothers-in-law of Scipio, trained like him in the liberal arts and Greek philosophy. Their motives were high, their measures were partly wise and partly illegal.[1] In 133 B.C., Tiberius was murdered, with many of his followers, by the aristocrats — an act that we can understand though not condone. On the last day of his life Scipio, whose later career might have suggested to his opponents a royal road to tyranny,[2] had spoken in defence of the Senate and denounced the agrarian laws of the Gracchan party; his death, as Cicero

[1] See the judicious account by Tenney Frank, *A History of Rome* (New York: Henry Holt, 1923), pp. 192–210.

[2] Scipio had destroyed Numantia without consulting the Senate; see Hammond, p. 15. It is significant that no such criticism comes from Cicero. Scipio is apparently for him the type of the Ideal Ruler. See Frank, *Lit. Roman Repub.*, pp. 210–244, who gives in the chapter "Cicero's Response to Experi-

implies,[3] may have indeed been brought about by those of his own household. In 121 B.C. came another "purge," as we have learned to say, in which Gaius Gracchus preferred suicide to murder and in which many of his followers were slain. That meant civil war — a series of civil wars, in which the victory of Sulla, his aspirations to sovereignty, and the inheritance of those plans by Julius Caesar and the fateful First Triumvirate in 60 B.C., led the way to the new civil war, to Caesar's exaltation and swift overthrow and to yet another war of citizens, whence issued the orderly triumph of Octavian — and the death of the Republic.

## I

A judgment on these events we should expect from Livy. He began his history between the years 27 and 25 B.C., after the downfall of the Republic; and he had no doubt that he had fallen on evil days. In the splendid preface to his work, he displays in a few pages his desire for the truth, his witty and sagacious handling of myth, his moral reading of history, his patriotic enthusiasm, his poetic mind, his religious reverence, and his outspoken pessimism. In words that Jacques de Bainville in his recent work, *La Troisième République* (*1870–1935*),[4] calls "passages éternels," Livy paints a picture of a kind of moral avalanche which has rolled down the years until it has reached "these times of ours, in which we can endure neither our vices nor the remedies for them."[5] Livy, like Cicero, could add to Polybius's "Rise and Triumph of the Roman State" a new volume, suggestive of Gibbon, on "The Decline and Fall of the Roman Republic."[6]

---

ence" an admirable exposition of the natural changes in Cicero's political attitude. He was not a turncoat for knowing enough to put on waterproof when it rained.

[3] *De Re Publ.* VI 12.

[4] Pages 316–317.

[5] *Praef.* 9. Cicero uses strikingly similar words (*De Re Publ.* V 2: nostris enim vitiis, non casu aliquo, rem publicam verbo retinemus, re ipsa vero iam pridem amisimus. Cf. *De Div.* II 4, a passage written hardly a year before his death.

[6] Livy, speaking of the "recent" introduction of luxurious living, with avarice and moral laxity in its train (*Praef.* 12), has in mind, as we see from a

Livy's life, outside the writing of his great work, was utterly uneventful. He was not, like Polybius and Cicero, a statesman; he had not taken part in the affairs of which he wrote. He was born at Patavium, the modern Padua, near Venice, in 59 B.C. Only the year before, the First Triumvirate had been formed; he was a lad of ten when Caesar crossed the Rubicon. When he first began to think of things political, he must have been aware of the tide that was sweeping the Roman world to monarchy. His attitude was fixed as he approached his great design of scanning the whole scope of Roman history. His sympathies are set forth unmistakably in his preface, which, unlike most prefaces, was written before he began his work. The district of Patavium had taken the side of the Senate in the conflict that ensued after Caesar's assassination, and was treated harshly by Asinius Pollio, the friend of Caesar and the legate of Mark Antony. This bitter experience may have helped form Livy's mind. Augustus dubbed him a "Pompeian," but with a wise tolerance he did not stop the writing of a work that certainly promised no propaganda for his own designs.

Of the one hundred and forty-two books that Livy finished of his *History*, only forty-five have been vouchsafed us by those jealous gods who sent their lightning on so much of Roman literature. More than that, they aimed their bombs with a fiendish accuracy.[7] What we most desire is, of course, Livy's account, and his analysis, of the history through which he had lived. What remains is the beginning of the story

---

later passage (XXXVI 6. 1–2), the spread of Greek influence after the Second Punic War. This is the very moment on which Polybius had set his finger (XXXI 25).

[7] The recovery of the lost "decades" of Livy's history has been one of the forlorn but irrepressible hopes of later ages. See Canon (W. L.) Collins, *Livy* (Ancient Classics for English Readers), 1876 [1880], p. 7. Early in 1924 scholars were startled by the announcement from a previously irreproachable Italian scholar that he had at last brought them to light; but his ridiculous imposture was quickly detected. See E. Chatelain, *Revue des Études Anciennes*, XXVI (No. 4. October–December, 1924), 314–316; Rand, *Classical Weekly*, XVIII (1924), 25 (October 27). I received a copy of the article of my revered friend about a week after I had sent mine to him. Other palaeographers doubtless saw the fraud the moment they saw the "facsimile."

down to the very time when Polybius came to Rome. We thus have Livy's version of the Rise and Triumph of the Roman state, but not that of its Decline and Fall. We may at least compare his views on the ideal government with those of Polybius and Cicero. It is perhaps no wonder that they are strikingly akin.

Moreover, it is a mistake to think that the history of Ideal Empire does not begin till the Augustan Age. It begins with Romulus, and the other early kings, a period that lasted for some three centuries and a half. Myth and poetry are part of its foundation. Myth and poetry and a reading of Greek traditions are part of the Roman story down to the period that Polybius knew when he found the Roman republic at the acme of its greatness. But myth has a way of turning into history in the thought of those of a later time, and the ideas underlying the myths are a vital, indeed the most vital, part of the record, since they explain the ambitions and the achievements of men.

Livy does not fare very well in the judgment of modern historians. Even Macaulay can declare, "No historian with whom we are acquainted has shown so complete an indifference to truth" [8] — a tragically ironic remark, in view of what our more recent authorities have to say about Macaulay. Livy is, for such critics, a picture-book historian, in contrast with that careful examiner of firsthand sources, Polybius.[9]

I will attempt no elaborate defence of Livy, but simply applaud his good sense in not attempting to unravel the *Dichtung* and the *Wahrheit* that were woven into the record of

[8] "Essay on History," in *Critical and Historical Essays* (Boston, Houghton and Mifflin, 1900), p. 258. Macaulay courteously adds, succumbing to Livy's charm and giving the devil his due: "On the other hand, we do not know, in the whole range of literature, an instance of a bad thing so well done."

[9] A notable instance is Polybius's investigation of the treaties between Rome and Carthage (III 22). He goes to the archives, not all of which had been destroyed by the Gauls when they sacked Rome in 390 (387) B.C. (Livy VI 1. 2; cf. note 33), and begins with the earliest treaty, drawn up in the year of the expulsion of the house of Tarquin in 509 B.C. He translates the ancient document as best he can, remarking that the Latin was so antique that even the most scholarly Romans of his time had difficulty in making it out.

the earliest days of Rome.[10] Polybius, too, as we have just seen, though concentrating on recent Roman events, investigated with no little care certain points in the earliest history of Rome, as though he were reckoning with firsthand material and not a string of myths and thought. He thought of Numa, for instance, as one of those ideal kings whose government was based on justice, religion, and peace.[11] Nor was Polybius unaware of the moral and incentive value of the Roman stories of the brave men of old, who sacrificed their lives for their country.[12] He repeats the tale of Horatius at the bridge in a tone less sceptical than that of Livy.[13] It is also patent that Livy was no less keen to ascertain historic truth [14] and that he, too, could search among old documents.[15]

He could indeed tell a lively story. That makes him suspicious at once to the safe and sober collectors of facts and *Vorarbeiten*. Oscar Wilde in his delightfully mendacious

[10] *Praef.* 6: Quae ante conditam condendamve urbem poeticis magis decora fabulis quam incorruptis rerum gestarum monumentis traduntur, ea nec adfirmare nec refellere in animo est. With a pleasant irony he asks the higher critics of other nations whether in view of the Romans' conquest of the world it was not at least appropriate for them to select the god Mars as their founder. See Chapter I, note 75.

[11] See Chapter I, notes 83, 85. A skillful synthesis of his predecessors' eulogies of Numa as the Ideal King is made by Plutarch in his *Parallel Lives* of Lycurgus and Numa (Loeb), I, 306–401.

[12] VI 54–55. These tales gave the stuff for those ballads which, according to Cato in his *Origines* and Cicero (*Tusc. Disp.* I 3, IV 3; *Brutus* 75) and Horace (*Odes* IV 15. 25–32), were sung at banquets and which Macaulay, drawing from his mendacious Livy, sought to reproduce in his *Lays of Ancient Rome*.

[13] II 10. 11: rem ausus plus famae habituram ad posteros quam fidei.

[14] Cf. note 10. An attempt is frequently made to show that Livy did not appreciate Polybius. Mr. J. W. Duff, for instance, in his admirable *A Literary History of Rome* (I, 645), is "astounded" to find in Livy "the chilly pronouncement" that Polybius is "an authority in no wise to be despised" (XXX 45. 5: haudquaquam spernendus auctor). For "chilly pronouncement" read *litotes* and emphasize in the text the "more appreciative" utterance that Mr. Duff buries in a foot-note (XXXIII 10. 10): Polybium secuti sumus, non incertum auctorem cum omnium Romanarum rerum, tum praecipue in Graecia gestarum.

[15] See the old laws in patently ancient Latin that he quotes in various places in Book I (I 24. 3–9; 26. 6–8; 32. 6–14; 38. 1–2). Even if he took them from some ancient historian, they disprove the charge that he selected only what he could turn into something picturesque; for the old laws are not exciting reading.

essay "On the Decay of the Art of Lying," speaking of the difference between the ancient historian and the modern novelist, remarks that the one gives us delightful fiction in the form of fact and the other gives us dull fact in the form of fiction. That is a gross misstatement, as any modern novelist will agree. What Wilde ought to have said is that Livy could make fact so interesting that we conclude it must be modern fiction.

Livy also has the spirit of a poet and of a dramatist. His history, in which the destiny of Rome — *fatum Romanum* — is magically unfolded, has been called a "prose-epic," "own sister to the *Aeneid*" [16] — a compliment that the modern scientific historian is only too willing to concede. Livy likewise can set the narrative of the house of Tarquin in a tragic framework. The succession of high estate (ὅλβος), overweening pride (ὕβρις) and vengeance (ἄτη) is as patent here as it is in Greek tragedy; and both Lucretia and Tullia are characters for the tragic stage. The story of the defilement of Lucretia by Sextus Tarquin,

who wrought the deed of shame,

and of his death by her own hand was told many times after Livy. Ovid's swift and brilliant narrative has touches of pathos, but it is on a lower scale.[17] The gorgeous rhetoric of Shakespeare's *Lucrece* out-Ovids Ovid and almost descends to bathos. Only Livy and Chaucer [18] can give the shiver of tragic feeling that purges us with pity and fear.

Now Polybius has no liking for the tragic historians. He

[16] Duff, *op. cit.*, I, 637. Mr. Duff skillfully mingles criticism and eulogy in his account of Livy.

[17] *Fasti* II 721–852.

[18] With a delightful combination of piety and humorous (not quaint) caprice Chaucer canonizes some of Ovid's heroines and other glorious martyrs like Lucretia in his *Legend of Good Women*; the poem, as we read in Robinson's *Chaucer* (p. 566), is "a cross between the *Heroides* of Ovid and the *Legenda Aurea*." Chaucer was prompted to his design partly by Ovid's compliments to the fair sex, including his own heroines, at the beginning of the Third Book of his *Art of Love*, and for Lucretia he follows in the main (yet with glances at Livy) the story as Ovid tells it. In spirit he attains the tragic simplicity of Livy. He takes Ovid up as Shakespeare takes him down.

states emphatically that the purpose of history and that of tragedy are not the same.[19] The tragic poet portrays true characters and moves the hearts of his hearers by the calamities in which they are involved. The historian's business is to relate real deeds and words; he should not put fictitious speeches into the mouths of the persons, however heroic, whose actions he narrates. But surely there may be tragedy in human events, like the defeat of France in June 1940, or the disaster of the Athenians in Sicily. Thucydides does not distort the facts of history when he feels and makes the reader feel the tragedy that underlies them. The examples that Polybius cites from the historian Aratus suggest not tragedy but the cheap thrill of melodrama, superimposed upon events. When the events speak silently for themselves, the historian deserves applause and not blame if with reserve and a simple nobility of style he makes their tragedy audible.[20]

So with the speeches, in which Livy abounds. They were a well-recognized device for the description of character. The historian is concerned with character at every step. He forms his judgments of character, of course at that risk in which judgments are involved. But the interpretation of moods and motives is part of his affair. He is not more faithful to history but less, if he restricts himself to an irreproachable, and un-enlivening, rehearsal of acts and facts; for these are not the whole truth in the story of living men. If, then, we must know their temperaments and motives as well as we may, pages of psychological description are not nearer verity than is a single speech. Make a man talk if you would know what he is like. The things that he says indicate his qualities, some-times with shadings and blendings recognizable as he speaks but hard to be put in words of description. That is why the ancient historians at times, and Thucydides among them,[21]

---

[19] II 56.

[20] See the excellent remarks by Rose, *Lat. Lit.*, I, pp. 286–287, on Livy's introduction to the Second Punic War: "no less poetical if it happens to be true." See also Finley's chapter on the Sicilian expedition (especially p. 246) in his great book, wherein he erects a perfect Doric temple to Thucydides, on the heights.

[21] For this aspect, and all the other aspects, of the speeches of Thucydides,

thought it best to set forth character in the way that Homer connotes the beauty of Helen of Troy. It is a delicate art, which Polybius preferred to abjure. But we may spare Livy the criticism that he is a kind of posthumous ghost-writer for eminent men. Rather, recognizing that he is using a traditional device for describing character, we may examine the success with which he describes it.

There is also a larger scope that these invented speeches sometimes have. They may exhibit not only the character of the speaker, but, dramatically, an important episode or movement of the times in which he plays a part. At the beginning of his Fourth Book, for instance, Livy presents two speeches made in 445 A.D., over the law proposed by the tribune Canuleius to grant the plebeians the right of intermarrying with the patricians and to permit either patricians or plebeians to be elected to the consular office.

The one speech, short and sharp, gives the views of the consuls. The sentences, although in indirect discourse, shoot their arrows swiftly at the unpatriotic tribune, who was seizing the moment to call a strike when the hostile tribes round about Rome threatened an attack on the city; labor was not contributing to defence. The consuls foresee the demolition of all standards, both human and divine, if the measure passes; there would be a sorry melting pot of men and animals, that is, of the first families with the "little people," or *canaille*. Do not think the plebeians will be satisfied by this surrender, the speaker remarks; they will call for more and more. And beware! Canuleius is one of the Fifth Column, in league with the enemy, who jubilantly see their chance to climb the Capitoline and occupy the citadel. But they won't, if all good men will rally to the consuls' side.

Canuleius is allowed a speech over twice as long, phrased in the direct discourse, as though the eloquent words came from his very lips.[22] His points of attack are two — the pride of the

see Finley, *op. cit.*, Index, p. 343. On Livy, Frank, *Lit. Roman Repub.*, pp. 188–189.

[22] The eloquence is not quite Ciceronian. The sentences are generally briefer and simpler in construction.

consuls, who treated honest Romans like the scum of the earth, and their stodgy conservatism in a commonwealth that, built for eternity, had from the start been ever moving forward in its mighty course.[23] The consuls who had succeeded the kings were once themselves a dangerous innovation. They should be the last to say: "It never was done before." [24] The consuls are not the source of sovereignty. That resides in the people, not in a class; it reposes on freedom — *omnibus aequa libertas*.[25] If you want harmony in the state do not permit divisive practices or institutions. By this proud law of yours you rend society in twain and create two states instead of one.[26] The consuls' arguments are nothing but propaganda. Their appeal to high patriotism is a trick for keeping the people in subjection. If they isolate themselves in a holier-than-thou attitude, very well; we will recognize their wall of partition. They will find that we won't enlist.

How modern this sounds! Modern to Livy's readers and modern just now. Needless to say, Livy was not favored with stenographic reports of these speeches. He invents the language, but the language is true to the historical moment of which he writes. In his day the points of dispute between the patricians and plebeians had long since ceased to agitate the Roman state. Livy is recording an epoch as distant from his own time as the days of the Tudors are from ours. But his theme is the eternal battle between conservatives and progressives, as vivid in the times of Canuleius as it was in another form in the Augustan age, or under the Tudors, or at the present time. Some such sentiments as those that he sets forth must have been uttered by the consuls and their adversary Canuleius. With a sympathetic penetration into the actual-

[23] IV 4. 4: Quis dubitat quin in aeternum urbe condita, in inmensum crescente, nova imperia, sacerdotia, iura gentium hominumque instituantur?

[24] IV 4. 1–2: "At enim vero nemo post reges exactos de plebe consul fuit." quid postea? . . . (Under the kings) consules numquam fuerunt: regibus exactis creati sunt.

[25] IV 5. 1. Here are at least *liberté* and *égalité*; but the first families were not displaying much *fraternité*.

[26] IV 4. 10: id vos sub legis superbissimae vincula conicitis, qua dirimatis societatem civilem duasque ex una civitates faciatis. Thus the fundamental national sin is pride; and harmony is its salvation.

ities of the past, Livy recreates them, and in that act does more justice to historical accuracy than in merely chronicling the data that had been transmitted. He remarked in his Preface that his readers, little interested in a dim and distant past, would want him to hurry down to the living events of their own times.[27] But he was in no hurry. Instead, he pulled them back to events hopelessly remote, to show that these were just as much alive.

What of his own sentiments? In his Preface, he writes as a conservative, a last-ditch conservative, to whom the world is going to the dogs. But when he is back in his beloved past, his purpose is sympathetically and dramatically to do justice to both sides. There are touches of humor in his portraits of both Canuleius and his opponents. On the whole the consuls are the losers in this far-away debate, which marks a moment in the onward march of history.[28]

A speech which Livy surely did not make up is reported in his account of those famous Isthmian games at Corinth at which Flamininus, after defeating Philip of Macedon at Cynoscephalae, proclaimed the freedom of Greece.[29] The throng that heard it, hardly believing their ears, expressed their amazement that a foreign nation could cross the seas to establish justice everywhere on earth; it was a crusade to make the world safe for democracy. These words were quoted in an eloquent speech made by the Italian Senator Tittoni at the Institute of Politics held at Williams College in August 1921. The parallel to the action of our country in the last war did not escape the audience.

If one thinks that this high-sounding passage is nothing but propaganda on Livy's part, one can find it almost word for word in Polybius.[30] If the two historians followed a common

[27] *Praef.* 4: festinantibus ad haec nova, quibus iam pridem praevalentis populi vires se ipsae conficiunt. These were the readers who fed on thrills and scare headlines.

[28] Cicero, a conservative with an open mind, is altogether on the side of Canuleius, who after all was not proposing an innovation but seeking to annul the law on intermarriage enacted *inhumanissime* by the Decemvirs in 451 B.C. (*De Re Publ.* II 63).

[29] XXXIII 32.        [30] XVIII. 44–46.

source, then Livy, for once, chose a good source; for so Polybius thought it. Or, if Livy drew straight from Polybius, then again his source was good.[31]

Another speech — I will mention but one more that bears on our topic — is attributed to one of the ancient heroes. I was reminded of it by an address given by a distinguished authority on medicine and physiology some nine years ago, at a time when that blessed word "technocracy" was having its brief vogue. The speaker, Dr. Walter B. Cannon of the Harvard Medical School, preferred to invite our attention to what he called "biocracy," meaning the economic constitution of the members of the state in one harmonious organism.[32] I wrote him that this was the best speech I knew on that subject since the oration made by Menenius Agrippa to the plebeians, when in the year 494 B.C. they struck, quit Rome and ensconced themselves on the now tiny eminence that bore the imposing name of Mons Sacer. He told them the fable of how the other members of the body revolted against the belly, which, lying comfortably in the middle, fed without toil on the sustenance they brought it. And so they struck, refused to feed it, and consequently found their own strength dwindle away; for the belly not only received their contributions but furnished them their blood from the food it had digested. The plebeians saw the point and returned to the city.

Wondering whether this story were still a part of Roman history as presented in our textbooks, I examined the five or six that my library happens to contain, including that of Mommsen, and found it in none of them. Of course it comes merely from Livy, who found it in no archives.[33] But what

[31] Note that Livy quotes, incidentally, Valerius Antias and Claudius Quadrigarius (XXXIII 30). Incidentally, those who find Livy superficial and naive in his use of Valerius Antias would do well to consult the article on Livy and Valerius Antias by my master and friend, Albert Howard.

[32] Dr. Cannon's address "Biocracy" was published in *The Technology Review*, XXXV, 203–206 (1933). It later appeared in a revised form as a presidential address entitled "The Body Philosophic and the Body Politic" before the American Association for the Advancement of Science in 1940. It now is printed as "The Body as a Guide to Politics" in *The Thinker's Forum*, XV (1942), 5–47.

[33] For these had perished when the Gauls sacked Rome about 390 (387,

could be more symbolic of that "harmony of the classes" (*concordia ordinum*) which not only Livy but Cicero and Polybius recognized as the essence of the form of government that the Romans had, by dint of experience, evolved? It is a pity that the Romans' tradition of their history is no longer regarded as one vital element in the story of Rome that modern historians think safe enough to tell.[34]

It is plain even from the chance quotations that I have made that Livy's conception of the ideal government of Rome does not differ essentially from that set forth by Cicero and Polybius. Much more could be said on this matter, and more still on the acute observations on statecraft with which his work is strewn. Machiavelli found plenty of material in merely the first decade, to draw forth his *Discorsi* and to receive further elaboration, and transformation, in *Il Principe*. An instructive volume might be devoted to a comparative study of Polybius, Cicero, Livy, and Machiavelli, with Adolf Hitler's *Mein Kampf* thrown in for good measure, or for bad.[35]

Frank). It is Livy himself who betrays this fact and therewith his difficulty in presenting a satisfactory account of the previous historical periods. Written records (*litterae*), "the only trustworthy guarantee of history" (*una custodia fidelis memoriae rerum gestarum*), were brief and scarce, and the records of the pontifices with both public and private monuments were destroyed in the burning of the city — yet not all (he says *pleraeque* not *cunctae*: VI 1). So some remained, including the Laws of the Twelve Tables, enough records of treatises to keep Polybius busy, and, I should think, the old laws that Livy himself quotes (see note 15). For a more detailed, and competent, account of this matter cf. Frank, *Lit. Roman Repub.*, pp. 178–182. The present passage might have been written by a modern historian. But Livy reckons also with the body of oral tradition, which contains at least a skeleton of fact.

[34] They cannot pay attention to a mere legend, and though it may be symbolically impressive, such is the wealth of literary and monumental material when they arrive at the period of the historian who tells it, they have no space for it. *Sic transit Menenius Agrippa* — but no, Shakespeare's *Coriolanus* will keep him alive.

[35] See an interesting letter on Hitler and Machiavelli by Malcolm C. Sherman in the *Boston Herald* for November 2, 1941. *Mein Kampf*, one of the great books of our day, reveals at first an attractive picture of a young man passionately devoted to his race and to social justice, who eagerly absorbed all manner of books, not to learn history but to have history teach him: "Ich will sie [i.e. die Geschichte] dabei nicht lernen, sondern sie soll mich lehren" (Munich edition, 1939, p. 14, cf. p. 36). This is an epigrammatical equivalent of Livy's twofold precept quoted in the following note. But Hitler eventually turned that precept upside down, selecting for himself and his country a course disgraceful in its beginning, disgraceful in its outcome.

We may finally raise the question whether Livy's repub-
licanism prevented him forever from seeing any good in the
imperialism introduced by Augustus. The pessimism expressed in his Preface is, after all, not irremediable; for his
search in history for good examples "which for yourself and
for your state you should imitate" and for bad examples which
you should avoid [36] implies, however dark the present, a program of reform. He does see some good in Caesar Augustus,
"our imperator Caesar Augustus," who, he says, "gained us
peace on land and sea." These words occur in the passage that
praises Numa for closing the temple of Janus, an act which
betokened the establishment of peace and which in the long
series of Roman wars had occurred only once between Numa
and Augustus.[37] Some resemblance between Augustus and the
good King Numa is implied.[38] Nor does Livy's praise of the
virtues of the men of old imply necessarily a preference for
a republican form of government. It is true that he hails the
establishment of that form after the expulsion of the Tarquins. His Second Book begins with a kind of paean on
liberty.[39] But the reigns of the kings Romulus and Numa
were for him model administrations, and he says of Servius
Tullius that just and lawful kingly power perished with him.[40]
The reign that he condemned, as Polybius would condemn,
was that of the tyrant Tarquin the Proud.[41] Perhaps the mind
of Livy became more modern, more sympathetic towards the
new government of Augustus, as the pages of his history pro-
gressed to his own times, just as his mind, in his phrase, became ancient as it entered imaginatively into the life and the
achievements and the beliefs of the men of old.[42] But that we

[36] *Praef.* 10: Hoc illud est praecipue in cognitione rerum salubre ac frugi-
ferum, omnis te exempli documenta in inlustri posita monumento intueri;
inde tibi tuaeque rei publicae quod imitere capias, inde foedum inceptu foedum exitu quod vites.
[37] I 19. 2–3.
[38] See note 11.
[39] II 1. 1–6. Cicero points out the instances of license that followed in the
train of liberty (*De Re Publ.* I 62).
[40] I 48. 8.
[41] I 49. So Cicero, *De Re Publ.* II 46, 51, 52.
[42] Cf. Chapter I, note 37. The best appraisal of Livy that I know is by Ten-

shall not know, unless the lost decades of his history should some day be recovered.

## II

We come now to Augustus and his plans for the establishment of an Ideal Empire. In temperament he differed sharply from his great-uncle Julius Caesar, whose adopted son he found himself after the will of the great dictator was published, whose avenger he became, and whose plans for a new government he determined to carry out, in his own way. Caesar was modern by nature. He was ready for a sharp break with the past. Octavian was conservative. He could not and would not overlook the majestic tradition that had descended to him from antiquity; even in our brief glance at Livy we have seen something of its splendor. Augustus had come not to destroy but to fulfil. I am convinced, after the estimable writings of Hammond[43] and Buchan on Augustus,[44] that the new ruler was sincere in his plans for the state. It should also be borne in mind that although the republican form of government had lasted from its institution in 509 B.C. to the battle of Actium in 31 B.C. — an amazingly long stretch of four hundred and seventy-eight years — and although the idea of such a kingdom as Tarquin the Proud had ruled — that is, a tyranny — was obnoxious to the Roman mind, both visions of the ideal kingdom of Romulus and Numa and Servius Tullius and the philosophical arguments of Polybius repeated by Cicero still hovered before the imaginations of thoughtful men as a rational ideal.

---

ney Frank, *Lit. Roman Repub.*, chap. VI, "Republican Historiography and Livy." The reader will find there some of the points that I have raised, and others, subjected to a keen scrutiny. As a result Livy can shake off much of the opprobrium cast upon him in modern times.

[43] *Augustan Principate* and *Hellenistic Influences.*

[44] John Buchan, *Augustus*, 1937. Before reading any modern account of Augustus the reader would do well to see what Suetonius has to say. Suetonius was an expert collector of biographical matter of all sorts, truth, rumor and scandal, which he treated about as Livy treated the early history of Rome (note 10), seldom trying to distinguish fact from fiction. For an excellent translation, together with the latest critical text, see the edition by J. C. Rolfe (Loeb, 1920).

What difference does it make if the history of the kingdom is largely myth to us? Of some mythical element in the tradition Livy and his urbane contemporaries were well aware.[45] But to them there was also a solid base of history in the old record on which they built their own theories of the state. That is why we cannot neglect Livy's history of early Rome if we would understand the purposes of Augustus. But further it is clear, as I shall try to show, that the mind of Augustus was formed at least in part by the poetry of two of his associates and admired friends, Virgil and Horace. In the poetry of Virgil it is rather the vision that we see; in that of Horace the fulfilment.

Virgil was born in 70 B.C., somewhere near Mantua, in North Italy.[46] His district suffered, as Livy's did, from the confusions and dispossessions that followed in the wake of the battles of Mutina and Philippi. He had no more inclination than Livy, at first, to make a national deliverer out of Octavian. He was a talented lad and received a good schooling at Cremona and Milan before going to Rome. He was a poet both born and made. At the time when his boyish mind opened to poetry, and a mind like his opened early, the general flavor of contemporary poetry was Alexandrine. That is to say, the smaller poetic forms and the humbler or, if you like, more human themes were in vogue — such as love poems and romantic legends briefly told. Catullus and Lucretius had just startled the world of letters with poetry of high genius. They both began with Alexandrine themes and both, in virtue

---

[45] Cf. note 33.

[46] I still maintain the traditional view that the town of Andes mentioned in Donatus's *Life of Virgil* (based on Suetonius) as the birthplace of the poet was identical with the modern village of Pietole three Roman miles south of Mantua. See *In Quest of Virgil's Birthplace*, Harvard University Press, 1930. My friend, the late R. S. Conway, *vir optime de Vergilio meritus*, had presented weighty reasons for a site near Calvisano, some thirty Roman miles (so in the *Vita Vergilii* by Probus) from Mantua. We had a lively but amicable exchange of arguments. Unhappily he did not live to answer my latest statement in "Once More Virgil's Birthplace," *Harvard Studies in Classical Philology*, XLIV (1933), 63–93. We agreed on the essentials — that Virgil was born somewhere in a delightful region of Italy, which it is exciting to explore.

of their talents and their absorption of earlier Greek poetry, rose vastly higher than their starting point. Both of them left their imprint on young Virgil.

But Virgil's temperament was cast in a different mould. He was born to write epic. The vision of his country's high destiny was before his eyes; the craving to worship a hero possessed him. There was little in contemporary politics to satisfy such longings. All about him was turmoil and dark foreboding. He was no product of his age; he helped to fashion it and to open its eyes to what he prophetically saw. It is somewhat the fashion to settle Virgil's case by dubbing him a court poet, whose testimony to the history of his times is thereby excluded on two counts: first, he wrote for the court, versifying propaganda on dictated themes, and, again, he was a poet, a dreamer. No judgment could be less historic. Virgil took no orders from his masters: he gave them. A dreamer he was, undoubtedly; and his dream came true.

Something of this we may see in the mock-heroic poem written by Virgil, according to his ancient biographer,[47] at the age of sixteen and entitled *Culex*, "The Mosquito." That local inspiration may be partly responsible for the subject will be patent to anybody who has spent a summer night at Mantua. This is the story:

A shepherd drives his flock afield in the early morning and, while they nibble their fodder, he leans on his staff and dis-

---

[47] Donatus (*Vitae Vergilianae*, ed. J. Brummer, Leipzig, Teubner, 1912), p. 4, 57. I will not revive the controversy over the minor poems ascribed to Virgil in manuscripts, whose evidence is supported by Donatus and Servius. Taking this evidence on its face value (it goes back at least to Suetonius), I sought to show (*The Magical Art of Virgil*, pp. 34–67) that these poems, arranged in a plausible chronological sequence from his earliest efforts up to the *Bucolics*, illustrate the development of the poet from an Alexandrine to an Augustan. Though eminent Virgilian scholars in our hemisphere, such as Tenney Frank and Norman De Witt, accepted this point of view, the tide of criticism since then has flowed in the other direction. See e.g. for the latest utterance, T. R. Glover, *The Challenge of the Greek and other Essays*, Cambridge University Press, 1942, p. 223. The word of this eminent Virgilian, as does that of another dear friend, Mr. Mackail (who called me a fundamentalist), carries a particular weight. Most scholars would agree, I believe, that the *Culex* has the brightest chances for authenticity. I will not disturb the order of the lights in this little galaxy, but leave them either to shine through the clouds or to fade into darkness, as subsequent investigation may determine.

courses on the simple pleasures of the pastoral life. At noon
he seeks the shade of the woods and has his siesta. As he sleeps
a glistening serpent glides up and is about to inflict a sting; a
kindly mosquito, seeing his danger, stings the shepherd first.
Awaking, the shepherd squashes the mosquito and slays the
snake. In the watches of the night the ghost of the mosquito
appears to him, sadly but gently rebukes him for his unwitting
ingratitude, and tells of his adventures in the world below; he
describes the famous sinners in torture and those pious folk
who have gained the Elysian fields. Next morning the shepherd repentantly builds a little tomb, heaps flowers round
about, and adorns it with a neat epitaph.

It is a sprightly little *jeu d'esprit*, in its outline, though
needing the finishing touch. But it is just what a genius at
the age of sixteen might well have written. Virgil did not
revise it; he kept it as raw material for parts of his later works.
It prophesies them all — *Bucolics, Georgics,* and *Aeneid.* And
it is vastly important for the conception of Virgil's mind and
purpose that I am trying to set forth.

I will emphasize but two points. The rhapsody on country
life presages the great passage at the end of the second book of
the *Georgics.* It is an answer to those critics who see in the
*Georgics* obedient propaganda for the imperial program of
"back to the land." For long before Octavian had a political
interest in country life, young Virgil both knew farming and
loved nature. That we see as clearly in this juvenile poem as
in his later work; in both of them the spirit of his master
Lucretius is upon him.[48] Maecenas may have prompted him
to the writing of the *Georgics,* but Virgil, despite his complimentary phrase, is taking orders from no one but his
Muse.[49]

The galaxy of sinners and saints in the inferno of the *Culex,*
prophetic of that in the Sixth Book of the *Aeneid,* is no less
significant. The sinners [50] are well-known figures of mythol-

---

[48] See *Magical Art*, p. 39.
[49] *Ibid.*, pp. 177–178.
[50] Verses 231–257. Otos and Ephialtes, Tityos, Tantalus, Sisyphus, Medea,
Procre, Philomel and Tereus, Eteocles and Polynices.

ogy and tragedy. In Elysium [51] we find the heroines of Homer and of tragedy — Alcestis and Penelope — with the story of Eurydice and Orpheus told at length — crude matter for the poet's art when he told it again in his *Fourth Georgic*.[52] The heroes are those of Homer and of the later tale of Troy, nor are the great Romans of old forgotten — Horatius and Fabius and Decius and the rest. The latest in history are the two Scipios, whose triumphs the walls of Carthage were doomed to dread. This is a republican, not an Augustan, *inferno*. It is impossible that a later imitator of the Sixth *Aeneid* with the wealth of its heroes and the utterly different plan at its disposal should have taken no more than what the *Culex* contains.

Young Virgil, then, oblivious of the march of contemporary Roman politics, oblivious of the literary fashions of the day, buried himself in Homer and Greek tragedy,[53] in Hesiod,[54] in the poetry of his countrymen, above all Ennius and Lucretius. On them he fed his cravings to write of something great, of the greatness of ancient Rome, and of its heroes, no less noble than those of Greece.[55] The germ of the *Aeneid* no less than of the *Bucolics* and the *Georgics* lies latent in this boyish

[51] Verses 260–375. Alcestis.

[52] I find no reason, even after W. B. Anderson's counter-arguments (*Classical Quarterly*, XXVI [1933], 36–45, 73) for not accepting the statement of Servius that the last part of the Fourth Book of the *Georgics* originally contained a eulogy of Virgil's brother poet Gallus, for which, after Gallus' disgrace and suicide, the story of Orpheus was substituted. (See Serv. in *Georg.* I 1 and *Magical Art*, pp. 340–342.) In that emergency, Virgil might have found a convenient starting-point in his earlier rendering of the story. For possible echoes of it cf. *Georg.* IV 455 and *Cul.* 287; *Georg.* IV 489 and *Cul.* 294.

[53] For touches in the *Culex* cf. verses 292 on Orpheus and 339–342 on the gods' vengeance (ἄτη) that meets man's pride (ὕβρις), as illustrated in the fates that attended the Greek heroes on their return from Troy (342–357). This familiar theme is employed for another early piece (*Catalepton* 3) of which the subject is not so probably Alexander (*Magical Art*, p. 41) as Mithradates. This terror of the Romans was finally overcome; he committed suicide in Colchis in 63 B.C. A schoolboy's imagination would be impressed with this sudden περιπέτεια. All details in the poem fit this interpretation if we accept the easy emendation (though not approved by recent editors) of *exilium* (v. 8) to *exitium*.

[54] *Cul.* 95. *Magical Art*, p. 182.

[55] *Cul.* 358–360: Hic alii resident pariles virtutis honore. Heroes mediisque siti sunt sedibus omnes. Omnes Roma decus magni quos suspicit orbis.

*jeux d'esprit.* He had no hero as yet, though he treats reverentially the young Octavius — not to be confused with Octavian [56] — to whom he dedicates his poem. He sought a hero, until in the *Bucolics* after a series of minor champions — Pollio, Varus and Gallus — he found Maecenas and the young Octavian.[57] Caesar had first appealed to his imagination.[58] The *Bucolics* were written, approximately, between 42 and 38 B.C.[59] At the time of the battle of Philippi in 42 B.C., Virgil was whole-heartedly Caesarian. Of the two victors, Antony and Octavian, different heirs to the legacy of Caesar, the poet, owing to his admiration of Pollio,[60] might at first have had more sympathy with Antony; for Antony had not yet become the monumental traitor of his country, the polluter of the Roman way of life. From these facts it is plain that Virgil was an imperialist, or monarchist, as you will, before he was an Augustan.

When Virgil found his hero, he forthwith deified him: "O Meliboeus, a god hath given me this peace," says the grateful shepherd.[61] This is no fulsome compliment. In the popular religion of Greece and Rome, immortality was not the ordinary lot of men, but it could be won by heroic deeds; one may call it the ancient mode of canonization. Heracles and Dionysus were mortals at the outset, but deified at last for their different services to humanity. Beginning with Alexander, Hellenistic kings received the honor of Godhood, not merely as a pure formality. The practice had the sanction of popular approval; it seemed a fitting recompense to bestow.[62]

---

[56] *Magical Art,* pp. 41–42.

[57] *Ibid.,* p. 152. Maecenas, esteemed as his patron, does not seem to have quite the glamour of a hero for Virgil.

[58] Cf. *Ecl.* V and *Magical Art,* pp. 98–99.

[59] *Ibid.* p. 76.

[60] *Ibid.* pp. 102–103. This admiration is obvious even if the Child of the Fourth Eclogue is not, symbolically, the son of Pollio. If that, however, was the intention, as I believe, then Virgil's enthusiasm for Pollio was, for the moment, intense.

[61] *Ecl.* I 5: O Meliboee deus nobis haec otia fecit. Namque erit ille mihi semper deus.

[62] On Emperor-worship see Buchan, *Augustus,* pp. 279–283; Hammond, *Augustan Principate,* pp. 261–263 (an excellent review of recent literature);

Just so the Romans paid divine honors to Aeneas and to
Romulus; [63] and when the Roman government veered towards
monarchy again, it was natural, after the vogue of the Hellenistic practice, to mete out divinity to great rulers. Julius
Caesar, after his death, was translated to a heavenly star, and
his worship was fixed in the liturgy.[64] Lucretius, banishing
the traditional gods in Epicurean fashion to pleasant ineffec-
tiveness in the intermundial spaces, created his own divinity,
the blessed Epicurus.[65] Cicero planned his *Dream of Scipio*
on the assumption that great rulers went to heaven after
death.[66] Virgil, therefore, with an inborn passion for hero
worship and perhaps with the example of Lucretius in mind,
saluted as a god the young ruler who had brought peace to
the countryside long before the worship of Augustus, somewhat against that ruler's will, was formally decreed and practiced in the provinces.[67] He later is invoked, with even
greater fervor, among the other deities to whom the poet appeals for guidance in the writing of his *Georgics*.[68]

All in this is prophecy of what was soon to come. And yet
henceforth in that great opening book of the *Georgics,* Octavian remains a gloriously human youth, the deliverer indispensable for the shattered state, for whose continued presence the god implores the ancient deities of Rome. For the
world's scene is lurid and tempestuous with turmoil; the
gods above have suffered Romans to shed one another's blood
in two godless civil wars; [69] Mars rages throughout the world;

---

Lilly R. Taylor, *The Divinity of the Roman Emperor*, 1931; A. D. Nock, *Camb.
Anc. Hist.* X (1934), 481–489.

[63] See on Ennius, Chapter I, note 125; also Miss Taylor, *op. çit.*, pp. 42–43.
Note also Livy's self-protective reticence with regard to Aeneas (I 2. 6).

[64] Cf. Virgil, *Ecl.* V and Miss Taylor on it (*op. cit.*) p. 112 and in general
pp. 78–99. The date of the Fifth Eclogue is probably late in 42 B.C. or early
in 41 (*Magical Art*, p. 98).

[65] *De Rerum Natura* V 8: deus ille fuit, deus, inclyte Memmi, Qui princeps
vitae rationem invenit.

[66] *De Re Publ.* VI 26.

[67] Cf. Miss Taylor, p. 111: "Unofficial though it is, it is the first expression
that we have of worship for him and perhaps as strong an expression of the
sort as we have at any time from an Italian source."

[68] *Georg.* I 24–42; *Magical Art*, p. 198.

[69] *Georg.* I 491: Nec fuit indignum superis bis sanguine nostro Emathiam et

the horses of the chariot of state break from the reins and run wild.

This is the moment when yet another civil war was brewing, in which Octavian and Antony came finally to their clash at Actium in the year 31 B.C. But after that battle the tone changes abruptly, as the poet starts his Third Book. A new vision has come to him, a vision of triumph, of Rome's new conquest of the world. And at last he has found his epic and his hero. The theme is immortal and it catches up the poet in its immortality.[70] He sketches the plan for his poem, in which he will throw down the gauntlet to Homer. He will celebrate the victory of his hero-god over the hosts of Egypt and his widening conquests throughout the world. His lineage from Troy will be manifested, and the god that founded Troy, Apollo, whom Octavian invoked at Actium, will receive due homage. There will be an inferno, where the ill-fated envy of his foes will know all the tortures of the ancient myths. This, then, will be an epic on a contemporary theme, a mighty theme of the heroic present.

But it is hard to turn current events into epic. To appeal to the imagination, they need a background far remote and the mystery of legend; to give the present affairs mythological trimmings of that sort invites the sudden descent to the ridiculous from the sublime. It is wiser to set the present in the past, transposing time, which means little to poets and philosophers, and leaving space. With an aim from afar, the poet can better hit the mark though not aiming directly at the target. As Virgil pondered and mellowed his theme, the mythical and ideal elements in his design came to the front; the actual and contemporary faded into the background. When the whole plan was matured in the poet's mind, all that remained

---

latos Haemi pinguescere campos. There is a touch of reproach in the epithet *superi*, which Lucan freighted with irony in his savage indictment of the divinities.

[70] III 8-9: temptanda via est qua me quoque possim Tollere humo victorque virum volitare per ora. By a skilful repetition of the words in Ennius's epitaph (*volito vivos per ora virum*) Virgil intimates that the Rome of Augustus will attain the eternal nobility of that of Ennius's time.

of the actual present was a touch of eulogy in his First Book,[71] the panorama of Roman history that Anchises unrolls before his son as he visits the Elysian fields in the world below,[72] and the pictures on the hero's shield.[73] All these scenes, with a skilful art, are presented as prophecies. The inferno, particularly intended, in the poet's original plan, for the enemies of the victor, now serves as a storehouse for history. The rest is the legend of Aeneas, how after toils and tragedies and wars he built the walls of Rome.

And yet the poem from start to finish glorifies Augustus and the Rome that he had built. It is too crude to say that Aeneas "stands for" Augustus. The poet meant to suggest, not to identify, and with that delicate and impressionistic sort of allegory which he had displayed delightfully in his *Bucolics*,[74] and to which he, alone of poets, had the clue, he centred his attention on the ancient hero of his tale, transformed him from a legendary figure to a man, wrought for him a character strong and deep and Roman, and let Augustus glimmer through. And there is one skilful use of a repeated phrase, applied first to Augustus and then to Aeneas, whereby the poet leads us to infer: "Yes, these two are one." [75]

I can merely broach this alluring aspect of Virgil's art, of high importance for our present topic. Certainly no monarch could be paid a greater homage than first to hear the chant of ancient prowess from primeval times up to his own exploits and then to behold his worship and his own ideals merging with those of the founder of the race. Without a

[71] *Aen.* I 286–288. Nascetur pulchra Troianus origine Caesar, Imperium Oceano, famam qui terminet astris, Iulius a magno demissum nomen Iulo. This is prophecy, with a confirmation of the Trojan descent of Augustus. This note, already sounded in the first sketch of the poem (*Georg.* III 35–36), necessarily is heard again near the beginning of the *Aeneid*. It sets the key.

[72] *Aen.* VI 756–887. In the middle of the poem, this longer prophecy is appropriate.

[73] *Aen.* VIII 625–728. Here, too, two-thirds of the way along, a fairly lengthy prophecy is in place.

[74] See *Magical Art*, pp. 162–164. Cf. Nock, *Camb. Anc. Hist.* (1934), p. 476: "The *Aeneid* is an apotheosis of the Augustan system which is not the less effective for being indirect."

[75] *Aen.* VIII 680 (*stans celsa in puppi*), applied to Augustus in the description of the shield, and X 261, applied to Aeneas.

doubt, Virgil looks to one man to establish the destiny of
Rome. They who, somewhat naturally, suspect the poet of
egregious flattery have never read him — read his own words,
I mean; for only by hearing Virgil speak, and not some other
in his place, can we know what he thinks and how he feels.

What, then, is Virgil's ideal empire? That of a benevolent
despot, and not only benevolent, it would seem, but om-
niscient and omnipresent? By no means. Our all-important
document is the vision of Roman history which Anchises reveals to his son in the Elysian fields. This is not set forth in a
plain narrative, nor in a tale by one who reports what he has
seen, like that in the *Odyssey*, which Virgil could not slavishly
repeat; that he had done in the *Culex*, in a boyish way. Instead he envelops it in the mystic metempsychosis of Plato
and Pythagoras. This is not merely a clever device. It mirrors the higher reaches of the poet's imagination; for Virgil's
youthful interest in Epicurean science has been caught up
into Platonic idealism. He pictures a concourse of expectant
souls, purged of remembrance in the stream of Lethe, ready
for new reincarnations on this earth. We behold them, standing in a long line. We are given the feeling of dramatic sus-
pense, since the seer unfolds to us not history but prophecy.
There is the lineage of Aeneas in early Italy, the Alban kings,
Romulus, builder of the new city, translated to divinity, ancestor of the Julian line, with Caesar and Augustus last in the
succession, made gods themselves, like Hercules and Bacchus.
Then follows Numa, founder of law, exalted from a lowly
poverty to imperial might, then warlike Hostilius, breaker of
the peace, Ancus over-eager for popular acclaim, the tyrant
Tarquins and, with the new government, Brutus, no less
proud, who slew his sons in freedom's name, moved by patriotic zeal and inordinate ambition. Virgil distributes repri-
mands as well as eulogies. Decii and Drusi, Manlius and
Camillus, symbolize the early republic and its savage wars.
But then comes a dreadful civil war, fought by father-in-law
and son-in-law, Caesar and Pompey, harmonious now in the
quiet night of Elysium, but destined to plunge their knives

into their country's heart. Anchises chides these little boys and tells them not to train their minds to bellicosities. Caesar, Olympian by birth, should be the first to lay down arms. There is a self-protective advantage in the legendary setting of the plot. It is not Virgil who makes the reprimand — he merely echoes the words of Anchises!

The earlier conquerors, conquerors of Greece, are pointed out, Mummius and Aemilius Paulus, though with no fervent praise. Mighty Cato, the elder Cato, and Cossus call for mention. So do the Gracchi and their adversaries the Scipios, those two thunderbolts of war; and ancient simplicity is praised in Fabricius and Serranus, tillers of the soil and potent with their small possessions. The seer in his rhapsody follows no strict order in the images that throng and weary his mind in their intensity. Yet he must tell of Fabius Cunctator, he who alone saved Rome by going slow. Virgil is quoting father Ennius:

unus homo nobis cunctando restituit rem.

Then with the force of an oracle, a sermon on the mount, comes the great command to Rome. Others will excel in graving images of bronze or marble, better plead causes, or plot the turnings of the sky and the rising stars. Thy task, Roman, is to rule the nations with just sway, to build moral order upon peace, to spare the conquered and battle down the proud.[76]

One hero remains — Marcellus, who captured Syracuse in the Second Punic War. And with him walks a youth of his own name, resplendent in arms but sad of countenance. It is the son of Claudius Marcellus and the emperor's sister Octavia, a lad well-liked and destined by Augustus to succeed him, but he died of a mysterious illness in 23 B.C. The rest of Anchises' prophecy turns to a funeral dirge in honor of this ill-fated youth.

On the shield of the hero, a similar prophecy is engraved by its maker, the divine Vulcan. Only the fire-god could put

[76] Quoted in Chapter I, note 34.

so many scenes on a shield: but with the swift music of the poet's lines and the rush of his ideals, the reader is swept along, the art of magical illusion making all things possible. Here Aeneas can inspect the deeds of Italy and Roman triumphs, from the Alban kings to the victory of Actium and the conquest of all the far-off nations of the earth. Halfway along, the rites of religion ordained by Numa are pictured, and when monarchy deteriorates into tyranny, the house of Tarquin is overthrown *pro libertate*. A glimpse of an inferno is given, where Catiline is punished with the mighty sinners famed in legend; and then we see the abode of righteous men, wherein is Cato of Utica, last of the Romans of that republic which he and Cicero had vainly struggled to defend. These are bold symbols for a worshipper of Augustus to emblazon on Vulcan's handiwork; but, as before, this is not the poet's device — he is merely describing the art of Vulcan!

Such is the shield that Aeneas, little guessing its meaning, raises to his shoulders.[77]

As we look, then, on this ideal empire that Virgil presents, we find that the poet, like Livy, has searched his country's history for monuments of good to imitate and monuments of evil to avoid. It is an empire founded on justice, righteousness, law and order, religion and an ultimate peace. That means the recovery of the Golden Age, of which he dreamed in his Messianic eclogue and which in his *Georgics* [78] he found established in the peace of rustic happiness, not less real than in the good days of golden Saturn, before the age of war. It is an Ideal Empire and not an autocracy. Aeneas, in the vow that he makes before his final combat with Turnus, assures Latins and Trojans alike that in the new confederated state he claims no regal power — *nec mihi regna peto*.[79] That is a

[77] This is the way that Virgil "imitates" Homer, for whom Hephaistos crowds as many scenes on the shield of Achilles, glimpses of the works and the conflicts and the pleasures of man's daily life — all set in a framework of earth and sky and sea and obliterating for the moment the battles on the plains of Troy (*Iliad* XVIII 478–618).                    [78] II 458–540.

[79] XII 189: Non ego nec Teucris Italos parere iubebo Nec mihi regna peto: paribus se legibus ambae Invictae gentes aeterna in foedera mittant. Sacra deosque dabo. Enlightenment from abroad merges with native strength.

reminder to Augustus that he has come not to destroy but to fulfill.

## III

Horace, our plump little Horace, sleek little pig from the Epicurean sty, as he called himself,[80] was no less powerful than Virgil in building the ideal empire. If Virgil dreamed it, Horace, to whom Virgil was the half of his own soul,[81] saw the dream fulfilled. Horace at first had no heroes. He had many friends, including a special circle of the finest. He made himself an expert in that art of friendship of which genial banter is the outward and visible sign, sign of a devotion that needs no expression. At first the drift towards monarchy awakened no sympathy in him. Quite the reverse. He fought, as commander of a legion — what we should call a colonel today — on the republican side at Philippi in the army of Octavian and Antony. He was studying philosophy at Athens and fitting himself to transmute Greek lyric into Roman, when Brutus came and enlisted him and other young idealists to save the old republic. In vain. Horace did not even save his shield.[82]

On his return to Rome he was quick to utter in the resonantly defiant lyric verse of his Sixteenth Epode [83] both his devotion to the lost cause and his despair of the present age. With only too accurate a foreboding of yet another civil war, he saw no hope for his countrymen save to sail away and found a new commonwealth in that legendary island of the blest far out at sea; there the Golden Age, a somewhat ironically pictured Golden Age, awaited them. Virgil, whether he already knew Horace or not, recognized that a brother poet had appeared on the scene. In his Messianic Eclogue he

[80] *Epist.* I 4. 15–16.

[81] *Odes* I 3. 8: et serves animae dimidium meae.

[82] *Odes* II 7. 9–12. It is pathetic to see how many sober-minded scholars endeavor to defend Horace from his playfulness here. Cf. *Spirit of Comedy*, pp. 45–46.

[83] Several of the epodes are in essence lyrics. Horace's great model at the time was Archilochus, among the fragments of whose verse we note a lyric strain no less than stinging invective.

countered with his picture of the Golden Age that just had dawned in Italy as a result of the pact between Octavian and Antony at Brundisium.[84]  And not many months after that, partly for this poem, partly for Horace's sketches of the life of Rome that later formed his pleasant satires, Virgil presented the new poet to the patron of poets, Maecenas.

It was Actium that won over Horace, Actium and his love of Virgil.  Octavian became for him the savior of the state, appointed by high heaven to make atonement for the crime of civil war, to avenge the death of Caesar, and to execute vengeance for that Waterloo of the day, the defeat of Roman arms by the Parthians in 53 B.C.[85]  And yet Octavian receives no undivided eulogy from him.  In a majestic Pindaric ode,[86] he calls the roll of the heroes of old, attaching a contemporary and ultra-republican hero, Cato the younger,[87] to the lineage of Regulus and Curius and Camillus; and this comes swiftly down, at the end, to young Marcellus, the hope of Rome in Horace's own day.  Here is the same pageant of history that Virgil, taking a hint from Horace, it would seem,[88] displayed in the vision of Anchises.  Both poets declare to Augustus that he had come not to destroy but to fulfil.  Moreover, although he is the vicegerent of Jove upon earth,[89] he is a Roman citizen — the foremost of Rome's citizens and their father, *pater atque princeps*.[90]  It was not till 2 B.C., about a quarter of a century later, and after Horace's death, that these terms became official designations.  Horace, like Virgil, voicing a growing sentiment,[91] speaks for himself ahead of the statesmen, and yet with

[84] Cf. *Magical Art,* pp. 108–109.

[85] *Odes* I 2. 31–32.

[86] I 12.

[87] I 12. 35, cf. II 1. 24. Cato is as much of a hero to Horace as to Virgil. Here again is food for thought presented to Augustus.

[88] Virgil and Horace, brother-poets like Wordsworth and Coleridge, may well have taken ideas from each other or wrought out, each in his own way, ideas that they had talked over together. See a fine essay by C. T. Murphy, "Vergil and Horace," in *The Classical Bulletin* XVIII (1942), 61–64.

[89] *Odes* I 12. 51: tu secundo Caesare regnes.

[90] *Odes* I 2. 50: Hic ames dici pater atque princeps.

[91] The Roman people in devotion to Julius Caesar put up in the forum shortly after his assassination a marble column bearing the inscription PARENTI PATRIAE (Suet. *Iul.* 85).

a glance back at the old republic. The sovereign ruler for him, as for Polybius, is a fatherly king, not a monarch. And above all, this king derives his power from Jove to rule the world in justice; or as Horace pronounces with Roman brevity:

te minor latum reget aequus orbem.[92]

Justice and religion are the foundations of the state.

This praise of Octavian, proclaimed between Actium and the year 27 B.C., when the title of Augustus was conferred on the new ruler, attests a complete reversal of the poet's political views since that time of black despair in which his Sixteenth Epode was written. Some critics would explain this *volte-face* as a natural, but not admirable, act of acknowledgment for the poet's snug farm in the Sabine hills, and for the reception of the ex-slave's son into the best circles of Roman society. Horace has often been charged with propaganda. The brilliant Italian historian, Guglielmo Ferrero, in his Lowell lectures some years ago, could even declare that Horace's convivial odes were written in the interests of certain prominent vintners; for Horace was a crusader for the use of wine, hitherto not properly appreciated by his countrymen.[93] Perhaps, then, some of the apparently innocent phrases, like *vile Sabinum*, are really teeming with advertisements of some better brand. While somewhat doubtful about the necessity of this crusade, I should be the last to criticize Horace's art, if, as a by-product of his verses, plenteous casks of Falernian and other brands were carted up the road to the Sabine farm with the compliments of the rival vintners. But these commercial odors have long since been blown from Horace's wines; their superessential fragrance remains.

[92] *Odes* I 12. 57.
[93] *Characters and Events of Roman History from Caesar to Nero* (New York and London, G. H. Putnam's Sons, 1908), pp. 194–196: "This is the case [i.e. the presence of propaganda] with the odes of Horace. . . . He corroded the ancient Italian traditions, which opposed with such repugnance and so many fears the efforts of the vintners and the vineyard laborers to sell wine at a high price; in this way he rendered service to Italian viticulture." The whole chapter "Wine in Roman History" (pp. 181–208) is well worth reading when one feels blue.

But Horace did not stoop to flattery. He kept his independence. He refused the Emperor's invitation to become his private secretary. In his mode of life as in his mode of thought, he was bounden unto no man.[94] Virgil's heroes came on in sequence, vertically. Horace's great friends may be plotted horizontally; they accompany him on the same plane, through life. Virgil gave his whole soul to each of his heroes in turn. Horace gave one half of his soul to his beloved Virgil, the other to his beloved Maecenas, while comfortably keeping both halves for himself.

Horace, as we have seen, did not come round to the new regime without a struggle. We see that reflected in various odes.[95] One of especial interest, written, I take it, not long after Actium,[96] still has some flavor of his early hopelessness. He no longer bids his countrymen sail away to an Atlantis in the sea, but he declares that the Roman way of life can be cleansed of corruption only if citizens will bring their gold and jewels as an offering to Jove's temple on the Capitoline, or, preferably, cast them into the nearest sea. He contrasts the more enviable lot of Scythians and Getae, whose nomadic life he pictures as one of simple contentment and moral purity; long before Rousseau, Horace had discovered the happy savage. *If*, he declares, anyone wishes to remove the bloodstains from the state, *if* he would like to have his name inscribed on statues as "Father of our Cities," he must take our unbridled lawlessness in hand. For "what do gloomy criticisms help, if sin is not cut away by punishment, and what do vain laws profit without moral support?"

> quid tristes querimoniae
>   si non supplicio culpa reciditur?
> quid leges sine moribus
>   vanae proficiunt? [97]

[94] *Epist.* I 14: Nullius addictus iurare in verba magistri.

[95] Particularly I 14, on the battered Ship of State, written either before the battle of Actium or certainly not much later.

[96] III 24. Some of the points made are viewed in a new light in the six odes at the beginning of Book III, in some of Book IV and in the *Carmen Saeculare*. See e.g. note 120, below.

[97] Verses 33–36. *Leges sine moribus vanae* is the motto on the arms of the

Three points are worth noting in this ode of Horace, written before his complete adherence to Augustus. First, that the sovereign must be not a monarch but the father of his people; second, that the moral reform of the individuals who compose the state must precede the introduction of any system of government, however perfect on paper it may be; and third, that the ruler himself, to gain the respect of his people, must see that his engines of reform can run. In short, here is a little "mirror of the prince," all ready for the man, whoever he may be, who is destined to take over the government of Rome. Horace, no less than Virgil and Maecenas, is one of Augustus's counselors.

Horace's most conspicuous monument, a monument more enduring than bronze, takes the form, not of the epic that Augustus and Maecenas were constantly badgering him to write,[98] but of a series of six odes, all in his most majestic metre, the Alcaic, at the beginning of his Third Book. These are not ostensibly a eulogy of Augustus. The poet appears as the priest of the Muses at a sacred rite, orders the profane to stand apart and his hearers to keep reverent silence, while he speaks what he is inspired to speak to boys and girls — *virginibus puerisque*. His aim is first and foremost, as before, the moral reform of the Roman people, beginning with the rising generation. He prescribes in the first of the odes the art of plain living and of contentment with one's lot; in the second, for the boys, a soldier's training in hardship and in battles for his country, and a soldier's life of discipline, which inculcates reverence for sacred things. In the Third Ode, we find Augustus at the banquet of the gods; he has won his immortality — and he must work for it, like Bacchus and

University of Pennsylvania, altogether in the spirit of its illustrious patron Benjamin Franklin. The precept, widely applicable, has not always been observed in our federal legislation.

[98] *Odes* I 6, II 12. In Suet. *Vita Horatii* (Rolfe, Loeb, II, pp. 486–488) we learn that *Epist.* II 1 was intended as a response to the Emperor's playful insistency. "Are you afraid that you will get a bad name among posterity for seeming to be so intimate with me?" Augustus asked. The response was no less playful; for Horace's eulogies were not written to order. Cf. *Spirit of Comedy*, pp. 87–90. This letter is a masterpiece of banter.

Hercules of old, by the performance of mighty deeds.[99]  Romulus, too, is there, admitted by Juno herself, after some protest from that offended Queen, who goes on to prophesy the Roman's triumph over all the world, provided, *provided*, that they will promise not to rebuild the walls of their ancestral Troy.  Horace, before the publication of the *Aeneid*, is sounding that national and patriotic note which is one of the clearest strains in Virgil's poem.[100]  They both may be warning Augustus not to venture on Julius Caesar's grandiose, and unRoman, scheme of shifting the centre of the government to some eastern capitol like Alexandria or Troy; [101] for Caesar, ahead of his times as usual, prophetically saw what Constantine, some four centuries later, was destined, in his own fashion, to achieve.

In the Fourth Ode, the most imaginative of all, the Priest of the Muses exalts the spirit of poetry, which, merging with the high intelligence that he calls *consilium*, forms that sovereign virtue without which moral strength becomes brute force.  Such a spirit is vital for the individual, like the poet himself; it is vital for the ruler of the state; it is vital for the gods themselves, who by that grace overthrow the bestial giants, types of might without right.

In the Fifth Ode, the poet reproaches the Roman soldiers of Crassus, who, after their disgraceful defeat by the Parthians in 53 B.C., had calmly settled down in the Orient and taken Oriental wives.  In contrast with this ignominy, the poet tells of Regulus, who, sent home from Carthage to negotiate the ransom of the Roman prisoners, dissuaded the Senate from accepting the terms, and went back calmly to his death.  There may be legendary intrusions in this story, but the legend had become history.  It was one of the *exempla* of Roman heroism, a Roman self-sacrifice, the immolation of one's self to cleanse Rome of a stain.

[99] Horace accepts the doctrine of the Divinity of Heroes to which Virgil had contributed something in its application to the ruling house.  See note 62.

[100] *Aen.* XII 826: Sit Latium, sint Albani per saecula reges, Sit Romana potens Itala virtute propago; Occidit occideritque sinas cum nomine Troia.

[101] Suet. *Iul.* 79.

The last ode in this series is on the downfall of religion, prop of the Roman state. "Because thou walkest humbly with thy gods, O Roman, therefore dost thou rule." I quoted from this ode in the preceding chapter [102] to show how the later Roman poets' praises of their ancestors' virtues are backed up by Polybius, who witnessed them.

Moreover the decay of religion means the decay of morality. Morality cannot stand on its own feet. So Pope at the end of the *Dunciad*, picturing Chaos quenching one by one the lights of life, drily observes:

> Religion, blushing, veils her sacred fires,
> And, unobserved, Morality expires.

The night that spreads over the Roman world, as Horace pictures it, is quite as black as it seemed to Livy.

"What does not ruinous time degrade? The age of our fathers, worse than that of theirs, has brought us forth more sinful still, soon to give birth to a progeny still more vicious." [103]

With these words, which have not the ring of propaganda by a court poet, the Priest of the Muses concludes his sermon to boys and girls. His Mirror of the Prince, his establishment of the state, begins with the reform of the people who compose it. His method is not to tell them they are all right; he tells them they are all wrong.

In the year 17 B.C., the Secular Games were celebrated. They marked the end of an epoch, or *saeculum*, for the Roman state, with Augustus at its crowning-point. Sacrifices were offered during three days and nights to the chief deities above and below, with the third and last day devoted to Apollo and Diana — peculiarly Augustan deities. In the course of their rites a chorus of twenty-seven chaste boys and twenty-seven virgins, chosen from the first families of Rome, sang a festal

[102] Note 38. Cf. also *Odes* III 1. 5–6: Regum timendorum in proprios greges, Reges in ipsos imperium est Iovis.

[103] Verses 45–58: Damnosa quid non imminuit dies? Aetas parentum prior avis tulit Nos nequiores mox daturos Progeniem vitiosiorem. (On Livy, see note 5.)

or secular hymn or *Carmen Saeculare*; and Horace wrote that hymn. Many a friend of Horace, travelling to Rome before this war — τὸ πρὶν ἐπ᾽ εἰρήνης — has crossed over from the railway station to the Museo delle Terme to pay his respects to certain slabs of marble there — I hope they still are somewhere — engraved on which in beautiful Augustan capitals fragments of the official account of the *ludi saeculares* have been preserved. The words that this traveller seeks first of all read: CARMEN COMPOSVIT Q. HORATIVS FLACCVS.

Horace's *Secular Hymn* has been woefully misjudged. It is called frigid and mechanical, as though the emperor furnished his poet laureate with the points he wanted covered, in one-two-three-four order, and Horace manfully versified them all. There doubtless were conferences between him and his imperial master as well as with Maecenas. But if we read attentively what Horace had written before, we shall see in the *Carmen Saeculare* the flowering of those ideas about the state that had grown in his mind for years. Whatever he took over from his noble friends was mingled with his own reflections before these mounted from the "deep well" of his mind,[104] and were fashioned into poetry.

It is not the kind of poetry that summons us readers today to the upper heights of thought and feeling. Too much of either would be out of place. The poem is a liturgical hymn, actually sung in a rite, sung by the youthful chorus of fifty-four at Apollo's temple on the Palatine, and again after they had crossed the Forum and mounted the steps to Jove's temple on the Capitoline. The worshipper's heart is set on the music, on the spell of the rite, on the solemn procession of those who typified the purity and the nobility of the new generation, as they marched down and along and up again from shrine to shrine. A fine display of the poet's fancy or his in-

---

[104] The phrase is of course that of John Livingston Lowes, in *The Road to Xanadu*, a work that brought life to our knowledge of the poet's mind and death to the *Quellenforscher*. For a discriminating estimate of the *Carmen Saeculare* and a vivid account of the celebration see Buchan, *Augustus*, pp. 178–180. He remarks that "there was never a more independent poet-laureate" than Horace (p. 191). Cf. also Miss Taylor, *Div. Rom. Emp.*, pp. 177–179.

dividual intensity would be comically out of place. He is praying, in this hymn, with the rest of the people to the patron gods of Rome.

Of course he has something to say. I will half translate, into rude prose, and half interpolate, as I try to give his meaning.

He invokes the blessing of Phoebus and Diana, shining glories of the sky, as the chorus sings its chant to all the gods that guard the city of Rome. May the kindly Sun see nothing in his course greater than that city! For at last the foes on all its borders have been peaceably subdued. And may Diana, goddess of childbirth, protect the mothers among our folk and grant plenteous offspring; may she prosper the new laws on marriage and the other enactments of reform that the Senate have passed or are deliberating. We need abundant offspring, but they must be born into a firmly moral order.[105]

On such a basis the epoch about to begin will run its full stretch of ten and one hundred years till another secular festival.[106] May the three Goddesses of the Fates, true prophets of the foreordained, join coming blessings to those of the past. Hereby the Fates are constrained by their former favors to make the future safe for Roman destiny.

May Mother Earth, fertile in crops and flocks, crown Ceres with a sheaf of grain. Let the crops be nourished by wholesome streams and breezes from Jove on high. Happy farmers, like those in Virgil's *Georgics*, need the gods' help for their success.

[105] No birth control is thought of. Right education with the motto of *noblesse oblige* will produce the desired result. Hitler would agree, on the understanding that all "non-Aryan" elements have been purged from the pure Nordic stock; see *Mein Kampf*, edition of 1939, p. 145.

[106] Horace apparently wishes to fix the duration of the *saeculum* lest some imperial successor should be prompted to shorten it for his own glory — which is just what Claudius and Domitian did. In this the poet laureate may have carried out his ruler's instructions; for few poets would be inspired by the Muse to versify "one hundred and ten years" or few do it as neatly as Horace: *Certus undenos decies per annos Orbis.* That number itself, instead of the normal one hundred years, was arrived at after most learned research on the part of the Roman Committee on Religion, in order to adjust mere chronology to the majesty of Augustus.

May Apollo sheathe his arrows in peace, and may he and his sister, our Lady Moon, twi-horned queen of the stars, give ear, if Rome is their work and if the remnant saved from burning Troy came to the Tuscan shore, led by Aeneas, who was destined to bestow more than he had left behind. Here is where Horace pays homage to his Virgil, who had died two years before; he lets him add his bit to the *Carmen Saeculare*.

May the gods grant good morals to our docile youth — docile they will be if we have something to teach them, if we establish our program of reform. And grant peaceful repose to our old men — a wonderful and thoroughly Horatian petition, for which he needed no orders from anybody. Amid all this social improvement, let us not forget that tranquil harbor for which aged pilots have a right to steer. An inconspicuous part is this, but an important part, of the high celebration — one slight reminder of Horace's art of leisure, which seems a lost art for us today.

And hear the prayer of the ruler, offspring of Anchises and Venus.[107] For he can conquer his foe in war, but show mercy to the fallen.[108] What is this but Virgil's sentiment:

parcere subiectis et debellare superbos?

If Augustus ordered Horace's lines at this point, he passed on the order that Virgil had given him. It is this chivalrous treatment that makes the Mede fear Roman arms and Scythians and Indians come to him for counsel. Verily peace is crowned with law and order.[109] The ancient virtues come again, Faith and Honor and Conscience, and in their train Prosperity, with a cornucopia of Earth's blessings.

So if Phoebus and Dian listen to the entreaties of the guardians of religion and the chant of this chorus, and if they prolong the happiness of the Roman state into an ever better age, the youth and maidens may carry home a good and cer-

---

[107] Here Augustus is clearly identified with Aeneas. See above, note 75. On the reminiscences of the Secular Hymn and of Virgil's poetry in the scenes on the *Ara Pacis*, cf. Chapter VII, note 20.

[108] Verse 51: bellante prior iacentem Lenis in hostem.

[109] Virgil's *pacique imponere morem*.

tain hope that Jove on high and all the gods favor these rites with their blessing.[110]

*Explicit Carmen Saeculare.* It is a hymn of fulfilment and of progress — an outlook sometimes said to be a purely modern invention.[111] Horace's pessimism, his vision of a world sliding from bad to worse,[112] has changed to a reasonable hope.

I therefore cannot find in Horace's *Secular Hymn* a frigid compliance with the sovereign's command. Every line is full of meaning; the whole presents that ideal empire which Virgil dreamed and Horace saw fulfilled. If Horace's stateliness seems artificial to some of us, that is partly because we have slighted religion and morality, liturgy and authority, and the reverent study of our ancestral lineage in Greece and Rome and plucked them from our system of education and thus from the foundation of the state.

Space fails me to present the wealth of sentiment and the subtle art of the great Fourth Book, called forth by new successes of the Roman arms in the north. It is not one constant eulogy of Augustus. All the old delights of Horace's poetry reappear, and in the opening poem he professes to be called back by Venus to the lyric he had sworn he would abandon; the ode is a tribute to the younger poets of love, Ovid among them, whom Horace trusts to carry on.[113] The strength of the book, its firm backbone, is furnished by the odes of triumph.[114] For the brilliant campaign in the country on beyond the Brenner Pass, the strategy was planned by the Emperor and carried through by his stepsons Drusus and Tiberius. Drusus

[110] Most editors ruin the meaning of the four flowing strophes (one sentence) at the end of the hymn by putting a full stop after *aevum* (*v.* 68) or *auris* (*v.* 72) or both.

[111] Cf. J. B. Bury, *The Idea of Progress* (London, Macmillan, 1920), pp. 11, 18, and Rand, *Founders of the Middle Ages*, pp. 13, 14, 291. Let us hope that the Sather Lectures on this subject given at the University of California by Professor W. A. Oldfather several years ago will be published at no distant date. For the idea in ancient Greece, see Finley, *op. cit.*, pp. 82–83.

[112] Cf. note 103.

[113] Cf. "Notes on Ovid," *Trans. Amer. Philol. Assoc.* XXXV (1904), 128–147 (esp. 138–143).

[114] *Odes* IV 2, 4, 5, 14, 15.

is the hero, Tiberius receives a notably cooler praise.[115] They both have profited by the lessons they learned at the paternal hearth, and both father and sons derive their strength from their ancestral Rome, which ever could rise above disaster.[116] It is the Golden Age once more, or something better.[117] The ruler has called back religion and the arts that made the old republic glorious.[118] Reform, as elsewhere in history, takes on the aspect of a renaissance — and that was a keynote in the plan of Augustus.[119]

The sense of fulfilment that animates this book is even more certain than in the *Secular Hymn*. With a glance back at his earlier pronouncement on the vanity of laws without the support of moral sentiment, Horace can now declare that "morals *and* law have conquered spotted sin." [120] In the ode in which this verse appears, there is a deeper and more personal affection for Augustus than is found elsewhere. The ruler seems to have won Horace's friendship at last. And Horace is still the counselor. The mirror of the prince is flashed again before the ruler's eyes and before those whom he had chosen to carry on his mission.

Nor is the comfortable outcome of it all forgotten, after

[115] The ode on Drusus (IV) begins with his praise, which is sung in a stately, Pindaric style (*vv.* 1–24), attributes part of his glory to the lessons he had learned in the household of Augustus (*vv.* 25–36), and ends with a panegyric of the noble line of the Nerones, who had fought gloriously against Hannibal (*vv.* 37–76). Again many editors mispunctuate. The prophecy put into the mouth of Hannibal goes to the end of the ode; there should not be a full stop after *interempto* (*v.* 72). Tiberius's ode (XIV) begins with a eulogy of Augustus (*vv.* 1–9), sounds the praise of Drusus once more (*vv.* 10–13), and only then does the *Maior Neronum* appear (*vv.* 14–32), after which we learn that Tiberius owed his forces, his strategy and his favoring gods to Augustus himself, whose conquests occupy the remainder of the ode (*vv.* 33–52).

[116] IV 4. 53–68. See Chapter I, note 25, where a phrase from this noble passage is quoted, since its sentiments accord with those of Polybius.

[117] He says of Augustus (IV 2. 37–40): Quo nihil maius meliusque terris Fata donavere bonique divi Nec dabunt quamvis redeant in aurum Tempora priscum.

[118] IV 15. Every word in this closing ode is significant. For a motto take *vv.* 12–14: Et veteres revocavit artis Per quas Latinum nomen et Italae Crevere vires.

[119] Cf. the chapter *Respublica Conservata* in Buchan, *Augustus*, pp. 147–169, and Hammond, *Augustus Principate*, pp. 21–23 with the notes on pp. 209–210.

[120] IV 5. 22: Mos et lex maculosum edomuit nefas. See note 97.

so many conquests — the life of peace and merriment. Romans will sing their sovereign's praise "sober in the morning of the unbroken day, mellowed when the sun is dropped into the western bay." [121]  In the last of the odes, he begins with his favorite apology for not writing epic on his hero's battles. He tried, but Apollo strummed his lyre noisily and bade him stop. For he has paid his tribute in a different way. He pays it again in the next verses of this ode. He ends it, and all his poetry, in mirth — mirth mixed with reverence. The family gathers, and after due worship of the gods, they start to sing, amid the boons of merry Bacchus, of the righteous heroes of the olden time; they sing of Troy and Anchises and the offspring of kindly Venus. It is Virgil's song once more. Horace's last verses are a toast to his Virgil, half of his own soul.

## IV

In the light of the poetry of Virgil, who set forth his vision of ideal empire, and that of Horace, who saw the vision fulfilled, let us glance at the career of Octavian and note its relation, so far as we can, to the ideas of these friends of his, members of the literary circle of his counselor Maecenas.

The youth of Octavius is well pictured by Buchan.[122] He was a studious youth of frail health whom his great-uncle Julius Caesar befriended. Caesar saw something in the lad that merited attention. Octavius responded to this fatherly interest with an intense devotion, and after the dictator's assassination in 44 B.C. consecrated his life to avenging him, especially when he found that, by the terms of Caesar's will, he had been adopted into his household. Caesar had become his father: it was a father's death that he would avenge. That is the clue to his subsequent conduct in his relations with the Senate, and Cicero, and Mark Antony. That was enough. As Buchan observes, "We need not credit him at the age of nine-

---

[121] IV 5. 38–40: dicimus integro sicci mane die, dicimus uvidi, Cum sol Oceano subest.
[122] *Augustus*, chap. I.

teen with even the rudiments of the policy which made the principate." [123]

The same devotion to the memory of Caesar, as we have seen, was shown by Virgil in his Fifth Eclogue, written after the Second and the Third in 42 B.C.,[124] not long before Octavian and Mark Antony, and Caesar's ghost, met the regicides at Philippi and defeated them, thanks primarily to Antony — and to Caesar's ghost. In the ensuing years it became more and more evident to Octavian that Antony stood in the way of his revenge. Antony, too, was Caesar's avenger, but primarily in his own interests. Octavian also must have felt it his mission to carry out his father's plans, so far as he understood them, for the consolidation of the Roman state. The more that Antony became involved in the Orient, and in Egypt, the clearer that mission became. An immediate thorn in the flesh was Sextus Pompey, who inherited from his father's success in clearing the sea of pirates the ability to become one himself. Sextus' business was not settled till 36 B.C., and that not by Octavian himself, who had shown no marked capacity in military or naval affairs, but by his great general, and engineer, and admiral, Agrippa. During this period there was not much time for Octavian to think ahead and lay the foundations for an ideal empire.

A year before that, Virgil had begun the writing of his *Georgics*, which caught up the theme that, as we have seen,[125] had already engaged his youthful mind in the *Culex*, written when he was but sixteen years old and before he came to Rome. There is no evidence whatsoever that he knew Octavius at that time, or at any time before his introductory Eclogue, the first in the series as we have them, but the last, or next to the last, if I am right, in point of composition.[126] He now has found his ultimate hero, who at his request had brought law and order into the troubled region about Mantua. Meantime his hero's thoughts were centred on eliminating Antony, the Hitler of the day.

[123] *Ibid.*, p. 71.
[124] Cf. note 64.

[125] Cf. note 48.
[126] *Magical Art*, p. 151.

But not to all high-minded Romans a Hitler.[127] Not to
Pollio, Virgil's hero in his earliest Eclogues, and still his hero
in 39 B.C.[128] The great poem of the year before, whoever may
have been the Messianic child, is dedicated, with exalted
praise, to Pollio. Octavian was hardly "the centre of the picture." [129] Pollio was Antony's envoy at the Pact of Brundisium, when, with the wise Maecenas speaking for Octavian,
the threatening outbreak between Octavian and Antony was,
for the moment, quelled. Among the leaders, Pollio was the
poet's natural choice. Virgil had reason for fighting shy of
both Antony and Octavian. The latter had shown certain
qualities that did not presage a Prince of Peace. Above all
was the vice of cruelty, exhibited not only during the proscrip-
tions decreed by him and Antony and Lepidus, when three
hundred senators, Cicero among them, and two thousand
*equites* were purged away, but also on the battlefield at
Philippi, where Octavian had taken no glorious part, and at
the siege of Perusia, where Antony's brother Lucius was defeated.[130] We will not tarry with the youthful excesses of
Octavian, as chronicled by Suetonius,[131] one of whose sources
was a pamphlet, or book, on Octavian written by Mark Antony.[132] What an interesting work these "Memoirs" must have
been — the best-seller of the day, of which the largest number
of copies, presumably, were acquired by the Emperor Augustus. Be that as it may, Pollio, not Octavian, was Virgil's candidate in 40 B.C. for the ruler of the Ideal Empire.[133]

It was only a year or two thereafter that Virgil transferred

---

[127] About a third of the Senate favored him. See Buchan, *Augustus*, p. 114,
and for admirable characterizations of Antony, pp. 45–46, 87, 123.

[128] *Magical Art,* pp. 86, 123–124.

[129] As Buchan would have it (*op. cit.*, p. 93).

[130] Suet. *Oct.* 13–15, 27.

[131] *Ibid.* 68–71. We should of course balance this array of what Suetonius
calls "charges or slanders" with the evidence that he amasses for the ruler's
simplicity of living (71–77). Cf. Hammond, "Hellenistic Influences," p. 16:
"The keynote of Augustus' life was simplicity." See also the appraisal of Augustus's character, with all the lights and shades, by Buchan, *op. cit.* pp. 253–
258.

[132] *Ibid.* 68, 69. 1, 2. 3, 4. 2. Antony also wrote uncomplimentary letters
to or about Octavian (*ibid.* 7. 2, 69. 2).

[133] The Fourth Eclogue, though the imaginary setting of the poem is the

his allegiance, in full enthusiasm, to Octavian, partly for the protection extended to Mantua, and partly because plans for the Ideal Empire were indeed going on. But the planners were Maecenas, *l'éminence grise*, as Buchan aptly calls him,[134] Virgil and Horace. When the two poets, with their friends Plotius Tucca and Varius, later the editors of the *Aeneid* after Virgil's death, accompanied Maecenas and Fonteius Capito, Antony's man, to Brundisium on their fresh mission to Antony at Athens late in 38 B.C. or early in 37, they hardly spent all their time in the adventures described by Horace in his familiar satire;[135] there were some moments for discussing the political situation that caused the mission and for looking ahead to its ultimate object. And when Horace in his odes[136] tells Maecenas not to weary his mind with high concerns of state but join him at a modest dinner at his Sabine villa, we may well suppose that after the *vin du pays*, or a choicer vintage brought by Maecenas, had begun to flow, it was sometimes the high affairs of state that occupied their attention. We should note once more, with particular care, that Virgil's conception of an ideal empire began to form immediately after the death of Julius Caesar, is expressed partly in the Fourth Eclogue, and is further developed in the first two books of the *Georgics*, which began to occupy the poet's mind at least as early as 37 B.C.[137] Octavian, meanwhile, was busied mainly with eliminating the menace of Sextus Pompey.

Some time not long after the defeat of this pirate, Octavian, whose thoughts had been developing, must have taken part in the deliberations of these three friends of the Roman state.[138]

---

moment of the birth of the child, was obviously written after that event (*Magical Art*, pp. 103–106).

[134] *Op. cit.* p. 148.

[135] I 5.

[136] III 8; 29.

[137] *Magical Art*, p. 342.

[138] That Virgil led the way for Augustus rather than took orders from him I have taught in courses since 1903. See also *Magical Art*, p. 99. My friend Conway, who doubtless preached the same doctrine even earlier, expressed it in his *New Studies of a Great Inheritance* (London, John Murray, 1921), p. 227, treating Horace in the same way (p. 54). A. Y. Campbell, *Horace: A New Interpretation* (London, Methuen, 1924), pp. 99–100, approved Conway's ideas,

What were the guiding ideas when, with the help of these kindly tutors, as kindly as Polybius had been to Scipio, the young ruler had thought out his own policy? After Hammond's demonstrations,[139] we may dismiss the conception of a crafty monarch who fooled the people with the fancy that his sole object was to restore the republic, whereas his covert design was under the camouflage of time-honored republican titles — *imperator, tribunus, censor, pontifex maximus* — to get all the power into his own hands and, in the fashion of his father, act like a dictator. He could, according to this interpretation, proclaim aloud, "La république est restituée," and add *sotto voce*, "La république, c'est moi." No, his devotion to the usages and the heroes of the past is genuine. Let us accept the testimony of Suetonius,[140] that next to the immortal gods he worshipped the leaders of the olden time.

But this is not the whole story, nor does Mommsen's conception of a *diarchia*, evenly apportioned to Augustus and the Senate, fit the facts.[141] He was the ruler, and he made it plain that he was. Although he twice offered to resign in favor of the old regime, he saw the necessity of a single, central control; and although he rejected the terms *rex* and *dictator*, he was glad to be called "father of his country," *pater patriae*, and "chief citizen," *princeps*.[142] The new flavor in both these titles is nothing republican. Thus Augustus steered a *via media* between Caesar's monarchism and the old-fashioned government by the Senate.

It has been observed that he harked back to Cicero and Pompey rather than to Caesar.[143] Right enough — though to Cicero rather than to Pompey, let us say. What he found in Cicero — and we should see it more clearly if all of the *De Re Publica* were preserved — was the doctrine of Plato and Po-

---

and so Buchan *op. cit.*, in various places, *e.g.* in his characterization of Virgil and Horace (pp. 272–276).

[139] Summed up in the final chapter of *Augustan Principate*, pp. 195–197.

[140] *Aug.* 31. 5.

[141] Hammond, *Augustan Principate*, p. 4.

[142] *Ibid.* pp. 110–113.

[143] *Ibid.* pp. 111, 268.

lybius concerning the best form of government and its illus-
tration in the Roman state.[144] In that ideal form, as we have
observed, the king, as father, the nobles, as the best of men,
and the people, free in their rights and the ultimate source of
power, each perfomed its valid part harmoniously. The conception of the king as savior and father was not "a new thing
in Rome." [145] It was a familar idea that the Romans had
learned from Polybius, if not before, and could recognize in
their own primeval history, or thought they could, above all
in the Golden Age of Numa. Augustus, therefore, though at
first, as the avenger of his father, he may have cherished a
plan for the state like that of Caesar, came round to the very
doctrine which Polybius had taught young Scipio and which,
it well may be with Cicero's help, Virgil and Horace had absorbed. He was no reactionary and no rebel. In Elmer Davis's
pithy phrase, Augustus "restored as much of the republic as
the traffic would bear"; "he called himself 'leading Citizen'
and almost everybody was satisfied." [146] For he had come
neither to destroy nor to revert, but to fulfill.

Augustus was undoubtedly a ruler of eminent political
genius, who knew his own purpose and accomplished it. But
his temperament was outgoing and coöperative. He was also
fond of poetry, and even tried his hand at it, and good-
humoredly placed the right estimate on his performance.[147]
He was fond of his poets. His intimacy with Horace was most
jovial, and his jestings with him were, to put it mildly, highly
informal.[148] After he returned from his victories in 29 B.C.,
he listened with relish as Virgil and Maecenas took turns in
reading the *Georgics* to him.[149] While the poet was at work
on the *Aeneid*, the Emperor constantly besought him to let
him see any of the finished parts; when Virgil thought best,

---

[144] He wished to be known as the *optimi status auctor* (Suet. *Aug.* 28. 2).
[145] Buchan *op. cit.* p. 116.
[146] See his review of Buchan's work in *The New York Times Book Review*,
Nov. 21, 1937, p. 3. Also cf. Finley on Pericles, *op. cit.*, p. 163.
[147] Suet. *Aug.* 85. 2.
[148] Suet. *Vita Horat.* ed. Rolfe (Loeb) II 484–488. Cf. note 98.
[149] Donatus, *Vita Verg.* ed. Brummer, p. 6, 91–96.

he read him Books Two, Four, and Six — three of the best. In the Fourth, Augustus would see primarily great poetry of a tragic cast; in the others, equally great poetry of different tones, he would hear next to nothing of explicit eulogy of himself. But having heard, or surmised, that he was another Aeneas, he would become aware of many a trait indispensable for an ideal ruler. Virgil, while reading aloud his story of the founding of Rome, was constantly holding up to his imperial auditor a Mirror of the Prince. So thought Horace when, referring to this very scene, he remarked that the Muses gave gentle counsel to the Ruler, and that after giving it, were glad that it was given.[150]

Thus is it clear that not only law and order, political sagacity and good roads, not only philosophy and humanism, but poetry helped build the Ideal Empire.[151]

[150] Odes IV. 4. Vos Caesarem altum militia simul Fessas cohortes abdidit oppidis Finire quaerentem labores Pierio recreatis antro. Vos lene consilium et datis et dato Gaudetis almae. See above, p. 67.

[151] Hammond, *Augustan Principate*, p. 24: "Augustus modelled himself on the ideals of Cicero, the Stoics and Plato." Jaeger *op. cit.* (Chapter I, note 96), p. xvii: "Augustus envisaged the task of the Roman Empire in terms of Greek culture." We may ponder again the meaning of Horace's ode IV 4.

# CHAPTER III

## ROMAN HIGH SERIOUSNESS AND ROMAN LAUGHTER

WE have seen that poetry and philosophy played no small part in the building of Rome. Possibly my readers may think that we have had enough of seriousness. Nothing could be more serious than the mood in which a Roman lays the foundation of the state. Even Horace, Rome's foremost expert in laughter, becomes exceedingly sober when he considers the destiny of Rome and holds up the Mirror of the Prince to his sovereign. There is a twinkle in his eye now and then, and he does not leave out wine and song from the peace on which good order is imposed; but up to that point the building of the ideal empire is no affair for jesting.

This kind of seriousness, of course, we do not need to prove is eminently Roman. But I mean something more. Whether or not Matthew Arnold intended his "high seriousness" to include a subtler and richer essence than what I have in mind — he doubtless did — I venture to employ his expression for my purpose. I am thinking not merely of imagination, or intensity, or nobility of language, all of which we have seen illustrated in various passages at which we have looked. Take that ode of Horace which I called the most imaginative of the six that make up his sermon to girls and boys.[1] There we have a principle propounded — the supremacy of the high intelligence typified by poetry — a principle deeply felt by Horace and presented with his careful art. It is a cosmic principle, applying to man, applying to the sovereign, applying to the world of the Olympians. To set off these high ideas, to

[1] IV 4. And see Chapter II, note 150.

brighten their foreground with gentler colors, there is a little legend, sparkling with humor and fancy, in which the infant Horace plays the part of the babes in the woods. All this is excellent; no touch of the prosaic or the banal appears.

But the quality of high seriousness is not there. For that we need a flight away from any earthly event, or experience, or any ideal principle wrought out by human thought. With such matter the poet may begin and with art and imagination so mold it that, as in the ode of Horace at which we just have glanced, it is transmuted into poetry. But more than that, there must come a moment when, of a sudden, whatever the nature of the incident or the idea, we find ourselves lifted from the earthly plane to an indefinable region of thought or emotion or both, in which the starting point slips wholly from our consciousness. In the twinkling of an eye the vision comes, a "bright shoote of everlastingnesse," and in the twinkling of an eye it may vanish. But its presence is the most real of all experiences. "High seriousness," or any other term, cannot describe it.

There are not many such moments in Roman poetry, or any poetry; but they occur, and may serve as a gauge of the poet's immediacy of feeling, of his originality, whatever his models may have been. Catullus, "tenderest of Roman poets nineteen hundred years ago," — whose emotions, intense and richly diverse, spring up spontaneously and flow into forms so natural that they seem to be created in their course — Catullus has these sudden shifts from the actual into the eternal, these flights that make the unknown known.

"Let us live my Lesbia and let us love, and reckon the mumblings of aged censors all at a farthing's worth. Suns may set and rise again. We, when once our brief light is spent, we must sleep one never-ending night."

> Vivamus, mea Lesbia, atque amemus,
> Rumoresque senum severiorum
> Omnes unius aestimemus assis.
> Soles occidere et redire possunt:

Nobis, cum semel occidit brevis lux,
Nox est perpetua una dormienda.[2]

With this last line the light of life goes not only for these
Roman lovers but for us. We are surrounded with the blackness of the long, last night and think of nothing else. This
is not a very bright shoot of everlastingness, but the color is
of no significance, if it be everlasting. It is everlasting, to
repeat my paradox, for the moment. In the next, we return
to actuality, to the passion of the lovers, which is all the more
intense because it is set on such a background, and because a
flicker of humor plays about the lines at the very end of the
poem, but not until those lines.

Da mi basia mille, deinde centum,
Dein mille altera, dein secunda centum,
Deinde usque altera mille, deinde centum,
Dein, cum milia multa fecerimus,
Conturbabimus illa, ne sciamus.
Aut ne quis malus invidere possit,
Cum tantum sciat esse basiorum.

The purpose of the uncountable thousands of kisses, for
which no special apology had seemed required, is to prevent
some envious rival from working a spell, casting the evil eye,
on the lovers — something that he could not do unless he knew
the mathematical value of their bliss.[3]

In a poem like this we have sure material for an estimate
of Roman originality in poetry. The supreme literature of
all time is Greek literature, of which the "educators" of our
day have robbed our schools. The great Roman authors proclaim clearly enough the inferiority of their own writings.
But we go too far if we think of Roman literature as a faded
copy of the Greek. Some of it is just that. But some is not.
The instances that I am citing here are for the most part what
may be called test cases, because the moment of high seriousness springs from the experience of a Roman mind reacting

[2] *Carm.* 5.
[3] Some editors, blind to the character of this poem, give it vulgar titles, such
as "The Kisses."

on Roman, or Italian, matter. We hardly need track out a
Greek source for the simple ideas or emotions expressed by
Catullus in the present poem. Its flavor is Italian; Italian
is the fear of the evil eye, and the word for kiss, *basium*, used
first by Catullus in Latin literature,[4] may have been brought
up by him from the country.[5] It is not the simple material,
but what is done with it, what it brings forth, that counts.
Only the poet himself could open up that momentary glimpse
of the eternal. Even if he found it in a Greek poem that he
reproduced — a most unlikely possibility — he is no less a
creator for making eternity shine through a Latin translation.
If just this one poem were all that we had of Catullus, we
should recognize his greatness and know by his example that
it is worth the while to search for similar originality among
other Roman poets.

Nor is the search in vain. In Virgil we have already seen [6]
that in the solemn prophecy of history made by Anchises to
his son in the Elysian fields the tone can change swiftly from
fervent panegyric to audacious humor when Caesar and Pompey are addressed as little boys.[7] The pomp and glory of Rome
vanishes as we look down on the earth-shaking Civil War from
the summit of Arcturus and find it nothing but a squabble

---

[4] If we may judge by the complete citations made in the *Thesaurus Linguae
Latinae*. After Catullus instances are rare (only one in Phaedrus and one in
Petronius) until *basium* flourished in Martial.

[5] My old master, Eduard Wölfflin, told us in his lectures at Munich in 1899
that it was a country expression that Catullus brought up to Rome from his
native Verona. Otherwise we might expect it somewhere in the numerous
plays of Plautus. The scholiasts of a later age drew distinctions in their fashion. Donatus (on Ter. *Eun*. III 2. 3) calls *basium* a mark of chaste affection,
*osculum* of duty, and *suavium* of passion. Servius (on *Aen*. I 260), illustrating
this doctrine, declares that, according to some, an *osculum* was given to sons,
a *basium* to a wife, and a *suavium* to a mistress. He adds that these distinctions are not true, since *basium* is most commonly used of an impure and lascivious kiss. Even learned scholiasts sometimes could not tell the difference.
If that difference was observed in Catullus's times, he may have chosen the
word with a purpose; for Lesbia, who received the full fire of his passion, was
a pure and radiant wife to him — until he found her out.

[6] *Aen*. VI 756–886.

[7] *Ibid*., 832: Ne pueri, ne tanta animis adsuescite bella Neu patriae validas
in vescera vertite viris. The alliteration adds pungency to the humor.

between two children anxious for a fight.  Nor is this merely
a descent from the sublime to the ridiculous.  War becomes
ridiculous; but above it the poet, without uttering a word, in
one of his speaking silences, reveals his vision of unending
peace.

Again, in a later book of the poem,[8] the hero, who in search
of allies has left the Trojan camp near the mouth of the Tiber,
sails up the river to the spot where Evander, an exile from
Arcadia, had made a settlement.  It was the site where later
the city of Rome was founded.  The king points out to his
guest the notable places in his primitive capital and the notable events that had occurred there; for the art of the poet
suggests that the country was already rich in history.  They
come at last to the king's mansion on the Palatine; it is a modest house, though Hercules had deigned to rest there:

> This threshold Hercules the victor crossed,
> And this the palace that then sheltered him.
> Dare thou, my guest, like him to scorn display,
> Fit thou thyself, like him, for life divine,
> Nor come disdainful to a poor estate.
> He spoke, and 'neath the rafters of his hut
> He brought the mighty hero to his bed —
> A bear-skin quilting on a pile of leaves.[9]

Now this rude hut is set by the poet on the very spot where
Augustus had his palace.  Here, then, is another of those skilfully veiled intimations, conveyed by prophecy, that Augustus is the hero of the *Aeneid* and that the hero of the *Aeneid*
is Augustus.  If especial significance is the oracular mandate
delivered to the hero:

> Dare thou my guest to scorn display —

> Aude, hospes, contemnere opes et te quoque dignum
> Finge deo rebusque veni non asper egenis.

The sovereign must know that playing the part of the hero in
this epic means more than bowing to compliments; if he, like

---

[8] *Aen.* VIII 306–369.
[9] Repeated from *Magical Art*, pp. 430–431.  See the whole chapter, "Simplicity from Imperial Rome."

Hercules — and Hellenistic kings — would win his immortality, he must obey the poet's rules for a good and simple life.

Furthermore, the poet's noble praise and his noble imagination are but incidents in his magic, which, hovering all along over Evander and his guest as they move like spirits through Augustan Rome, now comes in a flash that wipes out all the later splendor. In place of

The smoke and wealth and din of Rome,[10]

magic restores the simple temples and the ancient groves and the cottage about whose eaves at daybreak the choir of birds wake the hero on his couch of leaves.[11] There is no Greek source at this point for Virgil's magic. We start with Rome and, soon, so bright is the vision of what lies beyond, that terrestrial Rome has vanished.[12]

Horace, Quintilian remarks, in the course of his judicious compliments, sometimes can rise.[13] His flights may be in general like those of the little Matinian bee to which he likens himself,[14] But now and then, despite his disclaimer, the spirit of the eagle is upon him. It comes, I am sure, at one moment, when he breaks forth into a dithyramb, a Dionysiac ode, the wildest mode of ancient poetry in both its verse and its rush of emotion.[15] Horace's verse is not wild, and at first when

[10] Horace *Odes* III 29: fumum et opes strepitumque Romae. Tennyson neatly makes this line modern with: "The dust and din and steam of town" (*In Memoriam* 89).

[11] *Aen.* VIII 456: et matutini volucrum sub culmine cantus. One can hear chirpings at the beginning and a chorus at the end of this exquisite line.

[12] For other swift flights into the empyrean, see what Virgil makes of the rustic's philosophy, and of the Ivory Gate. Chapter IV, notes 22 and 35.

[13] *Inst. Or.* X 1. 96: Lyricorum idem Horatius fere solus legi dignus. Nam et insurgit aliquando et plenus est iucunditatis et gratiae et variis figuris et verbis felicissime audax. From these few words and Petronius' *curiosa felicitas*, the best *bon mot* in literary criticism (118. 5), and Horace's own *Musarum sacerdos* and his own *Romanae fidicen lyrae*, and his own *splendide mendax* (properly interpreted), an epitaph could be constructed that would fill Horace with content *per omnia saecula saeculorum*.

[14] *Odes* IV 2. 27–32.

[15] Horace notes Pindar's bold creation of words and his triumph over metrical laws in the dithyramb; *ibid.* 10–12: per audaces nova dithyrambos Verba devolvit numerisque fertur Lege solutis. Horace hardly means that Pindar's

"winged with a new spirit" he sings his praise of Caesar in groves and caves, one wonders whether a more suitable place for such a rhapsody might not be the imperial palace. But Horace continues:

Even as the sleepless Maenad stands wrapt upon the heights, looking out over Hebrus and Thracia white with snow and Rhodope where barbarian foot has wandered, so would I stray and look in wonder on banks of streams and the lonely woods.[16]

At once the human scene and imperial Caesar are forgotten, nor do they appear later in the ode. We are with the poet on far-off snowy heights. He is communing with nature in a mood of elemental wonder, or rather surrendering himself to nature, in the manner that may seem to some moderns the exclusive privilege of Romanticists. But the Classical poets could be romantic too, as Wordsworth testified by his praise of Horace in his poem called *Liberty*.[17] The ancients had as many visions of nature as moderns have, but we must look at their different forms of poetry to see all the shadings. For

---

verse contains no metrical elements; the familiar measures are there, but are swept along in the stream. Pindar is master of the kind of free verse that is difficult to write; we are only too familiar nowadays with the kind that is easy.

[16] *Odes* III 25. 8–14: Non secus in iugis Exsomnis stupet Euhias Hebrum prospiciens et nive candidam Thracen ac pede barbaro Lustratam Rhodopen, ut mihi devio Ripas et vacuum nemus Mirari libet.

[17] Verses 87 ff.:

> Who more wise
> Than the industrious Poet, taught to prize . . .
> That life — the flowery path that winds by stealth —
> Which Horace needed for his spirit's health;
> Sighed for, in heart and genius, overcome
> By noise and strife, and questions wearisome,
> And the vain splendours of Imperial Rome? — . . .
> Give *me* the humblest note of those sad strains
> Drawn forth by pressure of his gilded chains,
> As a chance-sunbeam from his memory fell
> Upon the Sabine farm he loved so well;
> Or when the prattle of Blandusia's spring
> Haunted his ear — he only listening —
>                        (and five more lines).

Horace would smile at the thought that his life was that of a pet canary. He heaved no sighs over the pressure of gilded chains. His romanticism was not tinged with sentimentality. He would be none the less grateful for such homage from the great romantic, who at his best (not here!) was veritably nature's priest; (cf. *Spirit of Comedy*, pp. 79–80). Our Romantic poets did not revolt

nature in pastoral poetry — the only kind which modern critics tend to dwell upon — has not the majesty appropriate for epic verse, nor is epic the place for the wild abandon with which the dithyrambic poet revels in his kinship with mountain fastnesses or glistening fields of snow.[18]

There is another form of high seriousness of which Matthew Arnold speaks; he calls it the "grand style," meaning nothing grandiose but, on the contrary, the expression of the tragic or the sublime in terms of the barest simplicity. There are no Latin verses, so far as I remember, to match the instances that Arnold quotes from Homer, as in the words addressed on the battlefield by Achilles to young Lycaon, Priam's son, who grasps his knees and begs for life. It is the moment when Achilles, aroused to frenzy, is wreaking vengeance for the death of Patroelus. Becoming strangely calm, he says:

Now is there none that shall escape death, whomsoever the god casts into my hands before Ilion, none of all the Trojans, and most of all, none of the sons of Priam. So friend, die thou, too. Why weepest thou so? Patroclus, too, is dead. And he was much thy better.

> ἀλλὰ φίλος θάνε καὶ σύ. τίη ὀλοφύρεαι οὕτως;
> κάτθανε καὶ Πάτροκλος, ὅπερ σέο πολλὸν ἀμείνων.[19]

Still, Horace, too, can set forth a moment of calm in the midst of tragic emotions or tragic happenings. It is the heroic

---

against the Classics; they revolted against the "Neo-classical" poetry that had preceded their own period. To understand either movement completely one must know at least as much ancient poetry at first hand as both these families of poets knew.

[18] On pastoral scenery, see *Magical Art*, pp. 164–166, and for the most delightful bit of pastoral description that I know in any poetry (Theocritus not excepted), — with its music and its quiet art and its fidelity to the scenery that the poet knew well — turn to Virgil, *Ecl.* I 46–58 — on the farm that "the fortunate old man" now has as his own again. For a translation of part of it, with a comment, see *Magical Art*, p. 147. As an example of epic scenery, take the lines on the mountains, Athos and Eryx and Father Appennine (*Aen.* XII 701): Quantus Athos aut quantus Eryx aut ipse coruscis Cum fremit ilicibus quantus gaudetque nivali Vertice se attollens pater Appenninus ad auras (translated in *Magical Art*, p. 165). Shelley's *Passage of the Apennines*, beginning: "Listen, listen, Mary mine, To the whisper of the Apennine," is a nursery ditty in comparison, though it tries to exalt itself at the end.

[19] *Iliad* XXI 97–107.

calm of Regulus, who forced the Senate to reject the terms he brought from Carthage and then, refusing to kiss his wife and children farewell, as though he were no more a Roman, hastened away, "a glorious exile." [20]

And yet he knew what the barbarian tortures had in store for him; still, he brushed aside the protesting throngs of his kinsmen and the people in the way, with little concern as if he were leaving his clients' long disputes after the case was over, on his way to his villa in Samnium or the sea-side of Tarentum.[21]

This passage may well have been in Andrew Marvell's mind, when in his "Horatian Ode upon Cromwell's Return from Ireland" he wrote of the martyred King:

> He nothing common did or mean
> Upon that memorable scene,
>   But with his keener eye
>   The axe's edge did try.

> Nor call'd the Gods, with vulgar spite
> To vindicate his helpless rite;
>   But bow'd his comely head
>   Down, as upon a bed.

There are strains of sombre poetry, partly inspired by Lucretius, in Horace's Epicurean odes; for the term Epicurean did not mean to the Roman poets, or to Epicurus himself, what it popularly connotes today — vinous carousing at a dinner of epicures. Wine was there, and ointments and the brief flowers of the lovely rose, but Horace, in Tennyson's phrase, would "spice his fair banquet with the dust of death." This is the tone of *Solvitur acris hiemps*,[22] *Aequam memento rebus in arduis*,[23] *Eheu fugaces, Postume, Postume*,[24] and *Diffugere nives redeunt iam gramina campis*.[25] This last is the ode that was singled out by Matthew Arnold as one of his

---

[20] *Odes* III 5. 41–56.

[21] There is a moment like this in the *Aeneid* (XI 96–99), when the hero, after the last rites have been paid for young Pallas, bids him forever hail and farewell and "saying no more, he turns to the high walls and makes his way back to camp."

[22] I 4.

[23] II 3.

[24] II 14.

[25] IV 7.

best beloved poems. In one of his sternly philological lectures,
A. E. Housman, foremost Latinist of our day and perhaps
our foremost poet, read a translation of this ode into his own
verse. He read it in a neutral tone, as though it were the
usual prose version, and added shamefacedly, "Perhaps the
most poetical of Horace's odes." [26]

It would not seem that the marriage of Poetry and Philology was consummated in Housman's mind. They dwelt in
separate mansions of the palace, bowing to one another in its
courtyards now and then. One was his play and one his work
— but which was which? Moreover, there are few obvious
echoes of the ancients in Housman's poetry. And yet I cannot
but wonder whether something of the exquisite precision and
overpowering finality and something of the defiant pessimism
of Housman's poetry may have been attained after long pondering on this very ode of Horace.

> Nos ubi decidimus
> Quo pater Aeneas, quo dives Tullus et Ancus
> Pulvis et umbra sumus.[27]

Death is not the only background on which Horace sets his
"Eat, drink and be merry," and the philosophy of Epicurus is
not his only creed. To be an Epicurean meant, for Romans
after Lucretius, to devote one's self to a strict and scientific
search for the laws of nature, with the corollary that no immortality is destined for individual lives. These are resolved
into individual atoms, which unite with new formations in
the immortal changes of universal matter and universal motion. Both Virgil and Horace embraced this philosophy fer-
vently in their youth. Virgil's hero worship and his vision of

[26] I was given a copy of this translation some twenty years ago by H. T. Deas,
now Fellow of Gonville and Caius College. It appeared as early as 1897 in
*The Quarto* and again in *The Trinity Magazine* in 1922 (see A. S. F. Gow,
*A. E. Housman, A Sketch*, 1936, p. 68) and now has become generally accessible
in *More Poems*, published in 1936 after Housman's death in that year. Mr.
Deas was among Housman's auditors at the time, and so was my friend
Arthur D. Nock, to whom I owe my statement of what took place.

[27] *The Shropshire Lad* appeared only a year before the translation of
Horace's ode. Horace's (momentary) pessimism is not quite of the same order.
Housman's defiance is more in the spirit of Lucan.

empire impelled him, whatever the final outcome of his thought, to Plato and the realm of the ideal. Horace, so some sober-minded critics assert, was converted to Stoicism when he witnessed thunder and lightning from a clear sky.[28] Stoic he was, at the proper moment, and at the proper moment Epicurean, or what you will. He took truth where he found it, and with reverence and with mirth molded it into his stable philosophy of life. Let us not, ye gods forfend, call him "eclectic." "Eclecticism," like "syncretism" and "epistemology," and many other high technical terms of philosophy, is but a tip to the reader that the sage can talk familiarly of matters most abstruse, when really he is talking abstrusely of matters most familiar. Let us call Horace independent — *nullius addictus iurare in verba magister —* [29] and if we must assign him to a school, it is that which he himself founded, the school of Horace.

Horace's study of Lucretius bore fruit of two varieties. Lucretian science went into his satires, those familiar talks, which he so called, *Sermones.*[30] In his odes, he turns into lyric those moments of high moral satire that make Lucretius the master among Roman satirists of the high moral sort. Such poems likewise breathe the calm and contemplative air of the choral odes in Greek tragedy. That is why, I believe, Horace consecrated his lyric poetry to Melpomene, the muse of tragedy.[31]

[28] *Odes* I 34.

[29] *Epist.* I 1. 14.

[30] "Horace Talks" again, in lively fashion, in the translation of H. H. Chamberlin, Norwood, Mass., The Plimpton Press, 1940.

[31] When Horace in an ode on the meaning of real wealth (III 16) remarks: "Increasing wealth is attended by care and the hunger for more. Rightly have I dreaded to lift my head for all to see, Maecenas, glory of the knights," he is not commenting on his own moderation but that of his patron, who, despite his greatness in the Roman state, chose to remain in the social order a simple member of the equestrian class rather than to acquire the technical nobility of the senatorial order. Horace says "I" while meaning "you," because he speaks as the leader of the chorus in a Greek tragedy, declaring those general truths in which the issue of the play is involved. So, for instance, in one of the best, and simplest, of his odes (II 10), he counsels moderation, with a strange sense of prophecy, to Licinius Murena, who soon was to be implicated in the conspiracy of Fannius Caepio against Augustus. Horace is a coryphaeus of life.

In one point Horace and his beloved Lucretius are worlds apart. Death is to Horace an evil, since it shatters the fine pleasures of life; gather them while we may. He faces it bravely, prepared to endure what it is wrong to emend.[32] Lucretius welcomes death as the sovereign boon, which brings the peace of an endless sleep. He rebukes as childish the traditional, dark view of death to which Horace returned.

This then should we ask of such a man, what is there so bitter about it all, if the conclusion of the matter is sleep and rest, why any one can pine away in never-ending grief? [33]

Lucretius had two aims in life — to know the truth, and knowing it, to set men free. The truth he knew, no doubt about it: it was the science of Epicurus, as much a god to him as Augustus was to Virgil and to Horace. Men were fast bound, Lucretius saw, by two obsessions — the fear of the gods and the fear of hell; and Epicurus, by relegating the gods to the intermundane spaces, out of harm's way, and by resolving both hell and human beings into atoms, relieved mankind of both these fears. He had the fervor of a prophet, proclaiming the deliverance that his god had brought. With an eye single to this aim, he wrote in a rush as the verses came. Sometimes they came roughly, but for that he did not care; his earnestness burns latently in them all, coming into sudden blaze at least-expected moments. And when the fire has consumed all the stubble, there is no brighter light in Latin poetry. He scorned rhetorical adornment, as sugar on the brim of a cup of wholesome wormwood. But such was his training in the arts, and such the power of ancient rhetoric to put a message into the proper form, that all unawares he obeyed its laws. His poems, said Cicero acutely, show many lights of genius,

---

So Seneca must have thought; for not a few of the choruses in his tragedies are shot through with familiar ideas and phrases from Horace. For an example, take the chorus of the Thebans in Act I of *Hercules Furens* (125–202).

[32] *Odes* I 24. 19 Durum: sed levius fit patientia Quicquid corrigere est nefas.

[33] *De Rerum Natura* III 909: Illud ab hoc igitur quaerendum est, quid sit amari Tanto opere, ad somnum si res redit atque quietem, Cur quisquam aeterno possit tabescere luctu.

and yet great art as well.[34] Lucretius was a poet *malgré lui* —
a rare phenomenon, so far as I am aware, in the history of
poetry.

I will refrain from quoting all the great passages on which
every good anthologist seizes. One will find the poet, like
Virgil, taking that far-off view of human activities which
renders them very small. Sheep grazing on a distant hill make
but a spot of white upon the green. Troops moving on the
plain with glittering arms, and the earth shaking with the
marchings of the might of men, and the echoing cries tossed by
the mountains to the starry firmament, and cavalry wheeling
about or making a mighty charge across the plain — all these
from a certain place high up on the hills seem to stand still
and make one spot of brightness on the plain.[35]

Lucretius, working with what some smaller minds conceive
to be a wooden and mechanical ordering of the universe, never
lost the zest of exploration, although the whole had been ex-
plained. At one point he prepares the reader for a surprise,
something at which he will at first recoil in fear and incredu-
lity. But be patient. There are many surprises all about us,
he says, although they cease to be surprises to our blunted
senses.

Take the pure radiance of the sky and all that is therein, the
wandering stars, the moon and the exceeding brightness of sunlight, if they all of a sudden were set before our mortal eyes, what
could be called more marvellous than they, or what less likely for
mankind to believe? Nothing, I think; so amazing this vision
would have seemed. And yet, tired and sated with that sight, we
none of us deign to look up to the shining temples of the sky.[36]

The heavens are too much with us. They have faded into
the light of common day. And so will fade later, the poet de-

---

[34] *Epist. ad Quint. Fratr.* II 9 (11)3: Lucreti poemata, ut scribis, ita sunt
multis luminibus ingeni, multae tamen artis. Cf. "La Composition Rhétorique
du Troisième Livre de Lucrèce," *Revue de Philologie* VIII (6oe, 1934), 243–266.

[35] II 317–332.

[36] II 1023–1039. In similar vein, the noted biologist E. G. Conklin remarks
in his Rice Institute Lectures (p. 195): "The development of a human being,
of a great personality, from a germ cell is surely the climax of all wonders,
and yet it is so common that it has ceased to excite wonder."

clares, the fearsome surprise that he thinks we are now able
to stand — the truth that there must be other worlds out there
in the infinite space, on beyond the flaming ramparts. How
Lucretius would revel in the metagalaxies that Harlow Shapley has taught the world of science to see! The data of that
ancient scientist were scanty and he lacked a laboratory, but
in his undaunted search for truth and in its method of reasoning his mind calls to the modern scientific mind as deep to
deep. It is no less the mind of a poet, whose sense of wonder
is not the romantic wonder at something fabulous, but the
primitive, Homeric wonder at something familiar. That may
be why Lucretius the poet, seeing all things new, favored the
Epicurean tenet that actually a new sun is born of new-formed
atoms every day.[37]

Lucretius, having solved the universe in all its parts, declares that to keep our world going, even for its present course,
an infinite supply of matter is necessary.

Lest upon wings of fire the ramparts of the world scatter suddenly, set free throughout the mighty void, and other things follow in like manner, and lest the thundering vaults of heaven
plunge from on high, and the world swiftly withdraw beneath our
feet and, as all things mingle with the downfall of the sky that sets
the atoms free, shoot off through the deep inane, so that in the
twinkling of an eye no relics appear but spatial wilderness and
unseen elements —

*desertum praeter spatium et primordia caeca.*

For in whatever part thou shalt assume that matter gives out, that
part will be the gate of death for things, and there all the throng
of matter will press forth.[38]

[37] V 660–666. Curiously, the conception of a round earth about which the
sun revolves apparently seemed less scientific to Lucretius than that of a flat
earth with a brand-new sun, atomically composed every morning and resolved into its atoms after finishing its diurnal course. He states the rival
hypothesis, but with the intensity of both his science and poetry, he makes
what to us is a quaint fiction thrill with truth. And why indeed should one
except the sun from the general mortality of natural phenomena? The sun
that once has bloomed forever dies. So Milton could make vividly poetic
both the Ptolemaic and the Copernican hypothesis. Some scientists may not
like the idea, but daring poetry is the life of science.
[38] I 1094–1113.

This swallowing up of our little world in the void is indeed predestined, Lucretius knows, at the end of the brief cycle of history in which he lives. Sure, then, of this truth, he can destroy it before its time. He takes joy in the process that annihilates the universe and proves his theory. He waves a wand even more potent than that of Virgil when he made the Roman of Augustus vanish before our eyes.

And yet, behind annihilation something remains. At least the mind of the thinker is there, to witness the havoc he has wrought in the fulfilling of nature's law. But he also witnesses another apocalypse of destruction with a somewhat different outcome. The Third Book opens with the praise of the divine founder, Epicurus, the guide of human souls from darkness to the light, their father, discoverer of truth, on whose golden words we feed as bees sip honey.

"For as soon as thy philosophy that arises in thy divine mind, begins to call aloud the story of the birth of things, fled are the terrors of the soul, the ramparts of the firmament give way, and I see things tossed about throughout the void. The majesty of the gods appears and their tranquil abodes we see, where — to quote Tennyson's rendering —

> Where never creeps a cloud or moves a wind,
> Nor ever falls the least white star of snow,
> Nor ever lowest roll of thunder moans,
> Nor sound of human sorrow mounts to mar
> Their sacred, everlasting calm.[39]

"But," the poet goes on, "nowhere facing them down below appear the tracts of Hell, nor does the earth block us from making out whatever is going on beneath our feet throughout the void. Then at this sight a kind of divine pleasure and a shivering awe seize me, since, by thy power, Nature in every part stands openly revealed." [40]

[39] *Lucretius*, 106–110. Tennyson is not in fashion in the present age; he has become a Mid-Victorian. Nevertheless, in his poem on Lucretius, as in that on Virgil, he has put into brief compass, and in what some day will again be recognized as poetry, more profitable reflections on the works and the temperaments of these ancients than, to the best of my remembrance, can be found in any critical essays of like extent.

[40] III 14–30. See *Les Esprits Souverains*, pp. 19–20.

Therefore, despite the crimes of priests, the gods remain. On beyond science is the genius of the master who discovered science. There comes in the poet's mind at this thought a thrill, despite him, of religious awe before such revelation.

May Marcus Tullius Cicero appear for a moment in the company of those high poets who know how to dissolve the actual into the ideal? I am not going to quote from Cicero's verses, least of all from those on his consulate; for there is little that is poetic there. He could manage rhythm smoothly, after his mastery of the rhythms of prose, and he had fed his heart and soul, as few of his contemporaries had, on the poetry of father Ennius and the other master poets of old. Their depth and strength of feeling he had imbibed; it comes to expression in his prose, above all in the last book of the great work that we have found so momentous in the building of Rome, his *De Re Publica*.[41]

In that last book is recorded the dream of Scipio that he tells his friends as they listened to his discourse on the State the day before he died. In his dream he mounts to the upper world in that ancient galaxy, the Milky Way, where the spirits of his two fathers meet him. They point out to him the spheres, misnamed planets or wanderers, and the starry heavens above them. He listens to the music of the spheres, not heard in our brute earth. He looks down in amazement on that little globe, in which the Roman empire occupies one tiny spot. They speak to him of the impermanence of human fame, which even on earth cannot climb across Caucasus or swim across the Ganges. And in point of time, what hero was known to the generations that preceded him, or how long

[41] The *Somnium Scipionis* is today often published separately, though better read along with the few remaining fragments of this book, and it was separately transmitted in antiquity, along with the commentary of the learned Neoplatonist Macrobius. It became one of the "best hundred books" in the Middle Ages, had an important influence on the dream literature of that period, for instance on *The Romance of the Rose*. Cf. "Ovid in 'Le Roman de la Rose,' " p. 114. The *Somnium* helped Dante in the composition of his *Paradise*, and it was one of Chaucer's favorite books; his Chaunticleer quotes it, with flooring effect upon Madame Pertelote, one of his seven wives.

amongst the folk to come shall his praises be heard? For the
world shall perish by flood or fire and a new cycle of history
begin, and even if the memory of one little man can pass
through these, it can in no wise survive for more than one
year, the one Great Year, made up of thousands of our little
years, since it is determined not by the revolution of one of
the lights of heaven but by the conjunction of them all in
the same positions whence they started on their course. "So,"
he says at the end, "knowing that you possess an immortal
soul, make it by service to your state worthy to claim its immortality and enter these celestial abodes. For souls weighed
down by the corruptions of the body, souls that violate the
laws of gods and men, must, after they are freed from their
bodily chains, be driven about the earth for many ages."

> Then he departed; and I was loosed from my sleep.
> Ille discessit; ego somno solutus sum.[42]

In this amazing little work, the only complete part of
Cicero's discourse on the state preserved to us — preserved because Macrobius in the fifth century of our era wrote a commentary on it full of Neoplatonic lore, which travelled with
it down the Middle Ages, where it was one of the great, essential books — Cicero has made Platonic immortality, after a
Platonic purgatory, the hope of every man of high spirit, if
only he will make the god within him his true self and thus
prove worthy of the highest prize.

The style of the work is no less amazing. The measured,
musical sentences with metrical cadences at their closes, and
all the way along, are no less poetry than verses of iambics or
of dactyls. The spirit is sombre and profound and what we
are pleased to call mediaeval. A passage like the following,
on the impermanence of earthly fame, may be arranged antiphonally, like verses of the Psalms. One may hear it, in
imagination, chanted by some mediaeval choir:

> Sermo autem omnis ille et angustiis cingitur iis regionum quas
> vides: nec umquam de ullo perennis fuit.

[42] VI 29.

Et obruitur hominum interitu: et oblivione posteritatis exstinguitur.[43]

Here is indeed "high seriousness" and a view of our little world like that which Dante with Beatrice saw from the summit of the skies. Cicero has transcended not only that mighty year of his consulate, but all the world of man.

## II

The *vir Romanus* as a species of the *genus homo* was surely equipped for laughter. For the complete definition of man, as pronounced by Greek philosophers, by Boethius and by all the Middle Ages, is that of a mortal, rational animal capable of laughter: *animal mortale, rationale, risus capax* — a most luminous definition, as Rabelais would agree.[44] And yet as we examine the portrait busts of various worthy gentlemen of the Republic, including that of the elder Scipio, we cannot fail to note an uncanny resemblance to the American business man of the less gentle sort, some minor robber baron of 1870. No gleam of laughter rests upon such a face.

Polybius tells a good story to illustrate the generosity of his pupil, the younger Scipio, and incidentally, the shrewd and

---

[43] VI 25. The sombre earnestness of this passage and of the whole Dream attest, whatever Cicero's views on the immortality of the soul, something more than a "brief toying with Platonic myth" (Frank, *Lit. Roman Repub.*, p. 218). Rather, we have here the ideal, and the real, Cicero. We should point to the height to which he climbed rather than to his lapses from it.

[44] Aristotle notes that laughter is an exclusive characteristic of man — οὐδὲν γὰρ γελᾷ τῶν ἄλλων (*De Partibus Animalium* III 10, Loeb, 1932, pp. 280–282). He does not, at least not in his *Categories* (Loeb, 1938), incorporate this trait in a logical definition of man. The elements in such a definition were furnished by the Neoplatonist Porphyry in his commentary on Aristotle's *Categories*: ἐστὶ δὲ γένος μὲν οἷον τὸ ζῷον, εἶδος δὲ οἷον ὁ ἄνθρωπος, διαφορὰ δὲ οἷον τὸ λογικόν, ἴδιον δὲ οἷον τὸ γελαστικόν, συμβεβηκὸς δὲ οἷον τὸ λευκὸν, τὸ μέλαν, τὸ καθέζεσθαι. (ed. Busse, IV 1, p. 2. 20). The genus is *animal*, the species is *homo*, the *differentia* is *rationale*, the *proprium* is *risibile*, while accidents are "white," "black," and "to sit." The Latin terms are those of Boethius in his translation of Porphyry (*ibid.* p. 20). He wrote two commentaries on this work, the first based on the imperfect translation of Marius Victorinus, the second on his own improved version. He replaced Porphyry's analytic definition with a synthetic statement beginning: *Fit ergo huiuscemodi hominis definitio* (Ed. Prim. I 4, ed. Brandt, 1906, p. 11. 28); he likewise adds *mortale* to the definition (*ibid.* I 20, pp. 61. 16, 68. 11). The authority of Boethius fixed *risus capax* as an essential human trait for all the Middle Ages and, let us hope, for all time.

somewhat humorless business sense of the old Romans.  Scipio
had inherited a legacy from his grandmother on the condition
that he should pay to the two daughters of the elder Scipio,
his grandfather by adoption, the half of the dowry that their
father had put aside for them, amounting to fifty talents in
all, or some $54,000 of our money; the other half had been
paid by Aemilia during her lifetime.  By law Scipio had three
years in which to pay his half, in three instalments, the first at
the end of the first ten months.  When that day arrived, the
husbands of the two ladies, Scipio Nasica and Tiberius Sem-
pronius Gracchus, father of the reformers, went round to the
bank for the first payment.  I hardly suspect that these gentlemen needed money, but they wanted to be paid on time.  To
their surprise, the banker handed them over the entire twenty-
five talents.  "You're mistaken, my good sir.  Only a third is
to be paid at this date."  "On the contrary, gentlemen, I have
instructions to turn over the entire amount to you."  Amazed
and incredulous, they went straight to Scipio to have him
rectify the error.  Think of the interest that he was losing —
for two whole years and more!  It took them some time to
understand that he had meant what he had done.  When he
bade them see the banker again, they walked away in deep
silence, dumbfounded with admiration for his noble spirit
($\mu\epsilon\gamma\alpha\lambda o\psi\nu\chi\acute{\iota}\alpha$) and ashamed of their own pettiness ($\mu\iota\kappa\rho o\lambda o\gamma\acute{\iota}\alpha$),
though they were second to nobody at Rome.[45]

It might appear that the noble Roman, whose character
combined something of a New England conscience with Scot-
tish thrift, needed instruction in the art of laughter.  Indeed,
according to the satirist Lucilius, admittedly the foremost wit
of Rome in Scipio's day, there was one Crassus who laughed
just once in his lifetime.[46]  He just comes under the philos-

---

Plato, the most subtle master of laughter in history (see W. C. Greene, "The
Spirit of Comedy in Plato," pp. 63–123), thought that neither gods nor statesmen should over-indulge in it (*Republic*, III, 388 E–389 A).  But this is not to
condemn laughter in itself.

[45] Polybius, XXXI 27.

[46] Macrobius, *Saturnalia*, II 1. 6: Crassum illum, quem Cicero auctore Lucilio
semel in vita risisse scribit.

ophers' definition of a man — so as by fire. Possibly some absolutely one-hundred-per-cent old Romans never deviated into mirth.

There is surely some laughter in Roman literature. Could it have been restricted to the proletariat, including slaves? Plautus was a commoner, Terence was an African slave.[47] His name, Publius Terentius Afer, suggests that he might have been of negro extraction. If so — it is not at all certain — he was a worthy predecessor of Alexandre Dumas *fils,* master of the same subtle elegance in comedy. Horace was the son of an ex-slave, and never ashamed of the fact. Then there is Phaedrus, a Greek slave from Pieria, who at the end of Augustus' reign and the beginning of Tiberius', turned some of Aesop's fables into neat iambic Latin verse and added some of his own.

Well, let us have a specimen of proletariat literature, written by a real slave. These are no simple stories of animals, these fables of Phaedrus. They present a panorama of human failings with pride as the worst, as in the Catholic rating. They seemed a safe sort of literature for the age of Tiberius and his high favorite Sejanus, but covert satire may lurk beneath. Sejanus could smile to see a monkey made a man, but he grew serious at the suspicion that he was being made a monkey. I will cite but one fable, not aimed particularly at Sejanus, but good for any politician then or now.

### The Bat — An Allegory

The birds and beasts once fought in dubious fray;
Now Mars to these and now to those would sway.
A bat, observant of the changing tide,
Took his stand always on the winning side.
Here, he spread wide his pinions like a bird;
There, furling them, became a mouse absurd.
But when the smoke of battle cleared away,
His fraud was patent as the rising day.

[47] For the purposes of our present discussion I am assuming that a basis of fact underlies the life of Terence by Suetonius; cf. Rolfe (Loeb), II, 452–463. But the reader will be entertained and enlightened by an essay from W. Beare ("The Life of Terence," *Hermathena* LIX [1942], 20–29), who dissolves Suetonius' sources into a mass of guesses made by previous scholarly biographers mainly on the basis of Terence's text.

Damned by both parties for the nasty trick,
He fled the light and dwelt in darkness thick.

### MORAL

Qui se duabus partibus commiserit
utrubique ingratus vivet et turpis sibi.

The man who tries two parties to control
Will lose both votes, and loathe his little soul.[48]

But back to Crassus, the man of one laugh. Lucilius, who recorded this event, was a member of the circle of Scipio, where he doubtless spread mirth as Horace did amongst the company of Maecenas. The one laugh that Crassus begat must at least have been prolific of laughter when Lucilius reported it to the club. Old Cato, as we saw, had a tart wit; he made Polybius laugh.[49] He must have made the whole town laugh in his speech on the Oppian Law.[50] This was a sumptuary enactment directed against the fair sex and passed during the heat of the Punic War. Poor woman was not allowed to wear more than a half-ounce of gold, or to wear a robe of diverse colors, or to be driven in a carriage in city or town or nearer than a mile thereto, save for the purpose of going to church. No wonder, when an age of prosperity returned, that Roman matrons demanded their former rights. Some senator was found to propose annulment. Dissension grew rife. The women held mass meetings, lobbied out of doors and picketed the Senatehouse; old Cato could hardly make his way through the crowd of them when he came to speak against the bill. His oration, naturally, was a fight from the last ditch, and though his objections were buried in that ditch, he had at least relieved his mind and shot out a few epigrams.

He fears not so much the present bill as the consequences to which it may lead (you will recognize in that argument a favorite conservative technique). "For," he bellowed, "if women have their way in this affair they will proceed to clamor for the vote and run for senator and where shall we be then?

[48] *Fab. Nov.* X  (ed. Ioh. P. Postgate, Oxford, Clarendon Press, 1919).
[49] See Chapter I, notes 42–44.
[50] Livy XXXIV 1–8.

Once make 'em our equals and they'll prove our superiors." [51]

There are plenty of other *bons mots* from the old Republic at the expense of the fairer and the stronger sex. Three from Plautus occur to me at the moment, but I will pass them by; discretion is the better part of valor. Why do male wits have just three targets for their shafts — doctors, lawyers, and women? Why do we all, except George Meredith and Horace, and the high wits whom Meredith commends, neglect the mighty man, the funniest thing of all?

Besides the wit of the old Republic there was plenty of Italian mirth, then and all through Roman history. One of the most pleasant discoveries for a reader of Latin literature to make is that the ancient Romans were likewise Italians. In some writers the carefree merriment, the rapid unconventional talk, and the irrepressible song of the Italy we used to know — the Italy that one day will return — are patent, for instance, in Plautus and Catullus. In others, the reputedly formal classicists, like Virgil and Horace, one can readily find many a delightful native scene. In Horace, there is the pious country woman who crowns her household gods with simple myrtle and sacrifices to them a most Italian animal, a little black sow; [52] there is the festival of Faunus, where the rustic who has sweated his strength in digging out the earth, now in the heavy dance stamps it lustily, for revenge; [53] and then there is Horace's little donkey — one occupant of Italy that Romans never conquered — and Horace himself as they trot all the way to Tarentum or up the hills to the Sabine farm.[54] In Virgil, the underlying charm of his *Bucolics* is the glimpse of Italian landscape amid his Arcadian idyl; the *Georgics*, though epic in tone, though looking ahead to the ideal Roman Empire, is

[51] *Ibid.* 3. 2: extemplo, simul pares esse coeperint, superiores erunt. They order these things better in France, as Cato would agree. Women do not possess the suffrage; they merely direct from the background. The French may feel that something of woman's value as a supermasculine ideal and something of the irony of her charm are lost when she gains the "right" to fight with men in the dusty arena of politics.

[52] *Odes* III 23.

[53] *Odes* III 18.

[54] *Serm.* I 6. 104.

all the way Italian, exultant with that native strength and industry and joy that the poet builds into his contemporary, and
Italian, Golden Age. Even in the *Aeneid,* the epic of all
Rome, there is one book, the Seventh, conspicuously Italian;
and the major theme, more and more prominent in the second
half of the poem, is the fusion of primitive Italian virtues with
the foreign culture brought from abroad. For thus did Aeneas
build his city.[55]

The mirth of Italy, moreover, found expression in various
dramatic performances, to which the tired Roman conqueror
could turn for relief. So Augustus,[56] like President Wilson in
our times, frequented shows of no high seriousness. Not all
the Roman comedies, or tragedies, of the early Republic were
taken over from the Greek. The primitive forms of drama
were rendered artistic with the help of Greece, but the contents were often pure Roman, or, better, pure Italian. Naevius, a contemporary of Plautus, wrote many such.

We wish we knew more about this extraordinary man, besides what the scattered fragments of his works can tell us.
He was not imported from abroad. He was born in Campania, a southerner, to be sure, but he fought in the First
Punic War and wrote an epic on that great campaign, em-
ploying the simple ballad verse called Saturnian, the national
measure of Italy. Naevius wrote tragedies, some on Greek but
some on Roman subjects, set both in modern and in very ancient times. He was not a favorite with the Roman nobility,
particularly the Metelli. He wrote lampoons on them, and
they put him in jail. The plain speech of an Aristophanes and
the ridicule of contemporary politicians on the stage were no
longer possible; the Roman heroes did not like cartoons.

And yet I wonder if the same aristocrats who imprisoned
Naevius did not turn up at some of the little comedies that he
wrote. They all are lost for us, but a number of the titles,
both Greek and Latin, have come down with the fragments.
I select a few, which may somewhat suggest Broadway.

[55] Chapter II, notes 79, 100.
[56] Ovid, *Tristia* II 509–514.

*Akontizomenos*, "Shot"; *Agitatoria*, "Female Charioteer," "Chauffeuse"; *Agrypnuntes*, "Wide Awake"; *Ariolus*, "The Medium" (this he wrote, incorrigibly, in prison); *Carbonaria*, "Charcoal-vender"; *Commotria*, "Lady's Maid"; *Corollaria*, "Flower-girl"; *Dementes*, "Fools"; *Dolus*, "Trickery"; *Personata*, "Masked"; *Proiectus*, "Exposed"; *Quadrigemini*, "Quadruplets"; *Tarentilla*, "Little Girl from Tarentum," and so on. For all of these fragments and titles we are indebted to the patient grammarians of later ages, who were gunning for unusual words and forms. We are grateful for the titles, which they quoted with scholarly propriety, and for specimens of the racy, colloquial vocabulary of Naevius in which he may well have held his own with Plautus. Some bits of wit and humor appear, despite the grammarians; the liveliest and longest, and it is only five lines long, from the *Tarentilla*, a name that suggests both *tarentella* and *tarantula*, pictures a gay coquette surrounded by a bevy of lovers to whom she distributes her favors all at once.

To one she nods, to one she winks, makes love to one and grabs another. With one her hand is busy, to another she gives a kick, to another she holds her ring to see, and pouts her lips at another, with another she sings and yet to another her fingers flash a message.

Not even Julius Caesar, who could dictate to seven stenographers at a time, was capable of such multiverse attention. Of course the maid of Tarentum understands the art of talking with the fingers, unknown to us, except to the deaf and dumb, but common enough among the ancients.[57]

Naevius must have done something to unbend Roman dignity — he and a whole troupe of jolly writers for the stage.

[57] It is lucky for us that the Maid of Tarentum was expert in the *loquela digitorum* and that for this reason Isidore of Seville in discussing this matter in his encyclopaedia (*Orig.* I 26. 2) quotes, and saves for us, these verses of Naevius *de quadam impudica*, as he calls her (Warmington, Loeb, II, pp. 98–101). He also cites a Biblical instance, the no-account person (*homo apostata, vir inutilis*) mentioned in Proverbs 6. 13: Annuit oculis, terit pede, digito loquitur. Sacred and profane references lie down together peacefully in the *Encyclopaedia Hispanica* of St. Isidore.

And off the stage there were men of wit, who loved a joke for a joke's own sake. Let us come down the centuries for a moment to a time not far from the fall of Rome in A.D. 410. It was then that Macrobius wrote his *Saturnalia*, "The Feast of Saturn," or "Christmas." It was a Pagan Christmas party, at which a group of friends gathered, Symmachus, the famous prefect of Rome, and Praetextatus, and Virgil's commentator Servius, and other survivors of the follower of the Emperor Julian, who had tried to turn back the hands of the Christian clock. They meet to celebrate the great feast of old Saturn, when everybody, slaves included, returned to his democratic Golden Age. The merriment is learned; the talk drifts finally to Virgil, when Servius, naturally, has much to say. But first other themes are broached, just as in Cicero's discourse on the state; [58] the technique of the dialogue, with a very different subject, is still maintained.

One of their topics is the art of jesting; they praise the wits of old and gives samples of their jokes.[59] The banqueters agree that Plautus and Cicero top all the rest. Plautus and laughter seem to be synonymous terms. They could tell a play of Plautus by the *iocorum copia*, the wealth of jests it contained. All the *bons mots* of Cicero were collected by his faithful secretary Tiro. The master was aware of his reputation as a wag. He knew of good stories that were attributed to him just because they were good ones. He said that a class of higher critics had arisen who just as they would say, "This verse is Plautus's and this one cannot be," so they could pick out every time the joke of genuine Ciceronian flavor and that which lacked it utterly.

I will repeat but one of the authentic witticisms, certified by Macrobius.[60] Cicero was dining out one day, and his host put on some very mediocre wine. "Try my Falernian," he said, "a vintage of forty years." Cicero took a sip and gravely remarked, "It stands its age well" — *bene fert aetatem suam.*

---

[58] Chapter I, notes 102–110.

[59] *Saturnalia* Bk. II. The book is incomplete at the end. How many more jokes Macrobius knew we can only guess.

[60] *Saturn.* II 3. 2.

Cicero had a quick and pungent wit, which he exercised at the expense of his opponents, notably Verres, who perhaps had at least a more intelligent appreciation of art than Cicero lets us suppose. One might make an anthology of his brilliant *bons mots* that would compare favorably with a similar assortment from any of the professional satirists. He had more wit than humor; he is nearer to Pope in spirit than to Horace. He left his victims covered with ridicule, not ashamed of their folly. Pompey, once his idol, whose exalted career he had helped to effect by his speech on the Manilian Law, became the target for his satire after the "First Triumvirate" in 60 B.C., which by one of the ironies of history was the fruit of that very speech. He affixed to the great general, who possessed little of the sense of humor, the pompous soubriquet of Sampsiceramus, a petty potentate of Caelo-Syria, and confided to his bosom-friend Atticus that Pompey was aiming at tyranny.[61] When at last he joined his forces in Epirus, he remarked caustically that he knew whom he was running away from but not whom he was following. No wonder that Pompey, as Macrobius declares, did not relish this pointed epigram, or his retort, when the Pompeians told him he had come too late, that he couldn't be too late, since he found that nothing was ready.[62]

The great Augustus, what time he was not extending the bounds of the Roman domain, was always cracking jokes. We may better understand from this why he was anxious to have Horace for his private secretary; he wanted somebody with whom to banter. Suetonius tells us that he was fond of clear and simple speech, with lively, colloquial phrases, in contrast with the sober Tiberius, who favored a highbrow and slightly

---

[61] *Ad Att.* II 17. 1: Turbat Sampsiceramus. Nihil est quod non timendum sit, ὁμολογουμένως τυράννιδα συσκευάζεται. This was only one year after the First Triumvirate was formed.

[62] *Saturn.* II 3. 7: Pompeius Ciceronis facetiarum impatiens fuit, cuius haec dicta ferebantur: "Ego vero quem fugiam habeo, quem sequar non habeo." Sed et cum ad Pompeium venisset, dicentibus eum sero venisse, respondit: "Minime sero veni; nam nihil hic paratum video." Macrobius gives us two more jibes from Cicero, which aroused Pompey to one flash of epigram: "I wish Cicero would go over to the enemy, to gain some fear of us."

archaistic style.[63] The curious will find Augustus's jokes recorded in a recent article.[64] A few, quite properly, are not included, among them one that Macrobius well calls a rough one — *iocus asper*.[65]

I will not chronicle all these jests, lest I receive the compliment once given in a review by one learned German to another, on writing the first really serious treatment of laughter. I certainly will not weary you with a complete list of the famous wits — among whom even Hannibal appears — chronicled by Macrobius. Let us add merely that Julius Caesar, who tried his hand at everything, including a Latin grammar, made an anthology of witty sayings, including some of Cicero's. He was one of those critics of finer taste, who when something spurious was given him as Cicero's, would cast it out. This we know since Cicero so informs us.[66]

I have spoken thus far of simple human laughter, spiced with wit. But there is also high mirth, that rare spirit of comedy that George Meredith alone has interpreted to our times. Alas, that so few read Meredith today! The comic spirit, as he shows it to us, above all in his *Egoist*, and his *Essay on Comedy*, hovers about human pride and self-importance, and with a "slim, feasting smile," points out the self-importance of one who takes himself too seriously. The comic imps perch on his shoulders, all unbeknownst to him. They view him not with scorn, but with a quiet laugh at his folly; for if high laughter degenerates into sarcasm, its strength is withered. The quiet laughter, even of the eyes alone, is un-

---

[63] Suet. *Aug.* 86.

[64] R. S. Rogers, "Augustus the Man," *Class. Journ.* XXXVI (1941) 449–463.

[65] *Saturn.* II 4. It happened that a young man from the provinces appeared in Rome bearing a striking likeness to Julius Caesar. He became the talk of the town, and Augustus summoned him to his presence. "Tell me, young man, was your mother ever in Rome?" "No, your Majesty," replied the provincial. "You see," said the Emperor, "my father often was." Macrobius adds that he admired Augustus' good temper in taking such jibes more than the wit he displayed in perpetrating them. Macrobius and his circle, in the spirit of Plato (see note 43 and *Laws* V 732 B, XI 935 B), did not relish vulgar jests or those that betrayed a bitter temper or were aimed at some personal defect. One such he cites from the old martinet who taught Horace, his *plagosus Orbilius* (ibid. II 6. 4).

[66] *Ad Fam.* IX 16. 4.

answerable. The victim must fold his tents like the Arabs, and silently steal away. One of the protagonists in such a comedy of life, in Meredith's estimation, is Terence. His gentle irony is true to that of his master, Menander. He, too, has an "amenity that is like Elysian speech, equable and ever gracious; like the face of the Andrian's young sister":

adeo modesto, adeo venusto, ut nil supra.[67]

Worlds separate the comedy of Terence from that of his predecessor Plautus. A large infusion of Greek culture must have intervened between them. Indeed it started earlier than Plautus, when in 240 B.C. Livius Andronicus, a slave, brought out a play adapted from the Greek, presumably to celebrate the closing of the temple of Janus at the end of the First Punic War. The stolid Romans, if stolid they were, must have been educated with incredible swiftness. When we read that at the performance of Terence's *Hecyra*, or "Mother-in-law," the crowds ran away to witness a rope-dancer's antics, we conclude, too hastily, that rope-dancing was better suited to the Roman temperament. But they sat through the young man's *Andria*, the first of his plays, brought out in 166 B.C., the year after Polybius arrived, and they sat through all the rest. His *Eunuchus* was the success of the day and netted its author a considerable sum. No wonder. It is lively in action and superb in the portrayal of character. Thais, the courtesan, is great-souled for all that, — yes, μεγαλόψυχος — and Chaerea is as charming a scapegrace as ever appeared on the stage, Beaumarchais's Chérubin not excepted. These are persons, not the stock characters that are generally appropriate in the comedy of manners of the later Greek stage whence Terence took his plots.

For, after all, that is perhaps what we do, act little parts in life, though taking ourselves quite seriously. All the world's a stage, where lawyers and statesmen, divines and professors strut in their brief roles. The persons in a comedy are worse than those in real life, though not utterly bad, as Aristotle pro-

---

[67] Cf. *Spirit of Comedy*, pp. 39–41; *Esprits Souverains*, p. 12.

foundly observed.[68] It does us no harm to see ourselves so portrayed in conventional plots with an inevitably happy ending. Within the conventional frame there is plenty of place for acute moral observation and for a genial cynicism as cleansing to the beholder as the pity and fear of tragedy. *Fabula de nobis narratur.* Yet it all ends in pleasure; for it all comes out well. Molière, a French Terence and something more, observes at the end of *Monsieur de Pourceaugnac,* "la grande affaire est le plaisir." We are amused as well as chastened. The problem play of our times, which runs after tragedy and either terminates in melodrama or leaves a bad taste in the mouth, would seem to the elegant Terence, and the elegant Molière, a comical failure in art.

Terence's own art is seasoned with comic irony. For this the audience must know more about the situation than the character in the play can know. The man on the stage, proceeding on a slender basis of information, as we often do in life, forms a well-reasoned plan of action, but the spectators know that he is building a castle in Spain, or in Cloudcuckooland; and seeing the pit towards which he is steering, they laugh, with the comic imps, at his self-important stride.[69]

Another potent source of merriment, as it is of tragedy in this world of ours, is misunderstanding, or better still, a complex of misunderstandings. In the *Andria,* the slave deceives his master; the master deceives his slave; the rival of young Pamphilus deceives himself in thinking Pamphilus in love with the maiden whom he himself would marry, while Pamphilus' heart is set upon another goal; and finally his father, master of the slave, is woefully mistaken in thinking that the truth proclaimed by the slave is falsity. In the *Hecyra,* the mother-in-law misunderstands her daughter-in-law, the husband misunderstands his wife, everybody misunderstands the mother-in-law, and the aged fathers of the married pair mis-

---

[68] *De Arte Poetica* 5 (1449 a): ἡ δὲ κωμῳδία ἐστὶν ὥσπερ εἴπομεν μίμησις φαυλοτέρων μέν, οὐ μέντοι κατὰ πᾶσαν κακίαν.

[69] On comic irony and the preparation of the audience as elements in early Roman comedy see Tenney Frank, *Lit. Roman Repub.,* pp. 106–123.

understand everybody else. The *Hecyra* failed, at first, because the audience was insufficiently prepared for these complexities.[70] For us, who like to solve riddles on the stage, the play seems all the better.

Another masterpiece of Terence — they all are masterpieces — is his *Adelphi,* "The Brothers," with its portraiture of the two old gentlemen and their different views on the proper education for the young. We witness the comic downfall of the Puritanic curmudgeon who had devised a system of airtight, logical rigidity. The imps perch on him and he repents. The piece is a worthy companion for Fielding's *Tom Jones,* which it may have helped to inspire. It won the signal honor of being produced, in the year 160 B.C., as part of the funeral rites of the hero of the day, Aemilius Paulus, victor at Pydna over Philip of Macedon.

How curious, from our point of view, that a comedy should form part of a funeral rite! That is because we do not understand the nature either of ancient religion or of the Catholic Sunday, when the solemn and mystic rite of Holy Mass is followed by human festivity. For the ancient Romans, like the Catholic Church, knew that if the rite is sacred, its solemnity is only intensified by an escape into everyday freedom and joy. After the tragic trilogy comes for relief the satyr-play. After the solemnities for which Horace wrote his *Secular Hymn* came scenic games and the contests of the circus.

How much is there original in the plays of Plautus and Terence? We know that they both took their subjects from the plays of the masters of the New Greek Comedy, the comedy of manners, of ordinary human incidents, as opposed to the political comedy of the writers of the age of Pericles, of whom Aristophanes is the master. He, too, is among the elect of George Meredith, and well he deserves his high estate. But among the playwrights of the Greek New Comedy, there is not, if we may judge by the fragments of their works, which is all that we have, any striking difference in tone. Menander, Philemon, and Diphilus are the greatest names. Menander

[70] *Ibid.* pp. 118–120.

excels in poetry and philosophic acuteness, but there is the same substratum in them all. In their view of the *comédie humaine* laughter is tinged with pathos and with sympathy, even if it does not attain the high domain of Plato's *Symposium*, where comedy and tragedy are met together.

Plautus, however, though starting with the Greek New Comedy, seems to show a character all his own. His rollicking, splash-dash humor seems more like the free spirit of Aristophanes, more like Italian vivacity, than the calm propriety and self-contained observation of life conspicuous in Menander. Terence is more nearly like the Greek masters. But did he do no more than translate them? Of course there was a certain advertising value in the proclamation of the playwright that his piece was taken from the Greek. His audience would know that it was *comme il faut*. But both Terence and Plautus, each in his own way, made some impress on their models, just as Lucretius colored Epicurean science with Roman gravity and high poetry. Plautus gives us a drama of action, Terence, like Racine, a drama of psychology. Plautus scatters open-handedly of his store; Terence, in his economy of phrases and of incidents, knows with Racine, as he declares in *Bérénice*,

le secret de l'art est de faire chose de rien.[71]

But, once more, is all this but a translation of Menander and the other masters of the Greek New Comedy? In spirit it doubtless is. Yet it is something to catch that spirit and embody it in another language. How much of the beauty of Helen of Troy survives in a Bohn translation of Homer? [72]

[71] Frank, with due attention to experts like Prescott and Leo, has given a masterly discussion of both Plautus and Terence in chapters II and IV of the work to which I am so often turning. He treats them both as if they were occupied with something more than mere translation.

[72] A test case is furnished by Terence's *Phormio*, the plot of which, we know, was taken from Apollodorus. But who was he? There were several of the name. The one from whom Terence drew, apparently, is chiefly known to fame because he furnished the models for the *Phormio* and the *Hecyra*, which after two attempts finally held the Roman stage. Curiously, the plot of the *Phormio*, in various of its features, closely resembles the *Aulularia*, or "Haunted House," of Plautus. And yet, again, the difference in spirit between

We know that Terence practiced *contaminatio*, whatever exactly that may mean. It involves, at any rate, the combination of scenes or parts from different plays, and the neat juncture of them requires a delicate art and may involve an alteration of the dramatic design.[73] In any case, a slave from North Africa deserves some praise for producing at the age of nineteen, a year after Polybius came to Rome, a play of such neat, colloquial Latinity, of such Attic elegance and of such delicate irony as *The Woman of Andros*. Terence's critics maintained that he palmed off under his own name the work of certain men of eminence. Terence declared himself only too willing to accept that soft impeachment, were it true.[74]

I have called Horace the expert on laughter among the Romans. Terence is a close rival, and I have devoted more attention to him because to many, though they think they know him well, he is an undiscovered country. Everybody is acquainted with the "old familiar Horace," with his Falernian, with the nymphs of his Sabine farm, and with his song, for which those nymphs often furnished the music. *Wein, Weib und Gesang* is a motto too vulgar for his triple jollity. His satire is devoted not to cudgeling villains but to casting a mellow spotlight upon fools. Strange that Meredith did not include him among the intimates of the Comic Spirit! [75] Horace is *par excellence* the master of banter; Au-

---

these two plays is obvious. Had Terence refashioned Apollodorus with the help of Plautus's play? These questions cannot be answered till some entire Greek play comes to light that Terence took as a model for one of his own.

[73] I have tried to show that is the case with the *Eunuchus* (cf. List of Books), pp. 54–72.

[74] *Adelphoe*, Prolog. 15: Nam quod isti dicunt malivoli homines nobiles Hunc adiutare adsidueque una scribere, Quod ille maledictum uehemens esse existumant Eam laudem hic ducit maxumam quom illis placet, Qui nobis uniuorsis et populo placent. According to Donatus in his comment on this passage, the *nobiles* in question were Scipio Africanus, Laelius Sapiens, and Furius Philus. Suetonius has accumulated all the rumors he could find about this matter; see *Vita Terenti* 3–4, ed. Rolfe (Loeb), pp. 456–459. The Romans, apparently, had a match for the Shakespeare-Bacon controversy, if it is still a controversy, of our day.

[75] See *Spirit of Comedy*, pp. 39–40. The points made in the rest of this paragraph summarize matters treated in this work (pp. 39–91) and in *Esprits*

gustus and Maecenas, Virgil and Tibullus, his slaves; and the bailiff of the Sabine Farm knew that well. He could banter with himself, and with a sly use of the first person, in a fashion that only Ovid among the ancients appreciated,[76] mean really the third or the second; dreadful to relate, the shafts pointed at his breast hit our own. One of his delightful arts is historically to magnify, or to mythologize, his own experiences; he is an ancient lyric poet on the field of Philippi, when he throws away his little shield, as three great lyric Greeks had done, and he is an Homeric hero on that same field, when Mercury wraps him in a cloud and carries him to safety. He makes over his country farm into a fabulous realm of the Golden Age, where Faunus, the pastoral god, works miracles, and, other deities assisting, rescues the poet from a falling tree. And the Spirit of Poetry scares away a wolf, while Horace sings of Lalage, or covers his infant body with leaves as he falls asleep in the woods of Mount Voltur, or the Muses walk in his company, whene'er he mounts the rising Sabine hills.

All this for Horace is *jeu d'esprit*. For Horace at heart is deep and serious. But he knew, as Cicero, a prince of satirists, knew,[77] and as Erasmus, Horace's disciple in his *Praise of Folly* knew,[78] that seriousness needs laughter for its own relief. It was Horace's art, and his pleasant philosophy of life, to speak truth with a smile.

The Romans, according to the *fable convenue*, gave to the

---

Souver., pp. 29–40. Horace's banter with Virgil is so nicely done in two familiar odes (I 3 and IV 12) that scholars unversed in the art of banter think that he must be addressing some other Virgil. Among them is not Mr. Glover (*Camb. Anc. Hist.* X [1934] p. 538).

[76] See Chapter IV, notes 45 and 54.

[77] For instance, take the pleasant scene at the end of De Oratore I, where debate on a high theme ends in laughter and genial banter. It is time for the siesta, and Scaevola, the great lawyer, who had invited a guest to his villa, has to go. But he would have been glad to hear Antony talk on — Antony had been arguing against the view upheld by Crassus (and Cicero) that a liberal education is a necessary precursor of the orator's career. "For," said Scaevola with a smile, "he didn't trouble me so much when he picked our civil code to pieces as he delighted me by admitting that he knew nothing about it." In general, on Cicero's genial, and serious, humanism, see Chapter I, note 100.

[78] *Spirit of Comedy*, pp. 92–117 (on Erasmus), esp. 113–115.

world law and order, military prowess, and good roads. That they gave, along with a conception of ideal government, consonant with that of Plato and Polybius and tested by experience. But Rome was built no less on the seriousness of high poetry and thought, on simple human laughter, and on the rare essence of high comedy. The noble Roman had verily learned how to laugh. He had mastered what is today one of the lost arts, the art of leisure, whereby the relative and interminable acquisitions of toil are harmonized in an immediate and absolute experience of tranquillity — one bright "shoote of everlastingnesse." The Roman likewise had learned not only to conquer the habitable world, but, catching the torch of discovery from the Greeks, to traverse the space far out beyond the flaming ramparts of the world.

# CHAPTER IV

# THE IVORY GATE

IN presenting Virgil's prophecy of the Ideal Empire and Horace's picture of its fulfilment, I doubtless have failed to satisfy some of my readers who wanted something more solid than poetry. I can only repeat my conviction that there is nothing more solid than the world of ideas. They abide, while the world of action and apparent fact is a mirage, full of gropings, inconsistencies, misunderstandings, and disappointments. These, of course, when acting on the intellect, perturb its clarity and suffuse its vision with mists. After such reflections I would invite the reader, despite his reluctance, to approach the Ivory Gate, and on the way to ponder somewhat more deeply than before on the mind and the art of Virgil.

When Aeneas and the Sibyl have heard the full revelation of Anchises in the world below, they are taken by him to the Gates of Hell. There are two gates, the poet explains. His words, as translated by Dryden, read:

> Two gates the silent House of Sleep adorn;
> Of polish'd iv'ry this, that of transparent horn:
> True visions thro' transparent horn arise;
> Thro' polish'd iv'ry pass deluding lies.[1]

If we think we can guess by which gate, after the true prophecy of Anchises, the hero and the Prophetess make their exit, we probably shall be wrong. They go out not by the Gate of Horn, but by the Ivory Gate. Many a reader has rubbed his eyes and looked at the passage again. Yes, Anchises sent them to the upper world by the Ivory Gate. What does the poet

[1] *Aen*. VI 893: Sunt geminae Somni portae, quarum altera fertur Cornea, qua veris facilis datur exitus umbris, Altera candenti perfecta nitens elephanto, Sed falsa ad caelum mittunt insomnia manes.

mean? Was it all a dream, then, and a false dream at that? Commentators have been busy with explanations. Aeneas and the Sibyl are real humans, with solid flesh and coursing blood. They can brush aside all sorts of dreams as they pass through the upper world. Aeneas strides on swiftly and finds his ships on the shore. The poet, with lines of wonderful rapidity, sets us again in the world of men, in the common light of day.

Yes, but, after all, why choose the Ivory Gate? An ingenious explanation was offered years ago by a great Harvard teacher who knew all Virgil by heart, Dr. William Everett. He pointed out [2] that the poet has in mind the ancient doctrine, repeated by Horace, that true dreams come after midnight, and false dreams in the hours before:

post mediam noctem visus, cum somnia vera.[3]

The Gate of Horn simply was not open at the time that Aeneas and the Sibyl left the shades. They took the open gate. The journey occupied just twelve hours. Perhaps we should reason that they had a long walk ahead to reach the ships at daybreak. Hades lies some distance below.

I wonder. I think they might have made it if they had started at 12.01 A.M. What is time to a poet after all? With his art of illusion he can erase time. Aeschylus, while a chorus sings, can bring Agamemnon all the way from Troy. Somehow I think it unsafe to track Virgil's chronology too closely. That is a matter, like the scenery in his *Bucolics* or the personal allegory in the *Aeneid*, over which he spread an impressionistic blur, leaving us to make out the contours of real

---

[2] *Class. Rev.* XV (1900) 153–154. This article is a spicy rejoinder to one by F. Granger earlier in the same volume (pp. 25–26). To the latter scholar the gates are symbolical respectively of the eyes and the mouth; the eyeball furnishes the gate of horn, the teeth the gate of gleaming ivory. He proves that the ancients believed, what none would deny, that the evidence of the eyes is preferable to that of the mouth received by the willing ears. His hypothesis has at least a comic value.

[3] *Serm.* I 10. 33. Dr. Everett gives instances in other authors of this familiar superstition, including various passages in the *Aeneid* where it is presupposed.

places or the characters of real persons veiled in a radiant haze.[4]

A much more profound study, learned and illuminating, has lately been made by another American scholar.[5] Drawing on Homer and Hesiod and Plato and still others, on the folklore of other lands and on art as well as literature, he sets before us the tangled maze of myths and fancies from which Virgil selected what served his own imagination, added what was required by the deepened Platonic and Roman religious sense, and from this wealth of suggestion fashioned his own picture of the gloom of Tartarus and that of the bright Elysian fields.[6] To him the long journey [7] is an allegory of the soul, a mighty soul, that must twice pass through the Gate of Ivory on its way from heaven to earth and back to its final abode in heaven.[8] And yet he declares that since deceptive dreams came, in the Roman view, from the Manes, and since Anchises was one of these, the poet suggestively presented Aeneas and the Sibyl as false dreams.[9]

[4] *Magical Art*, pp. 164–188; Chapter II, note 74. More fruitful is Dr. Everett's suggestion that the scenery of Virgil's beloved Bay of Naples, both its beauties and its horrors, lingered in the poet's mind as he composed his picture of the world below. I found it still possible eight years ago to ride on the back of a sturdy and somewhat demonic Italian guide through the infernal waters up to the light of day.

[5] E. L. Highbarger, *The Gates of Dreams, an Archaeological Examination of Vergil, Aeneid VI. 893–899* (The Johns Hopkins University Studies in Archaeology, No. 30, 1940). Whether the author's conclusions gain acceptance or not, his book offers new and valuable material for a study of Virgil's mind and art.

[6] *Op. cit.* p. 67, and chap. vii *passim*.

[7] Twenty-four hours rather than twelve (p. 25). Granted, on the understanding that Virgil can stretch hours to light-years or contract light-years to hours.

[8] *Op. cit.* chap. viii. Since Aeneas is portrayed by the poet as a prototype of Augustus as well as of "the noble Romans of all ages" (p. 114, and cf. above, p. 58), this mystical journey with its purging of the hero's heart is a most significant feature in the poet's Mirror of the Prince for Augustus (cf. above, pp. 80, 85). Aeneas, of course, in actuality ascends again not to heaven but to earth and the grim realities before him. Yet Aeneas, like Dante, emerges a deeply enlightened soul from the lower world. It is helpful to turn to Virgil after a fresh reading of Dante, to see what Dante found there and to find more there ourselves.

[9] *Op. cit.*, p. 81: "Vergil evidently considered Aeneas and the Sibyl 'false dreams,' and Anchises was now one of the Manes, of course." In this case, the symbolism Aeneas = Augustus loses much of its lustre.

That is the aspect of Virgil's picture of the Gates — whatever the underlying allegory, to which I think we cannot be blind. That Gate of Ivory has a connotation more solid than a dream. We recall perforce the brilliant parody of Pope in his *Dunciad*, wherein the Apocalypse of Dulness ends with the lines:

"Enough! enough!" the raptur'd Monarch cries:
And thro' the Iv'ry Gate the Vision flies.[10]

## I

The mind of Virgil would deserve our deepest study, even if he had not expressed his thoughts in noble poetry. That mind from beginning to end was a battlefield for the ancient conflict of which Plato speaks [11] between poetry and philosophy, or poetry and science. He had an early training in the Epicurean School and according to some of the ancients, like his commentator Servius,[12] and to some of the moderns, like Tenney Frank,[13] he remained in his heart of hearts an Epicurean — not of the frivolous but of the Lucretian school — to the end. But this is only one aspect of his thought. The other is an innate Platonism, which for him meant poetry. Hence the struggle in his mind between those mighty opponents. We remember that, according to his ancient biographer,[14] his

[10] At the end of Book III.

[11] *Republic* X 607 B: παλαιὰ μέν τις διαφορὰ φιλοσοφίᾳ τε καὶ ποιητικῇ.

[12] On *Ecl.* VI 13: nam vult exequi sectam Epicuream, quam didicerant tam Vergilius quam Varus docente Sirone. Here the reference is to Virgil's youth and his earlier work, but Servius maintains the same attitude in his comments on the *Aeneid*; see on VI 264: ex maiore autem parte Sironem, id est magistrum suum Epicureum sequitur. Huius autem sectae homines novimus superficiem rerum tractare, numquam altiora disquirere. This last remark is highly banal and hardly consistent with Servius' prefatory remark on Book VI: Totus quidem Vergilius scientia plenus est. In general, his comments on the "Epicurean" elements in the *Aeneid* are flat. He begins with Siro and implies that Virgil got no further. The author of the longer commentary (Servius Danielis), whether Donatus or not, has the same attitude in this matter (cf. on *Aen.* X 487: ergo secundum sectam (i.e. the Epicurean) sibi notam poetam locutum.

[13] *Vergil*, p. 109 and the last chapter. Frank presents *Servium in melius mutatum*. I should say, rather, that Virgil could never have been consistently Epicurean, but that the battle between science and the religion of the poet was with him to the end.

[14] Donatus *Vita Verg.* (Brummer), pp. 7–8.

purpose in making his voyage to Greece at the end of his life
was to put the finishing touches on his *Aeneid* in the most
congenial of environments, and then to devote the remainder
of his days to the study of philosophy — to see the conflict
through. But that was not to be. The poet was taken ill after
his arrival in Greece and died not long after his return to
Italy.

In each of his three major works there comes a moment,
whatever the subject, when Virgil deserts it for some upper
realm and speaks out on the great issues of life. The poetry
that issues from such a mood reveals, as we have seen,[15] one
of the rare glimpses of Roman high seriousness. In the *Aeneid*,
such a moment comes in the prophecy of Anchises. Another
is found in the song of Silenus in the Sixth Eclogue; and still
another in the praise of country life at the end of the Second
Georgic.

To the prophecy of Anchises I have already paid some attention. The Sixth Eclogue shows another cardinal quality
of Virgil's thought and art and originality. In that poem the
song of Silenus, which sounds far other than pastoral notes,
is prefaced by one of the most delightful little pictures in
Virgil's or anybody else's pastoral. The song is forced out of
old Silen by a trick. He is sleeping in his cave, sleeping off
his carouse, "his veins still swollen as ever," says Virgil, "with
the wine of yesterday."[16] Near him lie the garlands he had
worn, with a decent regard for the proprieties; for flowers,
wine, and ointment are the three essentials for a feast. His
hand is clutching his heavy tankard by its well-worn handle.[17]
Just now two shepherd lads and a woodland nymph, Aegle,
fairest of all the Naiads, steal up, bind up with a noose made

[15] Chapter III, notes 7–9.
[16] The god's life, it would seem, fell into two well-regulated halves — the day
after, and the day.
[17] Verse 17: et gravis attrita pendebat cantharus ansa. "Heavy," not from its
contents — it was empty — but from its size. "Well-worn," grasped actively on
the day, and passively, fondly, reminiscentially, on the day after; it had become
an anatomical part of Silenus. In every word in this line (excepting *et*, which
bows the others in) "all the wealth of all the Muses" flowers. There is languor
in *pendebat* and a somnolent (possibly rhonchial) assonance in *cantharus ansa*.

of the garland, and, to complete the charm, paint his face and brows with blood-red mulberries. He wakes, and sees that he is caught at last. The exquisite humor of this sketch shows that Virgil's laughter, when he chose to give it rein, had a keen delicacy that French lovers of Virgil, best of all Sainte-Beuve, can understand.

The song begins, while Fauns and the beasts of the field play about in a rhythmic dance and the stiff oaks nod their tresses. Did they quite understand its meaning? It is a song of creation, of creation by scientific law, atoms forming the elements, and elements the earth and the lights of heaven. But then come the legends — for science cannot explain all: the Golden Age, the flood, and tales of primal love, and tales of metamorphosis in this changing world. Of a sudden, the song is in praise of Gallus, brother poet of Virgil, as dear to him as Horace later was. His appearance seems nothing strange amid these marvels; for he in his own poetry had told of some of them.[18] The god sings till twilight; his notes are echoed from the valleys to the skies. Then Vesper, the evening star, bids the shepherds drive home their flocks, as he starts on his nightly course over Mount Olympus, who is far from pleased to have him come; for Olympus, too, has been listening.

This pastoral soars sky high, absorbing Olympus on the way. And yet, with Virgil's magic, incongruous elements are fused in a harmony. For it is Vesper himself who orders the shepherds home.[19] We end on *terra firma*. A matter-of-fact critic will point out the incongruous elements in Virgil's art and leave the matter there. But Anatole France, as a *poilu* in 1870, could make "comments upon that cosmogony, which the poet, by a delightful caprice, enshrined in an idyll." [20] To learn that one of Virgil's dear delights was to harmonize the incongruous and to recognize his triumphs in this daring art is the

---

[18] Some scholars have overemphasized the amount of allusions to Gallus' poetry in this eclogue. See *Magical Art*, pp. 143–144.

[19] Verse 85: Cogere donec ovis stabulis numerumque referre Iussit et invito processit Vesper Olympo.

[20] For the story, see *Magical Art*, p. 174.

beginning of wisdom for one who would understand our poet.

This power to elevate the subject while never leaving it is displayed by Virgil with a triumphant ease in the *Georgics* again and again, as in the praise of Spring and the praise of Italy in the First Book, and above all in the encomium of rustic simplicity at the end of the Second. Here Virgil, in contrast to the science of Lucretius, presents a philosophy of the country which has a place for simple, rustic faith and for a Golden Age of industry and well-won pleasures, a Golden Age not primitively remote but to men of good will accessible here and now. That was the life of the Sabines of old, of Etruria in its strength, and of the old Rome that girded its seven hills with a wall.

This pleasant picture is of course in harmony with the poet's vision of the Ideal Empire. And yet there is one touch that suggests the Ivory Gate. The rustics, says the poet, in their happy contemplative life have no interest in wealth or political power or the pomp and ceremony of kings or the discord that drives brothers to disloyalty. They care neither for Dacians and their confederates who swoop down from the Danube, *nor for affairs of Rome, nor for kingdoms doomed to perish.* In other words, they are not interested in the drums and tramplings of their nation's conquests —

non res Romanae perituraque regna.[21]

Did Virgil have some misgivings about the triumph of the Roman arms? Such reflections do not well fit the immediate program of Augustus. The poet, for the moment at any rate, is looking beyond all that. He sees a celestial city, a city of heavenly peace, far remote from even the majesty of the Roman Empire.[22] The contrast between the city of his vision and the actual Rome, however big and busy, may have started in him a course of painful wondering.

Virgil's mind was full of questionings, as Tennyson was

[21] *Georg.* II 498.
[22] This is one of those swift ascents from the temporal scene of which the Roman mind was capable. See Chapter III, note 12.

well aware.  Tennyson knew his Virgil, his Italian "Manto-vano," ever since his day began.  One of his best observa-tions [23] is that of the pulsing sadness — *sunt lacrimae rerum* — that underlies the outer triumphs of the epic story.  He ad-dresses the poet as

> majestic in thy sadness
> at the doubtful doom of humankind.

We may ask just here why Virgil, on his deathbed, ordered his final masterpiece to be burned.  Perhaps it was because he had not given it his finishing touches.  Half-lines remain which have a pathetic value for us but which he would have completed with something better than a gap.  Again there are faults in the structure, in the details of the plot.[24]  Virgil may also have felt that his magical art had not quite absorbed in-congruous elements into an integral pattern such as he had achieved in the Sixth Eclogue and in that artistically perfect poem, the *Georgics*.  It is no slight task to merge dissonance into harmony.  Then, too, the problem of identifying Aeneas with Augustus without the loss of the hero's own identity or the reality of the ancient story of Rome is nothing easy to solve.  An untold amount of patient pondering and experi-ment preceded the magic expression of a creative idea that in Virgil's musical lines seems to flow forth spontaneously.  At some point in the composition of the *Aeneid* he wrote to Au-gustus, in answer to his sovereign's numerous requests for some extracts from the work, that the task was so great that it seemed almost a mental aberration to have undertaken it.[25]

[23] See Chapter III, note 39.  Lucretius is sometimes called a pessimist.  He feels more profoundly than does Virgil the woes and the follies of mankind, but he masters them.  He is ultimately an optimist, rejoicing in the cosmos that his Master's science has established once and for all (cf. *Esprits Souverains*, pp. 22–23).  Virgil, with more of worship in his soul, aspires to the ideal world and gains it and then wonders if it is gained.  Temperamentally more sensitive than Lucretius, he is less sure of himself, less the master of his fate.

[24] Such as the inconsistencies in the story of the voyage from Troy as in-dicated elsewhere, and as perfected in the narrative of the Third Book, where the exact location of the goal is only gradually revealed.  I therefore would regard this book as one of the latest to be composed, though that is by no means the universal opinion.

[25] Macrobius, *Saturn.* I 24. 11: sed tanta incohata res est, ut paene vitio

Finally, is it blasphemous to inquire whether Virgil was as sure of his hero as he had been before? If there was a glimmering of any such doubt in the poet's mind, there may be a delicate sub-intention in the Ivory Gate. He read the Emperor his Sixth Book not long after the death of young Marcellus in 23 B.C. and only four years before his own death in 19 B.C.[26] Horace's first volume of *Odes* (I–III) had just appeared or was about to appear at the time of the reading. Horace had become a loyal supporter of the Emperor at that time,[27] but the note of calm assurance does not become permanent in his poetry before the *Carmen Saeculare* and the Fourth Book of his *Odes*. Virgil died just before the nation's satisfaction found expression in the Secular Games of 17 B.C. It would be interesting to know what feelings passed through the Emperor's mind as the mellifluous voice of Virgil ended the reading of the Sixth Book. Augustus might have had some vague wonderings about that Ivory Gate.

If, fulfilling our normal span, Virgil had lived from the year 70 B.C. to the beginning of our era, or a few years more, he would have seen various of his dreams pass out at the Ivory Gate. He would have asked himself whether, after the death of young Marcellus, any successor to the father of his people would be found who could maintain and strengthen the Ideal Empire. The Emperor was destined to several more bitter disappointments in his search.[28] His great general, Agrippa, was married to the widow of Marcellus, the Emperor's daughter Julia, of unhappy memory, and thus was taken into the family, but he died in 12 B.C. Then came Drusus, a great popular hero after his successes in the campaign celebrated by Horace in his Fourth Book, but he died in 9 B.C. His loss, as has been well said,[29] was an even greater tragedy for Rome

---

mentis tantum opus ingressus mihi videar, cum praesertim, ut scis, alia quoque studia ad id opus multoque potiora impertiar.

[26] Donatus, *Vita Verg.* (Brummer) p. 7.108. Cf. Chapter II, note 150.

[27] Chapter II, note 85.

[28] Tacitus chronicles the melancholy series (*Annals* I 3. 1–3). Cf. Hammond, *Augustan Principate*, pp. 68–74.

[29] Buchan, *Augustus*, p. 185.

than the death of Marcellus. Lucius and Gaius, the sons of Agrippa, succeeded him, but they died at the turn of the century. Tiberius, the elder, not the better, brother of Drusus, was left; he surely was not the Emperor's favorite, nor that of Horace, if we may judge by the meagre praise allotted him in his great triumphal odes.[30] Tiberius was the last resort.

And how about the Golden Age that the poet had proclaimed in his Messianic prophecy? It was a Golden Age of short duration, whoever the Child may have been. If Marcellus, the son of the Emperor's sister Octavia, he soon died. If Asinius Gallus, the son of Pollio, he lived to become a minor character in both politics and literature, whose chief distinction, I should say, was that he felt sure that he was the Child of the Eclogue.[31] And if, *horribile dictu*, the Child turned out to be the Emperor's scandalous daughter Julia, then the whole Golden Age flew out at the Ivory Gate. She played a part, nevertheless, in the Emperor's plans for the succession. Poor lady, married first to Marcellus, then to Agrippa, then to Tiberius, what romance was there in life for a soulful young woman, doomed merely to serve as a connecting link in the chain of imperial adoptionism? She managed to secure romance, and, along with her similarly unconventional daughter and Agrippa's demented son, became to her imperial father one of what he rudely called his three boils and cancers — his three headaches, as we more elegantly say today.[32] At the time of his death Virgil had seen one of the Emperor's high hopes for a successor come to naught. He had seen one of the seven conspiracies against Augustus, of which Suetonius tells,[33] flare forth. It was quenched, and with it a man of the

[30] Chapter II, note 115.

[31] Servius on *Ecl.* IV 11.

[32] Suet. *Aug.* 65. 4: nec aliter eos appellare quam tris vomicas ac tria carcinomata sua. This is one of those bits of vigorous and somewhat vulgar slang to which the Emperor was addicted; see Chapter III, note 63. It was too much for Quintilian. He remarks that just because Cicero called Catiline and his crew the bilgewater of the state, the youthful aspirant to eloquence should not follow one of the very ancient orators and call the state's enemies "boils." Quintilian was irreproachably Ciceronian. For a sympathetic account of Julia, see Buchan, *Augustus*, pp. 242–247.

[33] *Aug.* 19.

Emperor's immediate entourage, Licinius Murena, brother-in-law of Maecenas. Doubts and forebodings might have beset the poet's mind, lest his sovereign should not see his new Rome entrusted to strong hands.

Virgil, had he lived, would have met with other disappointments. He, who had planned to devote his remaining days to philosophy, might have seen that noble effort of the mind issuing through the Ivory Gate, with religion and morals in its train. After his vision of the rustic Golden Age what would Virgil have thought of Ovid, to whom "rustic" meant Puritan and boorish, to whom *rusticitas* was the cardinal sin in his gay world of intrigue? [34]

Perhaps we should leave the Ivory Gate shrouded in mystery, after all, in the fashion of Virgil's allegory, half-revealing, half-concealing the poet's mind, or rather, perhaps, exactly portraying a mood of doubt. It is not the doubt of bewilderment or the renunciation of choice. It is an inclusive doubt that shelters antinomic entities or emotions, like real and unreal, hope and fear, as equally valid, each demanding, at any rate, equal rights in poetry. Virgil, with an art possessed by few, may have given both of the contradictories a voice, when he makes Aeneas and the Sibyl issue through the Ivory Gate. [35]

A more modest solution is suggested by an article of faith accepted by the ancient commentators, represented by Servius, [36] that in exactly thirteen passages in Virgil's poetry there was simply no answer that human ingenuity could devise to the problem raised by the text. On meeting one of these *cruces*, the commentator could do no more than mark it with a cross and pass on. There was also the suspicion that Virgil had composed these passages expressly to stump his expositors. [37] Perhaps, then, the better part for us will be humbly to inscribe a *crux* on Virgil's Ivory Gate.

[34] See *Amores* I 8 and *Ovid and His Influence*, pp. 13–14.

[35] In fact, this is one of the moments of "high seriousness" in Virgil. See Chapter III, note 12.

[36] On *Aen.* IX 412: sciendum tamen et locum hunc unum esse de insolubilibus XIII, quae habent obscuritatem. The comment quoted in note 37 gives XII as the number; there may be a scribal error either way.

[37] In *Aen.* IX 361: sciendum est locum hunc esse unum de XII Vergili sive

## II

We pass herewith into the world of Ovid, a very blithe and modern world, detached from the age of Ideal Empire, which evaporated in his poetry. For Ovid was one of the most modern of men. The glamour of the brave days of old made, he asserted, little appeal to him.

> Laudamus veteres sed nostris utimur annis.

> We praise old times, but use the present age.[38]

And again:

> Prisca iuvent alios, ego me nunc denique natum
> Gratulor: haec aetas moribus apta meis.

> Let others praise the hoary past. But how
> I thank my stars I was not born till now.
> The present age is suited to my ways.[39]

Ovid is, by his proclamation, a poet of love, of playful love — *tenerorum lusor amorum.* Love is an appropriate topic in our present quest; for no human dream is more apt to glide out by the Ivory Gate. We will therefore spend a few moments with the love-poetry of the Romans:

> Omnia vincit amor, et nos cedamus Amori.

The four evangelists of love in Roman poetry, as Ovid declares,[40] are Gallus, Tibullus, Propertius and — Ovid himself.

---

per naturam obscuris, sive insolubilibus, sive emendandis, sive sic relictis ut a nobis per historiae antiquae ignorantiam liquide non intelligantur.

[38] *Fasti* I 225. This is a "statement" that Ovid takes down on his tablet from the god Janus's lips. In the fashion of the modern reporter he has secured an interview and is making the most of it. He begins by asking the god why he is the only one of the celestials who can see behind his back as well as in front. The interview is spiced with Ovid's wit — as well as with his genuine interest in religious rites. Let us note that the god adds temperately that both the old way and the new deserve our respect: mos tamen est aeque dignus uterque coli. The best introduction to the *Fasti* and to Ovid's knowledge of liturgy is the monumental edition of Sir James G. Frazer (London, Macmillan, 1929). For the general reader, the pith of his invaluable notes is given in his Loeb edition.

[39] *Art of Love* III 121–122.

[40] *Tristia* IV 10. 53: Successor fuit hic (i.e. Tibullas) tibi, Galle, Propertius illi; Quartus ab his serie temporis ipse fuit. This poem is Ovid's autobiog-

In point of technique, the use of the same metre, the elegiac, he is correct; for ancient poets are reverently attentive to the form, to the species, and to its laws. But the greatest of Roman poets of love, as Ovid was well aware, was Catullus, who, if we discount ordinary chronology, was the coeval and the peer of Sappho; his spirit really was not consorting with the Neo-Alexandrine poets of Rome in the days of Cicero and Caesar. We moderns are oblivious to form, and search for spirit. If we obey the maxim, perennially appropriate, of *cherchez la femme*, we may construct another royal line of succession, not of the poets of love but of their sweethearts, among whom Catullus' Lesbia and the fair bevy of Horace's nymphs rightly demand a place.[41]

Catullus, in his poems to Lesbia or about her, has given the history of a love, brief in time, eternal in its depths and heights, hardly to be matched elsewhere. It is the history of a pure, white soul, *anima candida*, transfused with passion, joy, and worship, with the keen bliss that turns to pain, with the fondness of a father for his child, with doubts and hate and loathing, when her baseness is revealed, with childlike gratitude for winning her again, with prayer to the gods for healing, and with a brave hardening of his heart, as he crushes the last vestige of his love, which, like the furthest flower in the field, falls before the passing plough.

Here, indeed, is the purging of tragedy, not on the stage but in a human heart. George Meredith, in *The Egoist*, writes: "Women have us back to the condition of primitive man, or they shoot us higher than the topmost star. But it is as we please . . . the poet's Lesbia, the poet's Beatrice; ours is the choice." The tragedy of Catullus is that he thought his Lesbia a Beatrice. His was not the lust of primitive man. His passion for her was pure, and shot him higher than the topmost star, until he knew her mockery and her vileness.

With the passing of Catullus, not only his love but all

---

raphy, written during his exile possibly at a time when he thought his death was impending. It is naturally an important document for the understanding of Ovid, as is his apology to Augustus (*Tristia* II).

[41] Cf. *Ovid and His Influence* (note 34), p. 10.

Roman love-poetry may seem to have floated out through the Ivory Gate. His successors made an art of what to him was sheer reality. They also told of sweethearts, of passion and success, of tears and infidelities and partings. Each had his chronicle of love, written partly from experience and partly from the ancient themes and topics into which experience was fitted. That is their art; and sometimes art makes truth appear like fiction.

And yet these poets have their charm. Of the great four of Ovid's canon, Gallus is known to us only by what others said of him, by Virgil above all, whose affection for his brother poet is proof enough that his poetry was worth while.[42] Tibullus, sweet and gentle, writes his loves in musical verse, as though the world's wars were in some other planet. If his poetry were suddenly discovered today in a French translation, all critics would hail it as a genuine product of the Romantic period. And so Propertius, if his books came similarly to light in German, would be called authentic *Sturm und Drang*. There is more virility in Propertius than in Tibullus, more tumult and more despair. There is also more genius; he felt more and more towards the end of his course the call to epic and the appeal of the old legends of Rome.

Horace is not of the elegiac canon. He, like Catullus, burst its bonds. Horace became Rome's lyric poet, and moulded all the measures of the light Greek lyric into stately Roman forms. Love is for Horace matter for comedy and playful banter and high seriousness. He had his loves, his jealousies, his hatreds in his hot youth. Such is his mastery of emotions that some might think he had no youth at all. He had no age. He was always wise and always a boy. He looked with that "slim, feasting smile" on the earnestness of the romantic lovers like Tibullus. His banter may take his own invented form of laughing at the third person in terms of the first. He pictures himself, for instance, as singing what ancient poets, with a nice technique, called a "closed-door" serenade; the other variety melts a maiden's heart and opens the door. So

[42] Cf. *Ecl.* X.

there he is, our plump little Horace, singing on the cold sill, out in the freezing rain.[43] Or, rather, there Tibullus is, and once was chased all night by his mistress's dog [44] — an episode that Horace, with extraordinary courtesy, passes by. Who else, I wonder, besides Chaucer has employed this urbane and admirably self-protective, while ostensibly self-revealing, form of ridicule? [45]

Horace's nymphs are legion. There are Chloe and Chloris and Tyndaris, the shepherdess in his pastoral; Rhode and Galatea, and Glycera, at whose call Venus herself comes in a pretty procession to her shrine; there are Neaera and Lyde and Lalage, whom he could sing while the Muses, guardians of the pure in heart, guided his wanderings in frozen Scythia or on the hot Sahara sands; there is Phyllis, the last, positively the last, of all his loves; there is Lydia, with whom he engages in an amoebaean debate that ends in reconciliation — a piece of delicate humor, turned into a little comedy not many years ago by a clever Frenchman, François Ponsard, for the Paris stage.[46] There are other types that Horace describes, Damalis the drunken, Pholoe of the fast set and her no less fast mamma, while poor Ibycus, the father, pays the bills for roses and champagne; there is Barine, maid of Barium, false, fickle and forsworn, and very popular, whom perhaps Horace had seen on his famous journey with Virgil and Maecenas; there is proud Lyce, now aging, abandoned by her cruel lovers, who deck themselves with green ivy and throw dry leaves to the east wind.

There are beautiful lads, as well — for whom the poet's

[43] *Odes* III 10. For more in this vein from Horace, see *Spirit of Metamorphosis*, pp. 215–217; *Spirit of Comedy*, pp. 50–53.

[44] I 7. 31: Ille ego sum, nec me iam dicere vera pudebit Instabat tota cui tua nocte canis.

[45] Cf. note 54. I cannot find my notes on Chaucer in which some years ago I had jotted down the instances I had observed. My friend Robinson now helps me out with the passage in the *Nun's Priest's Tale* "where Chaucer imitates Geoffrey of Vinsauf and wishes he had his powers of lamentation." He notes other passages as well. Here is a little quest for some Chaucerian versed in Horace and Ovid. He might also search the authors of the *aetas Ovidiana*; cf. Chapter VII, note 129.

[46] *Horace et Lydie, Une Ode d'Horace* (III 9), Paris, nouv. éd. 1908.

affection could have been nothing bestial — Lycidas "for whom now every youth is kindled, and maidens soon shall feel a modest glow"; Nearchus, sitting statuesquely with hands beneath his foot, while the breeze tosses his fragrant locks over his shoulders; and cruel Ligurinus, who will sigh one day as he looks in his mirror, "Ah why as a lad did I not have my longing at this moment, or why at this moment do not my cheeks return to life?"

We must not try too nicely to draw the character of each Chloe and each Lydia from the appearance of their names in different odes. Each is real in the momentary flash, and soon the light has passed. *Carpe diem, et carpe Lalagen.* You may never see her again — or you may. Many names and one essence, with various lights and shades. Study them all and you will find a composite nymph worth knowing. Her moods and her charms are various, but some of her traits are permanent. She is ever comely, dresses in simple taste, with hair done neatly in the fashion of a Spartan girl. Not too much perfume is on that hair, and not too elaborate garlands grace it — save on some very high and fast festivity, when roses are scattered and Falernian flows free. And she always brings her harp, that there its music may accompany her own clear voice, with Horace to join in, antiphonally, in a primitive symphony concert. Such was Horace's nymph. He could subscribe to Santayana's lines:

> And ever constant, though inconstant known,
> In all my loves I worshipped thee alone.

Yes, our little Matinian bee has been busy. Flitting from grove to grove he has gathered honey for our delectation and packed it in a little jar that we may label *Toutes Fleures.* I have suggested only a few of its flavors. The rest are for us to gather from his poetry, which to be relished can never be gulped but sipped at leisure through the years.

But what, oh what, have these fleeting amorosities to do with Augustus' enactments for the moral reform of Roman society and with Horace's grave protests that laws with no moral backing are in vain? We must recognize that the ancient standards are not our own, which draw their strength from the Christian way of life. The Roman family was built on sure foundations, but the column of its support was the wife — not the man. The man, like the youth, was free to take his pleasures with women of the lower sort. There was his domain of romance; for there he found freedom, of the lower sort.[47] A young man, in those days, did not inform his parents of his betrothal, as today. It was announced to him by the *pater familias*; his not to reason why. It was one of life's surprises, an unpleasant surprise, if he was already wrapt in romance — in willing chains and sweet captivity.[48] He must tear himself away; for he entered a new life as father of a family and was true to its obligations. He raised offspring and gave them his paternal care and fondness. But the world of romance, if he did not find it within, was his to seek without. He could be both centripetal and centrifugal if he wished. His wife, whether with romance or not, must ever be centripetal. That was why Julia rebelled.

Thus the only sexual crime was adultery. That was what Augustus proceeded to reform. For that there was punishment, naturally, for both woman and man, since the guilty man broke up another household. And that crime Horace consistently had lashed, and in an early satire, mistakenly called coarse, had ridiculed.[49] There had undoubtedly been a lowering of the old Roman moral standard ever since the Romans opened the door to the Greek way of life as they found it. Horace's *bon mot* that conquered Greece conquered its rude conqueror —

Graecia capta ferum victorem cepit —

[47] Cf. Buchan, *Augustus*, p. 254.

[48] So it seemed to young Pamphilus, in Terence's *Andria* (252–256). "Just now father passed by me down in the Square and nonchalantly remarked, 'Pamphilus, you're going to be married today. Go home and get ready' — as much as to say, 'Hurry off and hang yourself.' I was blasted!" (252–256).

[49] *Serm.* I 2. Horace calls a spade a spade, but the purpose of the satire is moral. Horace applies his device of using the first person to indicate the third and makes the offender ridiculous. See *Spirit of Comedy*, p. 61.

is true in more ways than one; Greek culture was accompanied by laxer morals. Our witness there is not merely old Cato but Polybius.[50] Catullus's passion, in itself crystal-pure, brought ruin to another household — if anything could ruin Lesbia. That was the evil at which Augustus aimed and, so far as one could, he hit the mark.

But let us not call Horace's poetical amours merely a metrical exercise after the Greek with no relation to his own sentiment; it is part of the Golden Age which the god Pan established on the Sabine Farm. It is part of Horace's laughter, as vital as his gravity. And he can change swiftly from gay to grave. All of a sudden we discover, in the deep heart of Horace, a reverence for the pure and abiding love of man and wife:

Happy they thrice and more, whom an unsevered bond unites, whose love, sundered by no vile reproaches, shall part them only with their dying day.

> Felices ter et amplius
> Quos inrupta tenet copula nec malis
> Divolsus querimoniis
> Suprema citius solvit amor die.[51]

Till death us do part. Possibly, as he wrote the lines, Horace may have thought of his ruler, who loved Livia his wife from the moment of their marriage, whatever its political significance, to the moment of his death.[52] After all, Horace's dream of love does not issue through the Ivory Gate.

## III

Ovid is Horace's aptest pupil in his school of wit. In his love poems, the metre and the species make him the fourth in the series of the Roman elegiac poets of love. In spirit and

[50] XXXI 25. 2–8. Young Scipio strengthened his character, says Polybius, by fighting against these vicious tendencies. Although one of the *illuminati*, he was as resolute as old Cato to maintain the virtues of ancient Rome.

[51] *Odes* I 13. 17–20. These verses, as some Freshmen learn, are written above two of the gates of Harvard College, a symbol of the unending love of her sons for *Alma Mater*.

[52] Buchan, *Augustus*, pp. 94–95.

in fancy he depends on Horace.  He catches up Horace's good-
humored ridicule of the romantic poets and carries it farther.[53]
He follows Horace in expressing this gay critique in terms of
his own experience.[54]  Adventures he presumably had, but he
treats them playfully, enlarging or reducing them at will.  He
creates from them a little world of intrigue, a world of fancy,
in which he takes extreme delight, as Horace did in his new
golden Sabine Farm.  One difference is patent.  Horace located his imaginary realm in a country valley.  Ovid did not
need to stir a step from Rome.  Horace, further, never unites
his nymphs into a single personage, although they all attest
a unity which only needs a name.  Ovid does, and calls his
whole experience Corinna, who owes her unity and her existence to Ovid's wit.  Her name does not veil that of some real
person, as Lesbia, Delia, Cynthia do.  Her maker must have
been highly entertained when a good Roman lady let it be
whispered that *she* was the only genuine Corinna.[55]  No, Corinna is a mythical heroine in an intensely modern age.  We
might suppose that she would name the poet's work.  But the
title is not Corinna but *Amores*, 'Les Amours.'  Ovid would
not over-Platonize in his merging of the many in the one.

This most intelligent adaptation of his own guiding idea
was complimented by Horace in the introductory ode of his
Fourth Book, published some four years after his *Secular
Hymn*, in which he had felicitated the Emperor on the success of his moral reform.  Unlike Cicero, who thought young
innovators were making the world dangerous for poetry,
Horace liked to consort with youthful bards whose verse was
sung all over town, and learn from them, with courteous
amusement, just what was what.  Ovid returns his compliment with no little fervor.[56]  A genre of love-fiction had been
perfected, for which many a later poet was thankful.

[53] See *Ovid and His Influence*, pp. 11–12; *Les Esprits Souverains*, pp. 42–43.
[54] See Chapter III, note 76.
[55] *Amores* II 17. 29: Novi aliquam, quae se circumferat esse Corinnam. And,
adds the poet gaily, "What wouldn't she give to become her?"  He apparently
resisted her blandishments (provided she ever existed).
[56] See Chapter II, note 113.

Herrick for instance, whom some have compared to Catullus, was spiritually far nearer akin to Ovid, with a dash of Horace and of Martial. Hence among his nymphs, Julia, Anthea, and the rest, appears Perilla, some intimate member of Ovid's household to whom he writes from exile. So in the familiar poem, "To the Virgins, to Make Much of Time," and thus to gather rosebuds while they may, there is included a small "Legend of those Saints that di'd for love," inspired by that admirable connoisseur of Ovid, Chaucer. Among these holy women are Saint Phillis and Saint Iphis, the latter of whom could have been suggested only by one of Ovid's less well-known tales of metamorphosis.[57] Herrick has Ovid's delight in the *nuance*, in watching a

> white cloud divide
> Into a double twilight.

He has Ovid's delight in little things, a little house *parva sed apta*. He knows the need of serious relief, and underneath his badinage is pure and simple piety:

> Lord, Thou hast given me a cell
>     Wherein to dwell;
> A little house, whose humble Roof
>     Is weather-proof;
> Under the sparres of which I lie
>     Both soft, and drie;
> Where Thou my chamber for to ward
>     Hast set a Guard
> Of harmlesse thoughts, to watch and keep
>     Me, while I sleep.

We have noted that painful closed-door serenade that Horace sang. Ovid has his,[58] a rather long poem in smooth and musical verse, part of it in strophes of six lines capped by a refrain. It lasts till cockcrow and the door opens not. But the lovers' woes will move no reader's tears. His appeals to the concierge, who is doubtless sleeping off a carouse, are staged for comedy. Won't he open just a tiny bit? The gallant

---

[57] *Met.* IX 636–797.
[58] *Amores* I 6. For a translation into verse see *Ovid and the Spirit of Metamorphosis*, pp. 218–219.

has learned in the grim warfare of love how to reduce his weight for this very purpose. He can slip in at the smallest crack; he is a product of the law of natural selection — only slim lovers survive. The tone of this poem is parody, not openly displayed as in a *Culex* or a "Battle of Frogs and Mice," but here and throughout this volume of *Amores* permeating the substance like a perfume, invisible but appreciable, by those who have the sense of smell. It abides amidst the gay intrigue, the infidelities, the arts of deception, the nimble somersaults from one attitude to its opposite. Ovid can be indecently audacious, but he is neither nasty nor vulgar. Nor do we ever quite know whether the poet, with his shield of parody, is speaking for himself. His wit allows him to skate on very thin moral ice. We have to laugh at his antics. If we reproved him, he would reply that just as the wise Aristotle declares that the persons of comedy are worse than those in real life,[59] so the protagonist in his drama of witty naughtiness was worse, oh very much worse, than the dramatist himself. Let us not make ready an answer; for he has blithely skated on.[60]

What we ask, as we float along the pleasant current of the *Amores*, is whether our poet had any serious moments at all. For all play and no work makes Jack a dull boy. There is dulness in unmitigated naughtiness and in unmitigated wit. As tragedy gains in depth by moments of comic relief, so from Ovid we demand a few touches of what we might call "serious relief," and that he gives us in flashes of true poetry, as in the lover's song to the dawn, distant precursor of the

[59] See Chapter III, note 68.

[60] In speaking of Ovid's sprightly version of Polyphemus' gigantic, pastoral wooing of Galatea (*Met.* XIII 750–899), Georges Lafaye, who knew his Ovid well, makes a sufficient comment in the words: "Ovid s'amuse" (*Les Métamorphoses d'Ovide*, p. 181). To that he adds, with similar understanding: "et pourquoi non?" These *mots* might serve as a double running-title, standing one on the left- and the other on the right-hand page, for all the *Carmina Amatoria* (and elsewhere). France above any other nation has understood what Ovid is about. Another excellent work is by Émile Ripert, *Ovide, Poète de l'Amour, des Dieux et de l'Exil* (Paris, 1921). See also the remarks on Ovid's influence on France in the seventeenth and eighteenth centuries, in *Ovid and His Influence*, pp. 160–162.

mediaeval *Aubade*.[61] Or again we find brief respite from wit,
when the blithe singer of the tender loves is suddenly revealed
as a sober head of a household, traveling with his wife over
hill and dale to witness a rare religious ceremony at Falisci,
her birthplace.[62] For, as we have seen, Ovid was devoted to
liturgy, as were most of the Roman poets of that time, nor
can a reader today who has not that devotion know the inner
secrets of Roman poetry.

Above all, we become aware, in the last book of these
many-faceted *Amores*, which contain in germ all the interests
of Ovid's mind, that all along his thought was occupied with
some work of larger scope, not epic, not panegyric of the
Ideal Empire, but tragedy, the very antipodes of the gay comedy that was flowing from his facile pen. The tragedy that he
wrote, *Medea*, favorably appraised by Roman critics, is lost
to us. Passages of tragic feeling meet us later in the *Metamorphoses*. For the moment, the poet effected a compromise
between love-elegy and tragedy in his *Heroides*, letters written
by the heroines of old to their loved ones at some moment of
distress.

In essence the *Heroides* are tragic monologues given a new
purpose, and a new unity, in an epistolary setting. Here and
there a true tragic note is sounded.[63] In most of them the
sentiment is pathos, in a few [64] Ovid's irrepressible wit provides that comic relief which is now welcome in the tragic or
pathetic background of the work. In all of them together we
find a delicate study of woman's moods, treated by Ovid with
a master hand.

Most skilful of all are the double letters, in which the
heroine's missive is in answer to one that her lover sends.

[61] *Amores* I 13.

[62] III 13. See *Ovid and the Spirit of Metamorphosis*, pp. 231–233.

[63] Particularly in *Her.* XI, a letter from Canace to Macareus, her own
brother, written as she was about to kill herself and her child of whom he was
the father. There is no gloating over incest in this poem. There is no multi-
fold employment of an "incest-motif" as in O'Neill's impressive, but futile,
attempt, in *Mourning Becomes Electra*, to domesticate Greek fate in New
England. Ovid adapts to the psychological purpose of his *Heroides* a myth
from Greek tragedy with the flavor of tragedy retained.

[64] As in *Her.* III, where Homer's Briseis finds herself at home in the circle
of Corinna.

Since in two of the three the lover is a suitor, and since he gains a favorable reply, his appeal is a model of Ovid's expert rhetoric in its most persuasive form. And the reply shows the power of gentle woman, after shivers of horror and of hate, to fabricate impressive reasons for the act on which she had determined all along. Did Ovid eavesdrop at Sparta? Paris and Helen in the flesh could not have been more lifelike than Ovid makes them, provided they had read his *Art of Love*. There have been at least two attempts in recent years, one cheap [65] and the other exquisitely French,[66] to show that Helen of Troy was one of us; but even Giraudoux would admit that Ovid, with hints from Euripides, had beaten all comers in that game.

Ovid's *Art of Love, Ars Amatoria,* is a sealed book to those who do not understand its overtones, or undertones, of parody. It is a rigidly didactic and exhaustively scholarly *Handbuch* to be put on the same shelf with the *Ars Grammatica.* But the very metre has a twinkle in its eye. Being a didactic work, it should appear in the stately, heroic hexameter, but Cupid, as the poet tells us in his *Amores,* would not permit him to sing of Gods and Giants but stole away a foot from every other line, making it elegiac. Solemnity in the elegiac couplet, prescribed for the canonical poets of love, is parody itself. The treatise is divided into three parts: I. Where to find her. II. How to win her. III. How to keep her. Part I, perforce, is a manual of Roman topography and private life. Colonnades, temples (certain temples), fora, theatres, amphitheatres, circuses, triumphs, banquets, all receive adequate attention. Interspersed, in Virgil's style, are set passages, or fables, such as the story of how the ancient Romans won their Sabine brides, told in rapid, sparkling lines, by the prince of narrators. One stroke there is, that hits the beauties of all times:

To see the show they come — to see and to be seen.[67]

---

[65] John Erskine's *Helen of Troy.*

[66] *La Guerre de Troie n'aura pas lieu.* Giraudoux is heir to the mantle of Anatole France, a perfect Ovidian when his wit is not spoiled by his bitterness.

[67] I 99: Spectatum veniunt, veniunt spectentur ut ipsae.

A code of gentlemanly conduct, a mirror of the lover, must be mastered by one who would win and keep. The Middle Ages understood it and made it over into a guidebook for chivalry, though they did not adopt its pervasive principle, *fallite fallentes*, "Deceive the deceivers." And yet the poet, in his gallantry, executes one of his *volte-faces*, and devotes the last book to similar counsels for the fairer sex, with a legend of good women and bad men. There had been two books for men. If women, with apparent discourtesy, receive only one, it is because they need less instruction in the subject.[68]

In point of art, this poem for its jewelled lines and faultless execution contests with Virgil's *Georgics* the prize awarded to the best book, not of the month, but of the years. Luckless are those who cannot hear those overtones, or undertones, of parody or mark its brilliant and incorrigible wit. Such readers find only stark lewdness and chilly rhetoric. And luckless are those who think the poet's *Remedies of Love* present the poet's recantation. Alas, those remedies are worse than the disease — and just as harmless, for those who have an ear for Ovid's laughter.

Are these two works monuments of the corruption of the age, stationed symbolically by the Ivory Gate? Not for those who know our poet through and through.[69] Ovid is enjoyable, if we know what we are enjoying. If one reads with sheer, lascivious gloating, or with nothing but indignation for what admittedly should never have been said, then the

---

[68] For a cool analysis of Book I, see *Ovid and His Influence*, pp. 35–41. The reader would find much instruction, and amusement, in submitting the remaining books and the *Remedia* to an even more minute scrutiny. Only in this way can one appreciate the exquisite parody with which Ovid has displayed the principles of didactic technique which he has learned from Lucretius and Virgil.

[69] It is far from the mark, indeed almost laughable, to call Ovid, as Buchan does (*Augustus*, p. 247), "a butterfly poet." Ovid's subtle spirit can easily elude such crushing condemnations. He was, in his terrestrial and modern aspects, essentially a wit, and one of the most brilliant of them all. Let us invite him to a banquet of the wits of high comedy, with Plato, Aristophanes, Horace, Walter Map, Nigel Wireker, Chaucer, Rabelais, Erasmus, Molière, Sterne, Fielding, Lamb, and Thackeray — I have already exceeded the sacred number nine, in fact we have, defiantly, the fatal thirteen. Two more, then, George Meredith to record the jests and Chesterton to pass the bowl.

cream curdles, and the wit evaporates, and only cold brutality remains. So, apparently, Augustus read some eight years after the book appeared, and in 8 A.D. banished Ovid to the frozen shores of the Euxine Sea. Two causes there were, the poet tells us, *carmen et error*.[70] The *carmen* was no worse in spirit and intent than the *Amores*, written some twenty years before. It *is* the *Amores*, grown from the special to the generic. That unnamed error was the cause; the poem was the pretext. The conduct of the younger Julia may have been involved, and with it the defeat of the Emperor's plans for the succession. The error, despite the learned gossip of modern scholars, remains a mystery, save that, whether the blame was really Ovid's, it was the kind of happening about which gossip clusters.[71]

## IV

There is another aspect of Ovid's temperament, in fact its very core, on which we have not touched. He was not lost in the shifting panorama of the world. He loved its changes, he loved in imagination to create them.[72] His spirit found itself in a poem on transformation, his *Metamorphoses*, completed, in preliminary form, at the time of his exile. Epic it was, despite the novel subject, novel as the subject that Milton chose for epic, a subject of the broadest scope, the story of transformations "deduced from nature's birth to Caesar's times." The long history has three periods, the world of the gods, the world of the heroes, the world of man; but tales of the recent poetry of the Greeks, or popular legend whether old or new, may be woven in wherever Ovid likes to tuck them. Various forms of poetry are absorbed into the swift-flowing story. We find ourselves reading pastoral or comedy or tragedy or oratory, but, just as we settle down to the ap-

[70] *Tristia* II 207: Perdiderint cum me duo crimina, carmen et error, Alterius facti culpa silenda mihi: Nam non sum tanti renovem ut tua vulnera, Caesar, Quem nimio plus est indoluisse semel. Whatever the real reason was, it wounded Augustus irretrievably.

[71] Nothing can be added to the brief statement given by Frazer (Loeb), pp. xi–xii.

[72] *Ovid and His Influence*, p. 56.

propriate mood, on flows the river through some other landscape. At the beginning of the poem Lucretian science con-
tends with the accepted myth in Ovid's sober chronicle of
the genesis of the world.

Then the mood changes when the gods appear. Ovid's
stories of the amours of the gods, his "divine comedies," shall
we say, may shock the sense of those who do not remember
that Homer has such scenes and that even the noble Virgil,
with Homer in mind, allotted comedy to Olympus, but tragedy to the world of men. Gods as well as poets must have
their play amidst their work. The philosophers' definition of
men must not be completely reversed to fit a god, as an *animal
superrationale, immortale, risus incapax*. Ovid's divine *jeux
d'esprits*, therefore, show the reverse side of piety. Piety
and pure religion shine through the story of Philemon and
Baucis, rustic folk who entertained deities unawares. Over
all hovers the spirit of metamorphosis, Ovid's spirit, coming
to a philosophic expression in the sermon of Pythagoras in the
final book.

> Cuncta fluunt omnisque vagans formatur imago.
> Ipsa quoque assiduo labuntur tempora motu,
> Non secus ac flumen; neque enim consistere flumen
> Nec levis hora potest, sed ut unda impellitur unda,
> Urgeturque eadem veniens urgetque priorem,
> Tempora sic fugiunt pariter pariterque sequuntur,
> Et nova sunt semper. Nam quod fuit ante relictum est
> Fitque quod haud fuerat momentaque cuncta novantur.

These lines were the starting-point for Shakespeare's sonnet
beginning:

> Like as the waves make towards the pebbled shore
> So do our minutes hasten to their end;
> Each changing place with that which goes before
> In segment toil all forwards do contend.

Ovid, like Shakespeare, is a spirit detached. This is a world
of chance and change. He revels in the flux and flow, but is
not bogged in it, like stolid souls to whom it is all commonplace. He delights in its shifts and moulds them to suit his

fancy. His mind dwells above the realm of circumstance, surveys it with sympathy and amusement, finds truth in myth as
well as science, and creates his own world of myth. He did
not, like Lucretius, contemplate raptly the natural law that
controlled the changes. He did not, like Virgil and his Plato,
ascend to the One from the Many; he contemplated the Many
in the One. He jestingly calls poetry falsehood, half in jest
and half in truth.[73] He prophesies, in the traditional way,
the eternal fame of his long poem, adding "if poets' prophecies
have aught of truth." [74]

That was Ovid's Golden Age, his mastery of time and circumstance, till his heavens crashed about him. He looked
bewildered at the ruins. It was not pleasant to leave Rome
and the Italian sky. At first he took his exile not seriously
enough. He mythologized his experience, in Horace's way.
He is an Aeneas, as he bids a sad farewell to his Roman Troy,
and a Ulysses as he sails the rough sea towards his new haven.
It was no haven of delight. He wearied his monarch, and
everybody else in Rome, with his pleas for recall. A decline
in health and in spirits becomes more and more marked during the ten years of exile that preceded his death in 18 A.D.,
four years after that of Augustus. And yet the Getic gloom is
relieved by bright poems of reminiscence on genial festivities
in town, or on his country garden, which he had loved to till.
He makes friends with the uncouth inhabitants. His ever-
curious mind prompts him to learn their language and in it
to write a panegyric of the Roman emperor.[75] His mirth has

---

[73] *Amores* III 12. 41: Exit in inmensum fecunda licentia vatum, Obligat historica nec sua verba fide.

[74] *Met.* XV 879: Siquid habent veri vatum praesagia vivam. For ampler, yet
still inadequate, analyses of the spirit of Ovid's *Metamorphoses,* see *Ovid and
His Influence* (pp. 54–76) and the introduction made to this analysis in *Ovid
and the Spirit of Metamorphosis.*

[75] *Ex Ponto* III 13. 17–40. This Getic poem in Roman measures (*nostris
modis*) — hexameters or elegiac couplets — would be one of the curiosities of
literature, had the fates been kind enough to preserve it. Ovid read it to an
admiring concourse, who roared applause as they rattled their quivers. Just
so the ancient Germans according to Tacitus (*Germ.* 11. 6) voted "Aye" by
striking spear on spear, and the Gauls, as Julius Caesar tells us (*B.G.* VII 21)
cheered a speech by a clash of arms. One of Ovid's auditors declared that a
poet who thus sang the praises of his sovereign ought certainly to be restored

not deserted him, nor his courage.  He gathers himself together, ready to take his fate when it comes to him by the
Euxine Sea:

> Fortiter Euxinis immoriemur aquis.[76]

He defies the tyrant to take jurisdiction over his mind, his
wit, his pleasant comrade all along the way.

> Ingenio tamen ipse meo comitorque fruorque
> Caesar in hoc potuit iuris habere nihil.[77]

He knew as well as his critics that this pleasant comrade had
led him into dangerous paths.  In anticipation of his death,
Ovid in the ancient fashion wrote out his own epitaph.  He
was a master hand at epitaphs, and none is better than his
own:

> Here I lie, jester of the tender loves,
> The poet Ovid, ruined by my wit.
> You who pass by, if ever you have loved,
> Pray that my bones may comfortably lie.[78]

But this is no exit by the Ivory Gate.  Or rather, let us
say, Ovid could find himself at home in a land of dreams in
which the true and the false commingle.  He who is known
as the first of mediaeval romancers may also be called the first
of mediaeval dreamers.[79]  He is not far from the kingdom of
the mystics, above the realities of temporal life, above the
fictions of poets.  His was a hitherto untrodden pathway to
the heights, which only Shakespeare travelled after his time.
That eminent critic of letters, Mr. Palgrave, called Ovid

---

by him.  Alas, who could translate Ovid's Getic numbers to His Majesty?
Perhaps — I hope not — we shall have to call this amusing episode one of the
poet's blithe fictions.

[76] *Ex Ponto* III 7. 40.

[77] *Trist.* III 7. 47.

[78] *Trist.* III 3. 73:
> HIC · EGO · QUI · IACEO · TENERORUM · LUSOR · AMORUM
> INGENIO · PERII · NASO · POETA · MEO
> AT · TIBI · QUI · TRANSIS · NE · SIT · GRAVE · QUISQUIS · AMASTI
> DICERE · NASONIS · MOLLITER · OSSA · CUBANT

[79] On the relation of *Amores* III 5 to the dream-literature of the Middle
Ages, see "Ovid in 'Le Roman de la Rose,' " p. 114.

"amongst world-famous poets, perhaps the least true to the soul of poetry." [80] Rather, he was the only one of his sort that antiquity produced. So in a different way, as we have seen, was Lucretius. The Roman temperament under the training of the Greeks had developed subtlety as well as strength. It might even lay claim to originality in showing to the world two masters of poetry each unique in his kind.

## V

But what thought Augustus when the end of his long life approached? I would not disagree with the general verdict that the end of the century and the beginning of our era mark a drop in moral vigor and in the glory of the Roman state. But if, once more, we lift up our eyes to the heights attained by few, or by one, the general lapse, regrettable at the time, calls for no tears as we look back upon it down the centuries. The Emperor, most probably, would admit the flaws in the structure he had reared, and the growing difficulty of his task.[81] And yet as his end approached, in the seventy-sixth year of his age, he drew up a momentous document, an account both of his deeds, *Res Gestae*, performed in winning the world for Rome and establishing his new constitution, and of the outlays made for the benefit of the state and of the Roman people. This record was engraved on two bronze pillars in front of his mausoleum in Rome; here was one epitaph that Ovid could not write, one of the most magnificent, indeed, in human history. The pillars of bronze are no more, but copies in marble were made for cities in the provinces; fragments of some of them, in Latin and in Greek, have luckily been discovered.[82] Here is no record of illusion or defeat. With a sol-

[80] *Landscape in Poetry*, p. 54. Mr. Palgrave also refers to the poet's "now faded supremacy." The French critics to whom I have referred have restored something of its lustre.

[81] Seneca recognized that the Emperor's one hope, constantly expressed, was for peace (*De brev. vitae* 4. 2: omnis eius sermo ad hoc semper revolutus est ut speraret otium). There is something wistful in this utterance.

[82] The most famous find was that of most of the Latin text with a Greek translation at Ancyra in Galatia (Turkey) by Busbecq in 1555. For an instructive essay on this humanist, scientist, and diplomat, see G. Sarton, "Brave

dierly brevity that bears the marks of truth and in its great
simplicity approaches grandeur, Augustus tells the story of
ideal empire fulfilled.

On his deathbed, Suetonius tells us,[83] he asked his friends
if he had played adequately the mime of life, and added off-
hand a Greek couplet:

> ἐπεὶ δὲ πάνυ καλῶς πέπαισται, δότε κρότον
> καὶ πάντες ἡμᾶς μετὰ χαρᾶς προπέμψατε.

> Since well the play ends, give us your applause,
> And with rejoicing send us on our way.

Then, dismissing them all, he enquired of newcomers from
Rome for the health of Drusus's daughter, who lay ill, and
answering his wife's kisses with his own, he died with these
words: "Live mindful of our wedlock, Livia, and farewell."

Whatever Virgil intended by his Ivory Gate, he would have
known, had he lived to see his sovereign die, that the Ideal
Empire had ended in sublimity.

---

Busbecq," p. 565. More fragments of the Greek version were found by Buckler
and Calder in 1930, and more of the Latin by Ramsay in 1914 at Antioch in
Pisidia, with a still greater number by D. M. Robinson in 1924. The best critical edition of the *Res Gestae Divi Augusti* from all these sources is by Jean
Gagé, 1935. Admirable photographs accompany the edition by Concepta
Barini, Rome, 1937, published in honor of Augustus at his Bimillennium and
included among the *Scriptores Graeci et Latini Iussu Beniti Mussolini Con-
silio R. Academiae Lynceorum Editi.* It is a pity that Benitus Mussolinus did
not sufficiently study the text as a Mirror of the Prince. The *Res Gestae*, along
with the jests of Augustus and fragments of his writings, has been skilfully
edited as a school textbook by Rogers, Scott and Ward, 1935.

[83] *Aug.* 99. 1.

# CHAPTER V

# DECLINE AND FALL

THE presence of a decline and a fall has seemed easy to trace in many periods of human history. We may think of Livy's picture of that avalanche that glided down the mountainside till it came to rest at the lowest level, the time of utter moral degradation, in which, to quote once more his words, "we can bear neither our disease nor the remedy for it." [1] Or, to present the other side of the picture, we have first the painful, but hopeful, ascent to the summit, then the brief breathing-space at the moment of triumph, and then the descent once more. These rises and falls of events are strangely similar to the experience of Sisyphus, doomed in the world below ever to push the huge stone up the hill, and ever to see it, once the top is reached, roll gaily down again. We may thus allegorize Homer's familiar lines, in which not only the words but the movement of the verse tells each moment of the story, particularly the heroic struggle of Sisyphus to get the stone up just one more inch to fixity, and the rapid rolling down again of the impudent stone, till it bumps to rest once more, maliciously demonstrating that the movement of human society is not "onward and ever upward." [2]

Moreover, unluckily for our praiseworthy cultivation of scientific accuracy, it is not always easy, in human affairs, to point precisely to a period of ascent or to an acme or to descent again. Polybius came at an acme, traced the steps in the ascent, yet was well enough aware that Roman society of the

---

[1] *Preface*, 9.
[2] *Od.* XI 593: Καὶ μὴν Σίσυφον εἰσεῖδον κρατέρ' ἄλγε' ἔχοντα

. . . . . . . . .

λᾶαν ἄνω ὤνω ὤθεσκε ποτὶ λόφον· ἀλλ' ὅτε μέλλοι
ἄκρον ὑπερβαλέειν, τότ' ἀποστρέψασκε κραταιΐς·
αὖτις ἔπειτα πέδονδε κυλίνδετο λᾶας ἀναιδής.

time was by no means perfect; [3] and he analyzed the elements in a decline of which he had seen only the beginning.[4] Livy's ideas, as we have seen, were identical, only that, when he wrote, the avalanche had not only thundered down the hill but crashed at the bottom in ruin. Of course, not all of his contemporaries shared this view. Indeed he may himself have later felt with Horace that, since the victory of Actium, history had moved uphill again to come to a broad plateau of peace, or with Virgil that this upward movement had started a dozen or so years before.

It is a perplexing affair. The watcher of events has to reckon with the course of human stones, which do not always obey the laws of gravity. Some gather moss as they roll, and some do not. Some roll so ambiguously that it is hard to tell whether they are going up or down; some just stay put. It is with trepidation, therefore, that I approach the topic of the Decline and Fall of Rome. I certainly must not venture on the highroad built by Gibbon once for all, or consider the necessary repairs in that road made by eminent scholars of our day. I am concerned, first of all, with the problem of selecting some reasonable starting point after the Augustan Age, where we may surely say: "Here beginneth the Decline."

I seem to have found one in the Latin style of Marcus Cornelius Fronto. To quote a passage from an excellent critic of Latin literature,

This amiable man, the teacher of Marcus Aurelius Antoninus, inflicted on his language the final injury, from which it never fully recovered, despite the efforts of St. Augustine and a few others. It was already artificial, more or less; he made it archaistic as well, and that in the very worst way.[5]

Here surely are the symptoms of decay. Though not all scholars command Professor Rose's vigor of language, most if not all would agree with his condemnation of that amiable man, Marcus Cornelius Fronto. I venture to differ completely from

[3] VI 57.
[4] Chapter IV, note 50. Both Livy and Cicero (*De Re Publ.* V 2) complete the picture.
[5] H. J. Rose, *Lat. Lit.*, p. 518.

this estimate. Having set out on a venture hazardous in all its
course, I might as well be audacious at the start.

Fronto [6] came to Rome towards the end of the Emperor
Hadrian's reign (117 A.D.–128 A.D.) from Cirta in Numidian
Africa. He had begun a political career in his birthplace and
continued it in Rome, rising to the office of a consul (a *consul
suffectus*) in 143 A.D. and then to that of a proconsul, with
Asia as his province; that was a high appointment, which illness kept him from accepting. Yet a far more important function had been assigned him by Hadrian. That emperor,
shortly before his death, had adopted Antoninus Pius as his
successor, along with his sons Marcus Aurelius and Lucius
Verus, as "Caesars," that is, princes — for such had become
the flavor of that good old republican title *princeps* adopted
by Augustus. To take charge of the lad's education, Fronto
was appointed in the field of rhetoric. Others besides Professor Rose have represented him as a fussy old pedant, whose
chief concern was to manufacture a style out of archaic words
and phrases assembled from the writers of the earlier Republic and fitted into contemporary Latin in a kind of mosaic appropriately called the *elocutio novella* — for surely such a style
had never been seen before. It is well, however, to remember, first of all, that Fronto, like Cicero, was embarked on the
career of a statesman and that he had been selected by the
keen-witted Hadrian, who had no special fondness for professors,[7] to teach his fosterlings the kind of rhetoric that future
emperors should know. Fronto must have made political
speeches that Hadrian liked; in fact his oratory won the acclaim not only of contemporaries like his ardent pupil Marcus

[6] The following estimate of Fronto has been presented, in briefer form, in
chapter XVII of the *Cambridge Ancient History*, XII (1939), 573–577.

[7] Hadrian was well trained in the liberal arts, including music and painting (*Script. Hist. Aug. Hadr.* [Loeb] 14. 8). He was a ready speaker and a
fluent poet and indeed thought himself better than the professors and the
philosophers, whose works he freely criticized; *ibid.*, 15. 10: et quamvis esset
oratione et versu promptissimus et in omnibus artibus peritissimus, tamen
professores omnium artium semper ut doctior risit, contempsit, obtrivit. cum
his ipsis professoribus et philosophis libris vel carminibus invicem editis saepe
certavit. But he made up for all that by giving them good salaries (*ibid.* 16.
8–11).

and Aulus Gellius, but of later writers, such as Sidonius Apollinaris, that cultivated Bishop of Clermont,[8] and the keen
critic St. Jerome; [9] to both of these the essential trait in Fronto's style was *gravitas*, "dignity" — the very quality that should
inform the soul of a future Emperor of Rome.

We should know nothing of the ardent pupil and his in-
spiring master were it not for another discovery of a palimpsest
manuscript from Bobbio by the eminent Cardinal Mai, in
1815, to match that of the *De Re Publica* of Cicero, the importance of which we have already seen.[10] Among the fragments is part of a collection of the letters of Fronto and his
correspondents. By far the larger part, and surely the most
interesting part, consists of the messages that passed to and
fro between the young prince and his teacher. The two were
bound together in an abundant affection and in the excitement of their common quest. It is the love of a teacher for a
pupil whose mind he was shaping for his high destiny; it is
the love of a pupil who, aware of that destiny, worshipped his
guide. Here, then, is another example of great teaching, to
set beside that earlier example we have seen; Polybius and
young Scipio seem to be reincarnate. Of course that was republican instruction; and yet Scipio, some think, was well on
the way to establishing the ideal kingdom — or as his enemies
thought, the degenerate form of tyranny.[11]

Although, with Marcus Aurelius, we are down in the Empire, long past the days of Catullus, the imperial lad loves his
master with the Italian fervor that Catullus lavishes upon his
friends, with a kiss on both their cheeks. He calls Fronto

---

[8] *Epist.* IV 3: Frontonianae gravitatis.

[9] *Epist.* 125. 12. Jerome during his eremitic experience in the desert took
up the study of Hebrew to mortify the flesh *ut post Quintiliani acumina,
Ciceronis fluvios gravitatemque Frontonis et lenitatem Plinii alphabetum dis-
cerem anhelantiaque verba meditarer* — a genuine penance for him, to give
up the mellifluence of the ancients for the gasping sounds of Hebrew. Note
that to St. Jerome Fronto is one of the royal authors.

[10] Cf. Chapter I, note 46. The Loeb edition by C. R. Haines, 1919, is of
special excellence. Previously the standard edition was that of S. A. Naber,
Lipsiae, 1867. Reference will be given in the notes to both H(aines) and
N(aber).

[11] See above, Chapter II, note 2.

"sweetest soul," "breath of me," "biggest thing under heaven"
— *anima dulcissima, anima suavissima, spiritus meus, mihi
maxima res sub caelo.*[12] The last exuberance has something
of the ring of slang, as does μέγα πρᾶγμα,[13] "big thing," "big
shot," and such is its flavor even in Demosthenes.[14] The
panegyric of the Emperor that Fronto in the traditional way
pronounced on his accession to the consulate calls forth from
young Marcus most explosive acclamations in Latin and in
Greek. He declares he is a lucky person to be given to such a
master.

O me hominem beatum huic magistro traditum! O ἐπιχειρήματα!
O τάξις! O elegantia! O lepos! O venustas! O verba!
O nitor! O argutiae! O χάριτες! O ἄσκησις! O omnia! [15]

The force of eulogy can no further go; few college professors
receive such compliments nowadays.

Fronto's fondness for his pupil is nothing less, though somewhat more temperate in expression. One of his epistolary
"Yours truly's" reads: *Vale meum gaudium, mea securitas,
hilaritas, gloria,*[16] and elsewhere he asks, "What is sweeter to
me than your kiss?" [17] The letter is most affectionate in tone.
Marcus replies that his teacher is winner in the world-contest
in love — *Tu quidem me . . . magis amabis quam ullus hominum hominem amat.* His pupil will do his best to repay
that passion, which, he says, far excels the longing that Socrates
and Phaedrus had for one another.[18] He fears, however, that
he has a dangerous rival in Gratia, Fronto's wife.[19] Such letters of banter attest the nobler element in the ancient affection

---

[12] *Ad M. Caes.* II 5 (I 118 H, 30 N).

[13] *Ad M. Caes.* II 3. 2 (I 130 H, 29 N); *Epist. Graec.* 6 (I 18 H, 253 N);
*ibid.* 7. 2 (I 32 H, 254 N).

[14] *In Lacritum,* 928 b. This is one of the possibly spurious speeches, but
it at least has a lively tone. Androcles had lent thirty *minae* to Artemon
and now after his death is trying to recover the sum from his brother, Lacritus
the sophist, a slippery customer. But he was also "something big, a pupil of
Isocrates" (μέγα πρᾶγμα, Ἰσοκράτου μαθητής).

[15] *Ad M. Caes.* II 3. 1 (I 128 H, 28 N).

[16] *Ibid.* I 8. 7 (II 1) (I 124 H, 24 N).

[17] *Ibid.* III 13 (I 220 H, 50 N).

[18] *Epist. Graec.* 7. 2 (I 32 H, 254 N).

[19] *Ad M. Caes.* II 2. 1 (I 112 H, 27 N).

of man for man; from its sordid side the lad's intimacy with
Fronto must have helped to keep him pure.[20]  The delight
of their common studies the master sums up in the phrase:
"I love life because of you; I love good letters with you." —
*Amo vitam propter te, amo litteras tecum*.[21]  And the boy declares that he often exclaims as he reads, "Oh how happy I
am!" — happy not at having a master who can teach him how
to express a maxim with greater rhetorical felicity, but because "I learn from you how to speak the truth." [22]

But what was this *elocutia novella*, the new style with which
Fronto would indoctrinate his pupil and the writers of his
time?  We may take as typical the alluring description given
by Walter Pater in *Marius the Epicurean*.[23]  It was something
"dainty and fine, full of the archaisms and curious felicities
in which that generation delighted, quaint terms and images
picked fresh from the early dramatists, the life-like phrases of
some lost poet preserved by an old grammarian, racy morsels
of the vernacular and studied prettinesses: — all alike, mere
playthings for the genuine power and natural eloquence of
the erudite artist, unsuppressed by his erudition, which, however, made some people angry, chiefly less well 'got-up' people,
and especially those who were untidy from indolence."  It
included "a certain tincture of 'neology' in expression — *nonnihil interdum elocutione novella parum signatum* — in the

[20] See *Meditations* I 16. 1, where he thanks his father for such protection,
and I 17, 1–2, where he thanks those of his family, his teachers and his
friends for the good influence that they shed on his life.  To Fronto he expresses a special debt for pointing out the evil qualities that characterize a
tyrant — envy, duplicity and hypocrisy — and the absence of human kindliness
conspicuous in aristocrats.  See also note 22.

[21] *Ad M. Caes.* IV 1 (I 74 H, 59 N).

[22] *Ibid.* III 12 (I 14 H, 49 N): meque saepius exclamasse inter legendum
*O me felicem*!  *Itane* dicet aliquis, *felicem te, si est qui te doceat quomodo
γνώμην sollertius dilucidius brevius politius scribas*?  Non hoc est quod me
felicem nuncupo.  Quid est igitur?  Quod verum dicere ex te disco.

[23] At the beginning of chapter v.  The first edition of this extraordinary
book appeared in 1885 — extraordinary for its insight into Roman religion
and Roman literature and extraordinary for its vogue.  The stream of its editions still flows; the last was in 1935.  The dainty world of Pre-Raphaelite
refinement has long since been shattered, but this book, its embodiment, is
still passed from hand to hand.  A little touch of exquisiteness does not harm
our generation.

language of Cornelius Fronto, the contemporary prince of rhetoricians."

The Golden Book in which Marius and the other lad discovered this exquisite style was the *Metamorphoses* of Apuleius, and what Pater says of this work is beautifully apposite. If we turn to Fronto, however, we can hardly find such a definition of style. His program with his pupil was anything but building mosaics from obsolete expressions. The phrase *elocutio novella* was indeed his,[24] but it refers not to a variety of style, but merely to the use of a *fresh* vocabulary, not the first words that come into your head, but the *best* words,[25] exact and striking and luminous.[26] This is nothing but the search for the *mot juste*, surely no reprehensible practice for one who is forming his style.[27]

The field into which Fronto would guide his pupil was indeed the literature of the Republic. As we noted in Chapter I, the works of the early period, save for Plautus and Terence, are preserved to us only in tiny bits. We can divine

[24] Writing his imperial pupil on a recent oration of his, he remarks that in general the sentences are splendid, though a few places could be corrected by a single word; for here and there is a bit not conspicuous for vivid phrasing: Pleraque in oratione recenti tuo, quod ad sententias (including both idea and form) attinet egregia esse; pauca admodum uno tenus verbo corrigenda; non nihil interdum elocutione novella parum signatum. (*Ad M. Ant. de eloquentia* 4 (II 80 H, 153 N). This last sentence is quoted by Pater as though it were affirmative, not negative. What did he think *parum* means? If the term *elocutio* designated a formal style, "neology," Fronto would have said *hac elocutione novella*.

[25] *Ad Ant. Imp.* I 2. 5 (II 42 H, 98 N): Praecipue autem gaudeo te verba non obvia sed optima quaerere.

[26] *Ad M. Caes.* IV 3. 3 (I 6 H, 63 N): insperata atque inopinata verba; *Ad M. Ant. de eloq.* 3. 8 (II 74 H, 150 N): verborum lumina.

[27] Something has been made of Fronto's *Encomium of Sleep* (*De Fer. Als.* 3 [II 4, 224 N]) as though the legend were told in the spirit of Apuleius's Story of Psyche. One must read the whole letter to see that Fronto is having a little fun with the asceticism of his former pupil, now (A.D. 162) on the throne of the Caesars. At least, he pleads, the Emperor ought to indulge in a siesta as of old. Fronto's tale, reminiscential of his rhetorical exercises performed with his pupil of old, is well and simply told with a touch of poetry in conception and phrasing (e.g. on the tiny drop of the herb of death with which Somnus flavored his mixture), but there are few unusual or highly colored words. Apuleius indeed created a gorgeously romantic style, but by his own genius, not from Fronto's laws. There is little similarity between the story of Psyche and the legend of Somnus unless one read them both in Pater's spell-binding translations (in chapters v and xiii).

the significance of the whole from what Polybius has recorded of the Roman state, and from what glimmers in the fragments of Ennius. Fronto had its entire wealth before him, and a happy hunting-ground it must have been.

Marcus was interested in this pastime. He reports on his reading and on his order of the day.[28] As many of the ancients did, he burns the midnight oil not by sitting up but by getting up to burn it. At least he arises at 3 A.M. and works till 8.oo. Then for an hour he walks in slippers back and forth before his chamber — quite the equivalent of our daily dozen. Then the reception at the Emperor's, for which he dons boots and cloak. Then the hunting of a boar, up a high hill, and home in the afternoon. Then books again, two hours on his couch, reading two of old Cato's speeches. "Don't think, dear master, you can find them at the Apollo Library, for I drew them out to take here. You'll have to suborn the librarian at the Tiberian [29] if you want another copy. Then I tried writing — poor stuff; I'll dedicate it to the Water-nymphs or to Vulcan. I've caught cold, whether from my early promenade in slippers or from my frigid writings I don't know.[30] Well, let's to bed. I'll pour some oil not into my lamp but on my head, to put me straight to sleep. I'm tired with that hunt and with sneezing all day long. Goodbye, dear, sweet master, whom I dare to say I want to see more than Rome itself."

On the next day, in the same merry spirit, he tells of rising at five and reading till 9 A.M., writing a bit better this time, and after His Majesty's reception, relieving his cold by swallowing honey water as far as the throat and ejecting it again.

[28] *Ad M. Caes.* IV 5 (I 178 H, 68 N).

[29] The first public library in Rome was established in 39 B.C. by Asinius Pollio, patron of Virgil and of Horace. Octavian opened another in 28 B.C. as a part of the Temple of Apollo, dedicated in that year. Horace was present on that occasion and along with the many petitions presented by Romans on that day, offered his poet's prayer. The Emperor also built one connected with the *Porticus Octaviae*, erected in honor of his sister Octavia. Vespasian added another in the palace of Tiberius — the one that young Marcus mentions. There were also several others in Rome at the time.

[30] Young Marcus may have stolen a jest from a familiar poem of Catullus (44).

"You'll pardon me, Master, for not saying 'gargled' (*gargaris-savi*); for I know the word is found in Novius." [31]

Again, he makes five volumes of extracts from sixty works. "Don't be startled at that sixty," he adds, "they include little Atellan plays of Novius and Scipio's little speeches.[32] He gathers maxims for his commonplace book — for rhetoric means a study of ethics, incidentally — and he clamors for more.[33] He has composed Latin hexameters and fashions a hendecasyllabic as he writes, inspired by a hot day.[34] The lad craves his teacher's criticism, and gets it.[35] At the end, when his pupil was twenty-four years old, Fronto can pronounce him well trained in the liberal arts, a finished Latin orator, and, above all, an expert in the art of making friends.[36] That is what rhetoric meant to Fronto — a training not only of mind and tongue, but of character. It is in essence the hu-

[31] Novius, about the middle of the second century B.C., wrote many Atellan plays, named from the town of Atella in Campania. They were originally a rude native farce dealing with life in small towns and abounded in coarse jests and gestures. Novius, with the example of the comedies of Plautus and Terence to help him, had made them somewhat more elaborate. But they remained exceedingly lively. One could hardly imagine that the author of the *Meditations*, once upon a time, had been versed in Atellan plays.

[32] *Ad M. Caes.* II 10 (I 138 H, 34 N): et Novianae et Atellaniolae et Scipionis oratiunculae. What were these "little speeches"? Scipio had become one of the eminent orators of the day, and so had his friend Laelius. Cicero finds it hard to distinguish between them, admitting the greater fame of Laelius but regarding the style of Scipio as more finished. Laelius had a fondness for antique expressions (delectari mihi magis antiquitate videtur et libenter verbis etiam uti paulo magis priscis: Cic. *Brut.* 83–85, in the *editio palmaris* of G. L. Hendrickson [Loeb], 1939). Scipio's speeches were so distinguished for the Roman qualities of dignity and majesty that he seemed more the leader of the people than their companion (gravitas . . . maiestas, ut facile ducem populi Romani non comitem diceres: Cic. *Lael. de Amicitia* 96). Not all of Scipio's speeches could have been brief affairs. I should infer that a goodly number of them was available in the days of Marcus Aurelius, and that he turned to the shorter and less famous ones to find something good in them, too. Fronto was training his pupil in seminary research; subjects: (a) Little Atellan plays of Novius, (b) the shorter speeches of Scipio. A man of catholic tastes, Fronto.

[33] *Ad M. Caes.* V 59 (I 54 H, 93 N).

[34] *Ad M. Caes.* I 8 (I 124 H, 24 N); II 10 (I 138 H, 34 N); II 5 (I 118 H, 30 N): *Nos istic vehementer aestuamus.* Habes en hendecasyllabum ingenuum.

"We are sweltering. Yes, I'll say it's hot here."

[35] *Ad M. Caes.* III 17 (I 108 H, 55 N); IV 3. 4–8 (I 6–12 H, 64–66).

[36] *Ibid.*, I 8 (II 1) 4 (I 122 H, 23 N); IV 1 (I 72 H, 59 N): Verum ex omnibus virtutibus tuis hoc vel praecipue admirandum, quod omnes amicos tuos concordia copulas.

manistic training which had come to Fronto from Plato *via* Cicero and which has been a vital element in all sound education down to the present time — or almost to the present time.

When he was twenty-five, there came a sharp turning-point in the life of Marcus Aurelius. He now proclaims an open revolt against rhetoric and turns to the pursuit of philosophy, which had long been appealing to his deeper self. He loved his old tutor as before, but his mind was set on serious things. He proved a good emperor and soldier, and in the midst of his German campaigns jotted down his meditations, whereby, unmoved by the world of circumstance, he was perfecting his Stoic character. We will leave him to his solitude, his inner triumph, and his outer disaster; he perished in the midst of war from one of those pestilences which, as the ever-lamented Hans Zinsser, with learning and urbanity, has shown,[37] have decided so many of the turns of history.

Fronto had borne his pupil's defection nobly. He wrote for him a short treatise *On Eloquence*, a rhetorical Mirror of the Prince for a prince who had turned philosopher. A philosopher, Fronto declares,[38] as Cicero had declared before him,[39] despises rhetoric at his peril; worthy thoughts demand a worthy diction. Marcus, touched by his tutor's appeal, begged him to select the letters of Cicero that would best improve his style.[40]

The range of Fronto's reading has often been falsely estimated. It has been restricted to the earliest writers, in whose antiquities he could poach for archaisms to his heart's content. Nothing could be wider of the mark. He studies these prim-

---

[37] *Rats, Lice and History*, p. 106.
[38] *Ad Anton. Aug. De Eloquentia* I 14–18 (II 66–70 H, 146–148 N).
[39] *Tusc. Disp.* I 6.
[40] *Ad Anton. Imp.* II 4 (II 156 H, 107 N). Marcus displayed from the start an enthusiasm for Cicero. See *Ad M. Caes.* III 14 (A.D. 143) (I 100 H, 52 N): Epistula Ciceronis mirifice adfecit animum meum. As Emperor (A.D. 161), he writes for "something of your own or of Cato or Cicero or Sallust or Gracchus or some poet — for I need refreshment. I want something that will uplift me and release me from my besetting cares. Perhaps you have some passages from Lucretius or Ennius — something sonorous (εὔφωνα), something that reflects character (ἤθους ἐμφάσεις)."

itives, among others, not for the rare word but, as we have
seen, for the right word — fresh and racy and luminous.
Hence the orator must search the best literature, and the
ancients will reward him for his pains. Plautus, whose rich
vocabulary is full of life, Lucretius who hits out ringing
phrases, Naevius and Cato and Sallust — all will help in the
forming of a style.[41] But not all the ancients, he declares,
have what he calls the clarion-note; some of them bellow or
shriek. Study, then, and discriminate.[42]

Such principles of style are not preciously archaistic. Cicero's interest in the early writers was as keen as Fronto's.
He, too, can admire the poetry of Ennius and the oratory of
Gracchus and the vigor of ancient style.[43] He, too, was on the
lookout for new turns of phrase [44] and luminous expression.[45]
Horace, likewise, despite his modernity, advises the search
of ancient poetry for rough diamonds of phrasing, which the
poet can make brilliant once more.[46] Such is the school of
"archaizers" to which Fronto belongs.[47] Nor was "the count

---

[41] *Ad M. Caes.* IV 3. 2 (I 4 H, 62 N).

[42] *Ibid.* III 16 (I 106 H, 54 N). Marcus had accomplished *plurimas lectiones*,
including comedies, Atellan plays and ancient speeches, among whose authors
few if any besides Cato and Gracchus could master that clarion call. This
reads like an onslaught on the primitive orators rather than a subservience to
them. Fronto has the aloofness of a critic rather than the extravagance of a
devotee.

[43] *De oratore* I 154; 193; where he praises the Laws of the XII Tables as the
embodiment of that *verborum vetustas prisca.*

[44] *Ibid.*, 155. His method of forming a style was to translate Greek orations
into Latin; to hunt for the *mot juste*, and to invent new expressions if the
Latin had them not: ut . . . non solum optimis verbis uterer et tamen usitatis,
sed etiam exprimerem quaedam verba imitando quae nova nostris essent, dum
modo essent idonea. Cf. *ibid.*, III 149.

[45] *Lumen, lumina* (very rarely *luminosus*) are frequent technical terms in
Cicero's rhetorical criticism; e.g. *verborum lumina* (*Orator* 95), *sententiarum
lumina* (*ibid.*, 85), *luce verborum* (*De Or.* III 24).

[46] *Epist.* II 2. 115: Obscurata diu populo bonus eruet atque Proferet in
lucem speciosa vocabula rerum, Quae priscis memorata Catonibus atque Cethe-
gis Nunc situs informis premit et deserta vetustas; Adsciscet nova, quae genitor
produxerit usus. Exactly Cicero's conception of a language living and growing
and picking up again, now and then, good elements temporarily abandoned.
A much more enlightened procedure than that of those Italian humanists who
disdained everything not "Ciceronian." Even that is something. Today we
just let language live and grow, not making artificial distinctions between
flowers and weeds.

[47] He is not one of those old-timers, of which every age sees specimens, who,

of mighty poets made up" for Fronto with those of the early Republic. Lucretius is to him sublime,[48] Horace a "memorable poet," whose wit he appreciated; [49] and Virgil a master in the niceties of words.[50] Ovid is not among his favorites. He mentions him not at all, as though his poetry had evaporated, like a dream flying out through the Ivory Gate.

Besides the earliest historians Fronto commends Julius Caesar, for his imperial style,[51] and devotes careful study to Sallust. In oratory, Sallust no less than Cato commands his respect.[52] But the supreme orator is still Cicero. More attention is devoted to him than to anybody else. His speeches have the true ring and nothing is more perfect in their kind than his letters.[53]

But with Cicero, Virgil, and Horace, Fronto's catalogue of great authors comes to a close. Indeed, despite Fronto's respect for Virgil and Horace, the authors on whom he would form the mind of his pupil are those of the Republic throughout its extent. In a highly significant passage [54] he passes discriminating judgment on a number of poets, historians, philosophers, and orators. They are all of the Republic — from Cato and Ennius to Sallust and Cicero. Those of the following century are treated to either ridicule or silence. What does this mean? Nothing less than a quiet republican revolution in letters. If the Empire is meant to be included

as Seneca remarks, "talk the Twelve Tables" (*Epist. Moral.* 114. 13: multi ex alieno saeculo petunt verba: duodecim tabulas loquuntur). Cicero would not quite like this remark. See note 43.

[48] *Ad Verum* (?) *Imp.* I 1.2 (II 48 H, 114 N): sublimis poeta.

[49] *Ad M. Caes.* I 8 (II 1). 5 (I 122 H, 23 N): Plane multum mihi facetiarum contulit istic Horatius Flaccus, memorabilis poeta, mihique propter Maecenatem ac Maecenatianos hortos non alienus. It would look as though Fronto's house in Rome was located in the famous Gardens of Maecenas on the Esquiline. For doubts on this matter cf. Platner-Ashby, *Topographical Dictionary of Ancient Rome*, p. 269. Yet cf. Haines, I p. xxxix.

[50] Aulus Gellius *Noct. Att.* II 26.

[51] *Ad Verum Imp.* II 1. 6 (II 136 H, 123 N) ; Caesari quidem facultatem dicendi video imperatoriam fuisse.

[52] Sallust is frequently quoted and imitated by Fronto (see Haines's index, II 341). He could sound the clarion call, along with Cato and Cicero; see *De eloquentia* III 2 (II 74 H, 149 N).

[53] See the preceding note and Haines's index (II 328).

[54] *Ad Verum* (?) I 1. 2 (II 48 H, 113–114 N).

at all, it is the Ideal Empire of Virgil and Horace and Augustus into which the strength of the Republic had been absorbed.[55] Fronto's reform keeps pace with the Neo-Attic movement in Greek literature; but though Appian the historian and Herodes Atticus were his friends, his own principles had another objective. He would return, not to a particular style, but to the best standards wherever found in the Republic and the Augustan Age. The style of Calvus, Catullus's friend, professedly "Attic," he dubs "quarrelsome," but that of Cicero "triumphant." [56] His revolt is against the degeneracy of the Imperial oratory and literary standards in the century that had preceded his own. He is no wistful Pre-Raphaelite shedding tears over the banality of his own times. He speaks rather as a humanist who looks for a Renaissance of culture now that an orator trained in the best tradition is about to ascend the throne.

What is behind all this politically or socially? It seems most strange that after so many years of Empire a mind like Fronto's should wish to erase so many years of its existence. But he had no political or social program to propound. The Empire was so firmly established that a man of letters could praise the virtues of the Republic in a fashion not quite safe

[55] *Ad Verum Imp.* II 1. 6 (II 136 H, 123 N); Postquam res publica a magistratibus annuis ad C. Caesarem et mox ad Augustum tralata est, Caesari quidem facultatem dicendi video imperatoriam fuisse, Augustum vero saeculi residua elegantia et Latinae linguae etiam tum integro lepore potius quam dicendi ubertate praeditum puto. Post Augustum nonnihil reliquiarum iam et vietarum et tabescentium Tiberio illi superfuisse. Imperatores autem deinceps ad Vespanianum usque eiusmodi omnes ut non minus verborum puderet quam pigeret morum et misereret facinorum. A clearly marked survey of a decline. Julius Caesar is responsible for the turning-point. He had the real oratorical fire (*quidem — quand même*), which simmered down into a pleasant elegance with Augustus, and evaporated under his successors until Vespasian came.

[56] *Ad Verum* (?) *Imp.* I 1. 2 (II 48 H, 114 N); Iam in iudiciis saevit idem Cato, triumphat Cicero, tumultuatur Gracchus, Calvus rixatur. Calvus comes out at the little end of the trumpet. For Fronto, the orator must not only be a *vir bonus dicendi peritus*, in Cato's phrase, or a consummate rhetorician; he must be aflame with some high moral passion. He should possess not merely goodness, but the *sublime et excelsum et amplificum ingenium* that the gods had given to Marcus; see *De eloq.* III 3 (II 72 H, 150 N). I doubt whether an Atticist would blow the trumpet that Fronto liked to hear. His estimate of oratorical style hardly differs from that of Cicero — or that of Quintilian. See note 95.

for a writer of the times of Tiberius or even of the closing years of Augustus's reign.[57] Fronto intended no protest against aristocracy or monarchy, or an aristocratic literary manner. Though some of the ancient phrases that he found may have survived in the popular language of the day, his object was not to cultivate a new colloquial idiom, or, according to the principles of some writers today, a proletarian style. He was interested primarily in a humanistic education for his Prince. He was no rhetorical pedant with a theory of words, but the tutor of a coming Emperor. He reverted to the Republic precisely as Virgil and Horace did, to incorporate its virtues in the upbuilding of good letters and of Roman character. He, too, desired the restoration of the Ideal Empire under the ruler whose mind he helped to form.

## II

I fear that Fronto, if I judge him rightly, nor am I alone in such a judgment,[58] has not shown us where to begin the story of decline and fall. What can Fronto himself do to enlighten us? I know of no passage in his works in which he declares that after him comes the deluge. Looking backward with his eyes, we see that he would end the great periods in the history of Rome with Virgil and Horace. The Secular Games indeed marked the end of a golden epoch, whence the world sank into something worse. Since it precedes the Frontonian Renaissance, we might call it, for the purposes of our momentary survey, the Roman Dark and Middle Ages. Let us contemplate both its gloom and any rays of brightness that still are shining. Perhaps it will give us some further clue in our quest of decline and fall.

As regards the political situation and the good and evil ways

[57] One might be tempted to end the true reign of Augustus with Ovid's banishment in A.D. 8 (on the exact date, see Rose, *Lat. Lit.*, p. 324). Ovid would agree. Though Augustus called Livy a Pompeian (*mit einem Tone*), Hadrian restored Pompey's tomb *magnificentius* (*S.A.H.*, (Spart.) *Hadr.* 14. 4) and Marcus Aurelius was profoundly impressed with the work of the regicide Brutus that Cicero had corrected (II 101 H, 52 N). This may be the treatise *De virtute*; see *Tusc. disp.* V 1 and Hendrickson, *Brutus* (Loeb), pp. 6-7.

[58] Best of all is Haines's statement, I pp. xxx-xxxiii, and II p. 81, note 1.

of the Emperors, in their course, I shall observe the utmost caution. I shall not attempt to whitewash Tiberius or to blackwash Tacitus. Knowing Tacitus from his own recorded words better than Tiberius, and having the highest respect for his qualities, I am tempted to put a possibly excessive trust in what he has to say. For the moment I will note merely that Augustus for some reason did not choose him first of all for his successor; Elmer Davis's *bon mot* may suffice, that "Tiberius wanted to be a President and ended as a Dictator." [59] I would not make Tiberius a monster from his youth; no more does Tacitus.[60] He was a silent man, and silence even more than speech is open to misunderstandings. He had his disappointments — one of them very great; if Julia had to marry him, he had to marry Julia.

No one, I believe, would question that in government the Ideal Empire went into a decline throughout most of the first century of our era. Kingship at times passed into its corrupted state of tyranny; Caligula, Nero, and Domitian, whatever slanders we may delete from their records, still must be put in the category of tyrants. Another earmark is the feeling, expressed in a famous dialogue by Tacitus, that oratory was on the decline.[61] Nor was he alone; others had harped

[59] In his review of Buchan's *Augustus* (Chapter II, note 146).

[60] In his masterly summary of the decline and fall of one whom he called *egregium vita famaque* at the beginning of his career (*Annals* VI 5).

[61] *Dialogus de Oratoribus*. It is still disputed whether this *libellus aureus* is by Tacitus. The style is nearer the accepted Ciceronian model than is that of his other works. But the symptoms are there — and the spirit. A style like that of the *Annals* did not spring in full armor from the author's brain. Mackail (*Lat. Lit.*, pp. 209–210) compared, with pertinent reservations, the development of Carlyle's style — and nothing could be better than Mackail's . description of the qualities of the matured style of Tacitus. If another composed the *Dialogus*, then he is one whom Tacitus would have been glad to meet. The larger argument in the work is the familiar *querelle des anciens et des modernes*. On that matter one of the speakers declares in words that make a good motto for a humanist, "Let us all enjoy what is good in our own times without censuring other ages" (41: bono saeculi sui quisque citra obtrectationem alterius utatur). The talk then breaks up with a bit of banter and with laughter, in Cicero's way. See Chapter III, note 77. Tacitus has a good word for antiquity in *Annals* VI 16. 2 (antiquis quoque et minus corruptis moribus) and for modernity in III 55. 6 (nec omnia apud priores meliora, sed nostra quoque aetas multa laudis et artium imitanda posteris tulit).

upon that theme.[62] It was evoked primarily by the painful awareness that thought and expression were no longer free. The state of oratory, therefore, is an index of the times. Cicero never wrote on the decline of oratory in the age of Cicero. He cried *"O tempora, o mores!"* as the foundations of the Republic were undermined, but in his dialogue called *Brutus, or On Famous Orators*, the march of oratorical progress from antiquity moves onward and upward to certain eminent speakers of his own day, with a precious little autobiography at the end. There is a touch of anxious foreboding at what may be in store,[63] but the deluge has not yet followed him nor was Tacitus aware that the proud waters had gone over his head.

For a judgment on the course of government in his century, and on the centuries before it, I would turn perforce to Tacitus. Not to mention various side remarks here and there,[64] there are two passages, one in the *Histories* and one in the *Annals*, which taken together give us part at least of his picture of the progress, or the decline, of the Roman state. Despite the length of these passages, particularly the second, I crave the reader's attention to them both, presented without omissions in my rude translations.[65] Let us bear in mind the charges frequently brought against Tacitus. A pessimist by nature, a disgruntled republican, incapacitated by his experience and by his sharp tongue to give a fair picture of the imperial system, he is said to employ his genius and his telling style for sarcastic slanders and diabolical innuendoes. What his real sentiments are, will become apparent, I hope, as one reads.

[62] E.g. Petronius, *Sat.* 1–5. Quintilian refers to a work of his *De causis corruptae eloquentiae* (*Inst. or.* VI *proem.* 3; VIII 6. 71). Tacitus may well be giving in the form of a little drama an answer to the plaints of an old-timer like Quintilian. His own style is another refutation.

[63] *Brutus* 328–329.

[64] An important case is considered in note 79.

[65] They both will be found, in the elegant French translation of Henri Goelzer (made for his edition in the series *Les Belles Lettres*), in *Esprits Souverains* (chap. v, "Tacite, maître de jugement souverain"), pp. 61–62.

That ancient and deep-seated propensity of humankind — lust of power [Tacitus observes] [66] — grew rampant with the growth of the dominion. For under simple conditions, equality of station was readily preserved. But when the world was mastered and rival cities and kings overthrown, and when men had leisure to covet power undisturbed, then the first struggle between nobles and commons flared forth. Now turbulent tribunes; now consuls over strong; and essays at civil war in city and forum. Anon Gaius Marius, of the dregs of the people, and Lucius Sulla, most cruel of the nobles, won their freedom by force of arms, and converted it to despotism. After them Gnaeus Pompey, less obvious — no better; and never after that was the issue aught save personal sovereignty.[67] The legions of citizens did not end strife with Pharsalia and Philippi, much less likely that the armies of Otho and Vitellius would have given up war of their own accord. The same wrath of gods, the same frenzy of men, the same motives for crime drove them to discord.

Here indeed speaks a satirist, with a depth and a savage strength unmatched in Roman letters. His theology is gloomy — yet not that the gods in themselves are vindictive like the "President of the Immortals," in Thomas Hardy's *Tess*; they are just, for they punish the frenzy of men. Men, indeed, are a bad lot, and always have been. The lust of power did not invade Rome along with Tiberius: it is *vetus ac iam pridem insita mortalibus* — an ancient and innate trait of us poor mortals, miserable sinners, as it is wholesome for us to be reminded now and then. So Tacitus's indictment is not specifically that of a disgruntled republican. The moment when avarice beset the triumphant state, according to Tacitus, was precisely that on which Livy had set his finger, that is, the very peak of its progress, the moment when Polybius had come to Rome.[68] Condemnation is allotted with even hand to Marius and Sulla; Pompey receives an added slap of sarcasm. The Emperors of Tacitus's own times, Otho and Vitellius, are put where they belong. For who would place them in the same scale of humanity as Marius and Sulla, Caesar and Pom-

---

[66] *Hist*. 2. 38.
[67] Numquam postea nisi de principatu quaesitum.
[68] See Chapter II, note 6.

pey? One thing is startling. Why is there no mention of Augustus, if Tacitus's mind was incapable of any but hard-crusted thought about monarchy? He here had a chance to excoriate Augustus as the founder of Empire, if such was his intention. Read through this passage again and you will find no antimonarchical or pro-republican sentiment expressed. In fact this passage is quite pure of politics. In it the satirist blasts human greed wherever he sees it; and he sees it everywhere. Nor is that necessarily pessimism — to know that human beings are not what they ought to be.

The longer passage is even more enlightening.[69]

Primitive mankind, not yet subject to base desire, lived without crime or fraud, and therefore without penalties or restraint. There was no need of rewards, since virtue was sought on its own account [that is, was its own reward]; and since men desired nothing contrary to right custom, they were prevented from nothing by fear. But after equality was sloughed off, and intrigue and force took the place of conscience and modesty, the rule of kings (*dominationes*) arose, and has remained eternally among many nations. Some at once, others after getting tired of their monarchs, preferred laws. These at first, as befitted man's lack of sophistication (*rudibus hominum animis*), were simple: fame has chiefly celebrated the laws of the Cretans, written by Minos, those of the Spartans, by Lycurgus, and the more elaborate and numerous laws that Solon wrote for the Athenians.

As for us, Romulus had ruled as he pleased; then Numa bound the people with sacred law and ceremonies; some enactments were made by Tullus and Ancus; but it was chiefly Servius Tullius who gave sanction to laws that even kings obeyed.

After the expulsion of Tarquin, the people devised, in opposition to the factions of the senate, many measures for preserving freedom and ensuring concord; they appointed decemvirs and, incorporating the best results of legislation elsewhere, they drew up the laws of the Twelve Tables; that marked the end of equitable legislation.[70] For there followed laws which, though at times directed against malefactors and apportioned to their offence, yet more often were put through with violence during factional strife, for the purpose of attaining illegal political power (*illicitos honores*) or banishing eminent men, or for other disreputable

[69] *Annals* III 26–28.
[70] That is, way back in 451 B.C.

purposes. Hence the Gracchi and a Saturninus, popular agitators (*turbatores plebis*), and Drusus, no less lavish in bribes in the interests of the Senate; the Italian allies were corrupted with false hopes and cheated by the veto.[71] And not even in the social war, or the civil strife that shortly ensued, did they abondon the practice of passing numerous and conflicting acts, until Lucius Sulla as dictator, annulling or altering former measures, and adding still more changes of his own, secured relief from this confusion — for not so very long, since the rogations of Lepidus soon caused trouble, and soon the tribunes were again given license to work up the people as they wished.

From now on courts were appointed not only with a general jurisdiction, but to have charge of special cases [e.g. Milo], and when the state was most corrupt the laws were most numerous.

How very modern that sounds!

Then Gnaeus Pompey was elected consul for the third time, to reëstablish order, but with remedies more burdensome than the abuses, alike author and transgressor of his own laws, he lost by arms what by arms he was protecting. Thereafter continuous discord for twenty years, no moral standard, no law; [72] the worst offences escaped punishment, and many virtuous acts brought ruin. Not until his sixth consulate (B.C. 28) did Caesar Augustus, established in power, abolish what he had decreed during the triumvirate, and give us laws whereby we might enjoy our princely ruler and our peace.[73]

Here is a wealthy document. Tacitus begins with the time-honored eulogy of a Golden Age of anarchy, which has echoes of Virgil and Lucretius and Stoic philosophy.[74] The need of law arises, and here one thinks of Lucretius again.[75] The

---

[71] That of the tribunes.

[72] Non mos, non ius. Tacitus has Horace's distinction in mind. See Chapter II, notes 97 and 120.

[73] Deditque iura quis pace et principe uteremur. Sallust (*De coniur. Cat.* 53) starts off with a similar survey (full of the First Person Singular), but he does not get very far. The influence of Sallust on Tacitus was not profound.

[74] See Furneaux's note on III 26. 1 (ed. of *Annals*, Oxford, Clarendon Press, 2nd ed. 1896) and Virgil, *Georg.* II 532–540; Virgil extends the Golden Age to the times of Romulus, the ancient Sabines and Etruscans — and to his own day, for one who understands the happiness of simplicity.

[75] *De Rerum Natura* V 1136–1155. The necessity of law is a byproduct of a tyranny, which reacts on its perpetrator: *Nec facilest placidam, ac pacatam degere vitam Qui violat factis communia foedera pacis.* Lucretius's political thought, blossoming from his atomistic cosmogony, is no different from that

rule of kings comes on, and is not condemned if it is accompanied by law. The mention of Lycurgus suggests Polybius and Cicero,[76] and among the Roman kings, though Romulus is not heralded as a lawgiver, as Livy makes him, good Numa has his usual place as the author of sacred law, and the legislation of Servius Tullius is praised, as in Livy and Cicero.[77] Here clearly is Polybius's conception of kingship founded on justice.

The downfall of Tarquin's tyranny, the principle of freedom, and the harmony of the different portions of the state are applauded, as Polybius, Cicero, and Livy applaud them, in a government no longer kingship but aristocracy. This happy regime culminates with the Laws of the Twelve Tables, in 451 B.C. Then comes that fatal moment of corruption, in accordance with Polybius's principle. The harmony of the state is disrupted by social strife. In the dissensions of patricians and plebeians at which he glances, Tacitus is obviously on the side of the patricians; he is no "liberal," as Livy and Cicero showed themselves to be.[78] If he is a disgruntled republican, it is to the very early Republic to which he would like to return, not to the age which Polybius saw and admired, nor to that of those champions of the people, the Gracchi, nor to that of Cicero, savior of the state, since that produced a Pompey. Nor does he regard the participation of the republicans in the Civil Wars as any fight for freedom. The man he does praise is Caesar Augustus, who brought Rome peace with his new order.[79] In a word, Tacitus is a monarchist, if

---

which Polybius and Cicero derived from Plato. Ancient thinkers might be bad boys in theology and metaphysics, but they were all fundamentalists concerning those ethical axioms that guarantee the well-being of the individual and of the state.

[76] Chapters I, note 80; II, note 11.

[77] Chapters I, note 62; II, notes 11, 12.

[78] Chapter II, note 28.

[79] Criticism of Augustus appears in Tacitus's citation of what people said for and against Augustus after his death (*Annals* I 9–11). Some would have it that though Tacitus ostensibly is reporting current conversation he intends, by one of his diabolical innuendoes, to cast a secret ballot with the detractors. But looking at the charges against the Emperor we must allow most of those that pertain to the earliest part of his career, and, admittedly, for all, or nearly

monarchy means Ideal Empire, founded on law and harmony and peace. He is of the party of Virgil and Horace. His condemnation of the Emperors from Tiberius down is based on his study of the early years of the first century of our era, and on what he himself had seen.[80] But a pessimist in politics he is not. In fact, with the accession of Nerva and of Trajan, he thought that the true Empire had been restored.[81] He meant to write of it, after tracing the causes of the preceding years, but his life was not spared for this task.

## III

Apart from Tacitus, was there anything else worth while in that century of Roman literature that Fronto scratched off his slate? May Tacitus' observation that it is possible for great men to exist even under bad emperors [82] be applied to literature as well as to history? I will not undertake a defence of that century; yet one or two bright spots may be made out in the gloom.

Let us note first of all two luminaries who belong in the same class with Fronto himself. We may call them literary dictators, the men who fixed standards of taste and introduced new literary modes. The Romans had always such dictators, if dictators is not too strong a word. Perhaps legislators, or counselors, would be better. Cicero is one, with Horace to follow him, and Cicero and Horace are closely bound in matters of literary judgment. So, under Nero, the great name is that of Seneca the younger.

Seneca was born in A.D. 4 and died in A.D. 65, at the behest

---

all, the *acts* of Augustus mentioned there seems to be good evidence. In the *interpretation* of the acts most divergent views would be expressed, as is always the case in popular estimates of eminent men. If Tacitus would induce us to believe that Mark Antony was tricked into marrying Octavian's sister and deserted her for Cleopatra in honest indignation at the trick, his innuendo is not so diabolical as naive. Poor Antony! Tacitus, I should say, is interested primarily in the psychology of popular judgments, in the ability of a human mind, or group of minds, to twist facts into agreement with one's preconceptions.

[80] In this he accords with Fronto. See note 60.
[81] *Agricola* 3. 3.
[82] *Ibid.*, 42. 5.

of Nero. That was an *annus fatalis* for the *intelligentsia*, the writers too intimate with those Stoic philosophers who, cherishing dreams of the old republic, were the political rebels of the day. Matters came to a head in that year with the conspiracy of Piso, which brought ruin to various men of high intellect who were, or were thought to be, implicated in it. Seneca is popularly known as a Stoic philosopher, a somewhat soft-shelled Stoic, in thought and practice, and as the writer of blood-and-thunder tragedies, held in higher esteem in the Renaissance and Elizabethan England than today. But he was also a traveler, a man of science, interested in everything. His letters do not always treat moral affairs; they contain interesting glimpses of the customs of his day.[83] His dialogues on ethical themes, such as "The Shortness of Life," "Mercy," "Anger," "Leisure," "Tranquillity," are full of apothegms, *sententiae*, born for quotation. That trait is no earmark of the Silver Age. The Romans had loved epigrams from the start. Montaigne, who was fond of Seneca, appreciated epigrams; though often compared to Horace, Montaigne is no less akin to Seneca.

Again, the Stoic's thought often approaches Christian teaching. Seneca has the sense of man's companionship with God,[84] if not God's fatherhood;[85] he proclaims the brotherhood of man, which knows no separation into bond and free;[86] he wel-

[83] One may cull the most instructive bits by following the references in the index to Dr. R. M. Gummere's edition (Loeb) of the *Epistulae Morales*. See also his remarks, vol. I, pp. xi-xii.

[84] *Ep. Mor.* 83. 1: Nihil deo clusum est. Interest animis nostris et cogitationibus mediis intervenit — almost "that we may evermore dwell in Him and He in us." But this intimacy with the Divine is pushed so far that man becomes his equal — *par deo surges* (*ibid.* 31. 9). With this utterance the cream curdles; Seneca has not attained to Christian Grace.

[85] God is the creator and preserver of the universe (*ibid.* 8. 28: Haec conservat artifex fragilitatem materiae vi sua vincens), but He is not as a father who pitieth his children. In fact Seneca's chief guide, and almost god, is philosophy. "Whether we are bound by the inexorable law of the Fates, or God as arbiter of the universe disposes all things, or chance drives and tosses human affairs with no fixed order, philosophy ought to protect us," he declares (*ibid.* 16. 15). Possibly his ultimate emphasis is rather on theology than Stoic fatalism or Epicurean chance (probably not this last), but the decision is kept in abeyance.

[86] The essence of life consists not in outer circumstance but in the intellect,

comes reverently that holy spirit which dwells in men's hearts.[87] He was claimed by Tertullian as *saepe noster,* "often ours"; [88] and such he was. In his essay "On the Happy Life," he remarked that to obey God is freedom: *Deo parere libertas est.*[89] So says St. Paul [90] and so says Tennyson:

> Ours are our wills, to make them Thine.

Did Seneca know St. Paul? They both were martyrs under Nero. Some later Christian writer, or teacher, published the letters that they were supposed to have interchanged; under the fiction, intended as a rhetorical exercise, lies some truth — a true appreciation of a certain spiritual affinity.[91]

Seneca's style is horrid, mere Silver Latin. This we know because we have been told so. Had we not been told, we should have found it enjoyable, certainly not difficult — an easy conversational style appropriate for essays. Seneca had been Nero's tutor, in those five years of gold, *quinquennium au-*

---

*animus, sed hic rectus, bonus, magnus.* It may be possessed by a Roman knight, or a freedman, or a slave. For what are they? Names that apply to a man's ambition or to the wrong that he suffers. Any one of them may mount to heaven from his little corner. Just rise, *et te quoque dignum Finge deo.* Seneca quotes Virgil (*Aen.* VIII 364), to whom he is devoted. His sympathy for all classes of mankind is not merely theoretical. He wants to help. (*De Vita Beata* 24. 3: hominibus prodesse natura me iubet . . . ubicumque homo est, ibi beneficii locus est.)

[87] *Ep. Mor.* 41. 2: sacer intra nos spiritus sedet. The whole letter is a beautiful expression of the divine immanence.

[88] *De Anima* 20: sicut et Seneca, saepe noster: Insita sunt nobis omnium artium et aetatum semina magisterque ex occulto deus producit ingenia. Seneca is *saepe,* not *semper, noster* to Tertullian. Seneca has all the moods of a poet, a dramatist of the emotions. We need not try to combine them into a system, but, as in Emerson, absorb them as absolutes, sympathetically, as they come along — *carpe diem.* He would regard the reflections of Professor Conklin quoted in Chapter III, note 36, as an extension of the whole passage from which Tertullian quotes. For teleology, if not theology, underlies Professor Conklin's exposition.

[89] *De Vita Beata* 15. 7. It is instructive to read this essay along with Cicero's *De Vita Beata* (= *Tusc. Disput.* I) and with St. Augustine's *De Beata Vita,* one of the Ciceronian dialogues of the period of his conversion.

[90] The theme of the Epistle to the Romans is the new freedom under the new law (e.g. 8. 2).

[91] These letters have at last appeared in a critical editon by C. W. Barlow in *Papers and Monographs of the American Academy in Rome* X (1938), with an excellent introduction.

*reum*, that preceded his ascension to the throne. Alas, that Seneca's five-year plan for Nero bore such awful fruit!

There are two writers of genius in the Neronian Age, both dying for the same cause and in the same year; needless to say, it was A.D. 65. They are Lucan and Petronius. Lucan, in his epic poem on the Civil War between Caesar and Pompey, has an epic without a hero. With the poet's republican fervor, Pompey should be the hero, but though large enough, he is not strong enough for the part. Caesar has full, epic vigor. But since he committed the crime of crimes in starting the Civil War, he becomes perforce the villain — although "a powerful devil, large in heart and brain," who, like Milton's Satan, threatens to upset the poet's stage and steal the show. And yet above the acts of men the poet, like Milton, sees some larger purpose working. With Lucan, however, it is not the eternal Providence whose ways he justifies, but the blind malevolence of the *Superi*, with whom, while the earthly conflict rages on the Emathian fields, the poet himself is waging a righteous war. What the outcome of his thought is we cannot tell; for the poem as we have it, and perhaps as its author left it, does not give the end of the story. It shows faults of flaming rhetoric, but also the marks of genius, which might have travelled far, had it matured.

Petronius is a mystery. He would be even more mysterious if we had nothing but the fragments of his master-piece that remain in which to spell out the intention of his work and his own character. But luckily Tacitus has devoted to Petronius one of those portraits in which, stroke by stroke, he sets forth with an eternal simplicity the traits of a subtle, degenerate, and fascinating nature, noble withal.[92]

Knowing Petronius through and through, by grace of Tacitus, we can better guess the nature of his *Satiricon*, in some twenty books, of which somewhat over two have come down to us. It is a picaresque novel, with nasty characters. It is a parody of a romance, whose hero, Encolpius, is a kind of Odysseus, driven over the seas by the wrath, not of a high

[92] *Annals* XVI 18–19.

Olympian deity, but of the lecherous scarecrow god Priapus. Poetry is mixed with the prose, in the manner of the Menippean satire that Varro cultivated, but the work calls itself not satire but *Satiricon* or *Satyricon*.[93] If Virgil's *Georgics* treats of farmers, this concerns satyrs; if so, they admirably act their parts in a novel satyr-play. Yet interspersed in the scabrous adventures are serious condemnations of the literary taste and the education of the day, there are poems on the Fall of Troy and on the Civil War — each with some subintention difficult to make out — and above all there is the Gargantuan banquet of the upstart Trimalchio, where we may learn not only low Latin, as vigorous as the vocabulary of O'Neill's *Hairy Ape*, but also comedy both low and high. For Trimalchio, funny enough in his vulgarity, likewise by his egoism draws bevies of the comic imps about him for their superior amusement. They smile at the solid self-satisfaction of one who is totally without a reason for being self-satisfied and who has a permanent genius for saying the wrong thing. How much of this work is dramatic and how much gives us the author? How much is parody? that we may never find out. Yet even in the few remnants of the work, together with what Tacitus has shown us, one of the most original, if not wholly admirable, of Roman characters is revealed, one of Horace's aptest pupils in the school of *nil admirari*.

The other rival of Fronto as a literary dictator and Imperial tutor was Quintilian; he was the tutor not of the tyrant himself — the more the pity — but of the grandsons of his sister Domitilla. In his introductory books on the education of the young, the education at home as well as in the school, Quintilian has written a manual for all time, more modern, because everlastingly practical, than some theories of education promulgated today. In his literary and oratorical principles,

[93] So in the oldest manuscript (*Cod. Bernensis,* 9th or 10th century, from Auxerre), and some others. The Renaissance spelling, and probably the ancient as well, was *Satyricon.* Since this is apparently a genitive plural, the original title was *Satyricon libri,* like *Georgicon libri,* or *Satyrica,* like *Georgica* — in English "Satyrics." An excellent edition, with annotations, is that by the late E. T. Sage, 1929.

Quintilian reacted sharply against Seneca and returned to Cicero — whom, incidentally, Seneca had praised.[94] Quintilian likewise, though admitting the use of philosophy, declared that the exercise of dialectic must be held in bounds, else it will consume oratorical strength with its subtlety.[95] When we think of the political implications of philosophy, we may recognize that something deeper than matters of literary style underlay the animosity of Quintilian for Seneca. Among the famous verdicts on Greek and Roman writers that he pronounced to form the taste of students of oratory,[96] none

[94] Not always, but he approves Cicero's encomium of philosophy (*Ep. Mor.* 17. 2) and regards him as the fount of Roman eloquence; *ibid.*, 40. 11: Cicero quoque a quo Romana eloquentia exiluit.

[95] *Inst. Orat.* XII 11. 13: haec pars dialectica, sive illam dicere malumus disputatricem (dialecticians would not favor this emendation), ut est utilis saepe . . . ita si totum sibi vindicaverit in foro certamen, obstabit melioribus et sectas ad tenuitatem suam vires ipsa subtilitate consumet. He has just likened oratory to a river that brims its banks with whirlpools as it flows. The orator who would move, instruct, and delight (*movere, docere, delectare*) in the traditional fashion (11) must not devote too much time to subtleties. This sensible doctrine comports both with Cicero's and with Fronto's views. See note 56.

[96] Quintilian does not always hit the mark, but whatever he says is worth thinking over. We must remember that he is primarily concerned with literature as material for the training of the orator. I will single out merely his judgment of Ovid (X 1. 88): Lascivus quidem in herois quoque (whereas you'd expect that at least in epic passages he would drop his frivolity) et nimium amator ingenii sui (as Ovid himself had remarked), laudandus tamen in partibus (a discrete reservation). Some years ago, in answer to an article sent him (Chapter II, note 113), the revered Basil L. Gildersleeve, who understood his Ovid, as well as all things Greek, sent me the following sonnet.

### OVID

'Too much, too much a lover,' said Quintilian
'Of his own genius,' writing of Ovidius.
And those who think it praise to be fastidious
That sentence harsh have blazoned in vermilion.
What soldier heeds the censure of civilian?
What care for Demos' judgment had a Phidias?
What right has Hodge to pass on fair or hideous
Or Attic cit to scoff at speech Sicilian?

Go on, go on Quintilian, stare and gasp
At any failings Ovid may have shewn.
Thine is the critic's, his the poet's sense.
For he who holds his muse in mutual grasp
Knows not which are her heart throbs, which his own
And loses selfhood in his joy immense.

is more searching than that on Seneca. He assured those who
censured his severity that he gladly conceded Seneca his good
points, despite those alluring vices of style that misled young
writers. He adds that Seneca's talents deserved a better ambition; the ambition that he desired he attained.[97] Ah, Quintilian, that is not even to damn with faint praise. As you say,
you have kept your barbed arrow till the last.

It is strange that Fronto has no good word for the writers
of the reigns of Nerva and Trajan. For then the Ideal Empire
had returned; and under that dispensation Fronto himself
was living.[98] With the new principle of adoption, which is
much like that of Scipio's day applied to a new purpose,[99]
Rome had an excellent series of rulers, as Gibbon declared
long ago,[100] down through eighty years of the following cen-

[97] *Inst. Or.* X 1. 125–131. John of Salisbury comes nobly to the rescue of
Seneca, though treating Quintilian with a Christian courtesy; see *Policraticus*
VIII 13, 763 b–764 c (Webb).

[98] See on Florus the historian, friend of Hadrian, Chapter VI, note 71.
Fronto appreciated Trajan. He alone of all the Roman emperors in his desire
for peace and his abstinence from vain glories may be likened to the good
King Numa (*Principia Historiae*, 11 [II 208 H 206 N]). It is a pity that we
have only tattered fragments of Fronto's preface to his account of the Parthian
War.

[99] Well stated by Galba in the speech in which he declares his adoption of
Piso Licinianus. Tacitus, who reports the speech (*Hist.* I 15–16) and is responsible at least for its language, emphasizes the uncertainty of family succession, especially in a family that was going to seed. Nero had the idea first;
he wanted a successor of his own stamp, and had selected an admirable coun-
terpart in Otho (*ibid.* 13).

[100] In the first chapter of the immortal *History of the Decline and Fall
of the Roman Empire*, London, 1776. To enjoy the full flavor of this work
one must read it in the first edition. The conscientious glossators who have
brought Gibbon up to date (Milman, Bury) may be used for consultation.
But there is nothing like feasting on the sumptuous pages of 1776 and brows-
ing on the original annotations, whatever their imperfection. For the same
view of Nerva and his successors, see Rostovtzeff, *A History of the Ancient
World* (Oxford University Press 1927, corr. 1928), vol. II, *Rome*, p. 231. We
find it before Gibbon in an unexpected quarter — not unexpected to those who
know the book — Fielding's *Tom Jones* (1749), not only one of the greatest
novels in our language, appreciated particularly by those familiar with the
ancient Classics and with the comic spirit, but a mirror of human life in many
of its aspects. In Book XII, 11, the King of the Gypsies, an uncouth monarch
with a delightful brogue, sets forth a theory of government that will hold its
own with the doctrines of Polybius; and thereto Fielding adds: "Mankind have
never been so happy as when the greatest part of the then known world was
under the domination of a single master; and this state of their felicity con-

tury; Nerva, Trajan, Hadrian, Marcus Antoninus Pius, Marcus Aurelius Antoninus, make up that new lineage of nobility. Whether the Senate and the people contributed their share to the harmony of the state is another question.

We need not dwell long on the chief writers of the day, who had all known the darkness of Domitian's regime and rejoiced in the sunlight of Trajan's. Pliny and Martial, Juvenal, Tacitus and Suetonius, each of them an interesting person to know and each of them making a distinctive contribution to good letters, helped each in his way to the building of Rome.[101] This galaxy may not shine so brightly as that of the men of letters who clustered about Augustus. Yet because of the bitter tyranny of Domitian, through which they all had passed, and because of the rebellion of the high-minded Stoics against that tyranny, they are animated with the strength of the old republic; in spirit they are more immediately akin to Ennius than to Virgil and Horace. Taken together, their writings enable us to see a picture of the age, its society, its amusements, its daily life, its literary and philosophical concerns, its politics, its government, fully as diverse, I should say, and more nearly complete than that which we have for the age of Augustus. It is invidious to call that the Golden Age and this the Silver. Let us name ages from their rulers, not from metals, though noting within each period the silver, the gold, the alloy. The greatest of the authors of Trajan's day, Tacitus, is one of the greatest in all Roman literature.[102] If he is silver, one is tempted to go off the gold standard. He is a judge of men, not morose or embittered, but discriminating, merciless, final. His eye is on the truth and he states what he sees. The world of men had come to judgment before him — it seems like the last judgment. His verdicts are a medicine for mankind. They have a tang of such relish that, for one, I would swallow any misjudgments with the medicine. If I err, I am

---

tinued during the reigns of five successive princes." Note: "Nerva, Trajan, Adrian and the two Antonini."

[101] For brief estimates of some of these see *Latin Readings*, pp. 63, 73.

[102] For more on Tacitus, see *Esprits Souverains*, pp. 53–64.

glad to err with Dryden, who put Tacitus on the same plane
with Polybius as an interpreter of human history.[103]

## IV

I fear that in this appraisal of Fronto's Dark and Middle
Ages of the first century of our era I have played the part of
a Balaam. At any rate, I know not where to mark the beginning of the pathway down. Why did not Fronto appreciate
Tacitus? Was it his style? But that, though not Ciceronian,
has the vigor of the primitives that Fronto so admired; and in
his *elocutio novella*, his choice of fresh and pregnant words
from which a garden flowers, he stands alone with Virgil.
Did Fronto reject both Seneca and Quintilian, because although they both, like himself, were Imperial tutors, they
did not fare so well as he? [104] *Tantaene animis professori-
alibus irae?* I will not press so discourteous a question. I will
leave Fronto with his own estimate of the preceding age and
will not begin the Decline and Fall of Rome with him.

At last, however, I will admit that we can point out a *facilis
descensus* in the reign of Marcus Aurelius' son, Commodus,
the gladiator-king. Poor Plato! In fulfilment of his vision, he
had seen a philosopher become king in the preceding reign.
But so had Commodus, and the son of a highly intellectual
father sometimes maps out for himself an entirely different
career from that of which he studied the domestic aspects
from his infancy.

The third century of our era, if we merely scan the course
of ancient Rome in its political and literary developments,
seems indeed one dismal wilderness. From the last chapter of
the Ideal Empire under Marcus Aurelius to the totalitarian
government of Diocletian at the end of this period, it is a
bleak descent.

[103] See Chapter I, note 4.

[104] He ironically calls himself a disciple of Seneca (*De Fer. Als.* 3. 2 [II 7 H,
224 N]), and then ridicules Seneca's childish jugglery (*Ad M. Anton. de ora-
tionibus* 2 [II 102 H, 155 f. N]) very much in the fashion of Quintilian (note
97). On Quintilian he has nothing to say, yet perhaps imitates him here and
there (Haines, II, p. 341) and evidently has the same conception of oratory
(note 95). Why not say so?

One resting-place on the way is the reign of the Emperor Gallienus, 260–268 A.D., who has been put in his proper light lately by a brilliant Hungarian scholar, who, pushing further the results obtained by other recent investigators, contributes an instructive essay to the final volume of *The Cambridge Ancient History*.[105] We now see that Gallienus was a competent ruler, who reformed senatorial procedure, reorganized the army, knew how to select good generals, fostered good letters, and effected a renaissance in art. He was a foe of Christianity, but found in a revival of ancient culture a better weapon than persecution. He was swift in action and successful in beating back the Germans from the frontiers. Athens was his intellectual Mecca and his court was frequented by Greek men of letters. One of his most enlightened acts was his patronage of the philosopher Plotinus, who revived the philosophy of Plato in a fashion adjusted to the religious needs of the times and etherealized by his own genius. The ideal ruler to whose example the Emperor Gallienus aspired, the prince that he saw in the mirror, was Augustus. Like him, he would be a *restitutor orbis,* and usher in a Golden Age.[106] In a word, his reign is a monument to the Pagan past of Greece and Rome, standing halfway between that of Marcus Aurelius and that of the Emperor Julian, who, towards the end of the ensuing century, sought to swing the world back from the Christian way of life to the vanished glories of Greece and Rome.

This rehabilitation of the Emperor Gallienus is accomplished by new studies of coins and inscriptions, along with a fresh consideration of the historical information furnished by Greek writers, rather than that contained in a Latin work, previously considered a highly important source for the annals of the third century of our era. This is the Imperial History, *Historia Augusta,* written, apparently, by various writers, Spartianus, Capitolinus, Lampridius, and others, and

---

[105] A. Alföldi, *C.A.H.* XII, pp. 181–193, 223–225.

[106] *Res publica restituta* is the essence of Augustus's ambition and, so far as the times allowed him, his achievement. See Chapter II, notes 139, 140; Chapter III, note 81. On Gallienus, Alföldi, *C.A.H.* XII, p. 187.

devoted to the biography of the Emperors from Hadrian on-
wards. We need not examine here the recent scepticism which
would resolve these authors into ghosts, but not ghost-writers,
and characterize the whole work as the propaganda piece of a
later age, possibly that of the Emperor Julian.[107] Avoiding an
encounter with the historians, we may at least observe that
these lives of the Emperors, whatever the number of authors,
are done in the manner of Suetonius, contain some excellent
and highly interesting matter, above all in the *Life of Hadrian*,
and serve, in some cases, as mirrors of the prince for Diocletian or Constantine. They furthermore are utilized, but only
most discreetly, by the critics who damn them. Behind them,
as Alföldi declares, lies some "Imperial History," [108] or some
set of Imperial biographies, written in the third century by
a follower, or by more than one follower of Suetonius. Some
of the lives are better than others. Those of the later emperors
are decidedly weak. They all illustrate Suetonius's omnivo-
rous appetite for truth, fiction, and scandal.

Now the Life of Gallienus in the *Historia Augusta*, pur-
porting to be written by a certain Trebellius Pollio, is one of
the inferior biographies; its object is to put Gallienus in a
bad light.[109] Yet not all is malediction. The biographer can
speak at least of the Emperor's occasional vigor in war.[110] He
also will not deny his wit or his eminence in oratory, poetry,
and all the arts,[111] and he quotes from a wedding hymn that he
wrote; the lines are well turned and have a touch of humor.[112]
Perhaps, then, various other bits in the life of Trebellius may
be historic in the core, though puffed with exaggeration or

[107] *C.A.H.* XII, pp. 598–599 (E.K.R.), 710–711 (the editors).

[108] He refers to "the author of the lost biographical history of the Emperors
on which our later chronicles and compendia depend" (*C.A.H.* XII, p. 224).

[109] *S.H.A.* (Magee), III p. 16.

[110] *Ibid. Gallieni Duo*, 11.

[111] 11. 6: fuit enim Gallienus, quod negari non potest, oratione poemate
atque omnibus artibus clarus.

[112] 11. 7–8. The writer remarks in conclusion (9) that it would be tedious
to go over all his poems and speeches which made him prominent among the
poets and orators of his time. That is all right for a poet or an orator, but
we demand something else from an Emperor (sed aliud in imperatore quae-
ritur, aliud in oratore vel poeta flagitatur).

given a malicious turn.[113] We learn among other things that
the Emperor spent elaborate thought on banquets, dress, ceremonies, and miraculous horticulture, with melons in winter,
fresh figs and apples in "alien months," [114] and new wine all
through the year. He made a jest of life and of the empire.
He publicly presented a hopelessly unsuccessful toreador with
a wreath, saying that it was a difficult feat to miss a bull so
many times.[115] Egypt revolts. "Well, cannot we get on without Egyptian linen?" Asia is overrun by the Scythians. "Well,
are we dependent on saltpeter?" Gaul slips out from his control. "Think you really that the Roman state is not safe without the cloaks of Arras?" [116] Here we may see a cynic, somewhat of the type of Petronius. He liked to make merry while
civilization went to pot.[117] Or shall we liken him to Horace's
just and tenacious man who amidst the falling world stands
undismayed? He is an interesting person, the author of these
*bons mots*, whether he was the real Gallienus or somebody
quite fictitious.

These lives of the Emperors, whatever the inaccuracy of
their report of facts and acts, have considerable significance
for the conception of the state that they record. Your new
Emperor is generally an Augustus who, with the help of Virgil's Messianic Eclogue, ushers in a Golden Age and restores
the Republic. Even the sons of Gallienus are a *novum Iovis
incrementum*, "new scions of Jove"; and here our evidence is
given not by Trebellius but by the Imperial coins.[118] That

[113] Alföldi, *C.A.H.* XII, 198: "The accounts in the H.A. of the pomp and
glory displayed at the decennalia of Gallienus may not all be true, but they
certainly preserve many genuine characteristics."

[114] 16. 2: ficos virides et poma ex arboribus recentia semper alienis mensibus
praebuit. The writer has not forgotten his Virgil (*Georg.* II 158: Hic ver
adsiduum atque alienis mensibus aestas).

[115] 12. 4: "Taurum totiens non ferire difficile est.

[116] 6. 4–6.

[117] 11. 7: Sic denique de omnibus partibus mundi, cum eas amitteret, quasi
detrimentis vilium ministeriorum videretur affici, iocabatur.

[118] *C.A.H.* XII p. 194. Few possessors of a dollar bill today — and their number is steadily diminishing — are aware that the green note is stamped with
two bits of Virgil — NOVUS ORDO SECLORUM (*sic,* cf. Ecl. IV 5) and ANNUIT
COEPTIS (cf. *Aen.* IX 625). The Golden Age, with Virgil, will therefore still
be with us, if we only knew it — that is so long as dollar bills shall last.

was "wishful thinking" on a magnificent scale in the black third century. To take but one instance from the *Historia Augusta*,[119] it is stated that Claudius II, the successor of Gallienus, had he only tarried longer in the state, would by his strength, his wisdom, and his foresight have brought back the Scipios and the Camilli and all the great heroes of old. He would have exhibited the manliness (*virtus*) of Trajan, the dutifulness (*pietas*) of Antoninus, and the self-restraint (*moderatio*) of Augustus. In other words, the ancient republican virtues are still the prop of Ideal Empire. The Mirror of the Prince is still held before the eyes of each new ruler, and as in the golden days of Numa, the power of one man to mould the habits of his subjects still operates; witness the simplicity and the self-mastery of Severus Alexander, according to the author of one of the better lives in the *Historia Augusta*.[120]

## V

That is all that I will venture to say about the dark third century, which Rostovtzeff, Baynes, and others have studied with much profit. Decline and Fall are relative terms. It depends on the observer. Rose-colored spectacles may make a dark prospect pleasant, while spectacles of black obscure the sun. Martial neatly makes fun of a certain Caecilianus; Mundungus we might call him, after Pope, who went round dolefully exclaiming, *o tempora, o mores!* "O times, O morals!" That is all right for Cicero, observes Martial,[121] when Catiline was plotting treason, and the fratricidal war of Caesar and

---

[119] *S.H.A. Div. Claud.* 2. 1–2.

[120] Lampridius (or whom you will). He describes the Emperor's *ordo diei* — one of many such accounts in Latin literature (*Alex. Sev.* 29 ff.). After the business of the day (30), he would read such works as Plato's *Republic*, Cicero's *Republic* and *De Officiis*, Serenus Sammonicus, a poet of the day and his friend, and — Horace. He also read the life of Alexander the Great, to whose traits he aspired, except his drunkenness and his cruelty towards his friends. Then follows an extended account of his good deeds and simple habits with the result that great men imitated him and noble ladies his consort (41. 2: imitati sunt eum magni viri et uxorem eius matronae pernobiles). Here is that Imitation of the Prince that in Roman tradition Numa had first inspired (Livy I 21. 2).

[121] IX 70.

Pompey was drenching the earth with blood. But why *o tempora, o mores* in this blessed age (it incidentally was still the age of Domitian) when mad wars have ceased and peace and joy are reigning?

> Non nostri faciunt tibi quod tua *tempora* sordent,
>   Sed faciunt *mores*, Caeciliane, tui.
>
> Not ours the *morals* that make you so bemoan
>   These *times*, my poor Mundungus, but your own.[122]

On the other hand, when a pessimist of noble character arraigns the age, as Charles Eliot Norton was wont to do, the rest of us were thanking our stars that we were living in the age of Charles Eliot Norton. For such a pessimism may have a moral effect. Gloomy utterances from a Lucretius, a Cicero, a Horace, a Juvenal, arouse the individual to make the times somewhat better. He may not succeed in that, but in the effort he effects his own improvement. In the blackest of times any one may build his own Golden Age, perforce. In every age you will find two sorts of men, those who are sure that they are the heirs of all the ages in the foremost files of time, and those who are convinced that we are going to the dogs. In every historical period two other historical periods exist, the primal Golden Age forever vanished, and the blessed Millennium towards which we tend.

I think I have made clear the point of view from which I have undertaken these venturesome studies of the building of ancient Rome. I am more interested in ideals than in their imperfect actualization in the rush of human life. A timeless view of events is more significant than the effort to determine their chronological or their causal sequence. While estimating literary periods, furthermore, or the various works within them, or the character of great actors of the past, it is more profitable to examine the ideals at which they grasped than their lapses from these ideals. The failures are common to our poor humanity in any period. The aspirations remain as

---

[122] See *Romantic Approach*, p. 3. Fielding makes the same observation, in language still stronger (Book VI, 1). See *Spirit of Comedy*, p. 93.

an index of the age and of the progress it had made in aspiration.[123] And so in the judgment of works of literature, we should sift gold from dross and concentrate our attention on the gold. That is the "truly critical" method — for does not criticism mean "the art of sifting"? It is uncritical to be left with dross after the sifting and to conclude that judgments extracted from the dross tarnish the gold; for gold it remains. Mr. Santayana, a critical spirit if ever there was one, observes, in his latest work, and we hope not the last, the *Realm of Spirit*: "My happiness lay in understanding the ancients (or thinking I understood them) rather than in contradicting them." [124] Another wise man had read literature in the same way. Quintilian, passing in review the writers of Greece and Rome profitable for the training of the orator, admits that the great authors had their faults, which some of their imitators blindly copied, but declares that it is better to pronounce a modest and cautious judgment of them, lest, as frequently occurs, one damn what one does not understand. And if, he adds, one must err on either side, he would prefer to have a perpetual pleasure in reading them than to mark down the many things he did not like.[125]

Of course there are bright ages and dark ages in human history. We may single out the best of them to study and enjoy. And so we may single out the solitary, lesser lights in some black night, who shine the brighter for its darkness.

[123] See Chapter III, note 43.

[124] *Realm of Spirit* (1940), p. 273. For further remarks on criticism, see the wise Fielding, *Tom Jones*, Book XI, 1 "A Crust for the Critics": "The word critic is of Greek derivation and signifies judgment. Hence I presume some persons who have not understood the original, and have seen English translations of the primitive, have concluded that it meant judgment in the legal sense, in which it is frequently used as equivalent to condemnation."

[125] *Inst. Or.* X 1. 26: modesto tamen et circumspecto iudicio de tantis viris pronuntiandum est, ne quod plerisque accidit damnent quae non intellegant. Ac si necesse est in alteram errare partem, omnia eorum legentibus placcre quam multa displicere maluerim.

# CHAPTER VI

# THE ROMAN CITY OF GOD

THUS far, perhaps to the disappointment of my readers, I have proved unable to locate the point when Rome began to decline or the moment when the great city greatly fell:

κεῖτο μέγας μεγάλωστι·

We saw that, in general, the third century of our era is no brilliant period in the history of ancient Rome, even after the rehabilitation of the Emperor Gallienus, and, as we may add, that of the great autocrat Diocletian.[1] We noted the signs throughout the century that the watchwords of the old Republic and the Ideal Empire were not forgotten. The Golden Age was constantly reappearing. The spirit of Rome still hovered over its ancient abode.

But these worthy ideals of antiquity are somehow out of place. The ghosts of Cicero, Virgil, and Horace still walk abroad, but their voices are faint. So intense was this pathetic dwelling in the past that the meaning of the grim actualities slipped away. The past was no longer absorbed into the present as in the days of the First Citizen who founded the Ideal Empire. Both became shadows, while a new power was forging ahead.[2]

This new power was the Christian faith, established in the Christian Church. For, as Mr. Santayana declares in his book on *The Realm of Spirit*, which I quoted in the last chapter and shall quote again,[3] Christianity was "a fundamentally new religion," or, in Buchan's oracular phrase, was " the greatest

[1] N. H. Baynes, *C.A.H.* XII pp. 658, 661.
[2] Rostovtzeff, *Ancient World* II p. 356: "All the authors . . . bear the stamp of weariness, disenchantment and despair. Christian literature alone was really alive."
[3] *Realm of Spirit* (1940), p. 212.

of historic convulsions." [4] If I have seemed reluctant to point to the moment when Rome began to decline and when it fell, it is not because I am unaware that there are definite periods in human history, which it is profitable to study, up to a certain point, as though they were animal organisms, to distinguish their characteristics, to examine their growth, and as in the case of an individual to trace their development from youth, to manhood, to old age, to death. At least this is one aspect of a profitable study of history. It is well to inspect the workings of social, political, and economic factors, as has been done most minutely by scholars in our generation and before. But when our eyes are on the third century of our era, I would submit that the most potent cause of the downfall of ancient Rome came not from within, but from without. The ramparts were of themselves decaying; but they crumbled before an engine of assault. One does not speak of "The Decline and Fall of the Dark Ages"; one looks rather at the revival of the light of learning in the Carolingian Renaissance. So in the third century we are concerned, for our present purpose, not so much with the tottering fabric of the state as with that new power that restored the Ideal Empire in a Christian form.

When we speak of a Roman City of God, one thinks inevitably of the famous work of St. Augustine, *De Civitate Dei*, and with St. Augustine we shall reckon, however briefly, in due time. But the idea of a kingdom not of this world, of a New Jerusalem, of a city not built with human hands but eternal in the heavens, was proclaimed at the beginning by our Lord, by St. Paul, by the author of The Apocalypse, or Revelation, of St. John the Divine. This heavenly City, in its earthly and visible form, was subject to no particular sort of government and to no particular economic or social organization. Our Lord made no pronouncements on any of these points. He did not declare that democracy in the sense that either our country or any other country has understood that term was the most Christian form of government. "Render unto Caesar," He said, "the things which be Caesar's, and

[4] *Augustus*, p. 343.

unto God the things which be God's"; [5] the Caesar was Tiberius. "Fear God. Honour the King," echoes St. Peter; [6] the King, who put him to death, was Nero.

This principle of respect for authority, whatever the nature of that authority may be, is elaborated by St. Paul.[7]

"Let every soul be subject unto the higher powers. For there is no power but of God: the powers that be are ordained of God." Horace, as we have observed, said something similar concerning Augustus:

Subordinate to thee he shall rule the broad earth in equity.[8]

In both cases, I take it, the emphasis is not primarily on the divine right of kings. In Horace it is on the king's obligation to walk humbly with Jupiter. In St. Paul, the words are addressed to the Christian community, who will have moments of restiveness under Nero. St. Paul, naturally, is not speaking as Nero's emissary, nor is he arguing for the Ideal Empire as the best of all possible governments. He is exhorting the followers of Christ, whose kingdom is not of this world, to conform to the political regime that they find.

There is, similarly, no prescription of any controlling social or economic scheme. Simplicity of life is commended. A particular young man is told — if he will be perfect — to sell all that he has and give to the poor and thus to have treasure in heaven. The young man, who imagined himself nearly perfect to begin with, is not quite induced to make this investment. This passage gives a character sketch, not a program of general liquidation. Our Lord adds, with the humor of the situation in mind, that it is harder for a camel to go through the eye of a needle than for a rich man to enter into the kingdom of God. When the disciples ask in amazement, "Who then can be saved?" he replies: "With men this is impossible, but with God all things are possible." [9] This does not mean that

---

[5] Matthew 22. 21.

[6] I Peter 2. 17.

[7] Romans 13. 1.

[8] *Odes* I 12. 57. Te minor latum reget aequus orbem. Cf. III 1. 5: Regum timendorum in proprios greges, Reges in ipsos imperium est Iovis.

[9] Matthew 19. 16–26. Our Lord, it would seem, does not suggest that male-

in answer to prayer the reformer will be told whether communism or other social systems will cure the woes of the world. Our Lord means, I venture to infer, that if the gospel of the new kingdom is accepted it will so work in the hearts of believers that in any of the relations of life mountains of injustice and dissension will quietly melt away.

The early Christians, incidentally, did try communism at first. They "had all things common; and sold their possessions and goods" and "laid them at the apostles' feet; and distribution was made unto every man according as he had need." [10] But the chapter following these words begins: "But a certain man named Ananias." Nothing could be more instructive. The common sharing of wealth had much in its favor. It seemed to flow naturally from the common sharing of brotherly love. But systems break down if the sentiments they incorporate no longer prevail. Or, to repeat old Horace once more,

What profit vain laws without moral support?

Quid leges sine moribus
Vanae proficiunt? [11]

It is therefore in the human heart, and in the human will, that the Kingdom of God must be built.

There is even no protest in the New Testament against the institution of slavery. The relation of slave to master should be that of a citizen to his ruler. The slave is exhorted not to mind being called a servant. For if he believes in the Lord, he is the Lord's freeman, just as a freeman who gives up his will to the Lord becomes the Lord's servant. [12] The two are on the same footing; they both have found a new service and a new freedom. The master of a slave, similarly, should treat

---

factors of great wealth should be liquidated. Like the poor, they will always be with us; and, *mirabile dictu*, they may attain salvation by God's grace.

[10] Acts 2. 44–45; 4. 35.

[11] *Odes* III 24. 35–36. A very significant ode, presenting a Mirror of the Prince to the coming ruler at some time before the chief power was in his hands. See Chapter II, note 97.

[12] Col. 3. 22–25.

his slave with kindness. Their worldly stations differ, but in the love of Christ they are the same; with God there is no respect of persons.[13] "So whatsoever ye do," St. Paul exhorts the slave, "do it heartily, as to the Lord, and not unto men." [14]

This attitude towards slavery would apparently have been the same even if slavery had involved the most diabolical maltreatment of human beings. Reform the slave-drivers and slave-driving disappears. As a matter of fact there are many redeeming features in this institution as practised in antiquity. Chances to rise above it meet us at every hand. This liberty was abused by the Imperial freedmen, and the Emperors who freed them, but in literature, as we have seen,[15] Terence and Horace would not have been known had there not been for a liberated slave or the son of a freedman an open road into the circle of the élite. Phaedrus did not rise socially so high, yet high enough to be marked out for destruction. And his fables were at once numbered with the classics by those who followed him. Epictetus, a slave from Phrygia, came to Rome and rose to the status of a philosopher. He had the honor to be expelled with the other philosophers by Domitian in

[13] Eph. 6. 5–9. On the "spuriousness" of Ephesians, see Nock, *St. Paul*, pp. 230–232. In the present matter, it is at one with Colossians, admittedly genuine, as it is also in its general argument (*ibid.*, p. 231). Professor Nock finds that it is "mainly a Pauline mosaic, and may involve a use of lost Pauline Epistles in addition to those which we know." "But the style of the letter is against it." For instance, "it has a sustained serenity which is quite unlike his way of writing." This is not the only problem in the way; yet finding enough sustained serenity in the Chapter on Charity in I Corinthians, I am willing to suppose that St. Paul could write steadily from calm heights the six chapters of the letter to the Ephesians, or perhaps to the whole Church, especially if he felt at the time that his end was drawing near. According to Canon B. H. Streeter in an admirable article on "The Rise of Christianity" in *Camb. Anc. Hist.* XI p. 257 the chronological order of the letters of St. Paul is: I and II Thessalonians, Galatians, I and II Corinthians, Romans, Philippians, Colossians and Philemon, "perhaps Ephesians, but only some fragments (mostly embodied in II Timothy) of the epistles to Timothy and Titus." St. Paul has increased his compass since the days when few scholars who cared for their scientific reputation would accept as genuine letters of his more than the sacred four admitted by Ferdinand Christian Baur.

[14] Colossians, *loc. cit.* note 12. St. Paul can practise as well as preach. He sends back to Philemon his slave Onesimus, who had become a helpful co-laborer with St. Paul. "But treat him not as a servant, but above a servant, and if thou count me as a partner, receive him as myself" (Phil. 16–17).

[15] Chapter III, note 47.

93 A.D. and afterwards he enjoyed the friendship of the Emperor Hadrian.[16] I doubt if in any subsequent period of history slavery has ever been so democratic. The ancients rated you by the level you had reached, not in inverse proportion to the distance you had traveled in reaching it.

In the new Christian community there was little need, at first, of pondering the relation of the faith in Christ with whatever was best in Pagan tradition. St. Paul had been a Pharisee, a man of cultivation. He quoted the Greek poets in his sermon to the Athenians just as he quoted the Hebrew prophets to his countrymen, to show that the prophecy had been fulfilled.[17] He wisely was all things to all men. Most of the followers of our Lord were humble folk, publicans and sinners; He came to call them and not the righteous to repentance. Even St. Paul appears to have made little appeal to the upper classes during his sojourn in Rome. Otherwise Seneca would have found him out — as the author of their correspondence imagined.[18]

## II

For many decades the Church was a subterranean force in Roman society. At first Christians felt no need of a new literature, save what was accessible to them in the Old Testament and, later, in the New. The impulse to create new modes of expression came from the persecutions of the second century, which proceeded in part from false charges, charges of immorality and political disloyalty, or treason, brought against the conduct and the rites of the suspected sect. Hence arose the Apologetes who wrote, some in Greek, some in Latin, to answer these charges and thus to set forth the nature of the Christian faith. We need not repeat this familiar story at any length.[19] But two points of prime importance concern us at

[16] S.H.A. (Spart) Hadr. 16. 10.
[17] Acts 17 and 26.
[18] See Chapter V, note 91.
[19] I have treated, superficially, certain aspects of it in Founders (pp. 38–49) and C.A.H. XII (pp. 590–597, 600–602). But we need a new study of all the Apologetes from someone who will read all their works and treat them as human documents.

the start as we come to a new era in the long building of Rome.

The first we may note in the *Apologeticum* of Tertullian, a work presented about 197 A.D. to the Emperor Septimius Severus. This writer, a priest of Carthage, one of the most interesting and many-sided characters of the early Church, so stiffly Puritanic that he drifted into the heresy of Montanus, so sure of new revelations from the Holy Spirit that he was not made a saint by the Catholic Church, was for all his Punic blood faithful to Rome and the Empire. He assures Septimius Severus that, while neither he nor any Christian will worship the Emperor as divine, they will pay truer homage to him by offering prayers for his welfare to the one true God; for the Christian Church still cherishes the mandate of our Lord to be loyal to the Government, so far as the fundamentals of the Faith will allow.[20]

The other point is the desire of certain Christian converts trained in the ancient liberal arts to absorb Pagan culture into the Christian way of life. This aim is apparent in a priceless little work, the dialogue called *Octavius* by Minucius Felix.[21] He, like Tertullian, probably came from Africa, the foremost centre of Latin literature in the early Church; he writes for the circle of his cultured pagan friends. Without mentioning the name of Christ or the articles of the Christian faith, he would show them that in spirit it is consonant with the highest ideals of the great writers of old. He quotes Virgil as St. Paul had quoted Aratus and Cleanthes.[22] He models his

---

[20] *Apol.* 30, an eloquent chapter, and the eloquence is sincere. Tertullian declares (30, 3) that the Emperor is great because he is subordinate to heaven: ideo magnus est quia caelo minor est. Here Dr. Glover, in his excellent translation (Loeb), scents "a distant memory of Horace" (*Odes* I 12. 57; see note 8); this may well be so. Tertullian had previously said that the Emperors would have believed in Christ if either Emperors had not been necessary for the world, or Christians could have been Caesars (21). This is Tertullian's way of saying, "Render unto Caesar the things that be Caesar's." On the loyalty of Christians Mr. Baynes remarks (*C.A.H.* XII p. 660): "Throughout all the persecutions no Christian had raised the standard of revolt." He refers to Tertullian, *Apol.* 35.

[21] See the translation by G. H. Rendell in the same volume with Glover's Tertullian.

[22] In his sermon to the Athenians, recorded in Acts 17. See Chapter I, note

dialogue, the *Octavius*, on the *De Natura Deorum* of Cicero. It contains reminiscences of many of the Roman authors from Ennius to Tacitus and Juvenal. Thus the essence of a new and Christian humanism is given in this work; in his style, Minucius is the first of the Christian Ciceros. He wrote, I now believe, after Tertullian's *Apologeticum* — though this point is still hotly debated — perhaps in the reign of the tolerant and cultivated Severus Alexander (222–235 A.D.).[23]

The noble Cyprian (St. Cyprian), Bishop of Carthage, a devoted follower of Tertullian, whose fiery essays he made over in a calm and Ciceronian style, contributed little of original thought to the building of Rome. In character and in principles he contributed much. Like his master, he was well read in the ancient authors; he, too, was a convert to the Church. In him, all the old Roman virtues were baptized. Moreover, in his work *De Catholicae Ecclesiae Unitate*, he voiced that spirit of union that the Church, and the world, most needed in those times of strife. In his teachings, true to the message of St. Paul, there is a foregleam of the new empire of Christ. He suffered martyrdom under Valerian in 258 A.D., and richly deserves his canonization.[24]

### III

Coming now to the reign of Diocletian at the end of the third century, we find Arnobius, another African, a teacher of rhetoric until his conversion late in life; to him we may devote a greater share of our attention, since his character and the purpose of his apologetic are [25] frequently misunderstood. His apology, *Adversus Nationes*, offers for Pagans trained in philosophy a novel approach to the Christian faith. Lucretius, whom he knew through and through, points the way. The human soul is as weak an instrument as Lucretius found it;

---

65. Professor Nock, after demolishing the historicity of this speech, adds: "At the same time, some of the speeches in Acts appear to rest on earlier documents and it is very likely that Paul did speak somewhat as he is represented." Very well; let it go at that.

[23] *C.A.H.* XII p. 597.                    [24] *Ibid.* pp. 600–602.

[25] I have only suggested what might be done with Arnobius in *C.A.H.* XII 607–609 and have added only a few details in the present account.

Plato was wrong, for all his eminence. But the soul has a deliverer, not in Epicurus, but in Christ. It can win its immortality through Him. This is not orthodox doctrine, and the work was put on that ancient *Index Librorum Prohibitorum* attributed to Pope Gelasius.[26] But St. Jerome admired it, and admirable it is for its scathing and witty attack on the absurdities of Roman religion, which Arnobius presents with such a wealth of information that it is today a precious source for rare myths and cults. He knows and praises Varro for his learning and Cicero for his fearless treatment of mythology,[27] nor is Plato, *ille divinus*, forgotten after all.[28] He knows the whole range of Greek philosophy and selects the best. He knows the whole range of Roman history. He makes us feel that the old Romans were better than their gods; thus are the ancient *mores* salvaged, to become a bulwark of a new Roman state.

These gods! The ancient myth-makers lugged them in to explain good Roman deeds. For instance Titus Tatius *opened* a new road in order to take the Capitoline — *viam pandere* is the phrase. He did not do it all alone. He did it, forsooth, with the aid of the goddess *Panda*, or *Pantica*, as some would have it.[29] Arnobius here discloses for us, with Varro's help, one of the essential modes of primitive Roman reasoning — to be added to those romances of the mind that Henry Osborn Taylor discussed in his brilliant lectures at Harvard, some few years ago.[30] This mode of thought, as satisfying then as any accepted scientific procedure was to be in any later century, was to explain all natural phenomena in personal terms.

[26] Gelasius is placed in a new and decidedly attractive light by A. K. Ziegler in his article cited in the List of Books; on the "Index," composed later than Gelasius, see pp. 8–9.

[27] V 8: Varro ille Romanus multiformibus eminens disciplinis et in vetustatis indagatione rimator.

III 6–7: arte omnes Tullii Romani disertissimus generis nullam veritus impietatis invidiam ingenue constanter et libere quid super tali opinione sentiret pietate cum maiore monstravit.

[28] II 36: Plato ille divinus multa de deo digna nec communia sentiens multitudini in eo sermone ac libro cui nomen Timaeus scribitur dicit.

[29] IV 1–3.

[30] *Fact: The Romance of Mind*, 1932.

Hence the legendary metamorphoses which traced the origin
of birds and beasts and flowers to human adventures, or mis-
adventures.  The early Italians, going further in this road
than the Greeks, so it would seem, devised a deity to justify
each circumstance, an eponymous hero not only for each town
but for each deed.[31]  Here is Plato's idealism, without the
sanction of Plato, set to work in the common experience of
ordinary men.  A satisfactory reconciliation of science and
religion, though not premeditated, was hit upon; for they
both are anthropomorphic.

Arnobius, I hope, will pardon this digression, for digression
is one of his strong points.  We will return to his ridicule of
the degrading absurdities of the myth-makers.  You laugh, he
says, you Romans, at the Egyptians, who worship beasts.  But
you are worse, who give your gods the forms of men and let
them act like beasts.  Would you not get excited if an artist
made a statue of Romulus with an ass's head or the saintly
Numa with a dog's, or if a pig's form were inscribed with the
name of Cato or of Marcus Cicero? [32]  There is a protest here
against the pollution of Roman men, falsely associated with
impossible gods.  Who is responsible?  The false and lying
bards, whom Plato rightly cast out of his Republic.  For all
that, the majesty of the ancient city survives.[33]

But there is a new empire in sight of which God is the sovereign,[34] *omnipotens imperator*.[35]  You taunt us with our
*novella religio*.  It *is* a new religion, since this is an age of
progress.  There has always been progress, ever since man rejected acorns for grain and abandoned his clothes of bark and
skins of beasts.  It is just as true of the arts of daily life, of gov-

[31] Take the deities mentioned by Varro that attended the growing boy in
the nursery — Edulia, Potina, Cuba, Ossipaga, Statanus, Abeona and Adeona,
Fabulinus. See *Founders*, p. 218.

[32] III 16: Quantas, inquam, irarum flammas suffunderent, excitarent, si
urbis conditor Romulus asinina staret in facie, si sanctus Pompilius in canina,
si porcina sub specie nomen esset Catonis aut Marci Ciceronis inscriptum?

[33] He calls the Romans *dominos rerum ac principes* (IV 1) and speaks of
Venus, with Lucretius in mind, as *Aeneadum matrem et Romanae domina-
tionis auctorem* (IV 27).

[34] II. 2-3.

[35] II 65.

ernment and of religion. You no longer deck the couches of
the gods for Saliarian feasts; [36] or slaughter only snow-white
bulls as offerings for your divinities, and certainly there are
no more human sacrifices nowadays.[37] This note of progress,
which has echoes of Lucretius, was caught up later by St. Ambrose and Prudentius, in their fight against the pagan conservatives of their day.[38]

What brought high-minded pagans of Arnobius' day to accept the new faith? One reason was the yearning for mysticism, purification, and immortality set forth in Oriental and
Egyptian rites and no less in Christianity. It was a ruling
passion of the age. They also became aware of the absurdities
of their own religious rites, especially when an Arnobius
with boundless learning and sarcasm pointed them out un-
mercifully. They saw also something pure, simple, honest,
convinced and brave in the Christian profession. They saw
a Divine Leader, more certain than the divinities of religion
and philosophy to whom they had turned in the past. All of
this was quite apart from magic, miracles, and theology. In
many cases, I can conceive, converts came primarily because
the ancient way appeared played out.

Arnobius did his part in speeding this process of conversion.
He is sometimes portrayed as a bitter sceptic and dismal pessimist. He can be as pessimistic as his master Lucretius when
he contemplates our drab humanity and man's foolish little
soul. He drinks the wormwood of Lucretius with no sugar on

[36] As we remember Horace's contemporaries did (*Odes* I 37. 1–4).
[37] II 66–69.
[38] Cf. Chapter II, note 111. Seneca makes an interesting point (in *Epist.
mor.* 90) in declaring that there has not been and cannot be any intellectual
progress in the history of inventions designed to make human life comfortable.
All that belongs to a lower sphere. Nothing counts but the intellectual life.
Mankind got on very well in the Golden Age, until monarchy changed to
tyranny and the age of inventions came in. Seneca is arguing against Posidonius
(and incidentally saving us at least the outlines of some treatise of his), who
recognized progress in the development of the mechanical arts (so Cicero,
*Tusc.* I 62), that is, as we should say, in the history of science. Seneca adopts
for his purpose the traditional idea of the Golden Age as a land flowing with
milk and honey and perpetual holiday. It symbolized to ordinary mortals
relief from toil — to Seneca, relief from "avarice." He philosophizes on the
theme on which Horace indulged in a little banter with his Virgil (*Odes* I 3).

the goblet's brim.  This is a wholesome draught for cheery evolutionists of our day or for those who delicately scratched the phrase "miserable sinners" from the latest American edition of the Book of Common Prayer.  But neither Lucretius nor Arnobius is ultimately pessimistic.  To the one, the imperfections of the world are but an incident in the perfect reign of matter and motion in an atomic universe.  To the other the blackness of the human heart fades before the cleansing light of Christ:

De profundis clamavi ad te.

A sceptic Arnobius is not; for nothing is clearer than his acceptance of the Christian faith, although he needed some instruction in theology.  His adaptation of Lucretius and of Plato for novel ends is skilfully performed; he is reconciling science and religion in his own way.  In the passage on progress and elsewhere he shows himself one of the greatest of Roman satirists in the vein of his Lucretius.

IV

With Arnobius's more famous pupil, Lactantius, we see the dawn of a new day breaking, and further progress in building Christian humanism into the structure of the Roman City of God.  His studies under his master and his profession as a rhetor were pursued in Africa, but the Emperor Diocletian gave him an appointment in Nicomedia in Bithynia.  He there was converted to the Christian faith.  He preserved a judicious silence during the persecution of Diocletian — or Galerius — in 303 A.D.[39]  At some time before the Edict of Tolerance, pronounced in 313 A.D., the greatest of Lactantius's works, the *Divinae Institutiones*, or "Training of the Christian," was written.  It is, partly, still an apology, but so broad is the scope of the work that it has rightly been proclaimed as the first systematic treatment of Christian faith and practice.

I will not stop to analyze its contents.[40]  I will emphasize

[39] Cf. Baynes, *Camb. Anc. Hist.*, XII p. 665.
[40] See *Founders*, pp. 54–62.

rather the atmosphere of hope and of a great deliverance that plays about this work. It bears a dedication to Constantine the Great.[41] The future emperor had not yet fought his way to the throne, but Lactantius may have singled him out as the victor, even as Virgil had found his final hero in Octavian before the latter's triumph.[42] Here, then, in Constantine is another Augustus, and with him the vision of an Ideal Empire has returned. Constantine, declares Lactantius, the first of Roman rulers to renounce error, will rule the world with justice once more and pass on to his sons the custody of the Roman name — *tutelam nominis Romani*. The phrase has an Augustan ring.

Here indeed is a different world from that of Arnobius. Curiously, Lactantius does not mention his master. The two differ greatly in temperament and in style. Arnobius's words rush out in crescendos. His favorite sentence is a question; he can have whole strings of them. The calm and reasonable Lactantius is master of his emotions and of his periods; he is the most Ciceronian of all the Christian Ciceros. Arnobius flourishes a bludgeon; Lactantius parries with a Damascus blade. Arnobius rushes into heresy impelled by his ingenious speculations; Lactantius glides into heresy unawares. Whether he omits his teacher's name intentionally or not, he had learned much from him. He is related to Arnobius as Cyprian to Tertullian.

It were hard to tell which scholar was better acquainted with the Classics of Greece and Rome. Lactantius of course wrote more and thus can make a larger display of his reading. Both certainly had read widely and read well, not omitting the author of the early Empire; for Fronto's restrictions no

[41] A translation of this impressive dedication is given in *Founders* (p. 50), with a note on its genuineness (p. 297). After the completion of the work Lactantius added another address to the Emperor, which is found in only two of the later manuscripts. Cf. Brandt's edition, p. 668.

[42] Or, since the son of Constantius Chlorus had by this time been made out to be the grandson of Claudius II, the proud *gens Claudia*, whose invincibility Horace had made Hannibal praise (*Odes* IV 4. 49–78), now had another scion on the Roman throne. So spoke the panegyricists of A.D. 310 and coins back up their language. See Magie *S.H.A.* III 178; Baynes *C.A.H.* XII 680.

longer hold at the end of the third century. We get from these two Christian writers a better picture of what was going on in the pagan schools of Africa than the accounts, or the works, of any of the pagans of that time can show. Lactantius has learned from Arnobius, or perhaps just by himself, how to make friends with the old authors. I will not repeat the long list of those to whom he refers.[43] He quotes them, he weaves their phrases into the context of his discourse. He thinks in their terms, and even when he refutes them, they linger in the background of his thought. Nor does he always refute them. They now and then supply fresh evidence for his point. In arguing on justice,[44] he backs his argument with the first two strophes of a very familiar ode of Horace:

Integer vitae scelerisque purus.

At the end of his work, in the vision of the final days of the world, the future reign of bliss, and the Last Judgment, a passage of no little eloquence and poetic feeling,[45] Lactantius calls suddenly on two pagan poets, neither of whom we should expect at that juncture. The one is Terence, with a line from his *Phormio*. With a touch of grim humor, the author tells sinners not to expect the dire discomforts anticipated by the slave Geta when his master gets back home —

molendum esse usque in pistrino, uapulandum, habendae
    compcdes,[46]

Grinding at the mill, getting floggings, wearing chains, —

no, not such unpleasantnesses are in store for the guilty, but rather the pangs of Hell.

The other unexpected poet is Lucretius. God the Father, Lactantius declares,[47] creator of the world from nothing, look-

---

[43] *Founders*, p. 52.

[44] *Div. Inst.* V 17 (18). 18.

[45] VII 27. 3.

[46] Ter. *Phorm.* 249. The presence of *usque* (unmetrical) shows that Lactantius used a manuscript of the Calliopian recension — an indication of the antiquity of that recension. Donatus was also acquainted with the reading *usque* (see W. L. Lindsay in his edition, *Script. Class. Bibl. Oxon.* 1926 *ad loc.*). It might well be read (v. Donatus) instead of *esse*.

[47] VII 27. 5–6.

ing down upon the wanderings of mankind, sent a guide to
open up to us the way of justice. Him let us all follow, to Him
give our devotion, since He alone, in the language of Lucretius, "cleansed the hearts of mankind by his words of
truth, and set an end to desire and to fear, and showed the
highest good to which we all are tending, and pointed out the
way, where, along a narrow path, in a straight course, we can
press on to it."

> veridicis hominum purgavit pectora dictis
> et finem statuit cuppedinis atque timoris
> exposuitque bonum summum quo tendimus omnes
> quid foret, atque viam monstravit limite parvo
> qua possemus ad id recto contendere cursu.[48]

Verily, this is a Lucretius come to judgment; yea, a Lucretius.
*Malgré lui*, he has been transformed into a prophet of Christ.
The pupil has gone further on the road that his master Arno-
bius laid out.

Among the old authors whom Lactantius knew with a special intimacy was naturally Cicero, who moulded his style and
helped to mould his thought. It is of particular interest to us
to note that one of the books most potent in this moulding
process was the *De Re Publica*, which, as we saw, not only
contains Cicero's own philosophy of the state but reproduces
that which young Scipio had learned from Polybius and
through Polybius and Panaetius from Plato. Lactantius is
our evidence that good old Republican doctrine still influenced thought in his day; and he, in turn, deserves our thanks
for quoting important sections of Cicero's work which are
not found in the old palimpsest fragments and which, therefore, but for him, would not be known to us today.[49] In some
places, while we may not be sure just where quotation ends
and interpretation begins, Lactantius's reflections may well
reproduce with sufficient accuracy the general context of Cicero's argument. Take the passage in which Cicero criticizes,

[48] *De Rer. Nat.* VI 24.
[49] See, for example, the passage cited in note 52. In some cases Lactantius is
giving the gist of Cicero's argument, or embroidering on it.

as Polybius and his pupil might well have criticized before
him, Plato's doctrine of social communism, including the
community of wives; for whether or not Plato may be somewhat jocose in the ideas to which his winged thought had
flown, Lactantius combats his reasonings, in an altogether
Ciceronian fashion, since they ill consort with the Roman
reverence for the family as an essential prop of the state.[50]

Of course Cicero must wear a winter garment of repentance
if he would enter Lactantius's Republic, the Roman city of
God. In discussing the ideas of justice, which for himself as
for Cicero and Plato is the foundation of government, Lactantius repeats in his own words the gist of the arguments of
Carneades, who, *via* the interlocutor Furius, appropriately
presents in the *De Re Publica* the same defence of injustice
that Thrasymachus had made in Plato's work.[51] Then, directly quoting Laelius's refutation of Carneades, he shows
where Laelius, too, along with Cicero and Plato, had fallen
short of the truth.[52] They labored well, but they had not the
right armor for defence, namely *pietas*, which means for
Lactantius the true knowledge of God, and *aequitas*, which
for him is not merely a legal term but an expression for the
equality of all men; [53] as we have seen, he finds Horace's
*Integer vitae* of use in presenting his argument. Of Plato he
says that he had dreamed God rather than known him —

[50] *De Re Publ.* IV 5 (Teubner ed. 1899, unfortunately omitted in Loeb) =
*Epitome* 33 (38) 1–5. This Epitome is not merely an abstract of the *Div. inst.*
but a summary statement of his arguments, often with new material. At the
beginning of the present passage Lactantius refers to Plato *quem deum philosophorum Tullius nominat*. Since it is not clear that Lactantius was profoundly versed in Greek, he probably drew heavily on Cicero for Plato's arguments on communism. He treats the same subject in *Div. Inst.* III 21–22.

[51] *De Re Publ.* III 19–21 = *Div. Inst.* V 16 (17). Cicero shows his originality
by matching Thrasymachus with Carneades. Plato's Thrasymachus is a delightfully human man of straw, especially when he perspires at the moment
of defeat (*Rep.* I 350 c–d). In assigning his part to Furius, who speaks in the
language of Carneades, Cicero recalls to the reader of his days the visit of
Carneades to Rome and its importance in the training of young Romans in
philosophy (see Chapter I, p. 18). Furius might have been in reality one of
the Roman youths who had imbibed a "realistic" philosophy from the clever
dialectician from abroad.

[52] *Div. Inst.* V 18 (19). 4–8.

[53] V 14 (15). 15.

*somniaverat enim Deum, non cognoverat.*[54] Whatever a Platonist of our times may think of this argument, it is plain that Lactantius, while unable to accept certain ultimate presuppositions of the pagans, treats their thought with respect.

In a similar passage, he quotes an eloquent passage [55] in which Cicero speaks of the true and eternal law the consciousness of which rules in all minds, spurring them to duty and guarding them from wrongdoing, that law which cannot be abrogated by either the senate or the people, which governs Athens as well as Rome, and indeed all peoples and all times, and which was proposed and established by God the master and ruler of all. Lactantius, though calling Cicero, after all, one who was far from the knowledge of the truth — *homo longe a veritatis notitia* — declares that he utters these words with a voice well-nigh divine, and inquires whether any Christian, though knowing, as he does, the sacraments of God, can write of His law as well as that.[56]

It would be most remunerating to examine all the quotations that Lactantius makes from Cicero's work *On the State,* considering of course not merely what editors of that work find germane for their purpose but enough of the content in Lactantius to show just what the citations meant to him.[57]

Even what I have cited will show, I hope, in what sense Lactantius may be called a Christian humanist, or, if one prefers, a humanistic Christian. I cannot attempt here any adequate discussion of humanism or to rush into that alluring domain where Werner Jaeger *suo iure* holds sway.[58] Let us try merely to think back to what Lactantius would feel about the matter. For a Christian like him, or any wholehearted Christian of his time, or any time, a new life had come to mankind with the presence of our Lord upon the

[54] *Ibid.* 13.
[55] *De Re Publ.* III 33 = *Div. Inst.* VI 8. 7–9.
[56] *Ibid.* 6, 10–12.
[57] Indeed this method might be more systematically followed in all editions of fragments of an ancient author's works, in case those fragments come to us, not on bits of parchment or papyrus, but as quotations embedded in some later author's work.
[58] See Chapter I, note 96.

earth, with His presence in the heart of His faithful, with His presence in the rite that made the Last Supper not a distant historic event but an immediate and perpetual reality.

No wonder that to some Christians then, and to some in later ages, or even to some of us today in certain moods, all human achievements in letters or in music or in art have seemed in comparison with that heavenly vision merely *parerga*, pastimes by the way. Lactantius, or any convert of his times, who had come from darkness into light

*puro e disposto a salire alle stelle*

had at the first a powerful feeling of revulsion; for the former things were passed away. In some, like Tertullian, that mood might lead to violent renunciations of the pagans and all their works, not without hard laughter and derision, yet with some glances backward in a gentler mood. In others, like St. Cyprian, the past was the past and called for no mention. The spirit of the antique culture had entered into his character. He had no time for either denunciation or further study of the ancient works; he labored to perfect a holy life, with meditations on the Holy Writ.

Again to others, Homer and Plato, Cicero and Virgil, had been so dear that they could not keep the door shut on them forever. They, and the whole program of the liberal arts, if shorn of false religion and false morals, could still be called upon to form the thinking powers and the tastes of the young. One could condemn the sin but not the sinner, retaining one's affection for so lovable a sinner, for instance, as Quintus Horatius Flaccus — or Lucretius, or Terence or Cicero — well, for them all.

Then dawns the thought that some have misconceived the ancient authors. The pagans spoke better than they knew. They now, as it were, baptized, can testify truly in the court of Christ. Thus far had Lactantius come on the paths of humanism; but some of the journey remains. For to us his interpretation of the old authors is charitably, or uncharitably, false. The art of allegory is attributed to them — ἀλληγορία

— veritably the art of making them say other things than they intended to. It was at least a courteous attitude towards pagan culture for those who had lived through the hostile reign of Galerius and were aware of the long tradition during which the Church suffered a state of persecution, either actually or potentially, according to the reigning emperor's will.[59] When once the empire had become Christian and when the last elements of intransigence had been absorbed, then could a scholar, certain of his faith, look back upon the ancient world, contemplate it in its own light, and without the need of sifting truth from error study each author's art and scope of thought for its own fruitfulness and for its own delight. To that stage Lactantius did not come; and so enough on humanism for now.

In the account of the Last Days given by Lactantius at the end of his works, one of the witnesses, Virgil, is invoked not to describe the tortures of Hell — though that he might have done — but to unroll a prophecy of the life to come. As Aeneas and the Sibyl had seen Anchises in the Elysian fields summon the centuries of Roman history to pass before them, so in Lactantius Virgil and the Sibyl — a late descendant of the Cumaean, with her oracles delivered in very late Greek verses — are bidden to foretell the life of the immortal human soul in purgatory and in heaven. Nor is Virgil's Fourth Eclogue less important than his Sixth Aeneid for this design.

"Then at the last," declares Lactantius, "shall come about those things that the poets say were done when Saturn ruled in his golden times." He then constructs from different lines of the Eclogue a picture in mosaic of the marvels of Virgil's Golden Age.[60]

By what right? some Christian contemporary might have asked. Some would say that all this is nothing but poetic fic-

---

[59] Baynes *C.A.H.* XII 655: "By the time of Trojan it had become established that the persistent avowal of Christianity carried as its consequences the penalty of death." The entire discussion of the persecution of the Christians is enlightening.

[60] *Div. Inst.* VII 24. 10–11. He welds together *Ecl.* IV 38–41, 28–30, 42–45, 21–22.

tion. But they, Lactantius insists, do not know whence the
poets took their imagery — *ignorantes unde illa poetae ac-
ceperint.*[61] These noble pagans of old had, in some shadowy
rumor, heard mention of the resurrection to come and of the
mystery of the divine sacrament. They could not quite perceive the truth. They saw through a glass darkly — but Christians saw face to face. Thus Lactantius was the first, at least
among Roman men of letters, so far as I can discover, to practise systematically that allegorical mode of interpreting the
Classics that dominated the Middle Ages. Moreover it is a
rare and subtle sort of allegory that he would make out in
Virgil and the rest. The old authors were not, like Dante,
fully aware of all four modes of meaning — literal, moral,
allegorical, and anagogical [62] — (luckily, we may say) — or
even of just two, the literal and the hidden or spiritual sense.
There was, however, beyond their own imaginings, some
higher sense of which they were not completely in command.
Once more, they spoke better than they knew. Like the
Pythian priestess they raved, not through Apollo's inspiration,
but by grace of the Holy Ghost. This view of poetry not as a
mere make-believe, but as an avenue, a darkly lighted avenue,
to truth is very rare, to the best of my knowledge, in later estimates of poetry throughout the Middle Ages. Ordinarily, one
would either note an allegory, that is, the real and spiritual
meaning, of which the poet was utterly unaware, or else call
his story a figment of the imagination. Thus John the Scot in
his commentary on Martianus Capella's *Marriage of Mercury
and Philology*, coming to a stretch of verse in that curious
work, notes simply: "These are poet's ravings and need no explanation." [63] How comforting for the expositor, especially
after wrestling with the ineluctable enigmas of Martianus's
text, to come to an oasis of poetry — *non ragionam di loro,
ma guarda e passa.* But what would Lactantius have said to
that?

[61] VII 22. 1.                                        [62] *Epist.* 13 (10). 7.
[63] *Annotationes in Marcianum* ed. Lutz, 20. 6 (p. 19): Poetica deliramenta
sunt . . . quapropter quoniam falsa sunt nulla indigent explanatione.

Lactantius, I take it, was also primarily responsible for the invention of a new form of poetry in which the spirit and the story were Christian and only the form was pagan. Thus Juvencus, in A.D. 330, six years after Constantine became Emperor in full right, converted the four Gospels into Virgilian hexameters — more impressively than one might imagine. Others continued in his wake; most skilful and poetical of all was Prudentius at the end of the century, who mastered all the metres, lyrical and epic, and what is more, had something poetic to say.[64] We cannot trace here the lengthy story of this wholesale baptism of pagan literature. We must not think that the new works were meant to replace the classics. They were intended primarily for pupils in the schools, who should not begin by feeding on the myths that their Christian masters had discarded. Juvencus illustrated the hexameter in a fashion theologically sound. In theology, Virgil led up to him; in art and in practice, he led up to Virgil.

One therefore sees the reason, or one reason, why the Emperor Constantine appointed Lactantius, now in his old age, as tutor for his son Crispus, and why it was that Lactantius may well have been behind the Emperor's famous speech, *Oratio ad Sanctos*, in which he expounded the hidden meaning of Virgil's Fourth Eclogue.[65] This was no display of Imperial exegesis, like the *Bibel und Babel* of his late Majesty Wilhelm II, but a state document of education. One has here, I should say, further evidence of the sincerity of Constantine's Christianity, to add to the powerful arguments of Mr. Baynes.[66] It also speaks for the eminence of Lactantius. He joins the ranks of the great teachers of emperors at whom we have been looking. Surely Rome stands foremost in the annals

[64] *Founders*, pp. 183–195, and on the new Christian epic, pp. 195–206. Also Chapter VII, note 33.

[65] *Ibid.* p. 273. The speech is preserved by Eusebius Pamphili, the noted church historian. He tells us that the Emperor's speeches, in Latin, were rendered into Greek by a staff of translators. He selects this *Oratio* as a specimen (*De vita Constantini* IV 3). The text is printed, after that of the *Vita*, in Migne, Patrol. Graec. XX 1231–1316.

[66] *C.A.H.* XII, Chapter XX and "Constantine the Great and the Christian Church," *Proc. Brit. Acad.* XV (1929).

of private tutoring. Rarely in recent times, at least, have private tutors had such pupils, or heads of state such private tutors.

We have then, in an ideal sense, a Christian Augustan Age, a Christian Ideal Empire, at the time that Lactantius, the new Cicero, was forming the ideals of Constantine and his son. Not that the world had become perfect, by any means. In fact it is the same black Age that Livy saw, at least when he was writing the preface to his histories. "These times of ours," Lactantius exclaims, "in which iniquity and malice have grown to their highest peak!": *nostra haec tempora, quibus iniquitas et malitia usque ad summum gradum crevit* — a *summa cum laude* for iniquity and malice.[67] Arnobius could not express a social pessimism more consummate — though he commanded a more vigorous choice of words. "But even this age," Lactantius proceeds, "is well-nigh golden in comparison with that to come." For learned men who had plotted the course of history declared that the final day was not far distant — somewhere within the next two hundred years.[68] But hold, there is one consolation, Lactantius adds. It follows of obvious necessity that the universal collapse cannot occur while stands the city of Rome — *incolumi urbe Roma*. These words echo those of Horace.[69] This is *urbs aeterna*, the prop of the world — *illa, illa est civitas quae sustentat omnia* — and when it falls, then shall we know that the end of all things is at hand. He summons up his courage to predict that day, for come it must.[70] But God grant that the ominous event may somehow be deferred.[71] The prayer of Roman Lactantius was answered in a way of which he could not dream; for the city still is standing.

[67] *Div. Inst.* VII 15. 7.
[68] *Ibid.* VII 25. 3–5.
[69] *Odes* III 5. 12.
[70] I have translated this eloquent passage in *Founders*, p. 62. Baynes *C.A.H.* XII 661: "Lactantius is not only a Christian, he is a Roman who shrinks in terror from the thought that one day according to the scripture of his religion the empire of Rome would pass, as had already passed the empires of Babylon and Alexander."
[71] VII 25. 8.

On the subsequent course of Christianity in the great fourth century, with its further absorptions of the best of pagan culture and the development of its own theology, we cannot further dwell. In view of the powerful influence of Cicero on its greatest men, Ambrose and Jerome and Augustine, I have been tempted to call it, so far as the West is concerned, the *aetas Ciceroniana*. I have broached this theme elsewhere,[72] and it richly deserves a thorough treatment by some younger scholar.

V

We come at last to the greatest name of all, St. Augustine. If I allow him only a tiny space in preference to Lactantius and Arnobius, it is because the significance of their work needs more emphasis, and much more still than I have given here, while all the world beholds, at least in its outlines, the towering eminence of St. Augustine.

Lactantius's prophecy of the downfall of Rome was fulfilled in an external sense just about a century after he wrote his *Divinae Institutiones*. In A.D. 410 Alaric the Goth captured the city and rode in triumph along the Sacred Way. The foes of the Church found their main charge against it only too spectacularly proved: Christianity had caused the ruin of the State. That crisis arouses Augustine to write the greatest of his works, greatest at least in its universal sweep, on the *City*, or *Commonwealth, of God, De Civitate Dei*; it is the outpouring of a philosophical and poetic mind determined to answer the ancient calumny once and for all and to build a new celestial Rome free from attack. He had achieved a similar purpose in a more picturesque and intimate fashion in his *Confessions*, in which he records his soul's ascent by the ladder of philosophy from the depths up to the peace of God — *inquietum est cor nostrum, donec requiescat in te*.[73]

The new work, *De Civitate Dei*, the fruit of his old age and

[72] *Founders*, p. 255.
[73] *Confessions* I 1. On the psychological as well as the philosophical importance of Augustine's Ciceronian dialogue *De Quantitate Animae*, see *Founders*, pp. 259–266.

of life-long meditation, with fourteen years devoted to its composition (A.D. 412–426), presents with imagination and high seriousness the essence of the Christian faith.[74] Augustine is the poet of the Church, as Plato is of Greek philosophy and Cicero is of the Roman Platonism of *Scipio's Dream.* All these poets write in prose, or what looks like prose on the printed page, until you read it.

As ever, Augustine's thought mounts ladders in its course, quick to pass from the Earthly City to the Celestial, quick to descend and quick to rise again. The first five books present his defence against the pagans. The earthly Rome had only itself to thank for its disaster. Then follow five books more in which he calls the history and the philosophy of the past to judgment. In the remaining twelve his thought is centered on the Christian faith, and like Lactantius he ends with the Last Judgment, Hell, and Paradise. Beyond these broad outlines there is not too rigid a system. Augustine's mind takes flights whenever, like Plato's mind, it is spurred by some novel or audacious thought to follow where it leads. The two cities are not separately built; throughout the work, the fabric of the one suggests its contrast in the other.

The *De Civitate Dei* has often been called a philosophy of history. That is a misnomer, if we have Hegel or Spengler in mind. We see here no general and philosophical principle, like thesis, antithesis, and synthesis, within which all the historical facts that an individual mind can master, or select, are arranged in a beautiful system, a mirror of the writer's thought, who thus creates the experience of mankind in his own image. Augustine, speaking of those who foretold one more persecution to succeed the traditional ten before the world came to an end, declares their views are thought out *exquisite et ingeniose,* but that these are prompted *non prophetico spiritu, sed coniectura mentis humanae,* which sometimes hits the truth and sometimes misses it.[75] A simple sort of philosophy of history, if such it may be called, had been

---

[74] For further details, see *Founders,* pp. 266–277.
[75] *De Civ. Dei* XVIII 52.

presented by the historian Florus, friend of the Emperor. Florus likens the Roman state to a human being, and marks the periods of infancy (*infantia*), boyhood (*adulescentia*), and young manhood (*iuventus*), or robust maturity (*robusta maturitas*); the latter period is attained in the age of Augustus, but it passes into senility in the century of his successors down to Trajan. With him, its youthful vigor is revived, and naturally flourishes unabated under Hadrian.[76] This is virtually the same reading of Roman history which, with one important difference, we have noted in Fronto [77] and to which Dante recurs in his panegyric on the heroes of Rome.[78]

But even this most simple and picturesque approach to a philosophy of history plays no part in Augustine's design. His aim, from the start, is merely to contrast the two commonwealths, the earthly, faulty, pagan city and the radiant City of God. He therefore presents a panorama of universal history. In the manner of the *Chronicles* of Eusebius, continued by St. Jerome, we find, in the earlier books, contemporaneous bits of the annals of Israel, Persia, Assyria, Greece, as well as Rome. Augustine makes Varro a constant companion, and Sallust, and Cicero, and no less Virgil; for to Augustine's poetic mind, Virgil has historical validity, since his thought is set on Ideal Empire. Among the rest, our old friend *De Re Publica* appears once. We owe to Augustine the same debt as to Lactantius for saving bits of Cicero's work that otherwise would have perished.[79] And we see that a hundred years after Lactantius, Cicero's analysis of the state still occupied the

[76] Hadrian was his friend. The two exchanged verses in a bantering spirit with one another. See *S.H.A. Hadr.* 16. 3–4. Lactantius sets forth Florus's historic scheme, but attributes it to Seneca (*Div. Inst.* VII 15: non inscite Romanae urbis tempora distribuit in aetates). Some have thought Lactantius was right in this attribution. See Brandt (ed. in *C.S.E.L.*) *ad loc.*

[77] Chapter V, note 55.

[78] *Convivio* IV 5. 80–104 (Moore). Dante traces the development of Roman History from childhood (*puerizia*) to the *maggiore adolescenza* of the republic to the hour of manhood when the first *principe sommo* (Caesar) appeared. Dante wisely says nothing of the old age of the Empire. The Roman state, by his theory, was ordained by God. For a fine exposition see W. H. V. Reade, "Dante's Vision of History," *Proc. Brit. Acad.* XXV (1939).

[79] He alludes to one passage from memory (*De Civ. Dei* XXII 6): Scio in libro Ciceronis tertio, nisi fallor, de re publica disputari nullum bellum

minds of cultivated men; indeed for both of these founders of Christian culture this majestic work is woven into the very tissue of their thought.[80] Its ultimate loss, therefore, was due not to Christian bigotry but to the inexplicable ravages of time.

For Cicero, Augustine of course had a deep respect. He could not forget the pagan sage whose essay, lost to us, on the value of philosophy had awakened in the young roisterer at Carthage a passion for serious thought.[81] Cicero is still to him that learned sage and prince of eloquence,[82] but he now does not hesitate to criticize him sharply. To take but two examples of Augustine's use of Cicero's work on the state, there is the famous demonstration that the Romans never had a *res publica* at all,[83] not a real *res populi*, if Cicero's definition holds. He calls a people an assemblage of a multitude associated by a common agreement on law and justice and by a common feeling of utility.[84] But how can there be any justice, Augustine asks, without a God to whom justice is referred? This criticism, as we saw, had been given by Lactantius, in a less striking form; [85] it is in line with Plato's discovery of the essence of the cardinal virtues in the world of ideas, and above all in the idea of the good; save that Augus-

---

suscipi a civitate optima nisi aut pro fide aut pro salute. For the meaning of *salus* he then quotes a passage, fairly long, found in another place (*alio loco*).

[80] Various Pagan writers have saved bits of the *De Re Publica* for us — such as Gellius, Nonius Marcellus, Servius — but they cite it merely for special points. But none of them, with the single exception of Ammianus Marcellinus, betray any appreciation of Cicero's thought. For that we go to Lactantius and St. Augustine.

[81] The Hortensius, an incentive (προτρεπτικός) to philosophy. On this and on the Ciceronian dialogues written at the period of his conversion to philosophy, see *Founders*, pp. 255–256. To cite one instance of his devotion to Cicero, the famous passage on God as the haven after the tumults of human thought (*De Beata Vita* I 1) is closely akin in spirit to Cicero's address to Philosophy as the harbor to which he had come after the storms of life (*Tusc. Disp.* V 5). All such harbors in ancient literature are explored by Campbell Bonner in his "Desired Haven," *Harv. Theol. Rev.* XXXIV (1941) 49–67.

[82] *De Civ. Dei* XXII 6: unus e numero doctissimorum hominum idemque doctissimus omnium Marcus Tullius Cicero.

[83] *Ibid.* XIX 21.

[84] *Ibid.* 24: Populus est coetus multitudinis rationalis rerum quas diligit concordi communione sociatus.

[85] Notes 53, 54.

tine centres these ideas in the Divine Person that embraces them.  Augustine proceeds to construct for the old Romans a more satisfactory definition of their community, in which the element of justice is left out.  In that sense they may have their Republic after all.  There is sarcasm in this courtesy, with the implication that Cicero had been dreaming of an ideal Republic, but knew not the way that leads to it.[86]

Again Augustine is concerned about the deification of Romulus.  It differs from that of the emperors, in which there is no danger to the Christian faith; for that was a mere mode of flattery, not a grave error that impinges on the truth.  Romulus was the only god the Romans ever really made.[87]  But Cicero had erred in seeking a proof of the true divinity of Romulus from the fact that his contemporaries lived at a stage in the world's history when men had long since become civilized; they must therefore have had good reason for accepting his godhead.[88]  A curious theory, this, for Cicero, thinks Augustine; for only Rome — not cultivated Greece — accepted the divinity of Romulus, and Rome was primitive enough at the time.[89]  The Romans deified their founder, Augustine

[86] The polity of Rome is no better than that of Greeks, Aegyptians and Assyrians: Generaliter quippe civitas impiorum, cui non imperat Deus oboedienti sibi, ut sacrificium non offerat nisi tantummodo sibi et per hoc in illa et animus corpori ratioque vitiis recte ac fideliter imperet, caret iustitise veritate (XIX 24).

[87] *De Civ. Dei* XVIII 24: nec postea nisi adulando, non errando, factum est temporibus Caesarum.

[88] *Ibid.*: ut Cicero magnis Romuli laudibus tribuat quod non rudibus et indoctis temporibus, quando facile homines fallebantur, sed iam expolitis et eruditis meruit hos honores. See *De Re Publica* II 17–19. Here we have the text preserved in the old manuscript (see Chapter I, note 48). Augustine's citation is letter perfect.  Editors, therefore, feel safe in putting into the text of Cicero the end of the last sentence (missing in the manuscript) exactly in the form in which Augustine gives it to us (see Loeb edition, p. 128).

[89] *De Civ. Dei* XXII 6: Quis autem Romulum deum nisi Roma credidit, atque id parva et incipiens?  Cicero's line of reasoning does seem peculiar. Homer certainly preceded Romulus, but how many of the neighboring undesirables who fled to the Asylum were versed in Homer?  At the same time Cicero seems to have felt that the long line of Alban kings indicated a continuous development of civilization in the midst of which occurred the divine birth and the deification of Romulus.  The Roman, therefore, does not look back to the founding of the City as the primal origin of his history, appropriately enveloped in myth; it was rather an interruption of the course of Nature which the will of the gods had designed.  See Chapter VIII, notes 7, 8.

continues, not from any love of error, but from an error of love. Christ, the founder of the celestial and eternal City, did not believe in God because through Him the City had its being, but rather it had to be founded because He believed in the being of God. Rome, already built and dedicated, worshipped its founder as a god in his temple; but our new Jerusalem placed its God Christ in the foundation of faith that it might be built and dedicated.[90] Thus has Augustine turned the traditional method of eponymous foundation upside down. He does not create, in the ancient style, an imaginary founder for a city whose early history is unknown. He begins with the Founder, even Christ, who built the eternal Rome anew as a City of God.

Roman history, along with Greek philosophy, has been thoroughly raked over in Augustine's work; the modes and causes of error have been mercilessly branded. Yet, just as we have noted in Arnobius and Lactantius, underneath is the implication that the Romans were better than their gods. It is in a magnificent passage from the *De Re Publica*, which Augustine has saved for us,[91] that Cicero repeats that "oracle," as he called it, of Ennius:

In men and ancient character the Roman State stands firm.

Moribus antiquis res stat Romana virisque.[92]

The light of this oracle is turned by Cicero on the blackness of his own times, when he declares: "By our own faults, not by some chance, we retain the republic in name, though the substance we have lost long ago."[93]

Here is the contrast between the actual and the ideal that

---

The attitude of Livy ("picture-book historian") is far more sceptical (I 16. 4, 8).

[90] *Ibid.*: Christus autem quamquam sit caelestis et aeternae conditor civitatis, non tamen eum quoniam ab illo condita est Deum credidit sed ideo potius est condenda quia credit. Roma conditorem suum iam constructa et dedicata tamquam deum coluit in templo; haec autem Hierusalem conditorem suum Deum Christum ut construi posset et dedicari, posuit in fidei fundamento.

[91] *De Civ Dei* II 21.

[92] *De Re Publ.* V 1. See Chapter I, note 133.

[93] *Ibid.* V. 2.

has led some scholars to surmise that Augustine may have taken his conception of a City of God from Cicero.[94] Not quite that, I should say; rather, he recognized in Cicero something germane to his own idea. He could ask Cicero with some asperity whether the Romans ever had a republic, and at the same time he could build the might of Roman men and character into the City of God.

With these few glimpses of Augustine's share in the building of the new City of God we shall have to be content. I have considered mainly the political foundations, for which he drew his material primarily from Cicero and above all from that magisterial work *De Re Publica*.[95] For the poetical and spiritual foundations, we shall come to him again, if all too briefly, in the next chapter. We must also examine more carefully the nature of the incorporation of Pagan culture into the Christian way of life. For the moment we may say with Lactantius, quoting his Cicero: "It is well. The foundations have been laid, as saith the illustrious orator [96] — *bene habet, iacta sunt fundamenta*." And to that Lactantius adds: "But we not only have laid the firm and suitable foundations for holding up the structure, but with large, strong beams have carried the whole building well nigh up to its top." [97]

[94] For discussions of this idea, see Schanz, *Gesch. der röm. Litt.* IV² (Munich 1920) § 1171. 2, p. 417).

[95] Significant is Augustine's unqualified praise of the younger Scipio, *morum optimorum maximaeque concordiae ille Romae Italiaeque liberator*, who fell a victim to the machinations of his political enemies. Augustine would not subscribe to the charge that he was plotting to establish himself as tyrant of the Roman state. Rather, *nullo illius urbis captus desiderio, ita ut iussisse perhibeatur ne saltem mortuo in ingrata patria fieret.* (*De Civ. Dei* III 21). Cicero was not the only pagan whom Augustine had studied with care. Varro, Sallust, and Seneca, among others, had furnished him with material for his judgment of ancient Rome. For a careful study of the ground that we have thus far traversed, the reader will find much of importance in the work of C. N. Cochrane, *Christianity and Classical Culture, a Study of Thought and Action from Augustus to Augustine*, Oxford, Clarendon Press, 1941. It is to be regretted that the Lowell Lectures delivered in 1930 by an eminent authority on St. Augustine, Professor George La Piana, have not yet been published.

[96] Cicero, *Pro Murena* 14: Bene habet: iacta sunt fundamenta defensionis. This phrase, picked up from a speech of no immediate significance for his theme and applied to it with a new meaning, is an indication that Lactantius had read widely in the works of Cicero.

[97] *Div. Inst.* VII 1: verum nos non solum fundamenta iecimus quae firma

Not quite to the top, we shall have to add, and never quite to the top, on this earth. But at least the foundation of the Roman City of God had been laid once and for all.

Meanwhile a curious situation confronts us. The Rome of Augustine was the ancient city on the banks of the Tiber, but the New Rome, whose presence Lactantius makes us feel, was the city of Constantine at Byzantium. What does this curious dichotomy mean in the history of ideas? We will examine its significance, as best we can, in the following chapter.

---

et idonea essent operi perferendo, sed magnis robustisque molibus aedificium totum paene usque ad summa perduximus.

# CHAPTER VII

# NEW ROME: EAST AND WEST

## I

WE are prone to two errors in our reading and appraisal of Greek and Latin literature. First, we are inclined to view the Greek and Roman masterpieces as pictures hung on the same museum wall. We look on this picture and on that and discover that the Roman art is palpably an imitation, garish in color, and cluttered with conflicting details, from which there should have been selected only what is appropriate for the design and what commands an unimpeded view from the Many to the One. This judgment is of course true. Neither Latin literature nor that of any other country displays the great simplicity of the best that Greece produced from Homer to Theocritus — a stretch of at least five hundred years.[1]

But we wrong all subsequent literatures in perpetuating this horizontal view. For that our schooling is partly to blame. We have our Homer and our Virgil on the same desk. We go to a Greek class at ten and a Latin at eleven. The two poets enter the same arena, and we are not slow to pick the winner. We modify our judgment when we have read enough of both the Greek and the Roman works to put them in their chronological order, to scan them vertically, to look on the contestants, not as wrestlers or boxers, but as the horsemen in the torch race made memorable by Plato and Lucretius, in which the torch was passed from one youth to the next as they sped on the course. So Werner Jaeger treats the humanism of the

---

[1] A super-enthusiastic eulogy of Roman literature is given by Augusto Rostagni, *La Letteratura di Roma republicana ed Augustea* (Istituto di studi Romani: Storia di Roma, XXIV), Bologna, 1939; the work is a product of the late Neo-Roman period in Italian history.

Greeks as it passed on through history. The Romans caught the torch, and from it lit their own.

The opposite error is to continue this vertical consideration of Greek and Roman culture after they had historically merged in one. From its earliest history, if we may believe the traditional accounts, Rome had turned to Greece for aid — aid from the Delphic oracle in times of stress or doubt,[2] aid from Greek lawgivers and makers of states when a change was contemplated in Roman government.[3] In the last half of the third century B.C. the rise of Roman literature, based in part on Greek models, induced a lively interest in all things Greek. That current towards Greek had been set in motion at least a half century before Polybius arrived and it flowed without ceasing straight down into the Empire.

This infiltration of Greek ideals into Rome is of course obvious in Latin literature. Not so the idea that the Roman state now had dominion over Greece. Dominant it was, ever since Corinth fell in 146 B.C., while Polybius and Scipio were yet alive. The Roman Empire had begun. But, curiously, one does not think of Athens and Sparta as dependencies of Rome, when one reads Cicero or Horace or Virgil. The might of empire, as they set it forth, is displayed on the frontiers, in the lands of Parthians and Medians, down by the undiscovered sources of the Nile, up in the icy regions of Germans and Hyperboreans. Greece seems, in Latin literature, like a fortified city that the current of invasion has swept around. That is because the great Roman authors were glad to admit the supremacy of Greek literature; the rude capturers bowed to the sway of captive Greece.

The universal sovereignty of Rome, in letters as in govern-

[2] The earliest recorded by Livy is the mission sent by Tarquin the Proud when disturbed by the omen of the serpent (I 56. 5); the latest mentioned in his pages is the visit paid by Aemilius Paulus, with young Scipio at his side (XLV 27. 6).

[3] The codification of the Laws of the Twelve Tables was effected c. 450 B.C. after a commission had studied systems of legislation elsewhere. So says Livy (III 31. 8), though modern histories of Rome suppress this suspicious assertion. Not knowing the arguments against it, I will merely raise a query whether the statesmen of Rome after some sixty years of experience with a growing democ-

ment, was first clearly and generally recognized, it would seem, in the reign of Hadrian. Trajan is a Roman of the old republican type. Hadrian is cosmopolitan, feeling himself at home in all parts of his domain, at Athens above all. The bilingualism of that day has a new flavor. A display of Greek letters on the part of a Roman like Cicero or Pliny is intended as a proof of elegance. But Suetonius, a younger friend of Pliny, became court secretary to Hadrian and writes in Greek or Latin as he will because both languages are serviceable media. By Hadrian's time, therefore, we may speak, I believe, of one world literature, namely Roman, with two main varieties, one Latin and one Greek. Plutarch, a good Greek and a good Roman, marks the transition. Born at Chaeroneia in Boeotia, he knew Rome and its emperors from Nero to Hadrian.[4] His famous *Parallel Lives* are a mirror of that Ideal Augustan Empire that drew its strength from the *mores* of ancient times. Plutarch begins at the beginning with Romulus, whom he pairs with Theseus; next comes Numa, whose appropriate compeer is Lycurgus. All this is in line with the tradition that we have been following in Polybius, Cicero,

racy (the beginning of the Republic is assigned to *c.* 508 B.C. by Rostovtzeff, Frank and others) might not have been intelligently curious enough to inquire how these things were ordered in Greece.

[4] According to Suidas (*Lexicon* ed. Ada Adler, Leipzig, Teubner, 1928–1938, Pars IV, 150. 27) Trajan appointed him a consul. But apart from the constitutional improbability of such an appointment, we may be more than suspicious of anything that Suidas has to say about Roman affairs. See notes 79, 80. John of Salisbury in the twelfth century had from some mysterious source learned of a treatise by Plutarch inscribed *Institutio Traiani*, prefaced by an *Epistola* addressed by Plutarch to Trajan (*Policraticus* ed. Webb, V 1–2, 539b–541b). It would be a pleasure to add Plutarch to the list of imperial tutors whose acquaintance we have made, especially since John also reports a tradition that Fronto (apparently our Fronto) was a grandson of Plutarch (*Pol.* VIII 19 792a). But the evidence is too dubious. However, Webb (*ad loc.*) inclines to the opinion of Wyttenbach that some ancient writer had composed a mosaic from various of Plutarch's works, with some extra touches, and that a translation of this work had somehow reached John of Salisbury. At any rate, the "institution" of the Prince, as described by John, tallies well enough with that of Plutarch (see note 5), save that John increases the religious emphasis. The four principles, according to him, that Plutarch would inculcate in his monarch are reverence before God, self-schooling, the training of his staff and of the aristocracy, affection for his people and the protection of their welfare (reverentiam Dei, cultum sui, disciplinam officialium et potestatum, affectum et protectionem subditorum). See note 130.

and Livy, just as Plutarch's discourse on government in the *Moralia* [5] is still of the ancient pattern.

Plutarch wrote only in Greek. In the reigns of Antoninus Pius and Marcus Aurelius, several writers of note were equally facile in both languages. There is Apuleius, Platonist, mystic, satirist, creator of one of the world's best romances and of a highly colored style appropriate for romance. He is as much Greek in feeling as Roman and as much Oriental as Greek. He was equally at home in Rome and in Athens and in his native Carthage. He wrote in Greek as well as Latin, poetry as well as prose. Only his Latin prose works have survived. Suppose it had been the other way round. Suppose we had only his Greek poetry. If that was as good as his Latin prose, would not the critics regard it as typical of the free spirit of Hellas, in contrast to the rigid formalism of Rome? Or what if he had happened to choose Greek for his *Metamorphoses*? There is new life there.[6] So is there in that gorgeously romantic poem, *Pervigilium Veneris*, "Keeping the Watch with Venus," which, whenever it was written, shows the spirit of Apuleius in verse.[7] Then there is Tertullian, who wrote in Greek as well as Latin. Had his seven books on Ecstasy (*De Ecstasi*),[8] written when the Paraclete was revealing new and startling visions to him, been preserved, and all his Latin works had

[5] 826 A. Περὶ Μοναρχίας καὶ Δημοκρατίας καὶ Ὀλιγαρχίας (*De Unius in Republica Dominatione* (H. N. Fowler, Loeb, X (1936), 305. The treatise is defective at both beginning and end. Herodotus (§ 3) and Plato (§ 4) are cited and the whole fragment breathes Polybius. The emphasis is on monarchy, but enough is said of harmony in diversity (§ 4) to indicate that the ultimate doctrine is Polybian. Highly instructive is the treatise Πολιτικὰ Παραγγέλματα (*Praecepta gerendae reipublicae*, Loeb, X, p. 158). Pending the completion of the Loeb edition (to be in fourteen volumes) the reader may turn with profit to the translation of *Plutarch's Morals*, published by Goodwin in 1870. Emerson concludes his sage and scholarly introduction to this work with the prophecy: "And thus Plutarch will be perpetually rediscovered from time to time as long as books last."

[6] *C.A.H.* XII 579–584.

[7] *Ibid.* pp. 586–588 (bibliography, p. 781) including the articles cited in List of Books. I still feel that, whatever the date finally assigned to this poem, Pater and Mackail (*Lat. Lit.*, p. 243 — though this may not be his latest view) were instinctively right in associating this poem, in style and spirit, with the age of Apuleius.

[8] *C.A.H.* XII 591.

perished, would he be classed with the legalistic theologians of Rome? And, perhaps most striking of all, the Emperor himself, Marcus Aurelius, Roman of the Romans, and yet fulfilling Plato's dream of a king turned philosopher, though not of the stripe that Plato had in mind — Marcus Aurelius wrote his masterpiece in Greek. But now, thanks to certain resuscitated fragments of parchment, containing the letters of Fronto, we have seen that, with his tutor's help, he had first perfected himself in Roman oratory.[9]

Such literary works as those that I have mentioned do not indicate a "Decline and Fall." Instead, they enlarge our preconceptions of the spirit of Rome, of the new Rome, which gained in vigor and in comprehensiveness not merely from the Christian faith, but in a wider sense, from the East. Intangible foundations were being laid, long before Constantine, which made his choice of a new capital at Byzantium not merely a shrewd political move, which Julius Caesar had anticipated in thought, but the outward and visible sign of a change in the spiritual habits of mankind.

## II

Whether or not Constantine applied the term "New Rome" to the new capital of the Empire at Byzantium,[10] which he rechristened with his own name, he certainly thought of the city as Roman. He bore the title of Augustus conferred on him by the Senate,[11] and by Lactantius who perhaps had thought of it first. The new Emperor had come to reëstablish the best of old Rome and to unite it with the living force of Christianity, whose emblem he inscribed on his standards to help him in the hour of need;[12] his profession of the new

---

[9] Chapter V, note 36.
[10] Baynes *C.A.H.* XII 697.
[11] *Ibid.* p. 685.
[12] The origin and resulting form of the *labarum* has been much discussed. See Baynes *C.A.H.* XII 683. I am indebted to A. D. Nock for references to A. B. Cook, *Zeus* (Cambridge University Press, 1925), p. 601, and especially to Alföldi's article "Hoc signo victor eris," pp. 1–18. The most important contemporary statement is that of Lactantius, *De Mort. Pers.* 44. 5. It may be that an ancient military symbol, whatever it was, was metamorphosed into the

faith was sincere.[13] There rested on him, perforce, something
of the aura of the old Imperial divinity, a legacy from his
pagan predecessors. Though of course his worship was not
sanctioned, like theirs, he was in a sense, as an heir of Augustus, God's temporal vicegerent upon earth. He was furthermore the father of his people, in that best form of kingdom
that Plato and Polybius and Cicero had described.[14] For over
a thousand years the new Roman empire lasted. Its citizens
were 'Ρωμαῖοι; and even today the word for "modern Greek"
is 'ρωμαίικα. This is an astounding conservatism for Hellas;
somehow it had become inoculated with Rome.

When does the Byzantine period in literature and art and
history begin? The date of Constantine's accession in A.D. 324
appeals with considerable reason to some historians.[15] Yet
others, with no less reason, would wait till the separation of
East and West. For under Constantine they were still united
in the new Christian Rome. A dramatic date is A.D. 529, when
Justinian I closed the schools of philosophy in Athens and
their masters fled to the sympathetic court of Chosroes I, the
King of Persia. Others would argue for a still later date. We
find the same difficulty in delimiting the Middle Ages in the
West.[16] In both cases we may be helped by forgetting exact
chronology. In both cases we know what we mean, or think
we do, by the terms Byzantine and Mediaeval. We may help
ourselves, perhaps, by thinking of the growth of a tree, and
of the seed whence it sprang. The seed is definite; it is the
Gospel of our Lord. The branches and their offshoots are
less definite. From one of them, Byzantine culture flowered;

---

Greek letters X and P, abbreviation for Χριστός. At the same time, Lactantius's
words seem plain enough: fecit ut iussus est et transversa X littera summo
capite circumflexo Christum in scutis notat. That is, he took the letter X,
tipped it around till it assumed the form of the Cross, +, and then curved
the top of the upright shaft so that it formed a P, a symbol both of the Cross
and of the name of our Lord.

[13] It was incidentally a sensible political move, but that does not explain
the mind of Constantine. He was as wise as a political serpent and as harmless as a Christian dove.

[14] Chapter I, note 55.

[15] E.g. Krumbacher, in his standard work, p. 2.

[16] See *Mediaeval Pattern of Life*, p. 63.

from another came that of the West. Both are parts of the Christian tree engrafted with scions from the fruitful stock of Greece and Rome.

Curious misconceptions of Byzantine civilization still prevail. We hear of its frozen fixity, its hieratic dogmatism, its autocratic bureaucracy, and of little else. An easy cure for this delusion is a cursory examination of Byzantine art.[17] Some study of art is necessary for the understanding of the literature of any country. The sight of the Duomo and the Baptistery at Florence gives us a new intimacy with Dante, or a walk about San Lorenzo and its library makes us turn to the sonnets of Michelangelo. Or, conversely, to form a picture of Dr. Johnson standing in the portal of Notre Dame de Chartres or on the steps of the Parthenon is to put a merciless strain on the imagination. Art and literature grow together and are mutually interpretative. And art sometimes can confirm in a flash what only after a long study we have learned from literature.

If I have made only a mention of Roman art thus far,[18] it is not that I am unaware of its importance. When the Apollo of Veii, a work of the sixth century B.C., was discovered not many years ago, what light was suddenly cast on the possibilities of culture in the early Roman Republic! Nor is this statue, most skilfully wrought in terra cotta, the only relic of its kind.[19] A line of such monuments, which we can inspect in the Museo di Villa Giulia, some earlier, some later than this Apollo, testifies to the continuity of a religious art, foreign in origin, which had come to be a part of Roman life. Again, when we look at the reliefs on the *Ara Pacis*, how much we learn of the nature of the government of Augustus, who appears not as a monarch enthroned but as a citizen, *princeps inter pares*, making sacrifice to the gods of Rome. And how intelligible, all of a sudden, becomes Horace's great Secular Hymn, written eight years before but showing scenes and

---

[17] *Crede experto*; a cursory examination is all to which I can lay claim.

[18] See the Preface to this book and List of Books, pp. 291–292.

[19] For a popular article by an expert, see C. D. Curtis in *Art and Archaeology* IX (1920) 275–277.

setting forth a spirit later to be carved on this Altar of Peace.[20] Then the Roman portrait busts of the Republic; Roman temples, theatres, aqueducts of a later date; Roman basilicas, triumphal arches, and monuments, like the majestic Trophy of Augustus placed in a beautiful site at La Turbie and recently restored by the generosity and the vision of a great American;[21] then the statues and busts of Caesar and Cicero and Augustus and all the later emperors; the houses and their equipments and all the monuments of Roman life, public and private, at Pompeii and Ostia; the frescos of the House of Livia or those of the Villa Madama that inspired artists of the Italian Renaissance — all these are vitally important in the building of Rome, and to present them all, in any adequate fashion, would have left us no time for our present quest.[22]

The inherent life of Byzantine art was first revealed to me not many years ago when Mr. Thomas Whittemore presented to us the results of his excavations, or rather exlavations, at Saint Sophia, one of the great monuments of the reign of Justinian I in the sixth century of our era, and one of the most magnificent churches of all Christendom.[23] The mosaics that he showed us in their original state were added in the reign of Basil I, founder of the Macedonian Dynasty at the end of the ninth century, or in that of his successor Leo VI.[24]

[20] Virgil, of course, no less than Horace, is carved into the *Ara Pacis*. See Eugénie Strong, *C.A.H.* X 518–550 and Lily R. Taylor, *Div. Rom. Emp.* pp. 177–179.

[21] Edward Tuck. See Ph. Casimir, *Le Trophée d'Auguste à la Turbie*, Marseille, Tacussel, 1932. The monument, one of the most splendid of the Augustan Age, was erected in b.c. 5 in honor of the Emperor and the successive conquests of b.c. 25, 16, and 15. With its art and its long inscription, it put in stone what Horace had already immortalized in verse (*Odes* IV) just as the *Ara Pacis* symbolized the spirit of the *Carmen Saeculare* and of the work of Virgil to which Horace had rendered due homage in that hymn. The restoration of the trophy at La Turbie (once *Tropaea Augusti*) was formally commemorated on April 26, 1934 (see the Paris edition of the *Chicago Daily Tribune*, April 23, 1934). See also *London Times*, April 19, 1934, pp. 17–18, and *Revue Internationale de l'Enseignement*, LXXXVIII (1934), 193–199.

[22] I would once more invite the reader's attention to Grant Showerman's *Eternal Rome*.

[23] See his work *The Mosaics of Saint Sophia at Istanbul*, Paris (Oxford Univ. Press for the Byzantine Institute), 1933, 1936.

[24] *E.g. ibid.* Pl. XII (mosaic in the narthex). Its original condition is shown in Diehl, *Peinture Byzantin*, Pl. XXII.

It was the eyes of the figures that especially attracted attention. The faces recalled those of Pompeian paintings, but they shone with a new life. Throughout Byzantine art, however rigid the figure may be, the eyes are alive and impart a kind of motion to an immobile body; [25] there is something most modern and realistic and yet strangely romantic, with a nineteenth-century romanticism, in some of these faces — a wild assertion, the reader may think; but if he will turn to some of the examples, he will recognize, I believe, the quality that I have in mind.[26] There is, further, in all periods of Byzantine art, a saintly majesty in the figures of emperors and an imperial dignity in the figures of saints, in keeping with the ancient conception of the divinity that doth hedge an emperor and that passed over to Constantine and his successors, only that in them this divinity was at once ennobled and humbled, since they were not gods, but the vicars of Christ.[27]

There is also in Byzantine art more of the utter sense of awe, of religious adoration before some unspeakable mystery, than I have noted in the art of the West. We see it there in the Annunciation by Botticelli, or, if not by Botticelli, then by one of his school who possessed the sense of awe. We see it supremely in Giotto, as in the frescos in the chapel of Our Lady of the Arena at Padua, which I had the rare privilege of studying all alone one golden morning many years ago. But in the Byzantine mosaics, frescos and manuscript illuminations, we find it all the way along.[28]

[25] Diehl, Pl. VIII (St. Vitalis at Ravenna, 6th century); Pl. LVIII a (ikon at the Cathedral of the Dormition, Moscow, 12–13th century); Pl. XLVIII (Baptistery of San Marco, Venice, 14th century).

[26] See Diehl, Plates LXXVIII–XC, taken from pictures in various manuscripts ranging from the tenth through the fourteenth centuries. An excellent specimen is found in a thirteenth-century manuscript of the Gospels at the Pierpont Morgan Library (M. 340, fol. 5$^v$) in New York; the picture is of St. Matthew.

[27] The saintliness of an Emperor may be observed in the figure of Justinian, and those of his *cortège*, in the sixth-century mosaic of the choir of St. Vitalis at Ravenna (Diehl Pl. IX). The imperial dignity of a saint appears in the figure of St. Demetrius in an early seventh-century mosaic at the Church of St. Demetrius at Salonica (Diehl Pl. XIII). So stately is the bearing of the Saint that even the nobility of his legs is apparent, covered though they are by his long robe.

[28] For a few examples, cf. the fresco of the Angel of the Annunciation at

Nor are humor and the comedy of daily life neglected in Byzantine art. For these we must turn chiefly to the manuscripts, some of which we may inspect without going abroad. In the Pierpont Morgan Library at New York, there are two Gospel Lectionaries, both written and adorned with pictures and illuminations towards the end of the eleventh century or the beginning of the twelfth. They both are in an elegant minuscule script, not by the same hand, but, if I mistake not, from the same atelier. They show a font of initial letters of an elaborate design, done in gold and in colors so vivid that they seem like jewels set into the page.[29] In one of these books there is a set of superb little pictures, some of them showing that sense of awe and that latent motion in stationary figures of which I have spoken.[30] There is also a little comic scene. The paralytic, healed, walks jubilantly with his bed upon his back towards a Pharisee, who surveys him superbly, knowing better than to accept the testimony of his eyes. A figure marked "a Jew," one of the common herd, is running excitedly towards a Sadducee, who turns away with bored indifference. The unknown artist has made from the Gospel miracle a little human comedy.[31]

The Empire of Byzantium abruptly ends with A.D. 1453, when Constantinople fell before the Turks. Not so Byzantine art. Long years before, the humanizing influence of Byzantium had spread abroad among neighboring peoples, some of them at times its bitter foes — Bulgars and Serbs and Rus-

Santa Maria Antica (7th century, Diehl Pl. XVII c), the painting of the Adoration of the Magi at Toquale Kilissé, Cappadocia (10th century, Pl. XX 6), the mosaic of the Dormition of the Blessed Virgin at Kahrié-Djami, Constantinople (beginning of 14th century, Pl. XL b). And in ikons of all the periods and in various countries, e.g. one of the Harrowing of Hell in the Museum at Leningrad (beginning of the 15th century, Pl. XCVI a).

[29] MS Greek 647, saec. XI/XII and 639 saec. XI/XII.

[30] MS 639, foll. 268ᵛ (the treacherous kiss of Judas), 271ᵛ (St. Peter as the cock crows), 280ʳ (the Deposition), 323ʳ (the Dormition).

[31] Fol. 19ᵛ. I have spoken of the Pierpont Morgan Library. Let me add a word on the small but priceless and growing collection of Byzantine work of art preserved at the beautiful estate of Dumbarton Oaks in Washington, now, through the generosity of its owners, a part of Harvard University, with its program of research mapped out and supervised by Wilhelm Köhler. I venture to predict that when the war is over, many a student will find profit and excitement in the rediscovery of Byzantium at Dumbarton Oaks.

sians. Splendid examples of Byzantine art remain today at Kiev, and holy ikons, Byzantine in their ultimate origin, are today, despite the new ideology of Russia, venerated in many a Russian home.

### III

Now, with this art fresh in mind, let us take a glance at certain episodes in Byzantine history of immediate importance for our present theme.[32] First of all, I should like, without even attempting an outline of that history, to suggest that it was not the prime mission of Byzantium to keep the Greek mind in cold storage for a thousand years; it is rather that the minds of a long line of critics of Byzantium have been in cold storage, each reverently preserving the frigidity of his predecessor. For myself, needless to say, I am speaking merely as an amateur, anxious to learn.

My second purpose is to bewail, with all possible vehemence, the tragic separation of East and West. And here two grievous rents in a once seemly and harmonious mantle may be deplored: the schism of the Christian Church and the disruption of the united culture of Greece and of Rome.

In the great fourth century, there is no break in the Roman Empire, from Constantine through to Theodosius, despite the effort of Julian to dissolve Christianity. For, as the Christian poet Prudentius said in a great line, that Emperor, though a traitor to God, was no traitor to Rome:

perfidus ille Deo quamvis non perfidus urbi.[33]

[32] The standard work on Byzantine history — with due attention to literature and art — is the Russian work by A. A. Vasiliev, translated into English (University of Wisconsin, 1928–29) and with the author's later improvements into French — *Histoire de l'Empire Byzantin*, 1932.

[33] The remaining lines in the eulogy of Julian by this Christian poet who passed his boyhood during the reign of the Emperor are also notable: Principibus tamen e cunctis non defuit unus Me puero ut memini ductor fortissimus armis, Conditor et legum, celeberrimus ore manuque; Consultor patriae, sed non consultor habendae Religionis, amans tercentum milia divum: Perfidus ille deo quamvis non perfidus urbi (*Apoth.* 449–454). These lines have the ring of Lucan. They also show well the Virgilian elegance and the old Roman strength of the foremost master of the new Latin poetry. See Chapter VI, note 65.

That is the age of those monumental figures in theology and in Christian humanism, Basil and Gregory of Nyssa and Gregory of Nazianzus. In the next century, after the fall of Rome, confusion reigns in the West.

In the next, under Justinian (A.D. 527–565), there comes a turning point; for Greece and Rome proceed to go their separate ways again. That great ruler felt himself thoroughly a Roman, the heir of the old Emperor of Rome, even though the City, deep in the dust, had lost its ancient glory.[34] Roman administration prevails in the provinces, and Justinian, in his *Pandects* and *Digest*, codifies Roman Law in the Latin language, but most of his new laws, the *Novellae*, he adds in Greek. He was also most vigorously Christian and bent on unifying the factions of the Church. And here again he is Roman; for he gives to one alone among the Patriarchs the title of Pope and Apostolic Father and assigns to the seat of the Archbishop of Constantinople a high, but the second place after the Most Holy Apostolic See of ancient Rome.[35] And yet Justinian in the new abode of Empire could not be deaf to the call of the East. As has happily been said,[36] in his religious attitude he occupied the position of a Janus, looking East and West — a hard position for a human to maintain. The Age of Justinian, great in poetry with Romanos, great in art with Saint Sophia, had slipped away from its Roman moorings. The ship of Byzantium was sailing its own course.

Among Justinian's successors Heraclius was a good general and kept the Persians at bay. His death occurred in A.D. 641. For over a hundred years the Roman Empire of the East was in full vigor. In the West, the Dark Ages were well under way. The successor of Heraclius in 641, Constantine III, stopped the invasion of the Arabs in Anatolia and effected a truce with them in A.D. 659 — an achievement as important for

---

[34] Vasiliev *Empire Byzantin* I 179: "Rome devint, pour un temps, une ville de second ordre, ruinée, sans importance politique, et le pope la choisit pour s'y réfugier." Of course the fifth century had been full of strife between the Eastern Church and that of Rome, but the rift did not become patent until Justinian.

[35] *Ibid.* p. 197.                    [36] *Ibid.* p. 196.

the safety of Christianity as the victory of Charles Martel near Poitiers in A.D. 732; and Constantine III held off the Bulgars in the north. These were strong monarchs who did much for the preservation and unification of the Empire. They were succeeded by the megalomaniac Justinian II, who stirred up dissensions again. He was dethroned and exiled after slices were taken from his tongue and his nose; [37] the second of his unhappy reigns terminated in A.D. 711, the very year when the Arabs had worked round into Spain.[38]

There then followed what might seem to some another dark and barbarous age, the age of Iconoclasm under the Isaurian emperors. Nobody likes to see beautiful symbols of veneration smashed by bigots or barbarians; but the Isaurians Leo III, Constantine V, Leo IV, were neither barbarians nor bigots. They were good rulers and protected the empire from assault. In a brief interlude under the cruel and selfish Queen Irene (A.D. 780–802), who ruled for her young son Constantine VI — conveniently putting his eyes out — the cult of images was temporarily favored, but not finally restored till the reign of Michael III in A.D. 843.[39]

That was a long time for Iconoclasm to prevail — over a century in all. Contrast the brief period of image-smashing in the war between Protestants and Catholics in the sixteenth century and the few years when churches as well as images were demolished during the French Revolution. There was some deeper policy, some deeper conviction, behind the ancient Iconoclasm. It was not an attack on the established religion; it may have been a protest against idolatry. So it would seem to Protestants of the sixteenth century, and to some

[37] Hence his agnomen of Rhinotmetos, in which he did not especially rejoice. Vasiliev remarks (I 256, note 2) that the tongue was cut "pas si complètement qu'il ne pût continuer à parler." If enough of his utterances had been preserved one might note a preference of the Attic style in his Glossotmetic Period.

[38] At least we may say that in his second reign this unfortunate monarch endeavored to strengthen the relations between the Eastern church and that of Rome, which he had done his best to disrupt during his first reign. But too late. (Vasiliev I 297–298.) In literature and in art the period from 610 to 717 was "la plus sombre" in all Byzantine history (ibid., p. 304).

[39] On Irene see Vasiliev I 312–313.

Protestants today; and support for that view may be gathered from some of the early writers of the Church in their attacks on pagan idolatry.[40] Again, the Emperors may have had some regard for the views of Jews and Arabs, to both of whom this fabrication of divine images was anathema; perhaps the Emperors sought to make the conversion of these races less difficult.

Another reason has lately been set forth with no little persuasiveness.[41] The opponents of the Emperors like the great theologian John of Damascus, who wrote his tracts in the second quarter of the eighth century, had appealed to the doctrine of the Incarnation as warrant for human representations of Him who was both God and man, and of the sainted persons associated with Him. To the Isaurian Emperors even that might have seemed blasphemy of the Most High; and furthermore, while holding all the tenets of the Faith, they regarded themselves as vicegerents of God upon earth; the odor of pagan imperial divinity clings to them still. Each in turn is the Pope of the Church with the Patriarchs subordinate to him; hence the expressive term nowadays applied to such a doctrine and such a policy — Caesaropapism.[42] The army supported the Emperors. The monks bitterly opposed them. The regular clergy wavered. Whatever the final analysis of its origin and its essence may be, Iconoclasm proved a powerful and workable doctrine for over a hundred years.

Its effect on art is of no little interest. Art did not stop. No churches were destroyed. But pictures must be restricted to the portraiture of human beings and human scenes. This secular imperial art was meant to replace religious art in the churches and public buildings and on coins. A broad field

---

[40] A paper read by Dr. Paul J. Alexander at a Byzantine seminary held at Dumbarton Oaks, Washington, in October 1941, on "The Theoretical Foundations of the Iconoclastic Controversy" is destined, let us hope, to be published before long as part of a book entitled "The Patriarch Nicephoros I of Constantinople (806–815) and his Writings."

[41] In the article by G. B. Ladner.

[42] *Ibid.* p. 149. "Iconoclasm was but an outgrowth and indeed the climax of the caesaropapistic theory and practice of the State, as represented by some of the most successful Byzantine emperors."

was thus opened which must have led to interesting developments in the scenes depicted in frescos and mosaics during the
long stretch of a hundred years. Alas, it all perished when
the Iconophiles came in again; the human art of the Icon-
oclasts was now itself iconoclazed.[43]

All things considered, the age of Iconoclasm is no decadent
or unprogressive age. The later stage, including the period of
reaction under Queen Irene, was weaker than the first. It occupied the years when the Carolingian Renaissance was in
full flower in the West. Communication between East and
West was by no means sundered; no Chinese wall prevented
the influence of the one from penetrating to the other, either
at this or at any later time. Queen Irene was not averse to the
marriage proposals of Charlemagne,[44] and that enlightened
Arab monarch, Haroun-al-Rashid, sent him an elephant.[45]
In 827 the Emperor Michael presented Louis the Pious with
a copy of the mystic work of Dionysius the Areopagite, St.
Paul's disciple.[46] We have learned to call the author Pseudo-
Dionysius, who wrote under the spell of the later Neo-platon-
ism. To the French of the ninth century the work came
straight from their spiritual patron Saint Denys. And the
myth became history, as myths sometimes do; for the treatise
on *The Celestial Hierarchy*, thanks to the translation by John
the Scot, proved a vital force in mediaeval mystic thought.
How powerfully do just these three incidents that I have
cited show that despite the wars of armies and theologies,
there was still the craving for a confederate humanity in the
"Middle Ages," East and West.

If we may regard the years from the death of Irene in A.D.
802 to that of Michael III in A.D. 867 as a tolerably insignificant period, if not notably one of decline, the ensuing Macedonian Dynasty of the ninth and tenth centuries (A.D. 867–
1025) is one of vigor and progress. The Emperors strength-

[43] *Ibid.* pp. 137–139.
[44] Vasiliev I 354–355.
[45] Einhard *Vita Karoli* 16. 3.
[46] See Dom M. Cappuyns, *Jean Scot Erigène* (Louvain and Paris, 1933),
p. 136.

ened their power. Theirs was still an absolute monarchy of the Caesaropapistic sort, which they found no difficulty in accommodating to the renewed cult of images. They perfected the imperial bureaucracy. They greatly enlarged the army. It was an age of economic activity, and prosperity. The new ecclesiastic mosaics and frescos, like those at St. Sophia to which I have alluded,[47] are of the highest order. There is also a revival of interest in the old Greek authors, both pagan and Christian.

From the death of the last emperor of the Macedonian line, Basil II, in A.D. 1025 till the accession of the Comneni in A.D. 1081, we have another of the static periods, succeeded by one of eminence in both literature and art. In A.D. 1204 occurred the Latin capture of Constantinople by Baldwin of Flanders, a sad by-product of the Fourth Crusade. That did not mean that the West had recovered New Rome. Baldwin did become emperor but found the throne a shaky seat. The Crusaders split the imperial domain into several Greek and Latin states, with a goodly share of the allotment to Venice. The Empire itself was unscathed. With Theodore Lascaris to guide it, it winged its way to Nicaea. After the house of Lascaris fell, Michael Palaeologus brought the Empire back to its ancient seat. He captured Constantinople in A.D. 1261, and there the dynasty he established ruled till the Turks came in A.D. 1453. That was the end of the New Rome of the East.

To illustrate the revival of the Greek authors in the age of the Macedonian rulers, I will single out Constantinos VII Porphyrogenitus (A.D. 912–959), since he, as I indicated in our opening chapter,[48] deserves our boundless thanks for saving what he did from Polybius's History, including that priceless story of young Scipio's education. The part from Polybius was only one item in the volumes of extracts that the Emperor prepared, partly with the help of his learned staff, on history, on agriculture, and on medicine. No merely pedantic curiosity prompted these collections; they served an imme-

[47] See note 24.
[48] Chapter I, note 7.

diate need. Alas, only a handful of these compilations has come down to us.

The series of excerpts in which those from Polybius are contained is preceded by a noble introduction written by the scholar who edited the work for his imperial master. Here is the gist of what he has to say.[49]

The Kings of old or their high-minded subjects, who were inured to toil but who knew the delights of a literary leisure, were afire with the love of letters and the passion for immortal fame. But the writing of history is an endless task, and since human character has a tendency to degenerate and men cease to take an interest in the records of the past and the pursuit of exact science, the knowledge of history becomes shadowed in oblivion. For the huge tomes of ancient authors give our modern readers a fright. Therefore our Emperor Constantine Porphyrogenitus, most orthodox and Christian of monarchs, with an eye for beauty and a keen sense of the practical, thought it a fine service for the general weal to make a collection of those books throughout the world that were packed with varied wisdom.[50] Then, to relieve the reader from too great a burden of boredom, he has selected the parts that would most surely rivet their attention by their attractive style and form their minds by their noble sentiments. There-

[49] Modern editors of Polybius naturally rescue these precious fragments from the Byzantine scrap heap and assign them, as well as may be, to their proper places in Polybius's work. But for the sake of that enlightened man Constantine VII Porphyrogenitus they should be studied in their context. See Chapter VII, note 58. A notable achievement is the critical edition of the *Excerpta Historica iussu Constantini Porphyrogeniti confecta*, 1903–1910. Here Polybius, of course, is one among many. It is still a pleasure, therefore, to turn to the early editions of Polybius, like that of the great Casaubon, where the introduction, which I have summarized, is followed by the excerpts from Polybius as given under the headings arranged by Constantine. A delightful affair is a translation by a French Benedictine, Dom Vincent Thuillier (Paris, Gandouin, 1727–30), with a military commentary by M. de Folard, Chevalier de l'Ordre Militaire de Saint Louis, Mestre de Camp d'Infanterie, with tactical diagrams. The frontispiece presents a medallion with a magnificent portrait of Claude le Blanc, Ministre et Sécrétaire d'État de la Guerre (and possibly a handsome contributor to the costs of printing). The work is pronounced "très-utile non seulement aux Officiers Généraux, mais même à tous ceux qui suivent le parti des armes." It is pleasant to think that Polybius was an I.D.R. for the soldiers of France in those days. It is a pity that young Louis XV was not fed with other portions of the *Histories*. There might have been no French Revolution if he had been.

[50] That is, I take it, he first assembled a collection of complete editions of the "best books." It is a pity that this library of manuscripts written in the tenth century or earlier has not come down to us in its entirety.

fore he has, from these varied excerpts, formed fifty-three treatises, in such a way that all fruitful lessons of history are included in them. The present treatise is the fiftieth in this collection, and it treats of *Virtue and Vice*.

There follow a list of the authors excerpted. In all there are twenty-seven. From antiquity come Herodotus, Thucydides, Xenophon, Polybius, Diodorus Siculus, Dionysius of Halicarnassus, Nicolas of Damascus, and, for Jewish history, Josephus. From the second century of our era, Appian, Arrian, and Cassius Dio; from the third, Herodian and Dexippus; from the fourth, Eusebius and Eunapius; from the fifth, Zosimus, Priskos, and Malchos; from the sixth, Malalas, Prokopios, Agathias, Menander Protektor, and Theophanes; from the seventh, John of Antioch and Theophylaktos Simokattes; from the eighth there are none; from the ninth, Nikephoros Patriarches and Georgios Monachus — a noble army of historians, ancient and modern, pagan and Christian, each with his morsels of virtue and vice for the spiritual sustenance of the gentle reader in the days of Constantine VII Porphyrogenitus. It is Livy's program for a moral reading of history with abundant examples of virtue and of vice exhibited on illustrious monuments.[51]

Others of the collections on history and government have a somewhat different purpose. When we see the titles "On Embassies," "On Military Strategy," "On Speeches made to Soldiers," "On Plots laid against Emperors," [52] we are suddenly aware that Constantine's historical lessons are intended not only for his subjects but, in a very special sense, for the ruler. He is constructing one of the familiar Mirrors of the Prince, an elaborate mirror, with a bibliography and laboratory practice provided — well, not so much a mirror as a shield. If all fifty-three of these vade-mecums were extant, we should behold the Emperor armed cap-a-pie. A Byzantine *Il Principe* would be before us, which we could add to the

[51] See Chapter II, note 36.

[52] For the complete list see Krumbacher, *Byz. Litt.* p. 259. Krumbacher's account of this remarkable man, an Augustus, a Maecenas, and a Livy in one, is admirable (pp. 252–264), and so is the brief sketch by Vasiliev, I, pp. 447–479.

ancient precursors of Machiavelli to whom I have already referred.[53] And yet these compilations were not solely for the
benefit of the Prince. They pointed the way up for those who
would ascend. They were good for anybody; for all members
of the state, high and low, had been moulded into an organism complex in its parts, simple in its one and indivisible
essence. Constantine could teach Hitler and Stalin lessons,
many lessons, in totalitarianism.

The same sense of tremendous, unshatterable unity meets
us in another work compiled for the Emperor. Scholars cite
it by a Latin title for convenience — De Caeremoniis — but
something like "Institutions" or "Ordinances" would better
express its significance.[54] Ceremonies are indeed described,
but the author is no mere aesthete, fond of fuss and feathers.
His purpose is "better to set forth the dignity of the Imperial
order of life, which has won the admiration both of our citizens and of those abroad," [55] and to hold up this splendor as
in a clear and newly polished mirror [56] to those who come
after, lest they forget.

The work has the strength of ancient Rome. The memory
of Constantine is kept alive by the holy office celebrated an-
nually for him, and the tombs of the emperors whose bodies
lie in the Church of the Holy Apostles are reverently designated.[57] Not only the call of the distant past but the sense of

[53] Chapter II, note 35.
[54] The title in the early editions is: Ἔκθεσις τῆς βασιλείου τάξεως (De Caeremoniis aulae Byzantinae). The inscription in the only manuscript (Leipzig
Rep. I 17) is: Κωνσταντίνου τοῦ φιλοχρίστου . . . σύνταγμά τι καὶ βασιλείου
σπουδῆς ὄντως ἄξιον ποίημα. This is adopted in the long-awaited edition by
A. Vogt (Les Belles Lettres, 1935). Here Σύνταγμα is translated "Traité," which
is one of its meanings. Possibly it also suggests "institution," "ordinance," or
"collection." Vogt's edition makes available, with improvements, part of the
material amassed in the monumental commentary by J. J. Reiske, Bonn, 1829
(repeated in Migne Patrologia Graeca 112). Since Vogt cites Reiske's pages in
the margin, I will make my references to R(eiske) and to M(igne).
[55] The undertaking is dear to the author (despite what others may say of
the superfluity) ἅτε διὰ τῆς ἐπαινετῆς τάξεως τῆς βασιλείου ἀρχῆς δεικνυμένης
κοσμιωτέρας καὶ πρὸς τὸ εὐσχημονέστερον ἀνατρεχούσης καὶ διὰ τοῦτο θαυμαστῆς
οὔσης ἔθνεσί τε καὶ ἡμετέροις. Praef. pp. 3–4 R, 73–76 M.
[56] Praef. p. 4 R 77 M: οἷόν τι κάτοπτρον διαυγὲς καὶ νεόσμηκτον.
[57] II 6 (532 R, 997 M); I 42 (642–649 R, 1189–1209 M).

living and regal presences would touch the hearts of the faithful as they walked from tomb to tomb. There lay Constantine the Great and Helen, Justinian and Theodora, Heraclius and Fabia. Some of the tombs had formerly rested in other churches, but they now were gathered under the shelter of the Holy Apostles. From one the remains of Constantine V, Copronymus or Cabalinus, had been torn out by Michael and Theodora [58] and the marble used for another structure. Another tomb of ill omen retained its occupant, the "filthy and accursed corpse of the Apostate Julian," yet suffered still to lie in a cylindrical sarcophagus, "of the color of porphyry, or Roman" —

> perfidus ille deo quamvis non perfidus orbi.

This is a Christian book. The Emperor is the head of the Church, but the State does not dictate religion. The Emperor is King in Christ the King Eternal. He is His Vicegerent upon earth. At the impressive celebration on Candlemas, he receives ($\delta\epsilon\chi\epsilon\tau\alpha\iota$) the Patriarch of Constantinople in due state, the service starts at his orders, he places the offertory on the altar, goes to his private oratory when the service begins and, when the Patriarch has been duly called by the proper assistants, the Emperor receives the sacred elements at his hands. The Emperor is above the Patriarch.[59] The splendor of this service and of those for Christmas and Easter and the other feasts of the Church must have been indescribably impressive. Ecclesiastical visitors from Italy, and other countries, who attended these offices must have felt like country cousins at a dinner of high society. Such rites are no device for bolstering up the power of Church and State; they emanate from that power itself. The Christian empire of which they are the outward and visible sign is like the tree described by Virgil, with its roots going as deep into the earth as its branches rise high

---

[58] Evidently Michael III, the Drunken (842–867), and his pious mother. It would seem that Theodora was mainly responsible for this act of purification.

[59] I 27. 6 (150–152 R, 385–389 M). It is almost as though the celebrant had become a server, or servant, serving His Majesty with the Bread and the Wine instead of dispensing them to him by the Divine Grace.

into the heavens.[60] Constantinople seems indeed the seat not only of the Roman Empire but of the Roman Church.

Other functions besides religious are described in Constantine's book of Ordinances — that on the election of an Emperor,[61] that on the promotion of a prefect,[62] and many more. Even the cutting of the hair of the Emperor's son has its due ritual.[63] These ceremonies are often attended by acclamations, or concerted cheers, an ancient practice going back to the early Roman Empire [64] and a most effective psychological device for strengthening loyalty, as in our national hymns.[65] Constantine's work is full of them. They touch the heart most

[60] *Georg.* II 290: Altior ac penitus terrae defigitur arbos, Aesculus in primis, quae quantum vertice ad auras Aetherias tantum radice in Tartara tendit.

[61] I 43 (217–225 R, 471–479 M).

[62] I 53 (265–268 R, 528–532 M).

[63] I 23 (620–622 R, 1153–1157 M). Of course this was a highly significant ceremony. The locks of the young prince were caught in a gold napkin. The high officials from the city and the provinces who were to receive portions of the locks held a long strip of cloth made up of different napkins sewn together. They tore it apart at the proper moment and wrapped each his portion in one of the napkins thus released. Reiske has an illuminating note on ancient, mediaeval, Oriental and more recent analogies; for instance when that attractive personage, Queen Christina of Sweden (who did more than anybody else to keep romance alive in the sixteenth century) abdicated the throne, her royal robe was torn in bits by the spectators, who of course were not incensed against royalty, but coveted precious souvenirs.

[64] Nero introduced the practice of rhythmic applause, which he had heard at Naples from certain Alexandrians recently arrived there, and formed an *école de claqueurs*, with five thousand young men as pupils, to learn the latest styles, "the Bee-buzz," "the Tile Style," "The Crockery" (bombos et imbrices et testas: Suet. *Nero* 20. 3). Acclamations abound in the lives of *S.H.A.*, and at first seem a suspicious sign of lateness. Since, however, the Senate of Trajan's day started the practice of having them entered in the *Acta Publica* and graven on bronze (Plin. *Paneg.* 75), we should not be surprised at even the most extravagant forms as reported for the following century.

[65] Acclamations seem less appropriate in formal democracies such as our own. "O President, live forever!" would come with ill grace from members of the party out of power. In Italy there is (or recently was) a conflict of appeals. In April, 1934, I saw "Viva il Duce!" most frequently displayed on walls or even on the columns of a Church portico. "Viva il Re!" was altogether secondary, while one little Church in Naples bravely had emblazoned itself with "Viva il Rè Cristo!" It is astonishing that the Germans, with their profound studies in history and psychology, have devised nothing more elaborate than "Heil Hitler!" I did witness a kind of ceremony at Coblenz in June, 1934, in which a gathering of men, women, youths, and children shouted in concert at a leader's bidding a series of moral maxims containing such words as *Stärke, Tapferkeit, Ewigkeit.* Perhaps something more Byzantine has been developed for the *Führer* by this time.

deeply when devotion to the Emperor is attended by devotion
to the Church. They are often antiphonal. The Imperial
functionary exclaims: "Christ conquers. Christ is king"
(Χριστὸς νικᾷ, Χριστὸς βασιλένει). The people shout in response: "Christ will protect the King" (Χριστὸς φυλάξει τὸν
βασιλέα).[66]

The people's games are not forgotten, in particular the races
at the Hippodrome. Two of the four ancient factions, the
Greens and the Blues, *Prasini* and *Veneti*, are still going
strong; but the Reds and the Whites, and Domitian's Purples
and Golds, have had their day.[67] Amusements are a part of
loyalty, and are accompanied by acclamations.[68] Then there
are sacred feasts — feasts after the sacrament, and merry affairs
they were. For Constantinople was very pagan, and very human, and very Catholic, in following up sincere devotion with
having a good time. Sweet is pleasure after piety. A Christmas dinner is described, the like of which you and I have
never seen. Besides the good fare, the very sumptuous fare,
there are musical entertainments, and dramatic shows.[69]

The world-wide importance of the Byzantine Empire is reflected in these rites and ceremonies. There are rites for the
reception of ambassadors, from Persia among the rest.[70] The
Ambassador from without observes a formal style of saluta-
tion on his arrival: the Bulgarian envoy asks with due respect,
"How fares the God-crowned King, the spiritual grandfather

[66] II 43 (649–651 R, 1209–1212 M). The Western Church had made quite
as elaborate a use of acclamations. For instance at a synod in Rome in A.D.
495 Pope Gelasius was thus acclaimed at the end of the session: "Hear, O
Christ: life to Gelasius!" (fifteen times). "Lord Peter, do you preserve him!"
(twelve times). "May you reach the years of him whose See you hold!" (seven
times). "We look upon you as the Vicar of Christ!" (eleven times). "We look
upon you as the Apostle Peter!" (six times). "May you reach the years of him
whose See you hold!" (thirty-seven times). See Ziegler's article on Gelasius,
p. 28.

[67] I 64 (284–293 R, 555–565 M).

[68] The Greens and the Blues seemed born for the purpose of antiphonal
acclamation, which mingled with the chant; for this the tones are sometimes
stated; see I 63 (280–284 R, 548–555 M). Our efforts at community singing
have something to learn from Byzantium.

[69] II 52. 4 (741–747 R, 1360–1371 M).

[70] I 88–89 (396–408 R, 720–741 M).

of our God-appointed ruler of Bulgaria? How fares our Imperial Queen?" The Logothete replies with similarly courteous questions.[71] There are forms for letters sent abroad. Highly significant is the proper address to the Pope of Rome: "In the name of the Father and of the Son and of the Holy Ghost. So-and-so and So-and-so Kings of the Romans (the Eastern Romans), believing in the same God, to So-and-so, the most Holy Pope of Rome, and our spiritual Father." [72] The same formula is to be used by the Patriarchs (he calls them also Popes),[73] except that the title of "Father" is not used. Thus, though there are several Popes, the Pope of Rome would seem to be accorded a special reverence.[74] Theologically the Eastern Church had been sundered from the West in A.D. 867,[75] but there was still room for correspondence couched in a respectful tone. Equally courteous formulas were used in letters to Persians and Moslems and Russians.[76] The Christian Empire of Constantinople commands the attention of the world. In wealth and splendor, refinement and majesty, the City of New Rome was the Paris of the Middle Ages.

[71] II 47 (680–686 R, 1256–1264 M). The old Roman *Augustus* is no longer the designation of the Emperor — it could hardly be for the Vicegerent of Christ — but the Empress is still Αὔγουστα, a happy compromise. Another Latin title surviving appears in the account of the rite mentioned in note 63 — πραιπόσιτος. There are others still. Old Rome is hard to weed out.

[72] II 48 (686 R, 1264 M): Εἰς τὸν πάπαν 'Ρώμης . . . ὁ δεῖνα καὶ δεῖνα πιστοὶ ἐν αὐτῷ τῷ Θεῷ βασιλεῖς 'Ρωμαίων πρὸς ὁ δεῖνα τὸν ἁγιώτατον πάπαν 'Ρώμης καὶ πνευματικὸν ἡμῶν πατέρα. Did the Pope of Rome smile wryly at receiving a missive from the Kings of the Romans?

[73] *Ibid.*

[74] At least this much remains of the usage of Justinian. See note 35.

[75] By the act of the council of Constantinople of that year in which the Roman Pope Nicholas I was excommunicated and the *filioque* in the Creed was declared heretical. Nicholas for his part excommunicated the Patriarch Photius, who in 869 was deposed in Constantinople in the presence of envoys from Rome. In 879 he was restored, and a virtual separation of the Churches was affected. Relations were not absolutely broken off and Photius was once more deposed in 886; but the rift was there. It became an impassable chasm in 1054. On the ecclesiastical part of the career of Photius, one of the greatest scholars of his age, see Vasiliev I 382–383, 436–439.

[76] II 48 (689 R, 1265 M).

## IV

I have just used an unfortunate term. For what is there mediaeval about Byzantine civilization? With the inevitable ups and downs and varied splendors it pursued an even course from Constantine the Great to the capture of the City in A.D. 1453. To be sure, the Western Middle Ages, if you will permit me what seems a wild Hibernian absurdity, were not mediaeval. Nobody then thought of himself as middling. John of Salisbury calls his contemporaries *moderni*, a word first used, to the best of my knowledge, by Cassiodorus or one of his contemporaries.[77] It seems to you and me peculiarly appropriate to ourselves, who know not what terrific classification will be applied to this our age by our descendants. The term "Middle Age" was invented by the Italian humanists, who had to characterize the Gothic wastes that intervened between the splendor of antiquity and their own. They did not apply it to Byzantium, whence the light of Greek literature was restored to them. Why not be satisfied with just "Byzantine"? Why when the West is afflicted with a misnomer should we extend it to the East? Perhaps some even more audacious spirit will invent a new term to designate the Western portion of the Christian Age.

It is high time for us, at any rate, to turn our thoughts to the West. The spirit of Rome had said goodbye to the banks of the Tiber, and against Juno's wishes, and Virgil's, and Horace's had built a new city not far from its ancestral Troy.[78] The plans of Julius Caesar had prevailed. But did nothing remain behind after that Ciceronian age of Ambrose, Jerome, and Augustine? Let us pick up those threads again, and in

[77] *E.g.* Cass. *Inst.* I 16 (in the impeccable edition of R. A. B. Mynors, Oxford, Clarendon Press, 1937, p. 32): Quod si in his quae dicta sunt aliqua fortasse loca dubia sunt relicta nec explanatione plenissima satisfacere potuerunt, nequaquam vobis modernos expositores interdico. This sentiment is echoed by John of Salisbury, *Metalog., Prolog.* 825 A (the reference fits both Webb and by his courtesy, Migne *Patr. Lat.* 199): Nec dedignatus sum modernorum proferre sententias, quos antiquis in plerisque preferre non dubito. Surely both Cassiodorus and John of Salisbury were up to date — and are.

[78] See Chapter II, note 100.

particular take another brief glance at Augustine's City of God in the light of the New Rome of the East.

First of all, I breathe an air of comfort in beholding the old Roman heroes once more. In the East, they are conspicuous by their absence. The reverence for his ancestors displayed by Constantine VII Porphyrogenitus takes us back in the imperial lineage no further than Constantine the Great, the founder of the City. From Constantine on the Latin flavor began to evaporate from New Rome. No Latin authors are excerpted for the Historical Anthology of the later Constantine. Likewise that eminent scholar and theologian, the Patriarch Photius, was a separatist from Rome in letters no less than theology; anti-Latin is his gigantic encyclopaedia of excerpts.[79] So was Suidas in his mighty *Lexicon*, written in the tenth century after that of Constantine's work.[80]

Let us see what Suidas has to say about Cicero, Horace, and Virgil. Cicero, he tells us,[81] is "the orator, about whom we have written under the letter $\phi$, on Fulvia, wife of Antony. Look it up under *Fulvia*." We follow this cross-reference and find the story of how Fulvia, when Antony ordered Cicero's head cut off, took it in her lap, pulled out his tongue and fastened it to his head and then with a grim jest had it displayed on the rostrum. So much for Cicero. " Ὁράτιος; proper name. Horace had been mutilated in his legs and therefore did not gain the consulate either in war or in peace on account of the uselessness of his feet." On Virgil we read: "Οὐεργίλιος; proper name" — which is the best of the three comments and absolutely correct as far as it goes. I am afraid that the great authors of Rome had become less than the ghosts of themselves in the New Rome of Constantinople.

The revival of an interest in Latin literature on the part of the Eastern Empire seems due primarily to the Crusades. I will mention merely the historian William of Tyre, who at the end of the twelfth century had studied in the West, had

---

[79] On this see Krumbacher, p. 73.
[80] *Ibid.* p. 562.
[81] For the latest edition of Suidas, see note 4.

read Horace and Virgil, Ovid and Cicero, and wrote a good Latin style.[82] A later pro-Latinist is Maximus Planudes, who translated various Latin works into Greek at the end of the thirteenth century under the Palaeologi. They are precisely the works in vogue in the West at that time — the moral apothegms that went under the name of Cato, Ovid's *Metamorphoses* and *Heroides*, Cicero's *Dream of Scipio* with the commentary of Macrobius, Caesar's *Gallic War*, Boethius's *Consolation of Philosophy*, Donatus's shorter grammar, and St. Augustine's work on the Holy Trinity. This was a well-reasoned program for the Latin education of the East. It was an importation. We cannot hope to discover an independent tradition of the classics of Rome at Byzantium. Yet we do note the infiltration of Latin literature into the East at the end of the period, the while the West was gradually winning back certain Greek texts, the new Aristotle and something of Plato. The Italian Renaissance was not effected by the sudden outburst of Greek light from Constantinople when the Turks captured it in A.D. 1453. Through the two centuries preceding there had been various harbingers of the brighter day when both the Greek and the Latin classics again became cornerstones in a liberal education.

## V

But back at last to St. Augustine. We have examined in the last chapter the ancient theory of the state that, with natural modifications, he built into the foundations of the Roman City of God.[83] He was a Roman of the Romans. He was not bilingual, finding as a schoolboy the prescribed study of Greek, including Homer, "most sweetly vain," a bitter pill to swallow.[84] That attitude contained the germs of the final

---

[82] For a new treatment, much needed, of this interesting figure, see the article of A. C. Krey, "William of Tyre," pp. 158, 163.

[83] Note 96.

[84] *Confessions* I 14. He wonders why he did hate Greek literature so (see also 13) and concludes that "a free curiosity" is more effective in spurring children to learn than "a meticulous necessity." St. Augustine had anticipated the Elective System. He heaps maledictions on that "torrent of human custom" that subjects school-children to the immoral tales of the Pagan poets. They

separation of East and West. But while shutting out Homer, he opened his heart to Virgil and Horace and other Roman poets; for poetry was ingrained in his nature. The idea of empire was acceptable to him, but not the earthly Empire, extended by so many frenzied wars [85] and dependent on the will of one man.[86] Rather it is the Kingdom of the one true God, who shall give us "Empire without an end." [87] He is quoting Virgil, who helps him all along to build his City of God. Not an emperor, as in the East, but Christ, is His Vicegerent upon earth. With what humility could a Caesaro-papistic ruler say "Render unto Caesar the things which be Caesar's and unto God the things which be God's"? Christ's kingdom is not of this world. Any political or social formula here below would suffice if we are faithful subjects of the higher kingdom. Meanwhile he finds the Empire of Constantine adequate; he is our sole Augustus.[88]

In this Empire according to Augustine, as we saw, the ancient Roman character, *mores*, is part of the foundation; [89] that is why God permitted the Romans to extend the boundaries of their domain.[90] He commends Horace [91] and Cic-

---

are the inventions of Homer, who ascribed human conduct to the gods; he had better have ascribed divine qualities to human beings. And here he is but quoting Cicero (*Tusc. Disp.* I 65), whom your schoolmaster, he insinuates, seems reluctant to quote. The *Confessions*, one of the world's great books, may be read with enjoyment in the seventeenth century translation of William Watts repeated in the Loeb Classical Library with corrections by W. H. D. Rouse.

[85] *De Civ. Dei* IV 3 and III 10, where a quotation from Virgil reinforces his point: An ut tam multum augeretur imperium debuit fieri quod Vergilius (*Aen.* VIII 326) detestatur dicens Deterior donec paulatim ac decolor aetas Et belli rabies et amor successit habendi?

[86] *Ibid.* III 21.

[87] *Ibid.* II 29: Illic enim non Vestalis focus, non lapis Capitolinus, sed Deus unus et verus Nec metas rerum nec tempora ponit, Imperium sine fine dabit (*Aen.* I 278).

[88] *Ibid.* V 24–25.

[89] See Chapter VI, note 93.

[90] *De Civ. Dei* V 18. This is an old-Roman chapter.

[91] *Ibid.* V 13. He quotes *Epist.* I 1. 36 f. and *Odes* II 2. 9: Latius regnes avidum domando Spiritum quam si Libyam remotis Gadibus iungas et uterque Poenus Serviat uni. Augustine may well have felt that Horace was another Solomon come to judgment (Proverbs 16. 32: "He that ruleth his spirit is mightier than he that taketh a city").

ero,[92] and of course Virgil,[93] for calling their countrymen back
to first principles, and the divine philosophy of Plato is given
all praise; for his doctrine, with that of Cicero his faithful
follower, is nearest of all to Christian truth.[94] But they came
to ultimate frustration, owing simply to human greed and
pride. What they established was not an Ideal Empire, but
a new asylum in the fashion of Romulus, whither the riff-raff
of the nations congregated.[95] The people failed to heed their
own prophets and Virgil above all, despite his exhortation,
which Augustine quotes at the beginning of his discourse, and
quotes again, "to build character on peace, to spare the conquered and fight down the proud." [96] They saw the vision,
to which by only their own power they could not attain. And
yet, for all that, there are those moments of high seriousness
in Virgil, in which "this faint world melts before his eyes." [97]
When the mind of Augustine confronted the mind of Virgil
in that transcendent sphere, he could not have cast this *poeta
nobilissimus* [98] out from the republic of God.

Augustine had seen the fall of the terrestrial city, and he
was on his deathbed, in A.D. 430, when Genseric and the Van-
dals were sweeping through North Africa. The rest of the
century was for Italy a dreary stretch of turmoil till of a sudden, at its very end (A.D. 493), Theoderic the Ostrogoth seized
the Kingdom of Italy and by his firm rule restored in fact, if
not in name, something of the splendor of old Rome. His
foremost minister was Boethius, whose outer life resembled
that of Cicero. He was consul in A.D. 510, saw his two sons

[92] *Ibid.* IX 5. Here the quotation is from *Pro Ligario* 37: nulla de virtutibus
tuis plurimis nec admirabilior nec gratior misericordia est. Augustine, like
Lactantius (Chapter VI, note 97), was widely read in his Cicero.

[93] *Ibid.* V 12. This chapter contains three quotations from Virgil: *Aen.* VIII
646–648 (on Roman liberty); *Aen.* I 279–285 (on the lust for domination to
which the possession of liberty gave place); *Aen.* VI 847–853 (the famous lines
on the true mission of Rome).

[94] *Ibid.* VIII 3.

[95] *Ibid.* V 17.

[96] *Ibid.* V 12.

[97] Chapter IV, notes 7, 15; *Magical Art*, p. 420. In Ovid, too, he would have
found them, on occasion (Chapter IV, note 79), and in Lucretius (Chapter III,
notes 38–40); but he apparently knew neither of these poets well.

[98] *De Civ. Dei* X 27.

consuls in A.D. 522, attained the highest dignity, that of *Magister Officiorum*, then suddenly was condemned for treason and executed in his prison in A.D. 525. Was he guilty of secret negotiations with the Byzantine court in the reign of Justin I? I hardly think so. As an aristocrat of the old school, he defended the Senate, some of whose members may have been guilty of disloyalty to the King. Despite his knowledge of Greek, by temperament and training he was Roman; the spirit of Constantinople could have made little appeal to him.[99]

The inner life of Boethius was, like that of Marcus Aurelius, an oasis amidst a desert of political activities. Though he attended intelligently to the duties of state, he had no dreams of an earthly Ideal Empire. His aristocratic spirit held aloof from a democracy like that of Athens, but he was painfully aware that the monarchy, which theoretically he seems to have approved,[100] had submitted to its frequent degeneration into a tyranny. The poem on Nero [101] has a poignantly contemporary application. In presenting his defence against his accusers, he showed that in his acts he had upheld the cause of the Senate, the primitive bulwark of the State. There is an unquenchable patriotism in this "last of the Romans," but before his eyes the mighty men of the old Republic move as in a dream.

[99] On Boethius, see *Founders*, chapter v, "Boethius the First of the Scholastics"; *Esprits Souverains*, chapter vi, "La Rome de Boèce et de Dante." The edition to which line-references are made is that of Stewart and Rand, The Loeb Classical Library, 1918. Among recent works, the best scientific review of Boethius and his works is the article by Dom M. Cappuyns in the *Dictionnaire d'Histoire et de Géographie Ecclésiastique*, 1935–36, pp. 348–380. For the best analysis of the mind of Boethius, see the beautifully written book of Eleanor S. Duckett, *The Gateway to the Middle Ages* (1938), pp. 142–212 (with consideration also of Cassiodorus and Ennodius).

[100] *Cons. Phil.* I 5. 9: Si enim cuius oriundus sis patriae reminiscare, non uti Atheniensium quondam multitudinis imperio regitur, sed εἷς κοίρανός ἐστιν, εἷς βασιλεύς qui frequentia civium non depulsione laetetur; cuius agi frenis atque obtemperare iustitiae summa libertas est. These are the words of Philosophy, who is applying the words of Homer (*Iliad* II 204) to one "whose service is perfect freedom" (cf. on Seneca and St. Paul, Chapter V, notes 88, 89), but we may infer that the earthly pattern would conform to the heavenly.

[101] II m. 6.

Who knows where faithful Fabrice' bones are pressed,
    Where Brutus and strict Cato rest?
A slender fame consigns their titles vain
    In some few letters to remain.[102]

The mind of Boethius was occupied not with theories of the state but with the old poets and with Aristotle and Plato, whose works he had begun to translate and whose divergent philosophies he meant to demonstrate were not so different after all. In the very year of his consulate, he devoted himself to the translation of one of Aristotle's works on logic and remarked in the preface to that work that philosophy was for him a solace for life.[103] Boethius was a Christian, and applied the method of logical reasoning gained from Aristotle to vital problems of theology keenly exciting to the philosopher's contemporaries because of the bearing of these fine-spun reasonings on political affairs.[104] If Theoderic, an Arian heretic, took offence at Boethius' attacks on Arius, they may have been partly responsible for his condemnation; in that case his death may possibly be considered martyrdom.[105]

[102] II m. 7. 15–18.

[103] De syllogismis hypotheticis (Migne, Patr. Lat. 64, 831 b): Cum in omnibus philosophiae doctrinis ediscendis atque tractandis summum vitae solamen existimem, tum iucundius et veluti cum quodam fructu etiam laboris arripio quae tecum communicanda compono. He goes on to speak of the rare pleasure of sharing high thought with one who can understand (fit quoque iucundior disciplina cum inter eiusdem sapientiae conscios iubet esse sapientem). This is true friendship, like that which Lucretius craved (I 140–144). The friend was either Symmachus, his father-in-law (cf. beginning of De Arithmetica and Tract. I, V), or John the Deacon (beginning of Tract. II, III) or some member of the little group of philosophers to which they belonged (Tract. III, 1–11).

[104] There can be no longer any doubt that Boethius is the author of the theological tractates ascribed to him. See Founders, pp. 149–157. As stated there, I have now abandoned the belief set forth in a doctor's thesis that Tractate IV, De Fide Catholica, is spurious. A forthcoming Harvard doctor's thesis examines the matter with fresh evidence. Very valuable is Father Schurr's work; cf. Speculum XI (1936) 153–156. He describes the theological and historical background of the Tractates, assigns A.D. 523 as the date when those on the Holy Trinity, I and II, were written, and proves that Tract. II, an exercise after St. Augustine, preceded Boethius' independent treatment in Tract. I (pp. 224–225).

[105] See Founders (2d ed.) pp. 179–180. Few Boethian scholars have swallowed the bait that I flung out. See Schurr, op. cit. pp. 222–223, and Miss Duckett, op. cit. p. 194.

To the downfall of Boethius we owe his greatest work, the *Consolation of Philosophy*, written in prison in the last year of his life. The sudden stroke of fortune crystallized thoughts that had been mellowing for years. He set them forth in a work of art, part prose, part verse, suggesting various literary types fused for his purpose into a new form. The poems are in various metres, skilfully wrought out. His prose has the elegance of Cicero's, and at the right moments the deep, sonorous tones that we hear in *The Dream of Scipio*, a work, along with other works of Cicero's, that Boethius knew well. Augustine was no less a model for thought and style.[106] If there are no glimpses in Boethius' thought of an Ideal Empire on earth, he has wings, he tells us, that carry him to the heights of heaven where the King of Kings holds rule. There is his fatherland; from thence he came, and there he shall set his feet again. If one would take a downward glance at the night he has abandoned, he will know that the grim tyrants before whom the poor people of earth tremble are naught but exiles in a strange land. Here in one stately poem is a true, though tiny, image of St. Augustine's *City of God*.[107]

The poets, both Greek and Latin, with whose lines, along with Aristotle's categories, Boethius had stocked his mind, are numerous and varied.[108] They dwelt in his mind; for he did not transport his beloved library with him to his dungeon. Their words came to him as he put some compelling thought

[106] Boethius himself mentions Augustine as his source for *Tr.* I (Stewart and Rand, p. 4. 31–32); on *Tr.* II see note 102. A highly important article is that of E. T. Silk.

[107] *Cons. Phil.* IV m. 1. This poem takes us back to Philosophy's remark about that real fatherland which Boethius had appeared to have forgotten. See note 98. Of late the question that worried Glareanus in 1546 (*Founders*, pp. 137, 311), as to whether a Christian could have written the *Consolatio* at such a moment, has been raised again in letters from two friends, most competent judges, Lane Cooper and George Sarton, and by Miss Barrett in *Boethius* (p. 153). See my answer in *Speculum*, XVI (1941) 350, and better still Miss Duckett, *op. cit.* pp. 194–195. I may take this occasion to correct a misprint in my review of her work in *The American Historical Review*, XLIV (1938), 86. The passage "in which history passes into poetry" is on p. 269, not 209. Any one interested in either history or poetry or the radiant city of Tours should look it up.

[108] They are best discussed in the work of F. Klingner.

into poetic form. Theocritus had come to him one day as he wrote out one of his commentaries on Aristotle; he was about to read pastoral for diversion.[109]

In Boethius we see a new and a final sort of Christian humanism.[110] The bitter controversies of the fourth century are over. The ancient authors are no longer feared as foes, or allegorized into the semblance of friends. They are taken for what they are, as such are known and loved, and are recognized by the gatekeeper with a smile as they pass into the City of God. This final form of humanism I find it hard to distinguish from Plato's. The liberal arts for Boethius was not merely an introduction to philosophy; they are of the essence of philosophy itself.[111] Nor do the arts lead to the Roman goal of service for the State. That goal has crumbled. Nor do they lead only to service for the Church. For that they are useful, but more than that, Philosophy, their sum and culmination, discloses to the human mind the range of its own powers, which once upon a time gave it entrance to Plato's world of ideas as now for Boethius its goal was the City of God. In no other way did Dante, who well deserves the title of humanist that some have given him,[112] learn the liberal arts

[109] *Com. in Arist. Herm., Sec. Ed.* III. 9 (Meiser, Teubner, p. 234): Philo enim dicit possibile esse, quod natura propria enuntiationis suscipiat veritatem, ut cum dico me hodie esse Theocriti Bucolica relecturum. Here are two irrefragable postulates, (1) that Boethius was already familiar with Theocritus and (2) that on the day when he penned these words he intended to read him again. In the same way the thought of reading Virgil comes to him (*ibid.* 207): haec enim quae utrumlibet (alternate possibilities) vocamus talia sunt, quae cum nondum sunt facta et fieri possunt et non fieri, si autem facta sint, non fieri potuerunt, ut hodie me Vergilii librum legere, quod nondum feci, potest quidem non fieri, potest etiam fieri, quod si fecero, potui non facere. Apparently Boethius was human and could not spend all his time in turning Aristotle into his new, scientific Latin and adding his comments. I suspect that he rather looked forward to reading Virgil or Theocritus or some other delightful poet when the day's stint was done.

[110] See Chapter VI, note 59.

[111] That is why Boethius wrote treatises on arithmetic, geometry, and music, not merely because they were prescribed subjects in a liberal education. The same conception of the seven arts is just as apparent in the philosophical studies of John the Scot. Cf. "How Much of the *Annotationes in Marcianum* Is the Work of John the Scot?", *Trans. Am. Philol. Assoc.* LXXI (1940) 501–502.

[112] Cf. the article by G. G. Walsh, S.J., and his book, pp. 81–96. Before

from his old master Brunetto Latini, whose dear and good paternal image still filled his heart, as in the world above from hour to hour he taught him how man can make himself eternal:

> Chè in la mente m'è fitta, ed or mi accora
> La cara e buona imagine paterna
> Di voi, quando nel mondo ad ora ad ora
> M'insegnavate come l'uom s'eterna.[113]

Such was the precious legacy that Boethius passed on for the building of Rome in the mediaeval West. In his application of Aristotle's logical method to theological speculation, he was the first of the scholastics; [114] the influence of his thought on the philosophy of the Middle Ages from Alcuin to St. Thomas Aquinas is witness to that fact. In a more profitable way than he had planned he had reconciled Aristotle with Plato in his *Consolation of Philosophy*; there Platonism blossoms in the poetry and the imagination of the argument, to which Aristotle contributes his appropriate share. That title of "first of the Romans," appropriate in one sense for Boethius, may seem curiously ironic to those in quest of the eternal Rome. Rather, he was the first of the Romans to build human philosophy and human poetry and the unim-

---

Father Walsh, Professor J. B. Fletcher had been bold enough to call Dante a humanist (*Literature of the Italian Renaissance*, pp. 39–42: "A gospel of *humanism*, substantially after Cicero, and a proclamation of *nationalism*, — in these two fundamentals, Dante certainly preludes the Renaissance"). And before Fletcher, Étienne Gilson in a delightful chapter on "L'humanisme médiéval at Renaissance" (pp. 171–196) in *Les Idées et Les Lettres*, deals playfully (p. 195) with Burckhardt's recognition of Dante as the "first modern man," pointing out that the first modern man, therefore, was a mediaeval man. Petrarch generally receives that honorific title. A new turn to the dispute about humanism has been given by Jacques Maritain in his *Humanisme Intégrale*. Both Dante and Terence, so far as I can see, have a place within that fold: *Homo sum; humani nil a me alienum puto.*

[113] *Inferno* 15, 82–85.

[114] *Founders*, pp. 156, 317. Patch points out (*Tradition of Boethius*) that this title which I thought I was the first to use (in my doctor's thesis, *Fleckeisens Jahrbuch* XXVI [1901] 425) had already been employed by Arturo Graf, *Roma nella Memoria e nelle Immag del Med. Evo*, p. 322, in 1883. *Vivant qui ante nos nostra dixere.* At any rate, the term has come to stay. Due recognition to the influence of Boethius on mediaeval philosophy is given by M. De Wulf in the sixth edition of his great *Histoire de la Philosophie Mediévale*, Louvain and Paris, 1934.

paired tradition of ancient literature into the New Rome that passed from St. Augustine to Charlemagne.[115]

After the Dark Ages of the seventh and eighth centuries [116] comes Charlemagne, King of the Franks in A.D. 768, sole ruler after the death of his brother Carloman in A.D. 771, and crowned Emperor of the West by Pope Leo IV on Christmas, A.D. 800, in Rome. And Emperor of that New Rome he was. No Caesaropapism here. Charlemagne, a loyal son of the Church, received his crown from the Pope, even as his father, Pepin the Short, had been anointed King of the Franks by Pope Stephen II, and as he himself had the donation of Pepin renewed by Pope Hadrian I. The Pope had temporal power over the central part of Italy, and in virtue of the forged decretals of Constantine which granted Italy and all the West to Pope Sylvester I, Hadrian, unwitting of the forgery, claimed a temporal supremacy over Kings and Emperors — a false philosophy for the Vicegerent of Christ, whose Kingdom was not of this world. Not that it mattered much to Charlemagne, who ruled an Empire from Barcelona to the Elbe. He had, as we have seen,[117] the ingenious idea of marrying the Empress

[115] The course of Boethius' influence on mediaeval culture, with something on the Renaissance, has recently received a masterly treatment by H. R. Patch in his *Tradition of Boethius*. An item on the Renaissance is now added by E. T. Silk, who describes a girdle-book, a small fifteenth-century manuscript of the *Consolatio* attached to its leather casing so that it could swing from the belt and be pulled up whenever the traveller wished a sip of Boethius from that flask. One can see how Erasmus could write part of his *Praise of Folly* on horseback (if he did) and not lose his manuscript if his steed started up in a hurry. All other girdle-books (less than a score in all) are liturgical in character. The Boethius is a unique prize and Yale is its lucky possessor. Another mark of devotion to Boethius in the fifteenth century is an exquisite manuscript at the British Museum in five little volumes, each with a picture and beautiful ornamentation, containing the text of the *Consolatio* with Jean de Meun's translation. One picture was reproduced (partly) by J. W. Clark (*The Care of Books*, University of Cambridge Press, 1902) and several more are given by Patch. On another, and superior, manuscript of this Renaissance precursor of The Loeb Classical Library see "Ovid and 'Le Roman de la Rose,' " pp. 104–105.

[116] One should enter this period by Miss Duckett's *Gateway*, with especial attention to her treatment of Cassiodorus and St. Benedict, whose fourteen-hundredth anniversary will be duly celebrated in 1943, we hope, despite rumors to the contrary.

[117] Note 44. The fact that Irene was ruling, with no authority, as βασιλεὺs,

Irene and thus acquiring at a stroke the Empire of the East
with the Pope as the head of the Church. But the East quickly
disposed both of Irene and of Charlemagne's audacious plan.
He effected, at all events, the framework of such an Empire as
St. Augustine had approved, when the ruler was a Constantine
or a Theodosius.[118] At any rate Charlemagne had Augustine
much in his thought. Among the readings to which he listened at the dinner table, so his biographer Einhard states, he
delighted in selections from Augustine, especially from his
book on the City of God.[119]

In all ways, Charlemagne sought to make of his Empire a
New Rome of the West. That meant a revival, a Renaissance.
He commissioned Alcuin, the foremost of his scholarly assistants, to correct the text of Holy Scriptures, to collate the
best manuscripts available and restore the original form. He
revised the books of liturgy in the same fashion. The Sacramentary called Gelasian, which in the two centuries preceding had gathered interesting but extraneous matter in France,
was replaced by the Gregorian Sacramentary, the briefer form
in use at Rome.[120] To make sure that the monks of St. Benedict had the right form of their own Rule, he sought out the
autograph at Monte Cassino, and had a copy made, accompanied by the variants which that interesting specimen of
popular Latinity had acquired at various places in the course
of its transmission.[121] The general principles governing this

gave Charlemagne the chance, so he hoped, to continue the line that came
not from Romulus Augustulus but from Constantine VI back to Constantine
the Great. That was better than creating a new Empire of the West to coun-
ter-balance that of the East. See Vasiliev I 353.

[118] *De Civ. Dei* V 25–26.

[119] *Vita Caroli* 24. 2.

[120] On the "Gelasian" Sacramentary, which was composed probably before
600 and which may contain some of the liturgical compositions of Gelasius,
see Ziegler, *op. cit.* p. 9. In Gelasius's view, Church and Empire both derive
from God and both are subordinate to Christ as king and priest. They therefore are separate one from the other. There is no room for Caesaropapism
here. Gelasius approximates closely to Dante's position; see note 141.

[121] The "road-breaking and epoch-making" work of my ever-lamented master Ludwig Traube ("Regula Benedicti," *Abhandl. der königl. Bayer. Akad.
der Wiss., philosoph., philolog. u. hist. Klasse*, XXI [1898], 2d ed. by H.
Plenkers, *ibid.* XXV [1910]) was well called by Lindsay (*Palae. Lat.* II [1923]

truly philological reform were laid down in a famous Capitulary, a kind of encyclical, sent to the various monasteries, the centres of education in his realm, in A.D. 787.[122] In it he chastises the slipshod Latinity in which too many priests indulged, the corruptions, or lies (*mendacia*), as he vigorously calls them, that had been allowed to creep into the ancient, sacred texts — a heinous offense indeed for those who were supposedly the guardians of truth.[123]

Nor was this all. This Capitulary is entitled *De Litteris Colendis*, "On the Cultivation of Literature," and Charlemagne took that title in its broadest sense. Perhaps with the Institutes of Cassiodorus to guide him,[124] he sought to recover the works of the old classic authors who had made Rome great. His emissaries went to Italy for fresh texts, based on old manuscripts, of the Latin authors, which we should not be reading today but for Charlemagne's enlightened plan. Even in the script in which the new copies were made, we see in all the *scriptoria* of France the development of a clear and stately book hand, from which the old cursive traits were gradually weeded out. The old hands had their beauty — so did the new. A new rivalry sprang up among the monasteries. Art flourished, the most original kind of art in this period, art with a purpose commanded by the Emperor — the purpose to restore in forms of beauty the true and ancient texts.[125]

---

15) "the star to which every twentieth century editor of a Latin text must hitch his wagon." On Linderbauer's edition (Metten, 1922), which was the first to do justice to the wealth of popular Latin in the original text, see *Class. Phil.* XVI (1923) 81–84.

[122] *Mon. Germ. Hist.*, *Leges* II, ed. A. Boretius (Hannover, 1883). The letter may well have been written by Alcuin.

[123] *Ibid.* p. 79. 19: Nam cum omnibus hominibus vitanda sint mendacia, quanto magis illi secundum possibilitatem declinare debent qui ad hoc solummodo probantur electi ut servire specialiter debeant veritati. A most effective admonition. Even the most slipshod scribe would not care to be called a father of lies.

[124] *Founders*, p. 283. I favor this suggestion all the more after a new study of Cassiodorus in the light of Mynors' edition of the *Institutiones*. See "The New Cassiodorus," in *Speculum* XIII (1938) 433–447. Cassiodorus drew the outlines of a model library, both sacred and profane, which many a monastery would endeavor to procure. An Emperor of Charlemagne's propensities would want that and something more.

[125] The best account of Charlemagne as a restorer of the correct styles in

In one monastery, that of St. Martin at Tours, we note a
particularly deliberate effort to reform the different fonts of
letters — square capital, rustic capital, semiuncial — on the
patterns found in ancient manuscripts, and to give to the
minuscule, employed for the body of the text, a new clarity
and grace in harmony with the larger varieties.[126] This meant
a Renaissance of handwriting, the outward and visible sign
of the Renaissance in literature and in ancient culture that
characterized the times. The printed letters in our books today go back, *via* a similar reform brought in during the Italian
Renaissance, to the age of Charlemagne.[127]

Among the readings at table to which the Emperor liked to
listen were histories and the great deeds of the men of old.
Among these was Augustus, who served him for a model of
the Prince. Einhard, his architect and biographer, fashioned
his life of the Emperor in accordance with Suetonius's plan.
Various details show not that Einhard made over the Emperor's policies and his daily habits to conform with Suetonius's picture of the ancient Emperors but that Charlemagne
himself conformed his life to what he read of them.[128] He

---

art, literature, and liturgy is still, despite its age, that of Dom F. Cabrol in the
*Dictionnaire d'archéologie et de liturgie,* edited by him and Dom H. Leclercq,
Paris (1914), III, 656–825.

[126] See *A Survey of the Manuscripts of Tours,* pp. 8–9. New light has been
cast on the School of Tours and all mediaeval script by an expert in the arts
of both printing and writing, S. M. (which can stand only for Stanley Morison),
*Black-Letter Text,* Cambridge University Press, 1942. Though the materials
for his great and definitive work were destroyed by Hitler's bombers, his leading ideas, it would seem, appear in these "pages printed prematurely." Palaeographers, especially encomiasts of the script of Tours, will find a new world
opened up in them.

[127] In both cases we have an external and visible proof that the men who
lived in either of these periods believed that it was an age of *renaissance* when
the standards of the good old times were being revived. One would say of the
ruler, in Horace's words: *Et veteres revocavit artes* (Chapter II, notes 118, 119).
The testimony of the manuscripts may be matched with the inscription on a
famous bronze ring in Paris: RENOVATIO · REGNI · FRANC · CARLUS · IMP · AG
(Cabrol. *loc. cit.,* p. 786) and with numerous acclamations of their new Augustus by various Carolingian poets. For these reasons I cannot follow my revered
friend, the late Henry Osborn Taylor (*The Mediaeval Mind,* 1938, I, 211), who
wished to get rid of the term *renaissance* once and for all.

[128] Cf. the article on "Suetonius in the Early Middle Ages," H.S.C.P.
XXXVII 43–48.

wished above all to be a second Augustus, and Virgil also fostered his ideals. The poets of his court caught up the strain. In poetry, as Ludwig Traube aptly remarked,[129] this was an *aetas Vergiliana*. In a word, the Ideal Empire of Augustus's times had returned to men's imagination.

But this happy vision of a political Renaissance vanished with the death of Charlemagne; neither his son nor his grandsons could hold together the fabric that he had built. The revival of ancient Roman culture that he had called into being prospered. The course of poetry, humanism, philosophy derived from his reforms continued through the Middle Ages, receiving new streams and branches, passing over some shallows, but constantly gaining in strength. We cannot follow the river or the rivulets, though they lead through pleasant pastures,[130] but come at once to where they break into the sea of Dante's all-encompassing thought. For he as justly as Virgil, to whom he applied the words, may be called the sea of all wisdom:

Il mar di tutto il senno.[131]

Certainly none other in the Middle Ages had so gathered together both the intellectual gains of his own times, with their poetic values, and those that antiquity had transmitted.

[129] *Vorlesungen und Abhandlungen*, II (1911, Munich, O. Beck) , 113. The *aetas Vergiliana* comprises the eighth and the ninth centuries, the *aetas Horatiana* the tenth and the eleventh (a somewhat less appropriate term?), and the *aetas Ovidiana* the twelfth and the thirteenth (an exceedingly apt term, which might also be applied to part of the eleventh century).

[130] Especially fruitful for our theme are the works of John of Salisbury, with particular relation to the theory of the state. See note 4. John knew only the "Dream of Scipio" from Cicero's *De Re Publica*, but some extracts from the other books he could get indirectly from Lactantius and Augustine's *De Civitate Dei*; see Chapter VI, notes 49, 79. So could another writer of the twelfth century, Otto of Freising, whose *De Duabus Civitatibus* obviously is modeled on the *De Civitate*, yet is adapted inevitably to his own times. See Mierow's introduction to his translation, pp. 62–63. An excellent analysis of the political theory of John of Salisbury is given by John Dickinson (*op. cit.*). He shows that the principle of *concordia ordinum* is basic for John. On the supposed letter of Plutarch to Hadrian see p. xxi. For the thirteenth century on cf. the article of Hans Baron, 3–28.

[131] Especially fine is the last chapter in Henry Osborn Taylor's great book, *The Mediaeval Mind*, entitled "The Mediaeval Synthesis." So is the introduction to Grandgent's edition of the *Divina Commedia*, ix-xxxvi, and the further development in his *Dante*.

Long study and a long love of Virgil —

il lungo studio e il lungo amore [132]

had fitted Dante to write his poem, his "Comedy," as with a reasoned rhetoric and perhaps a touch of irony he called it. It may be that he knew the allegorizing commentary of Fulgentius in the late Empire or that of Bernard Sylvestris of Tours in the twelfth century. For they both had read into the *Aeneid* an allegory of man, and that, as Dante declared in his letter to Can Grande,[133] was his own subject: *subiectum est homo*. But he needed no allegory to teach him that the vision of Virgil was true. He had absorbed, not merely read, many another of the old authors, Christian and pagan.[134] He did not, like the Apologetes of old, spend time in sifting true from false; like a true humanist, he seized on what he knew was true. After the death of Beatrice his thought dwelt in Cicero's essay *On Friendship*, and in the *Consolation of Philosophy* of Boethius. He knew the *Dream of Scipio*, and like Cicero, could look down from a celestial height upon our little world, the little threshing-floor that makes us all so fierce:

l'aiuola che ci fa tanto feroci.[135]

Cicero's plan of the spheres and Virgil's of the world below may have furnished the initial spur to Dante's imagination for his vision of Hell and Paradise. Augustine, whose *City of God* had been through the Middle Ages a guide for political thought, as for that of Otto of Freising,[136] was naturally a guide for Dante. It has been said, somewhat sentimentally, that Dante's philosophy is that of St. Thomas Aquinas set to

---

[132] *Inferno* I 83.

[133] *Epist.* X (XIII) 8: Si vero accipiatur opus allegorice, subiectum est homo, prout merendo et demerendo per arbitrii libertatem Iustitiae praemianti aut punienti obnoxius est.

[134] On Dante's reading in the Latin Classics see the work of Canon Edward Moore.

[135] *Paradiso* XXII 151. Fletcher shows skillfully the influence of Cicero, Virgil, and Boethius in forming Dante's idea of *humanitas* (*op. cit.* pp. 25–33).

[136] See note 130.

music.[137] Dante had mastered the scholastic method and he
pays due deference to the *Doctor Angelicus*. St. Thomas appears high in the Heavens, in the Circle of the Sun, with those
who have spread abroad the light of theology; but the heart is
greater than the mind, and higher still in the Circle of the
Rose is Augustine with Benedict and Francis, along with rows
of little children, blessed by Christ.

Dante's political thought is reasoned out in his *Monarchia*,
one of his latest works.[138] The argument is briefly this.[139]
The human mind must realize its intellectual potency in
action, with universal peace as the goal. The necessary political government is monarchy and the Roman Empire was
ordained by God. Here Augustine's hints are developed into
a philosophical and humanistic principle. No theological criticism like Augustine's is bestowed on the Roman Empire; like
the Roman people it is the noblest upon earth.[140] The authority of the Monarch, therefore, depends immediately on
God. It does not come directly from the Pope. Pope and
Emperor both are divinely appointed. There is no chance
for one Caesaropapistic ruler. The Emperor is not Pope nor

[137] The best recent work on Dante's philosophy is that of Gilson, *Dante et la
Philosophie*. Learning and philosophical acumen are couched in Gilson's viva-
cious style. Even the index is alive. Important is the demonstration that Dante
cannot be affiliated with any of the schools or thinkers (Aquinas included) and
that for him philosophy is not the handmaid of religion. It is his study of
Aristotle that forms this independent attitude. Dante is a Christian philosopher, not a philosophic Christian theologian. See Index, s.vv. *Dante, Philosophie, Théologie, Thomas d'Aquin*.

[138] Cf. "The Latin Concordance of Dante and the Genuineness of Certain of
his Latin Works," pp. 36–38. There is nothing like making a Concordance
(especially in company with so active a confederate as Ernest H. Wilkins) for
giving one a feeling for the texture of a work. See his article "Methods in
Making a Concordance." We published the concordance (*Dantis Alagherii
Operum Latinorum Concordantiae*) in 1912. Gilson (*op. cit.*, p. 163), though
not referring to our work, seems inclined to select from the various dates proposed for the *Monarchia* one of the later ones.

[139] Gilson's analysis (pp. 163–200) lays bare the heart of this work.

[140] *Mon.* II 3. 5 (Moore): Quod quidem primo sic probatur. Nobilissimo
populo convenit omnibus aliis praeferri: Romanus populus fuit nobillissimus;
ergo convenit ei aliis omnibus praeferri. Thus is the supreme nobility of the
Roman people encased in a syllogistic coat of mail. The argument in this
chapter is backed up by no less than seven quotations from Virgil (with one
from Juvenal). St. Augustine, too, can cite his Virgil, though less exuberantly.
See note 93.

the Pope Emperor.[141] Dante brushes away the Donation of
Constantine as an unrighteous act; [142] how relieved he would
have been to know about the forgery! He finds no argument
in the crowning of Charlemagne by Pope Hadrian. Those
who make that point, he brusquely declares, say nothing. For
the usurpation of rightful power (*ius*) does not create it.[143]
The foundation of the Empire is natural, human right (*ius
humanum*), as the foundation of the Church is that rock on
which Christ built it. Both are by the ordinance of God and
both indestructible.[144] In essence Dante's solution of the
problem of the best sort of state involves a return to Augustine and Virgil entwined in one. For Virgil's City of Earth
has become more divine, and Augustine's City of God has become more human.[145]

In this treatise on Monarchy, we see, Dante the poet, whose
mind ranges high in the heavenly spheres, can descend to
earth, enter the lists with any scholastic, and topple him over

[141] *Mon.* III 12. 76: Non enim dicimus: Imperator est Papa, nec e converso.
Nec potest dici quod communicent in specie; cum alia sit ratio Papae, alia
Imperatoris in quantum huiusmodi: ergo reducuntur ad aliquid in quo habent
uniri. This *tertium quid*, he demonstrates in the following paragraph, is either
God or some substance inferior to God. Dante's views seem much like those
of Gelasius back in the fifth century. See note 120. Dante can quote with a
new fervor the precept of our Lord, "Render unto Caesar the things that are
Caesar's" (*Epist.* V. 9, 152–154 Moore).

[142] *Mon.* III 10. 1–10, 105–132. The Church cannot receive a material gift
or power *per se*; silver and gold may be given to the Pope, not as to a possessor
but as to a dispenser of such bounties to the poor.

[143] *Ibid.* III 11. 15: usurpatio enim iuris non facit ius.

[144] *Ibid.* III 10. 53–55: Ipse (Christus) est petra, super quam aedificata est
Ecclesia; Imperii vero fundamentum ius humanum est . . . (61–65): sic et
Imperio licitum non est contra ius humanum aliquid facere. Sed contra ius
humanum esset, si seipsum Imperium destrueret; ergo Imperio seipsum de-
struere non licet. And thus is the Eternality of Empire founded on a syllogistic
rock. In this chapter Dante's citations come mainly from Holy Scripture —
St. Paul, Song of Songs, St. Matthew; and yet Aristotle is also summoned to
witness, speaking as it were with a like authority.

[145] Gilson traces the tendency of mediaeval thinkers (like Otto of Freising
in his *De Duabus Civitatibus*) to absorb the Earthly City in the Heavenly (*op.
cit.* pp. 200–205 ff.). Dante's audacity, if that is the right word, in claiming
the divine sanction for the empire of pagan Rome was perhaps engendered by
his adoration of Virgil. Augustine had much the same experience. Possibly
we may say after all that his later thought was closely akin to Dante's. Their
different utterances on the Roman state should be studied side by side.

with a lance snatched from Aquinas [146] or Averroes [147] or
Aristotle, called reverently "The Philosopher," [148] the master
of those who know. Here is a most human and polemic Dante,
like Milton in his pamphlets. Nor does he handle Popes or
Emperors with gloves. There are human defects in some of
the heirs of St. Peter — above all avarice and pride. Christ
did not demand anything of St. Peter for his high office save
"Follow me." Nor did Matthew have to make a contribution
of gold or silver for his election to the place vacated by Judas
Iscariot.[149] Far different in Dante's day. The root of the
matter, he declares, laying his finger on the mythical cause
of actual corruption, was that fatal Donation of Constantine
to "the first wealthy Pope":

> Ahi, Costantin, di quanto mal fu matre
> Non la tua conversion, ma quella dote
> Che da te prese il primo ricco patre.[150]

The universe in which Dante lived, the universe that out
of the present and the past he himself created, is among all
those that the mind of man has fashioned one of the neatest,
best built, most beautifully ordered. It is a Greek *cosmos*.
No discarded material remains. It is the world of Aristotle
and Lucretius. And yet it is a boundless universe with free
flights for the imagination and for human sympathies. It is
the world of Plato and Augustine. Within it the ancient
Roman Empire is given a perpetual abode. Pagan and Christian imagery are woven inextricably in Dante's art. The old
has not been metamorphosed, or mutilated; it merges with

[146] *Mon.* II 4. 5.
[147] *Ibid.* I 3. 76.
[148] *Ibid.* I 3. 4: iuxta Philosophum ad Nicomachum; I 5. 13; quorum primum
ab auctoritate Philosophi adsumatur de suis Politicis, and in some sixteen
other places.
[149] *Inferno* XIX 90–96. Dante deviates into a rather familiar pleasantry here,
and paves the way with an apology for it (88–89: Io non so s'io mi fui qui
troppo folle Ch'io pur risposi lui per questo metro). All criticism is disarmed.
It is sometimes thought that Dante had no sense of humor. Satire he had, but
wit and humor he apparently thought beneath the dignity of his theme. In
the matter of humor, his mind is much like Juvenal's.
[150] *Ibid.* 115–117.

the new in a natural harmony. Dante can look down upon the earthly Rome from the heights, as Scipio did in his dream. But it is nothing transitory. It is after the poet with Virgil has climbed the ledges of Purgatory to the Terrestrial Paradise at the top, has been bathed in the stream of Lethe, and seen Beatrice revealed at last, that she promises him his sojourn there will be brief. For "soon thou shalt be with me endlessly a citizen of that Rome of which Christ is a Roman —"

> E sarai meco senza fine cive
> Di quella Roma, onde Cristo e romano.[151]

The poet has not, like Augustine, barred off the Terrestrial from the Heavenly City. While it is just as solid and just as human as before, it abides in Paradise, where Beatrice the divine will reveal it to her human worshipper. That is the last volume in Dante's complete history of the Rise and Perfection of the Roman Empire, a story that Virgil had only begun to tell.

[151] *Purgatorio* XXXII 101–102.

# CHAPTER VIII

## THE ETERNAL CITY

IN the year 416 of our era, Rutilius Namatianus, prefect of the city of Rome two years before, wrote a poem, called *De Reditu Suo*, describing his return from Rome to his ancestral estates in Gaul. He presumably was a nominal Christian, to rise to so high an office of state. Within he is bitterly pagan. He is one of those at whom St. Augustine aimed in his work on *The City of God*. The sacred city had indeed fallen before the barbarians, Rutilius meditates; the poison of the new sect has worked. He leaves Rome with a heavy heart. He stops to kiss the city gates, as he steps over the sacred limits. He cannot proceed on the journey without a prayer to his goddess; for such is Rome to him:

> Exaudi, regina tui pulcherrima mundi,
>   Inter sidereos Roma recepta polos!

> Give ear, oh beauteous queen of all the world,
> Rome that hast godhead in the starry sky.
> Mother of men, mother of gods, give ear!
> For heaven is near us where thy temples are.
> Thee, while the fates allow it, sing we now
> And ever sing; for life is little worth
> If we forget thee.[1]

For all her fates, Rome is still to this poet the mistress of the world. She established an empire that stands for order and law and intelligence.

> Less is thy rule than thy good right to rule.

> Quod regnas minus est quam quod regnare mereris.[2]

Her right to dominion preceded her might. And she has crowned her power with a rare beauty. She is adorned with

---

[1] V 47–52 (Loeb *Minor Latin Poets*, J. W. Duff and A. M. Duff, p. 768).
[2] V. 91–92.

fair trophies and temples, with arches and aqueducts, with gardens and with a climate of perpetual spring. So then, dear city, the poet prays, bind a garland of new verdure on thy sacred head, and crown thyself with a golden diadem. Rise above thy disasters, as thou hast risen in the past.

Here, then, is the worship of the Eternal Rome at the moment of her apparent downfall. Rutilius repeats the creed that every Roman heart had cherished for centuries. It is fixed in Cicero's reverence of the eternal state and of the eternal law, as we saw in those passages that Lactantius and Augustine have saved for us.[3] It is proclaimed by Livy in that speech on progress by the liberal Canuleius in 445 B.C.[4] It is the undercurrent of Polybius' praise of that perfect system of government that the Romans had developed without the aid of Greek philosophy, an idea that he shared with Cato.[5] Ennius in his exaltation of ancient character as the bulwark of the state that stands [6] and in his devotion to Romulus as the divine king and father of his country [7] hardly thought of Rome as one of the transitory phases of human history. Could a city founded by the son of a god, himself exalted to godhead, be mortal? The gentle Tibullus, in singing of the happy, pastoral simplicity before Romulus, declares that the walls of the eternal city were built by him.[8] The magnificent phrase of

[3] Chapter VI, notes 56, 57, 90. Cf. esp. *De Re Pub.* III 33 (= *De Civ. Dei* XXII 6): debet enim constituta sic esse civitas ut aeterna sit. That is evidently the way that Rome was founded, as Cicero makes plain in the second book of his work.

[4] IV 4. 4. Quoted in Chapter II, note 23. All the *fatum Romanum* is in the phrase *in aeternum urbe condita in inmensum crescente.*

[5] Chapters I, notes 11, 73.

[6] Chapters I, note 133; VI, note 93.

[7] Chapter I, note 126. Observe that we owe this passage to Cicero (*De Re Publ.* I 64), who elsewhere expresses a lively interest in the divinity of Romulus (Chapter VI, note 89).

[8] II 5. 23: Romulus aeternae nondum formaverat urbis Moenia. This seems to be the earliest instance of the phrase *urbs aeterna*, or *Roma aeterna*, common enough later in both works of literature and inscriptions. H. Last in *C.A.H.* X (1934) 456–458 states that it was "Augustus who first gave the city of Rome that character which is still conceded by phrases like 'The Eternal City.'" I venture to think that the feeling behind that phrase was strong in the Roman mind at the time when Polybius saw the state at what was to him the height of its greatness.

St. Augustine in the first sentence of his *City of God* — *in illa stabilitate sedis aeternae* — is of course applied to the heavenly city, but it cannot help harking back in his memory to his youthful veneration of the eternal terrestrial Rome.

Meanwhile the prophecy of Rutilius came true, though not in the way that he intended. Rome remained eternal, but what do we mean by Rome? And where is her abode? At times she was not by the banks of the Tiber. She has made strange flights, which we will follow as best we can.

The terrestrial Rome, a century before the time of Rutilius, had moved to Byzantium, even as Julius Caesar had planned. Its majesty and might, despite its reverses, persisted there down to the fall of the city of Constantine in A.D. 1453. It fell not only for a military assault but for the sin of pride. Autocracy, despite its unexampled permanence of over a thousand years, could not abide forever. Its strength was not the majesty of state, but its attachment to the new spiritual Rome, the Church of Christ. When that crashed, the Church remained without a political home; it had no earthly centre. Russia had greatly benefited by Byzantine culture. Kiev and Moscow were centres of that culture and under Ivan III the Great, in A.D. 1480, it looked as though the New Rome of the East might have winged its way after the fall of Constantinople to Moscow. Moscow indeed was called the Third Rome, and indeed an autocratic and theocratic and Caesaropapistic rule with all its virtues and its defects passed from Byzantium to Moscow and from Moscow to St. Petersburg, and flourished there down till the revolution of 1917.[9]

The New Rome of the West fared better. To be sure, its terrestrial location shifted. Under Theoderic its centre was Ravenna, under Charlemagne, Aix-la-Chapelle; at the end of the tenth century Otto II brought it to Germany, where it remained the Holy Roman Empire throughout the Middle Ages and long after — way down to Napoleon's time. When Dante speaks of the Empire, his eyes are cast towards the

[9] See a splendid article by W. Lednicki, "Russia and her Culture," *New Europe*, I (1941), 250–253, 280–285.

north. If we are inclined to smile at the Holy Roman Empire, remembering Voltaire's *bon mot*, we may read Dante's passionate appeal, in his letter to Henry VII, *Caesaris et Augusti successor*, to cross the Alps and assume his rightful domain. Verily the Ideal Empire of Augustus and Virgil's reign of Saturn have returned, somewhat prematurely, in Dante's imagination. He lures the Monarch down, all in vain, with quotations from Virgil and from Lucan.[10] The earthly empire that Dante would build, subordinate to the Heavenly City but plainly independent of the Church,[11] is nothing less than that of imperial Augustan Rome. And yet locally it still was across the Alps.

In saying, then, that the New Rome of the West fared better than that of the East, I am thinking primarily of the Pre-Christian literary Rome and of the impulse given to a renewed study of the Classics by Charlemagne and of the guiding force that the ancient models exercised on literary forms and ideals. The best of Greek literature had perished for the West. It was treasured in the East, but treasured so carefully that the West had no chance to inspect it, while the works of Roman literature had been erased from the Byzantine list. The West got the better end of the bargain; for glimpses of Plato shone through Cicero and Boethius and glimpses of Homer through Virgil; thus a longing for the vanished masterpieces of Greece was aroused and was sated at last in the Renaissance. In the East, though the finer treasure was there, it was reverenced so deeply that literary style was not suffered to depart far from its norm. Popular Greek literature was, at first, discouraged. It has life enough today, but there are still two dialects, the ancient and the modern. In the West, popular Latin was accommodated to the native speech of the countries to which it spread, and either produced some influence on them or absorbed them into its own essence in a new vernacular. Original spirits felt free to develop this new medium

[10] *Epist.* VII. He also in his fashion draws on Scripture, with a decidedly extravagant citation from either the Gospels or the Mass in honor of the Emperor (45, Moore): *Ecce Agnus Dei, ecce qui abstulit peccata mundi!*
[11] Chapter VII, note 145.

of expression. Poetry of the highest excellence in the various vernaculars resulted. What works has the East to match with *Beowulf*, the *Chanson de Roland*, the *Roman de la Rose*, with Chaucer and with Dante? Here are great writers trained in Latin literature, in Virgil and Ovid and Cicero's *Dream of Scipio*, all forming from these ancient models an individual art, in which they embodied their own imagination, high seriousness, and laughter.

With the emergence of new nations, vigorous and distinct, each with its own part to play, each conscious of its peculiar strength, there could be no system of government to control them all. But one bond of union they had in the Catholic and Apostolic Church. Here was the new Ideal Empire, the City of God upon earth. Within it one could obey the precept of Christ and of the early Church once more, to render unto Caesar, whatever Caesar's government might be, the things that belonged to him, and to God the things that belong to God.

But why, we may ask, should the fugitive spirit of Rome descend once more upon its birthplace? The victorious Church of the Fourth Century inaugurated its official and external empire in the city of Constantine. But that outer form has long since passed from view. A Moslem republic now occupies the spot that witnessed the majestic ceremonial of Constantine VII Porphyrogenitus. Possibly we can do no better than to say that the spirit of Rome is not to be pinned to earth at any place. In outer might and splendor the terrestrial Rome that all the Middle Ages knew had fallen to a lowly estate. Why bother with it further? Why not think only of the heavenly Rome, with both Pagan and Christian colorings in its radiance, just as Augustine and Dante in different ways beheld it? Because we are bound by two historical facts, or what look like historical facts. One is the word of our Lord, who built his Church on the rock of St. Peter.[12] The other is St. Peter's martyrdom, which occurred in the city of Rome.

[12] Nock *St. Paul* 44: "The Roman Church showed an unerring instinct for underlying truth when it canonized Peter and Paul as its two founders."

The place assigned by tradition was the Circus of Caligula and Nero, where in the fourth century, when the Church became free to hallow the sites of martyrdom, part of the ancient circus was transferred into a basilica in honor of St. Peter.[13] In Pagan Rome one finds the monuments of the dead outside the sacred line that bounded the city; the traveler can see them now along the Appian Way. The spot where a Christian martyr fell marked the place of the church which soon would be built to house his relics. For nothing could be more sacred than they. They were not entombed outside a city wall; their holiness called for the protecting walls of a sanctuary, to be enlarged and beautified as the ages rolled on, and to awaken in the hearts of the communicants of that parish an indescribable devotion and a proud loyalty to their own saint. That ancient basilica of St. Peter has long since crumbled, but near it is the mighty Vatican, where crowds of the faithful from afar and near offer their worship at the scene of Peter's death and of his triumph.

What other centre, then, could there be for the New Rome of Catholic Christendom than the Rome of Augustus, and Cicero and Ennius and all the ancient heroes from primeval times? The town without might be small and dingy, but what mattered that for the Roman City of God, founded on St. Peter's rock? Thence went the word that brought Charlemagne to Rome for coronation and Henry II, ruler of the Holy Roman Empire, for humiliation at Canossa. He was summoned in A.D. 1077 by Gregory VII, in whose day the Papacy reached its apogee, claiming temporal and spiritual power alike. One could almost speak again of a new Caesaropapism to match that of the East. No Emperor became a Pope, but a Pope wanted much to become an Emperor.

One firm bond that the Church possessed was the Latin language. In any part of Europe not only the priestly celebrants but the humblest worshipper could feel that the same words of the sacred Mass that he heard were being said or sung at the same hour in some distant nation, the native lan-

---

[13] Platner-Ashby *Top. Dict.* 118. Cf. Peebles, *La Meta Romuli.*

guage of which was unintelligible to him. The same was true
of the music of the Mass and of many of the hymns. Today it
gives one the thrill of corporate communion with the past to
see in some late manuscript of the Middle Ages, as once I saw,
the same tones of the dialogue preceding the Preface to the
Sanctus that one hears today, only written out in the square
notation of the period; and later I saw those tones in a manuscript of the tenth century, only embodied in light and airy
neums that look like tiny birds flying across the page.

And the Mass itself — what genius created the original plan?
There were many liturgies in the ancient Church, in which
New Rome both East and West contributed. The origins of
the great art are obscure, and many collaborated in the making. But who, I wonder, was the first to extract the right bits
from Psalms and Gospels and Epistles and Apocalypse and
make them seemly for the new rite? Who skilfully matched
the Old Testament with the New in the lessons chosen for the
Lenten Masses? Who made mystic the words with which our
Lord was welcomed humbly by the centurion and thus made
them seemly for the Priest to utter as he strikes his breast before receiving the sacred Body of Christ?

> Lord, I am not worthy that thou shouldst enter under my
> roof; say but the word and my soul shall be healed.

> Domine non sum dignus ut intres sub tectum meum; sed
> tantum dic verbo, et sanabitur anima mea.

Then there are two Greek words in the Latin Mass heard
everywhere today — *Kyrie eleison.* Even though they were
not added to the Latin Mass till the fifth century,[14] they may,
with the Greek phrases in the Reproaches on Good Friday,
answered antiphonally by their Latin equivalents,[15] stand as
a symbol of that happy time when Greece and Rome were fellow subjects of the New Empire of Christ. Liturgical creation
was a growing art; Fortunatus in the sixth century adds two

---

[14] *Catholic Encyclopaedia,* s.v. *Kurie.*

[15] One choir sings: *Agios o Theos;* another answers: *Sanctus Deus.* The first
choir: *Agios ischyros;* the second choir: *Sanctus fortis.* The first choir: *Agios
athanatos eleison imas;* the second choir: *Sanctus immortalis, miserere nobis.*

glorious hymns for the Holy Cross, sung on Good Friday, and St. Thomas Aquinas, a poet as well as the *summator* of theology, writes in the thirteenth century a whole mass for the Feast of Corpus Christi. Liturgy grew as a mediaeval cathedral grew, harmonizing new and at first discordant beauties from age to age. Whatever these variations, all faithful Christians in the West felt underneath them the majestic unity of Rome.

The Latin language was also a bond for the community of scholars in the Middle Ages of the West. It was the obvious international tongue for the different countries, employed with a success only feebly approached today by artificial dialects like Esperanto. Students went from school to school, from teacher to teacher, getting the cream of instruction, as in the happy *Wanderjahre* when Germany was free. It was the age of cosmopolitan careers. For the goal of a liberal education was the calling of the Church, and the Church was one and international. Let us take a notable example.

Gerbert was born of humble parents at the town of Aurillac in Auvergne in the middle of the tenth century. At the monastery of Aurillac he attracted the attention of a Spanish count, who took him to Spain, where he studied mathematics and natural sciences under Arabian teachers at Cordova and Seville. He went to Rome with another patron, met the Pope and Emperor Otto I, who appointed him a teacher at the Cathedral School at Reims. After a brief service as abbot of the famous monastery of Bobbio, he returned to Reims, helped raise Hugh Capet to the throne of France, and was elected Archbishop of Reims. Going to Italy again, he won the favor of the Emperor Otto III, who appointed him his teacher; Gerbert was one of those Imperial tutors, like Seneca and Quintilian and Fronto in ancient Rome. He next became Archbishop of Ravenna and, when Pope Gregory V died in A.D. 999, the Emperor secured Gerbert's appointment as his successor. The poor boy of Aurillac little dreamed that one day he would be the first French Pope of Rome. Genius could rise as quickly from poverty to eminence in the Middle Ages as in the days of Augustus when the son of a freedman became a jovial friend of his sovereign, or as in our own country, where the road from a log cabin may lead to the White House.

Gerbert's chief service to his day was to give wider vogue to the science of the Arabs. A representative of the mediaeval humanism of two centuries later was John of Salisbury, who died in A.D. 1180. His pictures of the humanistic school of Chartres in operation are priceless documents in the history of education. He, like Gerbert, illustrates the cosmopolitan culture of the Middle Ages. For, though born in England, he was trained in France, the great centre of learning, and ended his life as Bishop of Chartres. As I have already hinted, it was the golden age of the elective system, when, sure of your subject — the good old training in the liberal arts — you elected your universities and your teachers, wandering round to get the best. One must not think of university life in the Middle Ages as perfect in every part. Scholars there were, but also, as ever since, young men of humble intellects and unindustrious habits. Of these some Oxonian of the times remarked:

> Oxoniam multi veniunt, redeunt quoque stulti.
> Many fools to Oxford come, and many go back home.[16]

Nor were all students serious. There were the gay Goliard strollers, singing of wine, women, and song, whose verses have their own life in the renderings of Helen Waddell.[17] I say these merry writers were not serious. Some of them were highly serious in their daily tasks; only, like Horace and Erasmus, they could give their minds a vacation now and then.

> Sweet it is to play the fool in season:
>
> dulce est desipere in loco.

[16] Possibly it was not an Oxonian who composed this verse. At any rate it may be adapted to any age and any college (if the name will scan).

[17] *Mediaeval Latin Lyrics*, 1930. These are not translations, though the words have literal correspondence. The same elements are taken, and passing through a poet's mind come out as poetry. Deep calls unto deep. The selections include some bits from the ancient poets; for instance, the Virgilian *Copa*. These lyrics should be read along with the gifted author's earlier work, *The Wandering Scholars*, a learned volume in which learning (*heu, nefas, heu!*) is made as interesting as fiction.

In brief, New Rome, with the laughter and the high seriousness of the Old, had thoroughly domiciled itself again in
the Western Middle Ages. Mediaeval life, like mediaeval
education, is nothing spotless. Envy, hatred, malice and all
uncharitableness, along with all the other sins, flourished then
as now.[18] But my present concern is with the heights of the
ideals, from which one might descend, rather than with the
frequency and the rapidity of the descents. One thing is
clear. Thanks to the Catholic Church, the Latin language,
and the program of the liberal arts, a cultivated citizen of any
one of the countries of Europe would find himself at home in
any of the others. There was, therefore, an intellectual and a
spiritual Empire, of which they all were parts. One could see
the One through the Many — most clearly and most richly in
the poetry of Dante.

The Italian Renaissance saw something more than a revival of the Classics. Latin literature had been revived in the
days of Charlemagne, with more and more enlightenment up
to Dante's day. No better conception of Christian humanism
can be found in the Renaissance than he sets forth in both his
theories and his practice. The recovery of Greek literature
at the fall of Constantinople was not an unheralded event.
But the sudden accession of Homer and the tragedians, Aristophanes and Plato's *Republic*, to mention no more, opened
up before the minds of men a realm of gold as full of wonder
and of the incentive to explore as that which Columbus was
soon to find across the seas. Greek and Latin masterpieces
were united once more in the program of liberal training as
they were in the days of ancient Rome. What Dante would
have done had he known Homer and Aeschylus — just those
two — it is interesting to speculate. But, after all, we need
not regret what the fates allowed the Middle Ages, a chance
for the spirit of Virgil's Rome to speak again after the Christian centuries — with no fresh understanding of the Greeks
but with the voice of Dante.

Amid the splendors of the Renaissance in letters and the

[18] For an honest and careful portrayal of the darker aspects of the picture,

Arts, there can be no doubt where ancient Rome was sit-
uated — right where it had always been. Some might wonder
whether the Christian Rome had flown away, perhaps to join
the spirit of Constantinople somewhere in the Far East. We
should note that efforts had been made at various times after
the Latin conquest of Constantinople in A.D. 1204 to heal the
ancient schism of the Church and make the Pope of Rome its
head. Politics on both sides prevented.[19] The Church of the
Renaissance, at all events, commanded respect from abroad.
Its leaders were men of learning and polite deportment. In
such Papal rules as that of Nicholas V in the fifteenth century
(1447–1458) and Leo X in the sixteenth (1513–1522), if philosophers had not become kings, humanists had become Popes.

To be sure, in the abundance of wealth and lavish orna-
ment, the Church, as in St. Jerome's day, may have become,
in his words, "greater in power and wealth, but smaller in virtues": *potentiis quidem et divitiis maior sed virtutibus minor*.[20] Neo-Pagans flourished, we hear, drinking so deeply of
the ancient Helicon, or of the ancient Falernian, that the
draught became a Lethe for all Christian faith or feeling.
Some such there were; but the charge of Neo-Pagan is too
lavishly flung round, especially by those who have not followed
the course of Christian humanism. One of the victims is
Iacopo Sannazaro, who, with his brother poet Pontano, wrote
rich and musical Latin verse, as much a mother tongue to
them as their native Italian. Their poetry has many an echo
of Virgil and Ovid and Horace and Catullus and all the rest,
but they always have something of their own to say, and the
beauty of the bay of Naples is in their art; Sannazaro creates
nymphs for its islands and capes and for his villa, just as
Horace planted the Golden Age in his Sabine Farm. Sannazaro's "Hymn on the Nativity" (*De Partu Virginis*), one of

I would commend the various books of my esteemed friend Dr. G. G. Coulton,
with whom I locked horns in *A Romantic Approach to the Middle Ages*.

[19] See Vasiliev *op. cit.* II 350–352. One wonders what would have happened
at the Council of Lyons in A.D. 1274, if Thomas Aquinas, who was coming to
take part, had not died on the way.

[20] *Vita Malchi* 1.

the most famous poems of his day, and many days to come, is a precursor of Milton's art of weaving ancient colors into a fabric new and sacred.[21] Such poets are Pagan, if Pagan is the word for the architecture of San Lorenzo.

At any rate, the Church survived the luxury of the Renaissance, from which it gained in depth of ancient culture. It had survived the Dark Ages of Merovingian times. It survived the Reformation. As a corrective of morals, particularly in connection with indulgences, the protest of Luther seems deserved; it was met by a Counter-reformation — if that is the right term — within the Church, whether or no that movement preceded, or accompanied, or followed that which Luther started. The dates are not ultimately significant. A longing for more spiritual purity and cleaner practices was in the air. Such a vision came to the soldier Ignatius Loyola as he lay wounded at Pampeluna in 1521. Luther might have waited.

The illustrious Order founded by St. Ignatius Loyola worked out a system of education of vast significance for the topic of this book. Its contributions to the art of teaching are as momentous as those of the Order of St. Benedict have been to learning from the days of Cassiodorus to Mabillon and to Wilmart. The *Ratio atque Institutio Studiorum Societatis Jesu,* familiarly called *Ratio Studiorum,*[22] finally formulated

[21] This poem, in three books, is nearer to lyric than to epic, with much of the nature of one of the longer Homeric hymns. It is serious, reverential, and in places mystic. It is shot through with Virgil, whose Messianic eclogue is skillfully used for prophecy. The wealth of mythology absorbed into the story of the Incarnation by Sannazaro is not a ludicrous blasphemy; rather, all the images created by the ancient poets are summoned with the shepherds to worship at the crib. One of the admirers of the poem was the eminent person to whom in a poetical preface it was dedicated, Pope Clement VII. The last couplet reads, with a pleasant touch of banter: Rarus honos summo se praeside posse tueri; Rarior a summo praeside posse legi: "'Tis a rare honor by the Church's head To be protected — rarer to be read." Clement VII, though wobbly as a diplomat and responsible for a new capture of the City by the northern barbarians (in 1527), was a connoisseur of art and letters; he was also discovered by Henry VIII of England to be firm as a rock on matrimonial formalities.

[22] See Father Donnelly's recent book on *The Principles of Jesuit Education in Practice.* He has for many years been at Fordham University, professor of rhetoric, making a living force of what has generally become a lost art.

under Claudius Acquaviva, the head of the Order from 1581 to 1615, was based on the ancient liberal arts, among which the study of the Classics was an inseparable part. It is the ancient program of Christian humanism that had prevailed in the schools of the Renaissance, like those of Vittorino da Feltre and Guarino da Verona. Old Rome and New were packed by the Jesuits in a portmanteau, ready to be carried to any land and any government. Not all governments have welcomed the Society of Jesus, fearing some subversive propaganda underneath.

In our hospitable land, Jesuit and other Catholic institutions are the last refuge of the Classics as a fixed part of the College program. At the same time, Jesuit education has not only kept pace with the amazing development of the natural sciences in our times but has supplied, from its ranks, investigators of world-wide fame. Let us hope that the Catholic colleges, while hospitable to science, may hold firm against the encroachment of less meaty disciplines! For science may dwell peaceably with religion. As a wise man has said: [23] "Science is the reason, art the joy, religion the harmony of life." Finally, true to the original intention, the Jesuit institution, like other Catholic colleges, provides for the training not only of the mind and the soul but of the body; its athletic teams command respect.

The establishment of Protestantism in various countries of Europe, particularly Germany and England, and at first France, with its transmission to our own country in the seventeenth century, has naturally led to the disintegration of New Rome. When the Church was replaced by the Bible as the source of authority, the interpretation of the Bible led first to the formation of different denominations, determined by their modes of interpretation, in the freest of which interpretation became a matter for the individual conscience. Finally, with the rise of modern critical scholarship, no Bible was left to interpret, in the former sense. It remained a master-

[23] G. Sarton, "The History of Medicine Versus the History of Art," *Bulletin of the History of Medicine*, X (1941), 135.

piece of literature, especially in Luther's translation and in the noble English version which King James's scholars revised. Rather a library than a book, it contains in prose and poetry a record of the historical and the spiritual experience of the Jews, the gospel of our Lord, and the annals of the early Church. It long will be read with devotion, or it will be put away and rediscovered. In some Protestant denominations it is still a divine textbook. In some it is still true from cover to cover. In others there is no compelling reason to turn its pages, unless the spirit moves.

In education there has been a similar disintegration, so far as the old Liberal Arts are concerned. Once the pride of Oxford and Cambridge, they were brought over by graduates of Cambridge in the seventeenth century to establish again in the new college that bears John Harvard's name; they flourished in full vigor down to President Eliot's reform, since when all over our country they have fought a losing battle.[24] Worse still, with the growing disintegration of the Protestant Church, religion has been gradually squeezed out of education both in our public schools and in all but the Catholic colleges.[25] No doubt about it. The world is throwing treasures away and entering the Dark Ages again.

Some such gloomy thoughts as these were running in my head a few nights ago as I lay in my bed, when suddenly I went to sleep again and dreamed that I had ascended to a pleasant place in some starry sphere. It seemed like the Milky Way, or some Metagalactical Way, not without the savor of

[24] The danger in obliterating all vestiges of a liberal education in which the Classics play a significant part is beginning to dawn on more than one of our educational leaders today. See for instance the *Report of the President of Harvard University to the Board of Overseers*, Cambridge, 1942, pp. 24–26. The most eloquent plea delivered of late for the old training is Sir Richard Livingstone's *The Classics and National Life*, the Presidential Address delivered on April 22, 1941 to the [British] Classical Association, Oxford University Press, 1941. In similar vein is an address by C. S. Collier, *The Significance of Phi Beta Kappa*, delivered at the annual meeting of the Alpha Chapter of D.C. at The George Washington University, June 9, 1941.

[25] The evil of this situation, too, is becoming more and more apparent. See President Conant's Baccalaureate Sermon of June 7, 1942, "A Statement of Faith" (*Harvard Alumni Bulletin*, XLIV (1942), 530–532.

the heavenly rose high up in the Empyrean and yet suggestive of that greensward within castle walls where the sages
and poets of old, confined perforce to the inferno, seemed to
enjoy, by Dante's grace, the pleasures of the contemplative
life. In fact, as my eyes became accustomed to the mystic light,
I saw approaching a little company made up of some of those
whom Dante mentions [26] — Homer and Horace, Terence and
Ovid and Lucan, Plato and Cicero and Livy. When I saw
that Polybius, unheralded by Dante, came with the rest, the
dream nearly turned to a nightmare, lest these subjects of the
present discourses, who had often in recent weeks visited me
in nightmares, had come to demand condign punishment for
my misrepresentations of their views. My fears were strengthened when I saw that Dante, with his good guide Virgil, had
joined the company, and that St. Augustine had slipped down
from the Circle of the Rose — ah, hence that fragrance. As I
stood trembling, and thought I heard Virgil murmuring

> obstipuit steterunt comae vox faucibus haesit,

one of the band advanced with a dignity becoming his eminence and looked not ungraciously in my direction. It was
Marcus Tullius Cicero.

"My friends and I," he said, "have perceived the agitation
of your spirit, and have come to take part in a *disputatio* with
you."

"Master," I cried, "such honor is too great for me, but if
you vouchsafe it, let the *disputatio* be arranged in the fashion
that your auditor demanded in the First Book of your *Tusculan Disputations*. I will do the listening. Do you pour forth
a profuse strain of well-premeditated thought:

Sed nihil te interpellabo; continentem orationem audire malo."

"On the contrary," Cicero replied, "my friends and I desire
to converse with you. We are in touch with the events of your
day, and in fact have heard parts of your Lowell Lectures,
thanks to the Intermetagalactical Broadcasting Company, and

[26] *Inferno* IV or elsewhere.

while some of it was cut off by static and some — pardon me —
by soporific — " "Oh, I quite understand," said I. "We
should like to hear," he continued, "a clearer statement on
certain points, and about some of them my friends can speak
better than I. We have all come to understand each other
better here, where souls slough off their bodies, but we all still
have our specialties, you know."

"Gracious Master, as you will." "Good!" said Cicero. "Proceed."

"I was lamenting our times," I began. "*O tempora, o mores*,
if you understand what I mean." Cicero bowed gravely. "For
we see in our present economic and social and moral standards
the same disintegration that prevails in the course of modern
religion and education. Our fathers sowed the wind and we
are reaping the whirlwind. When three great nations, Germany, Italy, and Japan, all of whom have made notable contributions to human civilization, now wage wars without
declaring them" — at this I saw Polybius shudder — "flaunt
on their banners the motto that might makes right, and replace *superbia* with *humilitas* as the most deadly of the deadly
sins," — "What!" interjaculated St. Augustine — "not only," I
continued, "our present equilibrium but the moral balance of
over two millennia are overturned." "Exactly so," remarked
Cicero. "For if your contemporaries will examine, I will not
say the ethical ideals of antiquity, but the commonsense principles of action that all mankind thought no more than simply
decent, if you will trace them from Homer down in diverse
forms of literature, in diverse schools of philosophic thought,
as diverse as Platonic idealism and Epicurean materialism,
you can put together a code of simple moral principles held
as axioms. They are neatly assembled in the poems of our
friend Horace here, who, busy Matinian bee, flitted from
flower to flower and packed the honey in a small but comfortable jar." "Yes," added Dante, "the core of ancient ethics —
not all the articles — was taken over with approval by the
Church. You will find, for instance, in that eminently sensible work of St. Gregory the Great, on "Pastoral Care" (*Cura*

*Pastoralis*), and, a bit after my time, in the poetic, and no less practical, meditations of Thomas à Kempis, utterances that have the savor of the old poets, whom indeed these pious authors had known in school."

"This lineage of moral precept, of ordinary decency," I went on, "has now been snapped like a cord by the rulers of Germany, Italy, and Japan. Two sins, just two, as you, Holy Father Augustine observed, lie at the root of all the blunders and transgressions of nations — avarice and pride. Horace knows their symptoms and their cures."

"Increasing wealth," said Horace solemnly, "is attended by cares and by the thirst for more. . . . The more a man denies himself, the more he shall receive from the gods. Unclothed I fly to the camp of those who covet naught, and eagerly leave the party of the rich, more sumptuous as lord of a despised estate than if whate'er the industrious Apulian plows I were said to bury in my granaries, poor amidst great wealth — *magnas inter opes inops*. And again: God hath power to change high with low. He taketh down the mighty from their seat, and hath exalted the humble and meek. And again: Because thou walkest humbly with thy gods, hence, Roman, dost thou rule. Shall I quote more?" "No, that will do, Horace," said St. Augustine. "The resemblance of these sayings, in spirit and in form, to familiar words of the Old Testament and the New is plain enough. Horace's is not the kind of paganism to which Herr Hitler would return." "Right!" put in Dante. "Nor is his new 'Civic Communion' at Easter nearly so attractive as the Devil's Mass that my so-called Middle Ages knew. Even Rutilius Namatianus, despiteful of Christians and Jews alike, worshipped his goddess Rome not merely because she rules, but because she has the good right to rule."

"Master," said I, turning to Cicero, who thus far had been very taciturn for him, "may I ask what you think of the new Ideal Roman Empire that flourishes in Italy today?" "Ideal Empire," he replied, "is perhaps our poet Virgil's concern. He will speak if he wishes. As for me, I saw some good in the

grandiose ambition of the Italian *dux*. His soul was fired
with a passion to revive the glory of old Rome, and your
learned men are not sorry for the buried monuments of
antiquity that he brought to light. But his rule, like the tyrant's, was based on might; he was at once a builder and a
barbarian invader of eternal Rome. His family seems to be
ancient Republican — the Decii, you know — Publius Decius
Mus. Ah me, if he hadn't added that stupendous *agnomen* —
Publius Decius Montanus Mus."

"May I point out," Lucan spoke up, "if Virgil will only
agree, that my warning prophecy has been fulfilled? I coun-
seled Nero, with my tongue in my cheek, as he took his place
on the heavenly axis, to take care to sit in the middle, lest his
spiritual ponderosity by moving too far north or too far south
should upset the cosmic equilibrium.

> Aetheris immensi partem si presseris unam,
> Sentiet axis onus.

Now this modern tyrant has slid south nearly to the end of
the pole. Yet luckily, such is his lessened weight, and such
that of his northern partner that the world still revolves as
before."

"I fear we are jesting unduly," declared Cicero. "The foes
of peace and decency are by no means conquered as yet."

"May I have one word?" spoke up Phaedrus, who, as befitted a slave, had lurked unseen in the background. "By all
means," said Augustine. "We are all slaves and all free."

"Well, Masters," said Phaedrus, "even suppose they win —
they who have strayed from the path of ancient decency; they
cannot conquer. They can overrun lands but not the souls of
men nor human scorn. They cannot see why in the eyes of
your English Meredith or your French Balzac their hob-
nailed clatterings in the Place de la Concorde rouse laughter
unquenchable, and not subservient awe before imperial majesty. Perhaps one day when they find they have been strutting
a comic stage, these genial Germans, *ganz gemüthlich* and
*ganz wissenschaftlich* when they are not given too subtle a

rôle to play, will themselves break out in laughter or break out in revolt.

"And now if you don't mind I will repeat one of my fables —a humble affair, like all my servile poetry, but perhaps with some pertinence just here. It is the fable of the greedy man, one of the 'Haves' who wasn't happy.

"A fox, engaged in constructing a rather complicated system of dugouts for his residence, bored his way into a dismal cavern where lay a dragon guarding a hidden treasure. 'Pardon this intrusion,' said the Fox, 'but now that I'm here, and seeing that I have no interest in the treasure that you are so solemnly guarding, would you mind telling me just *why* you're doing this? Isn't it a rather monotonous task, and don't you ever wish for a nap?' The Dragon replied that he got nothing out of it, but that he was assigned to that duty by Almighty Jove. 'So you neither receive anything for yourself nor give to anybody else?' 'Such,' replied the Dragon, with all the gravity of Faffner, 'is the pleasure of Fate.' 'Don't get mad if I speak out my mind,' rejoined the Fox, 'but the Gods were certainly out of temper on the day when you were born.' "

"Many thanks, good Phaedrus," said I. "If you are destined to be slaves under the blessed New Order of Hitler, may we be such slaves as you. But what Rome eternal can we build, in the case the free nations win this war? If some magic power should sweep away the outer forms of nations and force the world to begin again with the harmony of religion, government, and education that you, O Dante, possessed in spirit and saw partly realized on earth, for one I could make myself at home. That would be putting back the hands of the clock, as our up-to-the-minute friends would say. They want us to throw it away and try their latest model. But the old clock will keep good time, just you wind her up."

"Yes, because she's set by eternity," replied Dante. "But you're right in saying my dream was only partly realized. My times were frightful, worse than yours, and so it is always with the Church militant there upon earth. You must face your world as it is. It is different from the compact little Europe that I knew. My countryman Columbus, Admiral of the Ocean Sea, was partly responsible for that. I see now a vast assortment of nations, each with its right to live and thrive in its own way. A new Roman empire, or a new British, or a new American empire would be unthinkably disastrous. You tried to form a family of nations at the end of the last war, but chiefly through the failure of your own country to abide by the covenant that it had recommended to the others, new dissension and not new unity was the outcome. The resolve to fight a war to end all wars is not an idle fancy that faded because you have become worldly-wise. It is the only goal for you now as then, and as in the days when my master Virgil and I dreamed of universal peace. You will have your chance once more. If you do not grasp it, after your chastening, you will be incredibly ungrateful and insensate." "I see," said I. "And forget not that your New Order," continued Dante, "must be established on the foundation of mutual forgiveness and good will. No race of men is so degenerate that you should find it impossible to offer for them the prayer that Christ raised on the cross for those who tortured Him to death. To think that ideals have perished because you have been false to ideals is a most comic form of self-conceit. The firmament does not crash when you fall down."

"Or even if it does," chanted Horace, "its ruins will strike the just man undismayed." "Yes, indeed, my tuneful Matinian bee," said Dante; "but what has good Cicero, who has not been able to get a word in edgewise, to say to all this?"

"Nothing except that in my little work on the state, which did have something of a vogue down the centuries, I drew my doctrine straight from the lessons that Polybius taught young Scipio there." "Ah, yes, my Cicero," spoke up Polybius, "but you expressed those ideas so much more eloquently than I." "Well, Polybius, do you begin, and when you like, I will take up the strain."

"Very well, then," Polybius said, "here is my new adjustment of our old theories to the modern age. Each nation in this new family will have the form of government that it considers best suited to its needs. Much may be said for what you call a constitutional monarchy, like England's, like Norway's, and, in bygone days, like Italy's, in which the King, in the fashion that I described after our Plato and our Aristotle, is father of his people. If instead the government is a democracy, whether your kind or some more socialistic or communistic sort, or an autocracy, or what you will, let a nation have it if it so desires, provided that it effects a harmony with justice among its people and that its presence does nothing to disturb the international peace. Each nation may change its status as it will, observing the principle of your French Renan that the existence of a nation requires a perpetual plebiscite, and heeding the warning of another Frenchman, recently recorded in a fine little volume for which you owe much to Helen Waddell, a knowing interpreter of your Middle Ages, O Dante — of their mysticism and of their fun."

"My Middle Ages, indeed!" exclaimed Dante. "Since when were we 'middling'? We called ourselves *moderni*. Read John of Salisbury, please. These later folk borrowed our word and think it applies only to themselves."

"Of course, of course," said Polybius. "When they learn from us to view the world *sub specie aeternitatis*, and *sub specie humanitatis*, they will orientate themselves more properly. But back to our muttons. Let me quote the French soldier.

" 'It is with régimes as with individuals: they have their youth, their flowering, their decadence and their death. The decadence of democracy is demagogy, its death dictatorship.' I, too, had said that, in other words. Now to continue.

"If identity in polity may not be demanded of the different nations, an economic identity or an economic equilibrium in their commercial relations would seem not only a possible but an indispensable reform. However long the period of adjustment or whatever the exceptions made for this nation or for that, the feeling that each and every country was getting a square deal in international business would be the surest guarantee of universal peace. It might be then that forms of government could be re-examined in the light of the economic stability secured, to see if it might not be possible, and desirable, to make them more nearly of the same pattern. But now it's your turn, Cicero."

"Well, if you insist," Marcus Tully replied. "What seems true of the economic relation of any one state with its neighbors would apply to the relations of its citizens in their commercial dealings with one another and likewise to the relation of social class to class. For, as you and I declared, the conception of a classless society is unfruitful and untrue. We are born free and equal, but we cannot stay so, after nursery-days are over; for we are not equally equipped with intelligence or the desire to rise. So long as the political and the economic structure of the government or the character of the administration of the government offers the individual any inducement to push ahead there will always be three classes of citizens on the basis of wealth and power and achievement of any sort. There will always be, to use most humble and unscientific terms, upper-dogs, dogs, and under-dogs. This classification presupposes four irrefutable maxims. First, a dog is a dog for all that; so second, be kind to under-dogs, ye top ones; and be hopeful, ye under ones, for, third, every dog may have his day; and fourth, let not dogs delight to bark and bite, though 'tis their nature to.

"Now these three classes, which in the course of social experience form themselves, are, of course, not mutually exclusive and are by no means permanent. The upper class was formed by those who had the strength to rise. They will stay on top just as long as its members contribute to the welfare of the whole society. The moment they are affected with pride and begin to despise those beneath them — that is, as our visitor from the tiny world below would say, to put on dog — they then give up the right to their place. They either decay in peace or are driven from their heights by attacks from below; under-dogs and just plain dogs arise in wrath, tear down the unworthy upper-dogs, and the social round begins again. I have descended to the *sermo plebeius*, Polybius, but you will understand."

"Indeed I do, most noble Roman. I'm glad to find that you don't talk periods all the time."

"Just so. Glance at my *Letters* sometime. A word more, since at last I have a chance to speak. Whatever the government of a state, these three classes seem bound to exist if the free and normal action and the rightful ambition of the individual are not impeded by some New Order bent on liquidation. Wealth may be liquidated, but not intelligence or power."

"Yes," spoke up Horace, "nor greed. And more than that, it's a shame to equalize wealth; for then the poor man hasn't the delight of knowing how much happier he can be than the rich. And think how the satirist will be hit. Now he feeds on wealthy egoists, though never invited to dinner. But then his 'slim, feasting smile' will be more slim than feasting."

"Good enough," smiled Cicero. "You certainly would lose your job. Even more serious, however, than that calamity is the prospect that in a strictly classless society the power that controls it, for some power there must be, will be either a single tyrant or an oligarchy. If a nation desires precisely that sort of government, as Russia apparently does today, no other nation should interfere, unless its own freedom is threatened by such a neighbor."

"Watch Russia well," put in Polybius. "They are fighting now not for an ideology but for their soil. And their generals, struggling against heavy odds, outstrip the Germans and everybody else in strategy and tactics. Even you Romans have something to learn from them."

"Thank you," said Cicero. "At all events it is likely that when the members of the new family sit down to dinner, their table manners will grow more and more alike; the totalitarian governments will then no longer eat with their knives. That is what my Livy and I meant by our phrase *concordia ordinum*, a principle well understood by the Schoolmen and by Dante and by Holy Church, to which some of my writings were vouchsafed to pave the way. For that harmony is what the 'blessed night' that precedes the morn of Easter brings to the Christian world — *fugat odia, concordiam parat, curvat imperia*. I thank you for letting me finish this little speech. *Dixi*."

"Good Cicero," said I, "I hope that is not positively your last word. But tell me, will there be no more wars? If none, won't you be sorry, O Livy, who described them so well?" "Not I," said Livy. "I only drew pictures on my page, except when I copied Polybius." "Not at all, my dear Livy," answered Polybius. "You got some facts that escaped me. I'll not regret the passing of war. There will be plenty of novelties to take its place. Some kind of world police there must be, with the latest military equipment, while all the nations are disarmed, except for their own police protection. If any nation again be guilty of aggression, it will, by that token, be guilty of civil war." "Oh, I know!" exclaimed Livy. "Let's revert to single combat, or triple-combat, if you like — Horatii against Curiatii, you remember, way back in the days of yore." "Not bad, my colleague. Men will never forget your description of that fight. I never could paint like that — quite as exciting as a football match." "See here," Horace spoke up. "Our guest has told us how martial football has become. Let international quarrels be settled by international games. In our day war was indeed a game — for Mars, who glutted himself with bellicosities —

> Heu nimis longo satiate ludo

said I to him. The Furies arranged these ghastly exhibitions, at which he always sat in the orchestra circle —

> Dant alios Furiae torvo spectacula Marti!

Now let's have football and invite the crowd — gate-receipts to go to the winner for strictly educational purposes. Many a national ruler, many a college president, would find that a happy solution."

"And now," said I, filled with a new hope for mankind, "I wonder if Dante will tell us what will become of the Church?"

"Gladly," said he. "But first I must thank Cicero for ap-

plauding our good Livy. I understood him — didn't I? —
when I wrote

> siccome Livio scrive, che non erra.

For he doesn't err, Cicero, if he agrees with you, does he?"

Cicero said nothing, but I seemed to see him nod his head.
And then Dante thus continued:

"The Church in your new Roman Empire may perhaps not
be of one form, at least as things look now. The most natural
candidate for universality, judging by mere geography, would
seem to be my Roman Catholic Church, since, unless I mistake, upon it, as still upon the British Empire, the sun never
sets. One obstacle to the world dominion of the Catholic
Church was removed by that Concordat some thirteen years
before this day, when a Pope cherished not only by all the
faithful but by all of your times who have worked with manuscripts at the Bibliotheca Apostolica Vaticana under his
kindly eye —" "Yes," interrupted Cicero, excitedly, "and a
friend of that great Cardinal, Giovanni Mercati, who gave the
world the final edition of the fragments of my poor *De Re
Publica*!"

"I know," continued Dante, "and even more important
than that, that great and scholarly Pope renounced all but a
nominal temporal power, only to make his spiritual power
more deeply and more widely reverenced. For over the world
in vastly different governments Catholics may with a new
meaning render under Caesar the things that are Caesar's, and
unto God the things that are God's."

"But," I ventured to interpose, "*o altissimo poeta*, there
are other Christian Churches like the Greek and the Russian,
different forms of the Church of East Rome, as well as the
Armenian and part at least of the Anglican Church who cherish the conviction that they too descend in a straight line
from the faith once delivered to the saints. Likewise the
Lutheran Church and the various forms of Protestantism believe that in revolting from the Catholic Church they have
merely peeled off accretions that subtle theologians and fussy

liturgists have plastered on the simple faith of Jesus of Naz-areth. There are also noble religions outside the Christian fold, those of the East — China and India and Japan — and in particular the Hebrew religion from which Christianity sprang under a Jewish leader. In all of these there are good and saintly souls, who in both faith and works often put Christians to the blush."

"Aye," interposed Augustine. "Think of St. Peter's words: 'Of a truth I perceive that God is no respecter of persons: but in every nation he that feareth him and worketh right-eousness is accepted with him.' Think of the words of Our Lord: 'Other sheep I have that are not of this fold: them also I must bring, and they shall hear my voice; and there shall be one fold and one shepherd.' "

"Verily may God grant," I continued, "that there shall be one fold. In recent years there have been many attempts among us to bring the Christian churches under one roof. But the problem of finding the least common denominator of the denominations has met with no solution — unless it be a zero. In war, at the front, or in some civic disasters, Protestant min-ister and Jewish Rabbi and Catholic priest have toiled to-gether for the wounded and the dying, knowing, with a rare sense of elevation, that their religious faiths have met at last on a common ground when dispensed in works of mercy for human beings in distress. But their creeds have surrendered not one iota of those articles that they hold dear. Perhaps that is all for which we can hope in peace as well as war — a kindly tolerance of others' beliefs, a strong and healthy toler-ance, not an indifference to beliefs, as though they did not matter. Father, forgive us, for we know not what we think."

"Many human dreams," Dante went on, "must perish be-fore the hard facts of life. To make actual the vision of Eter-nal Rome upon earth would itself take an eternity. But the vision abides. Your Santayana, and mine, says in his latest work, the keystone of his philosophy:

" 'Plato, who had the soul of a poet, knew perfectly how much he was sacrificing to the desperate enterprise of maintaining an impregnable and incorruptible city on earth; and the Church afterwards acknowledged that on earth it was but a Church militant; triumph, liberation, happiness could come only in heaven.'

"That is well said," continued Dante, "and bear in mind that the Church militant fights foes within as well as without." "Yes, indeed," spoke up St. Augustine, "I wrote a book on Heresies. One hundred and twenty-eight had been recorded in my time, and though some said there were only eighty, even that number may suggest your own epoch's fertility in dissension. The City of God of which I dreamed is indeed in the heavens above. For all that the Church below does well to struggle for unity. For thus it shows its vigor — *eppur si muove*."

"Master Cicero," I said, "Dante and Augustine have somewhat comforted me. But could you assure me that your works and the works of all this noble and ancient company are not bound for oblivion in the years ahead?"

"I should have no fear," he replied. "But please do not call us ancients. We are all of one company. The Greeks, our masters in everything, passed us the torch. We ran with it and handed it on. If works survive a bimillennium — as Virgil's and Horace's did (and mine, incidentally, though nobody noticed the fact) — they are not two thousand years old but two thousand years young." "Cicero," I interrupted hastily, "I am ashamed of my generation, and all the more so because, if my count is right, the two thousandth anniversary of your birth in 106 B.C. coincided with the year when I graduated from college in 1894. I can only plead in excuse that on your birthday, January 3rd, we were taking our Mid-year Examinations — " "Oh, I see," replied Cicero. "Say no more. I perfectly understand. Now if you need more comfort, this I say. In the building of your Rome, the ancient authors will lay the foundations for you as of old. Schools and colleges may find them out of date, but in Thucydides and Plato and Aristotle, in Polybius and Livy and Tacitus (and another author, *quem pudoris causa non nomino*) the principles on which your new confederation must be founded are set forth with a more durable modernity than in the studies of contemporary polity and society that now are driving us out. Fifty years from now these present studies will be ripe for the museum of curiosities, while the ancients who taught the principles of good government to your forefathers will teach them to your sons. And, in the art of life, have you forgotten what our Terence's George Meredith said about the Classic scholar?" "I know," broke in Horace. "It is in his chapter 'On an Aged and a Great Wine,' and it goes:

" 'Of all our venerable British of the two Isles professing a suckling attachment to an ancient port-wine, lawyer, doctor, squire, rosy admiral, city-merchant, the classic scholar is he whose blood is most nuptial to the webbed bottle. The reason must be, that he is full of the old poets. He has their spirit to sing with, and the best that Time has done on earth to feed it.' "

As Horace read, Cicero nodded approval and then spoke on: "And you certainly must not neglect a message, recently broadcast to us from your Livingstone. He will tell you what statesmen were brought up on me and my confederates here. It is a tract for the times and a banner of hope to defenders of Greek and Latin. Nor have a fear lest any one call you dull and pedantic. You did not kill the Classics — they cannot be killed. If you transmit to your students a sound knowledge of the Greek and Latin tongues, the only keys to our temples, and if you can translate us into your own language, not into jargon, you will open our doors and despite your explanations, our visitors will see our beauties with their own eyes. Though small your numbers you need only to have faith that the treasures you guard will shine out once more as they have cast their light on even darker days. In the Middle Ages, for instance, — oh, pardon me, Dante —" and Cicero stopped abruptly.

I then heard a voice, it seemed like Dante's, and yet the tones of St. Augustine were distinguishable, and those of Virgil, too, and Horace, and Cicero, and indeed all the members of that choir invisible, the grave and the gay, all speaking, or chanting, one chorus with many parts — and these are the words of their song: "There is an eternal Rome to which those of high spirit may mount without delay. All roads lead up to it. No one can follow all, but each may make some headway towards the goal. You each may build a little city in the skies.

"You may follow the path of history and, if you will, trace periods of decline and fall or plot the cycles that tell us what is coming next. These cycles may never get any deeper into historical fact than the cerebral cycles whence they sprang. But unless your readers take too much to heart your prognostication of woe and cry, 'Ah, mercy me, the end of the world is come!' your work will do no harm, since it will direct your generation to reading history, and to pondering on what history means, in the spirit of Santayana, And thus for more enlightenment, you may pass to some good novel, to which philosophy of history has paved the way.

"Or you may follow the course of human progress, though the end may be your disappointment — or your illumination. A light will dawn if you note the ideals that any age sets forth, rather than the deviations from the norm, and conclude that the only progress you can measure is that of some one man."

And then the voice I heard was that of Dante. "A man, like good Augustine, as I said of him, may go from bad to good, from good to better and from better to best, or, if he go the other way, like Tiberius in Tacitus's judgment, his age is not primarily to blame; for both these men had fallen on evil times and evil days. There is no progress in material improvements, even as Seneca, *saepe noster*, observed. Progress follows not the horizontal line of history, but the vertical line that guides a man's eyes to the firmament. When all eyes are thus star-ypointing, then of a truth will there be a heaven on earth.

"Whatever your religious belief today, or lack of a formal religion, it is at least a broken light from New Rome East and West. Even if your creed and rites are most simple in

character you will know them better if you compare them
with what the Greek or the Roman Church has treasured
from antiquity. For you of the West, the Catholic faith is nearest to your origins. Whether you accept that faith or not, a
study of the Roman Missal, the reading of the Mass from day
to day, the Mass appropriate for each day, and thus the
knowledge of the richness of the Christian year, will open up
new worlds. For even though you cannot accept the faith that
we hold dear, at least you should know what it is that you
cannot accept.

"So you need not be a Catholic or a Christian to make this
exploration worth the while. A good companion with whom
to start the voyage will be your Santayana, most iridescent of
the lights of America in days gone by. You he may

> Despise, but is himself so bright
> He'll flood your hearts with love and quench your hate.

"A Catholic in his youth, Santayana turned to the philosophy of nature, Lucretius somewhat assisting. His *summa
philosophiae naturalis* has appeared, volume after volume, and
none is more illuminating than the last. He who, by his own
declaration, was the only consistent materialist alive, now caps
the series with the book called *The Realm of the Spirit*. His
philosophy remains the same, but whether through the influence of his Plato, or his own spirit of poetry, a strange light
shines through his philosophy of nature. If his materialism
is as spiritual as some philosophers' idealism is matter-of-fact,
his honest intentions are not to blame. Like his brother-
materialist Lucretius, he did what he could. If he presents a
kind of materialistic allegorization of the doctrines of the
Church, the doctrines of the Church are only veiled by the
allegory. He has added to their mysticism, and perhaps to his
own.

"Here are his closing words on dogmas and creeds, which
he finds are at least

the companions and vehicles of a spiritual discipline. They do
not thereby become miraculously true; nevertheless they reveal

inner and outer harmonies established with long labor and sacrifice in the human soul. There they remain fountains of wisdom and self-knowledge, at which we may still drink in solitude. Perhaps the day may return when mankind will drink of them again in society.

"Santayana is a philosopher and a poet of timelessness. And timelessness is the last and best of T. S. Eliot's poems, *The Dry Salvages*; despite Kipling, the philosophy of East and West have met in this poem of the timeless sea. Many are the dissensions and frustrations, many are sins and follies in the warfare of the world. But Greece and Rome and the Church of Christ have built an *urbs aeterna*, whose timelessness is the right of its citizens upon earth. So Dante learned when his dear teacher, like a father, taught him the old disciplines, that make the mind of man eternal here and now."

I knew not then whether I was listening to all or only one of the choir, or whether I was merely lost in thought at what they had been singing. And yet at the end the voice of one was clear who, with his accustomed reticence, had not spoken before. But now Virgil said, "This vision does not issue by the Ivory Gate." And so I awoke, like Scipio from his dream: *illi discesserunt, ego somno solutus sum.*

# EPILOGUE

At the end of that last lecture of the course given at the Lowell Institute, I added the following remarks, which I venture to repeat here, thinking that some of my readers in search of good reading may find them useful.

"Ladies and Gentlemen of this courteous audience, now that we all have awakened, kindly accept my thanks. Rome was not built in a day, still less in shifts of time amounting to eight hours. At least I hope that I have pointed out how we each may build a small but eternal Rome.

"Perhaps you might like a few suggestions for your reading. Even if you know nothing of the languages, get the original texts along with accurate prose translations. For the ancients, The Loeb Classical Library with its translations into English, and the *Belles Lettres* series, with equally successful translations into French, will give you ample help. Learn the pronunciation of the language, and if the work is poetry, the metres of the poems it contains. Read the translation of a passage, not too long, to get the sense, and then the text to get the music. Perhaps that will spur you to master the elements of the language. The more of that you know, the richer your experience will become.

"Here are a few programs, to suggest others that you will make for yourselves, after reading some brief history of the different literatures.

1. Homer, Virgil, Dante, Milton.
2. Thucydides, Polybius, Livy, Tacitus, Gibbon, and Trevelyan.
3. Polybius, Livy, Machiavelli, and *horribile dictu, Mein Kampf.*
4. The Greek tragedians, Shakespeare, and Goethe's *Faust.*
5. Aristophanes, Plautus, Terence, Molière, Goldoni, Congreve. But I had better stop, even with Horace and Ovid left out in the cold. Oh, well, I will add one or two more —

6. Greek Lyric poets, Catullus, Horace, the Goliards (including Villon), Ronsard, and English lyric poets of the seventeenth century.

7. Ovid, Boccaccio, Chaucer, and Rabelais.

8. Begin your reading, of at least half an hour a day, with something from the Roman Missal, edited by Dom Cabrol with an English translation, or with something from your own service-book, whatever it may be.

"In all these programs top off with some of the poets of our day. After your course in the ancients, you will be better able to distinguish those of our day who flourish a contemporary flashlight, from those who have caught the torch to pass it on. Remember Santayana's maxim, declared in the preface to his collected poems, 'To say that what was good once is good no longer is to give too much importance to chronology.' Modern and ancient will lie down happily together, if each in his fashion has laid hold of eternity.

"Moreover, if we learn to make friends with the best spirits of the past, we need not worry about our ancestry, if that is one of our worries. We shall be taken into the family of Homer and Plato and Cicero and Virgil and all the rest, and thus tie ourselves to a lineage even longer in time and purer in blood than it would have been even if all our fathers had come over in the Mayflower. As Horace, the son of a freedman, remarked, soon after his merits had gained him entrance into the circle of Rome's Four Hundred, 'I am comforted by the thought that my simple life is happier than if my father, my uncle and my grandfather had all been Congressmen.'

"How long it will take to finish all these programs, or any one of them, it would be rash to predict. The reader will doubtless change any one that he starts to suit his taste. It matters not. Each road will lead to Rome and that right quickly. The sights along the way will be enough to fill the rest of our days with what President Eliot called the durable satisfactions of life."

# LIST OF BOOKS

# LIST OF BOOKS

THIS is not a carefully selected bibliography. If it were, it would not include so many references to my own writings. These I give that the reader may be enabled, if he wishes, to supplement the accounts of certain matters treated in this book with what I have said elsewhere. He will doubtless think, as I shall later, of numerous additions to make to the works that are cited here.

## I. EDITIONS AND TRANSLATIONS

### A. THE LOEB CLASSICAL LIBRARY

Most of the classical authors cited will be found in the Loeb Classical Library. This great scholarly undertaking was founded in 1910 by the late Dr. James Loeb and is now nearing completion of its original program of some four hundred volumes. Both texts and translations are of high order. The reader's attention is called particularly to the following items in the Library:

*Aristotle: Parts of Animals,* with an English translation by A. L. Peck (L.C.L. No. 323).

*Boethius: The Theological Tractates,* with an English translation by H. F. Stewart and E. K. Rand [and] *The Consolation of Philosophy,* with the English translation of "I. T." (1609) revised by H. F. Stewart (L.C.L. No. 74).

*Cicero: De Re Publica; De Legibus,* with an English translation by C. W. Keyes (L.C.L. No. 213).

[Fronto.] *The Correspondence of Marcus Cornelius Fronto,* edited and for the first time translated into English by C. R. Haines. 2 vols. (L.C.L. No. 112, 113).

[Marcus Aurelius.] *The Communings with Himself of Marcus Aurelius Antoninus,* a revised text and a translation into English by C. R. Haines (L.C.L. No. 58).

*Minutius Felix,* see *Tertullian.*

*Ovid's Fasti,* with an English translation by Sir James George Frazer (L.C.L. No. 253).

*Ovid: Tristia; Ex Ponto,* with an English translation by A. L. Wheeler (L.C.L. No. 151).

*Plutarch's Lives*, with an English translation by Bernadotte Perrin. 11 vols. (L.C.L. No. 46, 47, 65, 80, 87, 98–103).

*Polybius: The Histories*, with an English translation by W. R. Paton. 6 vols. (L.C.L. No. 128, 137, 138, 159, 160, 161).

[Quintilian.] *The Institutio Oratoria of Quintilian*, with an English translation by H. E. Butler. 4 vols. (L.C.L. No. 124–127).

*Remains of Old Latin*, newly edited and translated by E. H. Warmington. 4 vols. (L.C.L. No. 294, 314, 329, 359).

*St. Augustine's Confessions*, with an English translation by William Watts (1631). 2 vols. (L.C.L. No. 26, 27).

*Scriptores Historiae Augustae, The*, with an English translation by David Magie. 3 vols. (L.C.L. No. 139, 140, 263).

*Seneca: Moral Essays*, with an English translation by J. W. Basore. 3 vols. (L.C.L. No. 214, 254, 310).

*Suetonius*, with an English translation by J. C. Rolfe. 2 vols. (L.C.L. No. 31, 38).

*Tertullian: Apology; De Spectaculis*, with an English translation by T. R. Glover; *Minucius Felix*, with an English translation by Gerald H. Rendall based on the unfinished version by W. C. A. Kerr (L. C. L. No. 250).

### B. OTHER EDITIONS OR TRANSLATIONS

[Aristotle.] *Porphyrii Isagogue et in Aristoteles Categorias Commentarium*, ed. A. Busse (Commentaria in Aristotelem Graeca, vol. IV, no. 1; Berolini: G. Reimer, 1887).

[Augustus.] *Res Gestae Divi Augusti*, ed. R. S. Rogers, K. Scott, and M. M. Ward (Boston: Heath, 1935).

—— *Res Gestae Divi Augusti*, ed. J. Gagé (Publications de la Faculté des Lettres de l'Université de Strasbourg; Paris: Les Belles Lettres, 1935).

*Boethii In Isagogen Porphyrii Commenta*, rec. S. Brandt (Corp. Script. Eccles. Lat. XLVIII; Vienna, 1906).

[Chaucer.] *The Complete Works of Geoffrey Chaucer*, ed. by F. N. Robinson (Boston: Houghton Mifflin, 1933).

[Dante.] *La Divina Commedia di Dante Alighieri*, ed. and annot. by C. H. Grandgent (Boston: Heath, vol. I, rev. ed. 1933).

[Cicero.] *M. Tullii Ciceronis De Re Publica quae supersunt*, ed. Angelo Mai (Romae in Collegio Urbano apud Burliaeum, 1822).

*Constantini Porphyrogeniti Imperatorio De Cerimoniis Aulae Byzantinae*, rec. Io. Iac. Reiskii cum eiusdem commentariis integris (Corpus Scriptorum Historiae Byzantinae VIII; 2 vols.; Bonn: Weber, 1829).

*Constantin VII Porphyrogénète, Le Livre des Cérémonies* (Collection Byzantine, Assoc. Guillaume Budé), Tome I (text and, in a separate volume, commentary, by Albert Vogt) (= Bk. I, 1–46 [37]) (Paris: Les Belles Lettres, 1935).

Donatus, *Vitae Vergilianae*, ed. J. Brummer (Leipzig: Teubner, 1912).

*Excerpta Historica jussa imp. Constantini Porphyrogeniti confecta*, ed. Boissevain, De Boor, Büttner-Wobst. 4 vols. (Berlin: Weidmann, 1903–1910).

[Horace.] *Horace Talks, A Translation*, by H. H. Chamberlin (Norwood, Mass.: The Plimpton Press, 1940).

*Ioannis Saresberiensis Episcopi Carnotensis Policratici sive De Nugis Curialium et Vestigiis Philosophorum libri VIII*, recogn. C. C. I. Webb (Oxon.: Typ. Clarend., 1901).

*Iohannis Scotti Annotationes in Marcianum*, ed. Cora E. Lutz (Cambridge, Mass.: Mediaeval Academy of America, 1939).

Lactantius, *Divinae Institutiones et epitome divinarum institutionum*, rec. S. Brandt (Corp. Script. Eccles. Lat. XIX, Pars I; Vienna: Tempsky, 1890).

*Mediaeval Latin Lyrics*, translated by Helen Waddell (New York: R. R. Smith, 1930).

[Otto of Freising.] *The Two Cities, a Chronicle of Universal History to the Year 1146 A.D., by Otto, Bishop of Freising*, translated with introduction and notes by C. C. Mierow; edited by A. P. Evans and C. Knapp (New York: Columbia University Press, 1928).

*Plutarch's Morals*, translated from the Greek by several hands, corr. and rev. by W. W. Goodwin, with an introduction by Ralph Waldo Emerson (Boston: Little Brown, 1870, with several re-editions).

## II. Books and Articles

### A. ART AND ARCHAEOLOGY

Brehier, L., *La Sculpture et les arts mineurs byzantins*, Histoire de l'Art byzantin, publiée sous la direction de M. Charles Diehl (Paris: Les Éditions d'art et d'histoire, 1936).

Casson, S., "Etruscan Art," *Cambridge Ancient History,* IV (1920), ch. xii.

Diehl, Charles, *La Peinture Byzantine,* Histoire de l'Art byzantin (Paris: Van Oest, 1933).

Hill, Ida Thallon, *Rome of the Kings; an Archaeological Setting for Livy and Virgil* (New York: E. P. Dutton, 1927).

Peebles, B. M., "La Meta Romuli," *Rendiconti della Pontificia Accademia romana di Archeologia,* XII (1886), 21–63.

Platner, S. B., *A Topographical Dictionary of Ancient Rome,* completed and revised by Thomas Ashby (Oxford University Press, 1929).

Rodenwaldt, G., "Art of the Early Empire," *Cambridge Ancient History,* XI (1936).

—— "Art of the Later Empire," *Cambridge Ancient History,* XII (1939).

Scott (Ryberg), Inez, *Early Roman Tradition in the Light of Archaeology,* Memoirs of the American Academy in Rome, VII (1929).

*An Archaeological Record of Rome from the Seventh to the Second Century B.C.,* Studies and Documents edited by K. Lake and S. Lake, vol. XIII (Philadelphia: University of Pennsylvania Press, 1940), reviewed by G. M. A. Hanfmann, *Amer. Journ. Archaeol.* XLV (1941), 489–493.

Shaw, C., *Etruscan Perugia,* Johns Hopkins Studies in Archaeology, No. 28 (Baltimore, 1939), reviewed by Lily R. Taylor, *Class. Phil.* XXXIX (1942), 206.

Strong, Eugénie, "Art of the Roman Republic," *Cambridge Ancient History,* IX (1932), ch. xx.

Van Buren, A. W., "Art of the Augustan Age," *Cambridge Ancient History,* X (1934), ch. xvii.

Whatmough, J., *The Foundations of Roman Italy* (London: Methuen, 1937).

### B. OTHER SUBJECTS

Addleshaw, G. W. O., *The High Church Tradition: a study in the liturgical thought of the seventeenth century* (London: Faber and Faber, 1941).

Alföldi, A., "Hoc signo victor eris," *Pisciculi* (Festschrift for Father F. J. Dölger; Münster: Klauser and Rücker, 1939).

Bainville, Jacques de, *La Troisième République, 1870–1935* (Paris: Fayard, 1935).

Baron, H., "Cicero and the Roman Civic Spirit in the Middle Ages and the Early Renaissance," *Bulletin of the John Rylands Library*, Manchester, XXII (1938), 3–28.

Barrett, Helen M., *Boethius: Some Aspects of his Times and Works* (Cambridge: University Press, 1940).

Baynes, N. H., "Constantine the Great and the Christian Church," *Proc. Brit. Acad.* XV (1929).

Buchan, John, *Augustus* (London: Hodder and Stoughton, 1937).

Cappuyns, Dom M., *Jean Scot Erigene* (Louvain and Paris, 1933).

Conklin, E. G., "What is Man?" *Rice Institute Lectures* (Rice Institute Pamphlet XXVIII [1941], 153–281).

Dickinson, John, *The Statesman's Book of John of Salisbury* (selections from the *Policraticus* with an introduction). Political Science Classics, ed. L. Rogers (New York: Knopf, 1927).

Donnelly, F. P., S.J., *Principles of Jesuit Education in Practice* (New York: Kenedy, 1934).

Duckett, Eleanor S., *The Gateway to the Middle Ages* (New York: Macmillan, 1938).

Duff, J. W., *A Literary History of Rome* (London: T. Fisher Unwin, 1920).

Eliot, T. S., *The Classics and the Man of Letters*, The Presidential Address delivered to the Classication on April 15, 1942 (Oxford University Press, 1942).

Finley, J. H., *Thucydides* (Cambridge, Mass.: Harvard University Press, 1942).

Frank, Tenney, *A History of Rome* (New York: Henry Holt, 1923).

—— *Life and Literature in the Roman Republic* (Sather Classical Lectures, VII; Univ. of Calif. Press, 1930).

—— *Vergil: A Biography* (New York: H. Holt, 1922).

Gilson, E., *Dante et la Philosophie*, Études de Philosophie Medievale, ed. Gilson, XVIII (Paris: Vrin, 1939).

—— *Les Idées et Les Lettres* (Paris: Vrin, 1932).

Glover, T. R., "Polybius," *Cambridge Ancient History*, VIII (1930), 1–24.

Grandgent, C. H., *Dante* (Master Spirits of Literature, ed. G. R. Noyes and W. M. Hart; New York: Duffield, rev. ed. 1921).

Greene, William Chase, *The Achievement of Rome, a Chapter in Civilization* (Harvard University Press, 1933).

—— "The Spirit of Comedy in Plato," *Harv. Stud. Class. Philol.* XXXI (1920) 63–123.

Hammond, Mason, *The Augustan Principate in Theory and Practice during the Julio-Claudian Period* (Harvard University Press, 1933).

—— "Hellenistic Influences on the Structure of the Augustan Principate," *Memoirs of the American Academy in Rome* XVII (1940).

Hirzel, R., *Der Dialog, ein literarhistorischer Versuch* (Leipzig: S. Hirzel, 1899).

Howard, A. A., "Livy and Valerius Antias," *Harv. Stud. Class. Philol.* XVII (1906) 161–182.

Jaeger, W., *Paideia: The Ideals of Greek Culture,* translated from the Second German Edition [*Paideia: die Formung des griechischen Menschen,* Berlin und Leipzig: Walter de Gruyter & Co., 1936] (New York: Oxford University Press, 1939).

Ladner, G. B., "Origin and Significance of the Byzantine Iconoclastic Controversy," *Mediaeval Studies* (Pontifical Institute of Mediaeval Studies, Toronto, Canada), II (1940), 127–149.

Lafaye, G., *Les Métamorphoses d'Ovide et leurs modèles Grecs* (Université de Paris, Bibliothèque de la Faculté des Lettres, XIV; Paris, Félix Alcan, 1904).

Klingner, F., *De Boethii Consolatione,* Philol. Untersuchungen her. v. Kiessling u. von Wilamowitz-Moellendorf, XXVII, 1921.

Krey, A. C., "William of Tyre," *Speculum* XVI (1941) 149–166.

Krumbacher, K., *Geschichte der byzantinischen litteratur,* 2nd ed. (Munich: Beck, 1897).

Mackail, J. W., *Latin Literature* (New York: Scribner, 1895).

Maritain, Jacques, *Humanisme Intégral; problèmes temporels et spirituels d'une nouvelle chrétienté* (Paris: Aubier, 1936).

Moore, Frank Gardner, *The Roman World* (Columbia University Press, 1936).

Nock, A. D., *St. Paul* (New York and London: Harper and Bros., 1938).

Moore, E., *Studies in Dante,* First Series (Oxford: Clarendon Press, 1896).

Norden, E., *Aus altromischen Priesterbüchern,* Acta reg. societatis humaniorum litterarum Lundensis, XXIX (Lund: Gleerup; Leipzig: Harrasowitz, 1939), reviewed by A. D. Nock, *Class. Phil.* XXXIX (1942) 88–89.

Palgrave, F. T., *Landscape in Poetry from Homer to Tennyson* (London: Macmillan, 1897).

Patch, H. R., *The Tradition of Boethius, A Study of his Importance in Medieval Culture* (New York: Oxford University Press, 1935).

Rand, E. K., "The Ancient Classics and the New Humanism," in *Going to College: A Symposium* (Oxford University Press, 1938).

—— "The Humanism of Cicero," *Proceedings of the American Philosophical Society*, LXXI (1932).

—— "The Latin Concordance of Dante and the Genuineness of Certain of his Latin Works," *Twenty-ninth Annual Report of the Dante Society* (Cambridge, Mass., 1910), pp. 7–38.

—— "How Much of the *Annotationes in Marcianum* is the Work of John the Scot?" *Trans. Amer. Philol. Assoc.* LXXI (1940) 501–502.

—— *Les Esprits Souverains dans la littérature Romaine* (Sorbonne Lectures; Paris: Boivin, 1936).

—— "The Latin Literature of the West from the Antonines to Constantine," *Cambridge Ancient History*, XII (1939), ch. xvii, pp. 571–783.

—— *Founders of the Middle Ages* (Lowell Lectures; Harvard University Press, 1929).

—— *Horace and the Spirit of Comedy* (The Rice Institute Pamphlet XXIV, 1937, No. 2 (193)).

—— "La Composition Rhétorique du Troisième Livre de Lucrèce," *Revue de Philologie* VIII (60ᵉ, 1934), 243–266.

—— "A Romantic Approach to the Middle Ages," *Mediaeval Studies* (Pontifical Institute of Mediaeval Studies, Toronto, Canada) III (1941), 1–14.

—— "Renaissance — Why Not?" *Renaissance* (L'École Libre des Hautes Études, New York), I (1942), 1–13.

—— *Ovid and His Influence*, Our Debt to Greece and Rome, ed. by Hadzsits and Robinson (Boston: Marshall Jones Co., 1925).

—— "Ovid and the Spirit of Metamorphosis," in *Harvard Essays on Classical Subjects*, ed. by H. W. Smyth (Boston: Houghton Mifflin, 1912).

—— "The Metamorphosis of Ovid in 'Le Roman de la Rose,'" *Studies in the History of Culture*, in honor of Waldo Gifford Leland (ed. by P. W. Long for the American Council of Learned Societies; Menasha: Banta Publ. Co., 1942), pp. 103–126.

—— "Notes on Ovid," *Trans. Amer. Philol. Assoc.* XXXV (1904), 128–147.

—— "Sur le *Pervigilium Veneris*," *Revue des Études Latines*, XII (1934), 85–95.

—— "Spirit and Plan of the *Pervigilium Veneris*," *Trans. Amer. Philol. Assoc.* LXV (1934) 1–12.

—— "On the History of the *De Vita Caesarum* of Suetonius in the Early Middle Ages," *Harv. Stud. Class. Philol.* XXXVII (1926) 43–48.

—— "The Art of Terence's *Eunuchus*," *Trans. Amer. Philol. Assoc.* LXIII (1932) 54–72.

—— *Texts and Translations for Latin Readings*, Supplementary Set, with a foreword and commentaries by E. K. Rand, to accompany an album of ten phonograph records prepared under the direction of F. C. Packard, Jr., Harvard Film Service, Cambridge, Mass., 1941.

—— *Studies in the Script of Tours. I. A Survey of the Manuscripts of Tours.* (The Mediaeval Academy of America; Harvard University Press, 1929).

—— *In Quest of Virgil's Birthplace* (Harvard University Press, 1930).

—— *The Magical Art of Virgil* (Harvard University Press, 1931).

Richter, Gisela M. A., *The Metropolitan Museum of Art, Handbook of the Etruscan Collection* (New York, 1940) reviewed by G. M. A. Hanfmann, *Amer. Journ. Archaeol.* XLV [1941] 487–489.

Ripert, E., *Ovide, Poète de l'Amour, des Dieux et de l'Exil* (Paris: A. Colin, 1921).

Rose, H. J., *A Handbook of Latin Literature from the Earliest Times to the Death of St. Augustine* (London: Methuen, 1936).

Rostovtzeff, M., *A History of the Ancient World. Vol. II. Rome.* Translated from the Russian by J. D. Duff (Oxford: Clarendon Press; corrected impression. 1928).

Rowell, H. T., "Vergil and the Forum of Augustus," *Amer. Journ. Philol.* LXII (1941) 261–276.

Santayana, G., *Poems* (New York: Scribner's, 1923).

—— *Poems. Selected by the Author and Revised* (New York: Scribner's, 1923).

—— *Realm of Spirit* (New York: Scribner's, 1940).

—— *Realms of Being* (New York: Scribner's, 1942).

Sarton, G., "Brave Busbecq," *Isis* XXXIII (1942) 557–575.

Schurr, P. Dr. Viktor, Css. R., *Die Trinitätslehre des Boethius in Lichte der 'skythischen Kontroversen* (Paderborn: Schöningh, 1935).

Showerman, Grant, *Eternal Rome, the City and its People from the Earliest Times to the Present Day* (New Haven: Yale University Press, 1924), appropriately dedicated to Franz Cumont and George Lincoln Hendrickson "et mihi et inter se amicis."

Silk, E. T., "Boethius's *Consolatio Philosophiae* as a Sequel to Augustine's *Dialogues* and *Soliloquia*," *The Harvard Theological Review* XXXII (1939) 19–39.

—— "The Yale 'Girdle-book' of Boethius," *Yale University Library Gazette*, XVII (1942), 1–5.

Sorokin, P. A., *The Crisis of Our Age* (New York: Dutton, 1941).

Streeter, Canon B. H., "The Rise of Christianity," *Camb. Anc. Hist.* XI (1936) 253–293.

Taylor, Henry Osborn, *Fact: the Romance of Mind* (New York: Macmillan, 1932).

—— *The Mediaeval Mind: A History of the development of Thought and Emotion in the Middle Ages.* 2 vols. (London: Macmillan, 1911; 4th ed., 1925, reprinted 1938).

Taylor, Lily R., *The Divinity of the Roman Emperor* (Philol. Monographs publ. by the Amer. Philol. Assoc. I, Middletown, Conn., 1931).

Temple, William, Archbishop of Canterbury, *Christianity and Social Order* (New York: Penguin Books, 1942).

Traube, L., "Regula Benedicti," *Abhand. der königl. bayer. Akad. der Wiss., philosoph., philolog. u. hist. Klasse,* XXI (1898), 2d ed. by H. Plenkers, *ibid.* XXV (1910).

Vasiliev, A. A., *Histoire de l'Empire Byzantin,* traduit du russe par P. Brodin et A. Bourguina, préface de Charles Diel. 2 vols. (Paris: Picard, 1932).

Waddell, Helen, translator, *A French Soldier Speaks,* by Jacques (London: Constable, 1941).

—— *The Wandering Scholars* (Boston and New York: Houghton Mifflin, 1927).

—— *Mediaeval Latin Lyrics* (New York: Richard R. Smith, 1930).

—— *The Desert Fathers* (New York: Henry Holt and Co., 1936).

Walsh, G. G., S.J., "Dante as a Medieval Humanist," *Thought* XIV (1939), 384–400.

—— *Medieval Humanism* (New York: Macmillan, 1942).

Wilkins, E. H., "Methods of Making a Concordance," *Twenty-ninth Annual Report of the Dante Society* (Cambridge, Mass.), 1910, pp. 1–5.

de Wulf, M., *Histoire de la Philosophie Médiévale* (6th ed., Louvain and Paris, 1934).

Ziegler, A. K., "Pope Gelasius I and his Teaching on the Relation of Church and State," *The Catholic Historical Review*, XXVII (1942), 3–28.

Zinsser, Hans, *Rats, Lice and History* (Boston: Little, Brown, 1935).

# INDEX

# INDEX

Achaean League, hostages from, 5 ff., 18; democratic principles of, 6, 12.

Acclamations, in ancient Rome, 230; in Constantinople, 230 f.; in the western church, 231.

Acquaviva, Claudius, head of Jesuit Order and author of *Ratio Studiorum*, 264 f.

Adler, Ada, 212.

Adoptionism, imperial, 171 f.

Aemilius Paulus, Lucius, victor over King Philip at Pydna, 5; meeting with Polybius, 7; dies poor, 14; *Adelphi* at his funeral games, 110.

Aeneas, his founding of Rome, 3 f.; *see* Augustus.

*Aetas Ciceroniana*, 202; *Horatiana*, 247; *Ovidiana*, 129, 247; *Vergiliana*, 247.

Aetolian League, 6 ff., 14.

Agrippa, 123.

Alaric, 202.

Alcuin, influenced by Boethius, 242; chief agent in Charlemagne's reforms, 244; probable author of Charlemagne's Capitulary, *De Litteris Colendis*, 245; script of Tours, 245 f.

Alexander, 6.

Alexander, P. J., 223.

Alföldi, A., 174 ff., 214.

Allegorical interpretation, in Lactantius, 197 ff.; in John the Scot, 199; in Dante, 199, 248; *Aeneid* allegorized by Bernard Sylvestris of Tours, 248.

Ammianus Marcellinus, 205.

Ananias, 183; *see* Communism, Early Christian.

Anaxagoras, 28.

Ancient ethics through the ages, 268 f.

Anderson, W. B., 54.

Antoninus Pius, Marcus, Gibbon's estimate, 171 f., 177.

Antonius, the orator, 8.

Apollo of Veii, 216.

Apollodorus, 111 f.

Apologetes, 185 ff.; interpretation of the ancient authors inferior to Dante's, 248.

Appian, 157.

Apuleius, quotations from Ennius, 31; style described by Pater, 150 f.; bilingual, in prose and poetry, 213.

*Ara Pacis*, importance for Horace's *Secular Hymn*, 216.

Arabian science, studied by Gerbert, 261.

Aratus, 22.

Archimedes, 28.

Aristophanes, one of the elect of George Meredith, 110.

Aristotle, relation to Polybius, 10; admired by Cicero next to Plato, 20; on laughter, 98; persons of comedy worse than those in real life, 108 f.; *see also* Boethius; Dante.

Arnobius, *Adversus Nationes*, 187; unorthodox theology, 187 f.; praise of ancients, 188; ridicule of mythology, 189; progress in religion and science, 189 ff.; Lucretius's influence on, 187, 189 ff.; reconciliation of religion and science, 191; "pessimist and sceptic," 190 f.; satirical powers, 191; teacher of Lactantius, 191; use of Plato, 188, 191; of Cicero, Varro, 188.

Arnold, Matthew, high seriousness, 81; the grand style, 88.

Art, importance for understanding of literature, 216.

Art, Roman: Apollo of Veii, monuments at Villa di Giulia, *Ara Pacis*, 216; portrait busts, buildings, Trophy of Augustus at La Turbie, monuments of public and private life, 217.

Art, Byzantine, 217 ff.; mosaics at St. Sophia, 217; eyes, romantic expression, mystic awe, 218; majesty of Saints and Emperors, 218; in Morgan manuscripts, 218 f.; monuments at Dumbarton Oaks, 219; after the fall of Byzantium survives in Bulgaria, Serbia, Russia, 219 f.; low level in 7th century, 222; effect of Iconoclasm, 223 f.

Athens, 6, 22.

Augustine, St., *De Civitate Dei*, 181, 202 ff., structure and relation to Lactantius, 203; *Confessions*, 202; poet of the Church, 203; Platonic mind, 203; *City of God* not a "philosophy of history," 203; use of pagan authors, esp. Varro, Sallust, Virgil, Cicero, 204 ff.; preserves fragments of *De Re Publica*, 204; influence of that work on his thought, 205 ff.; Ciceronian dialogues, 205; on deification of Romulus, 206 f.; shatters eponymous foundations, 207; preserves Ennius's "oracle," 207; praises Scipio Minor, 208; on prescribed Greek, 235 f.; Roman poets used in his vision of the ideal Rome, 235 f.; especial use of Virgil, 237; no Caesaropapism, 236; Constantine as sole Augustus, 236; Roman *mores* in the City of God, 236 f.; Plato praised, 237; his death, 237; influence on Charlemagne, 244; a guide to Dante, 248 f.; his progress described by Dante, 281; the eternal Rome, 255; *De Trinitate* translated into Greek by Maximus Planudes, 235.

Augustus, dream and fulfilment of ideal empire, 50 ff.; resemblance to Numa (Livy), 49, to Pericles, 79; contrasted with Caesar, 50; Caesar's avenger, 74 f.; relation of career to Virgil and Horace, 74 ff.; not at first a hero to Virgil, 76; Virgil and Horace his counsellors, 66, 77; sincerity, 78; Republican element in his new empire, 78; influence of Plato, Polyb-

ius, and Cicero, 78 f.; interest in poetry, 79 f.; fond of banter, 66; and of new jests, 107; disappointments in establishing the succession, 123 f.; conspiracies against him, 124 f.; *Res Gestae*, 143; noble death, 144.

Aurelius Antoninus, Marcus, pupil of Fronto, 8; Italian warmth, 148; love for Fronto, 148 ff.; order of his day, 152 f.; training in rhetoric, 153 f.; in philosophy, 154; fond of Cicero, 154; turns to mystic Stoicism, 154; admires the regicide Brutus, 158; Gibbon's estimate, 171 f.; bilingual, 214; death, 154.

Averroes, used by Dante, 251.

Bainville, Jacques de, 38.

Banquet of the wits, 138.

Baron, H., 247.

Basil, 221.

*basium*, 84.

Barlow, C. W., 167.

Baur, F. C., 184.

Baynes, N. H., 177, 180, 191, 198, 200 f., 214.

Beare, W., 100.

Benedict, St., anniversary, 243; *Regula* revised by Charlemagne, 244; his Latin style, 245.

Beowulf, 257.

Bernard Sylvestris of Tours, allegorical interpretation of the *Aeneid*, 248.

*Bible*, its lessening significance as the authority of Protestantism, 265 f.

Bilingualism in the Roman Empire, 212 ff.

Biocracy, 47.

Black, N. H., 29.

Blake, R. P., *Preface*.

Bobbio Monastery, 18, 148.

Boethius, on laughter, 98; career resembling Cicero's, 237 ff.; hardly guilty of treasonable negotiations with Constantinople, 238; monarchistic in sentiment, but no Ideal Empire in his time, 238; for him it is the City of God, 238 f.; plan to reconcile Plato and Aristotle,

239; effected in *Consolatio*, 242; Christian philosopher and scholastic theologian, 239 f.; Christian martyr (?), 239; the poetry of, and in, his *Consolatio*, 240; perfect Christian humanist, 241; reader of Theocritus and Virgil, 241; philosophical import of the seven arts, 241; influence on mediaeval philosophy, 242 f.; girdle-book, 243; illustrated manuscripts of Jean de Meun's translation of *Consolatio*, 243; *Consolatio* translated into Greek by Maximus Planudes, 235; the *Consolatio* in spires Dante, 248.

Bonner, C., 205.

Botticelli, 218.

Boyden, A., 35.

Brutus, *De Virtute*, 158.

Bryce, J., *American Commonwealth*, 9.

Buchan, John, on Augustus, 50, 55, 69, 73 f., 76, 78 f., 123 f., 131 f., 138, 159.

Bury, J. B., 72

Busbecq, A. G., 143 f.

Byzantine history: beginning and end of the period, 215 f., 219; outgrowth of Eastern Christianity, 215; Byzantine civilization, misconceptions of, 215, 220; sketch of Byzantine history, 220 ff.; Isaurian dynasty, Iconoclasm, 222 ff.; Macedonian dynasty, 224; Constantine VII Porphyrogenitus, 225 ff.; Comneni, 225; capture of Constantinople by the Crusaders in 1204, 225; by the Turks in 1453, 225; neglect of Latin literature, by Constantine VII Porphyrogenitus, by Photius, by Suidas, 234; Latin literature revived during Crusades, William of Tyre, 234 f.; Maximus Planudes, his corpus of translations, 235; popular Greek literature discouraged, Greek classics preserved, 256, and restored to the West in Renaissance, 262. *See also* Art, Byzantine.

Cabrol, F., 246.

Caesar, Julius, anthology of witty sayings, 107; praised by Fronto, 156; *Gallic War*, translated by Maximus Planudes; quoted, 141.

Caesaropapism, at Constantinople, 223, 225, 229; *see also* Art, Byzantine; New Rome.

Calvus, 157.

Campbell, A. Y., 77.

Can Grande, 248.

Cannon, Walter B., 47.

Canuleius, a type of the progressive, 44 f.

Cappuyns, M., 224, 238.

Carneades the Academic, effect on young Romans, 17; criticized by Lactantius, 195.

Carthage, 13.

Casimir, P., 217.

Cassiodorus, praises the moderns (*moderni*), much as we, 233; edition of Mynors, 233, 245; treated by Miss Duckett, 243; influence on Charlemagne, 245, 264.

Catholic Church, as Ideal Empire, 257 ff.; martyrs, 258; Latin language as its bond, 258 f.; the Mass, and its music, 259 f.; as goal of liberal education, 260; during Renaissance, 263 f.; survives both Renaissance and Reformation, 264; Order of St. Benedict and Society of Jesus, 264 f.; last refuge of religion in education, 266 f.; Church militant, 271; Christianity, modern attempts at union of denominations, 278; a guide to Eternal Rome, 281 f. *See also* New Rome.

Catholic Sunday and Roman funerals, 110; worship and jollity in Constantinople, 231.

Cato the Censor, conservative, 17, 101; wit, 18, 101 f.; friendship with Polybius, 23 ff., with the younger Scipio, 24 f.; studied by Fronto and M. Aurelius, 154 ff.; *bon mot* on women, 101.

Cato, "Dionysius," *Moralia*, translated into Greek by Maximus Planudes, 235.

Catullus, high seriousness, 82 f.; as love-poet a peer for Sappho, 127;

his a disastrous love, 132; read by Marcus Aurelius, 152.

Chamberlin, H. H., 91.

*Chanson de Roland*, 257.

Charlemagne, Emperor of New Rome, 243; no Caesaropapism, 243; fidelity to the Pope, 243; not affected by decretals of Constantine, 243; plans to marry Irene and absorb the Eastern Empire, 243 f.; an *alter Constantinus*, whom Augustine approved, 244; admirer of St. Augustine, 244; reform of text of Scriptures, Sacramentary, Rule of St. Benedict, 244 f.; a renaissance of the ancient authors and ancient forms of script, 245 f., 256; imitation of Augustus, 246 f.

Chatelain, E., 40.

Chaucer, his Lucrece compared with Livy, Ovid, and Shakespeare, 42; Chaunticleer quotes *Somnium Scipionis*, 96; shows Horace's and Ovid's art of banter, 129.

Chosroes I of Persia, entertains the exiled philosophers, 215.

Christianity, takes over ideals of antiquity, 186 ff.; Heavenly City as ideal state, 181 f.; no prescription for government, 181 f., for social or economic scheme, 182 f.; failure of communism, 183; conception of slavery, 183 ff.; reconciliation of pagan with Christian ideals, 186 ff., 195 ff.; the strength of its appeal to pagans, 190; Christian humanism, 196 ff., 241 ff.; defense of the new faith by St. Augustine, 202 ff.; conversion of Constantine, 214 f. *See also* City of God; New Rome.

Christina, Queen of Sweden, her robe torn in pieces for souvenirs, 230.

Church and State: "Render unto Caesar," 181 f.; religion above the state, 182; so in Caesaropapistic Byzantium, 229; but the Emperor is above the Patriarch, 229; no Caesaropapism in West, 243; forged decretals of Constantine and temporal power of Pope, 243;

Gelasius, harmony of Church and State, 244; Dante's harmony of the two, 249 f.; he condemns the "Donation" of Constantinople, 250. *See also* Christianity; New Empire.

Cicero, an independent thinker, 19; influence of Plato, 19 f.; conference at Smyrna with Rutilius, 20 f.; his debt to Ennius, and *vice versa*, 31; poetical qualities, 31; a poet in prose, 96 ff.; preserves more quotations of Ennius than any other ancient author, 31 ff.; dramatic sense, 36; his tragic death, 36 f.; on the Decline and Fall of the Roman Republic, 38; a statesman-historian, 39; a liberal conservative, 46; defender of the Republic, 61; renowned as a wit, 105 ff.; satire on Pompey, 106; laughter and banter, 113; on Laelius and Scipio, 153; on rhetoric and philosophy, 154; interest in Ennius, Gracchus, and other ancients, 155; poet of Roman Platonism, 203; meagre fame in Byzantium, 234; *De Re Publica*: 18 ff.; a mirror of the culture in Scipio's day, 18, 26 ff.; Bobbio palimpsest, 18 f.; a monument to Cicero's humanism, 19; relation to Plato, 19 f.; setting of the dialogue not wholly imaginary, 20 f.; divine art of building, 4 f.; ideal state that of Polybius, 21 ff.; principle of *concordia*, 21; the ideal state manifest in Roman history, 23; this idea of Polybius also set forth by Cato, 23 f.; on Lycurgus, 25; mirror of the prince (Numa), 25 f.; *Somnium Scipionis*, 18; poetic quality, 96 ff.; view from on high, 97; despite of fame, 97 f.; musical and liturgical Latin, 97; "mediaeval" spirit, 97; compared to Dante, 98; vogue in the Middle Ages, 96; translated into Greek by Maximus Planudes, 235; inspires Dante, 248; *De Oratore*, a monument of humanism, 19; *Tusc. Disp.*, on Panaetius's adoration of Plato, 17; Book I compared with

Seneca and Augustine, 167; *De Amicitia*, inspires Dante, 248; *Leges*, sequel to *De Re Publica*, 19. *See also* Fronto; Arnobius; Lactantius; Augustine; *Aetas Ciceroniana*.

Circles in society, cause of tragedies, 37.

City of God, anticipations in Lucretius, 94 f., 237; in Cicero, 96 ff., 208; in Virgil, 85 f., 121; in Ovid, 142, 237; Roman poets contribute to Augustine's vision, 236; Roman *mores* part of this foundation, 236 f.; St. Paul and St. John, 181; Cyprian, 187; Lactantius, 201; Augustine, the two Cities contrasted, 203 ff.; the Heavenly founded by Christ, the Earthly by Romulus, 207; the Heavenly in Boethius, 238 ff.; harmony of the two Cities, in Dante, 249 f.; he completes the Ideal Empire of Virgil, 252. *See also* St. Augustine; Ideal Empire; New Rome; *Preface*.

Clark, J. W., 243.

Classless society, its injustice, 22.

Claudius II, a paragon, 177; assumed ancestor of Constantine, 192.

Clement VII, Pope, and humanistic friend of Sannazaro, 264.

Closed-door serenade, in Horace, 128 ff.; in Tibullus, 129; in Ovid, 134 ff.

Cochrane, C. N., 208.

Collier, C. S., 266.

Comedy: laughter a human characteristic, 98; not a characteristic of some Romans, 98 f.; proletariat humor, 100; homespun wit of Cato, 101 f.; Italian humor, 102 f.; Broadway humor of Naevius, 103 ff.; *bons mots* recorded by Macrobius, Plautus, Cicero, Augustus, Hannibal, *et al.*, 105 ff.; high comedy, Terence, 108 ff.; comedy at funerals, 110; Greek New Comedy, 110 ff.; rollicking comedy, Plautus, 111; *contaminatio*, 112; Horace, an example for Meredith, 112 f.; training of the Romans in laughter, 114. *See*

*also* Aristotle; Terence; Horace; Ovid.

Commodus, gladiator-king, 173.

Communism, Early Christian, *see* Ananias.

Conant, J. B., on liberal education, 266.

Concordances, value of, 249.

Conklin, E. G., the wonder of the natural (Lucretius), 93.

Constantine the Great, compared to Augustus, 192; sincerity of his Christianity, 200; fulfils prophecy of Julius Caesar, 214; regarded Byzantium as a new Rome, 214; received title of Augustus, 214; conversion, 214 f.; *labarum*, 214 f.; tombs of Constantine and Helen, 229; his "Donation" to Pope Sylvester attacked by Dante, 251; *see also* New Rome.

Constantine III, stops the Arabs, 221 f.; the Bulgars, 222.

Constantine V Copronymus, 229.

Constantine VII Porphyrogenitus, preserves extracts from Polybius, 9; *Excerpta Historica*, 225 ff.; educational value of this work, 226 f.; the twenty-seven Pagan and Christian authors excerpted, 227; mirror of the prince, 227 f.; totalitarianism, 228; *De Caerimoniis*, its national significance, 228 f.; splendor of religious services, 229 ff.; other functions, 230 f.; clipping of prince's locks, 230; acclamations, 230; games, 231; Greens and Blues, 231; feasts, 231; reception of ambassadors, 231 f.; especial homage to Pope of Rome, 232; courtesies to other nations, 232.

Conway, R. S., 51, 77.

Cook, A. B., 214.

Cooper, L., on Boethius, 240.

Corinna, Ovid's mythical, and modern, heroine, 133.

Coulton, G. G., 262 f.

Counter-reformation, 264.

Cornutus, teacher of Persius, 8.

Crassus, L. Licinius, the orator, 8.

Crassus, who laughed once in his life, 99 ff.

Criticism, less valuable than understanding (Santayana and Quintilian), 179.

Critolaus the Peripatetic, 17.

Curtis, C. D., 216.

Cyprian, St., *De Catholicae Ecclesiae Unitate*, 187; silence on pagan authors, 197.

Dante, quotes Ennius (from Cicero), 32; vision of history, 204; mirror of the Middle Ages, 247 ff.; Christian humanism, 241 f., 248 f.; devotion to Virgil, 247 f.; his Christian *Aeneid*, 248; pagan and Christian sources of the *Commedia*, 248 f.; explanation of his allegory to Can Grande, 248; relation to Thomas Aquinas, 248 f.; Ideal Rome, New and Old, 249 f.; harmony of Virgil and Augustine, 250; a Christian philosopher, not a philosophic theologian, 249; *Monarchia* a later work, 249; use of Aristotle, Averroes, and the Roman poets for philosophical arguments, 249 f.; condemns "Donation" of Constantine, 250; political attitude like that of Gelasius, 250; attacks on Emperors and Popes, 251; his sense of humor, 251; his universe, 251 f.; completes the Ideal Empire of Virgil, 252; appeal to Henry VII as a new Augustus and Messiah, 256; the voice of Rome, with nothing of Greece, 262.

Dark Ages, in the West, 221; in the East, 222, 224; a background for individual brightness, 179, *Preface*.

Davis, Elmer, *bons mots* on Augustus, 79, and Tiberius, 159.

Deas, H. T., Housman and Horace, 90.

Decline and Fall, of Rome, observed by Polybius, 145; by Cicero, 146, 207; by Horace, 68; by Virgil, 56; by Livy, 146; by Fronto, 157 f., 204; by Tacitus, 159 f., 161 f., 164; seen relatively, 177 ff., 181; not obvious in the Second Century of the Empire, 214; observed by Lactantius, 201; his prophecy of the fall of Rome, 201 f.; the fall, the capture of the City, 202; decline hard to define, 145 f.; decline relatively unimportant in a history of ideals or a timeless view of history, 178 f., *Preface*; Rome alive after its fall. *See also* Augustine; Rutilius Namatianus.

Deification of heroes and kings, 55 f.; of Romulus, distinguished from that of Emperors (Augustine), 206.

Democracy, possibly good, but not the best form of government, 12; an ancient crusade for (?), 46. *See also* Government.

Demosthenes, *In Lacritum* quoted, 149.

De Witt, N., 52.

Dickinson, J., 247.

Dictators, literary, 165.

Diehl, C., 217 f.

Dollar bill, Virgilian inscriptions on, 176.

Diocletian, totalitarian government, 173; rehabilitation of, 180; the Persecution of 303 not by him (?), 191.

Diogenes the Stoic, 17.

Dionysius Areopagiticus, pseudonymic, but very influential on mediaeval thought, 224.

Domitian, 172, 178, 184.

Donatus, commentary on Terence, 84, 112, 193; life of Virgil (*see* Suetonius); shorter grammar translated into Greek by Maximus Planudes, 235.

Donnelly, F. P., 264.

Drusus, tragic loss of, Augustus's ideal successor, 123.

Dryden, estimate of Polybius, 7; of Tacitus, 173; translation of Virgil quoted, 3, 115.

Duckett, Eleanor S., on Boethius, 238 ff.; her *Gateway to the Middle Ages*, 240.

Duff, J. W., *Preface*, 41 f.

Dumas, Alexandre *fils*, *alter Terentius*, 100.

Edict of Tolerance, 313 A.D., 191.

Elective system in education, argu-

ments for, in Augustine, 235 f.;
the mediaeval sort, 261.

Eliot, T. S., poet of timelessness,
*The Dry Salvages*, 283.

*Elocutio novella*, 173; *see* Fronto.

Emerson, Ralph Waldo, on the perpetual rediscovery of Plutarch,
213.

Ennius, career, 30 f.; fragments saved
in Latin quotations, 31; poet of
Roman majesty, 31 f., 35; satire,
32; poem on natural science, 32;
dramatic Epicureanism, 32 f.;
translation of Euhemerus, 33;
views of the ideal state agree with
Polybius, 33 f.; description of a
humanist, 34 f.; his "oracle,"
which Augustine preserved, 207;
praised by Fronto, 156.

Epicharmus, used by Ennius in his
poem on natural science, 32.

Epictetus, ex-slave and philosopher,
184.

Epicureanism: Epicurus treated as a
divine deliverer by Lucretius, 56,
95; his philosophy turned into
high poetry by him, 92; meaning
of Epicureanism for the Roman
poets, 89 f.; Lucretian science in
Horace's satires, Lucretian poetry
in his odes, 89, 91; struggle of
Epicurean and Platonist in the
mind of Virgil, 118 f.; Epicurean
philosophy baptized by Arnobius,
with Christ for the deliverer,
187 f.

Epilogue, suggested readings, 284 f.

Erasmus, disciple of Horace, 113;
companion for the Goliards, 261.

Erskine, J., vulgarization of Helen of
Troy, 137.

Everett, William, 116 f.

Fact, a romance of the mind, 188 f.
*See* Ideals.

Fabius Maximus Cunctator, Q., 7.

Ferrero, G., Horace's propaganda for
vintners, 64.

Fielding, H., *Tom Jones*, Polybian
theories of the King of the Gypsies, 171 f.; the polluted mind of
the denouncer of pollution, 178;
"A Crust for Critics," 179.

Finley, J. H., Jr., his temple to
Thucydides, 10, 12, 43 f., 79.

Flaminius, speech at Peace Conference, 14 f.

Fletcher, J. B., Dante as a humanist,
242, 248 f.

Florus, his "philosophy of history,"
203 f.

Fortunatus, hymns still in use, 259 f.

France, Anatole, reads Virgil in
camp, 20; an Ovidian *manqué*,
137.

Frank, Tenney, *Preface*, 17, 30, 33,
37, 44, 48 ff., 52, 109, 111, 118.

Frazer, J. G., 126, 139.

Friendship, the rare and philosophic
sort, in Lucretius, and Boethius,
239. *See also* Virgil, Horace.

Fronto, condemnation of, 146; defense of, 146 ff.; as tutor to Marcus Aurelius and Verus, 8, 147 ff.;
correspondence, 148 ff.; a teacher
like Polybius, 148; *elocutio
novella*, 147, 150 f.; respected by
Gellius, Sidonius Apollinaris, and
Jerome, 147 f.; romantic devotion
to Marcus Aurelius, 148 ff.; his
style, 151; what drew him to Early
Republican literature, 151 f.; not
archaistic, 155; few quotations
from Ennius, 31; range of his
reading, 154 ff.; fond of Cicero,
154, 157; of Lucretius, Horace,
and Virgil, 156; distaste for
"Silver" literature, 156; republican revolution in literature, 156 f.;
not Neo-Atticist, 157; conception
of oratory that of Cicero and
Quintilian, 157; not anti-monarchical, 158; humanist, not pedant,
158; praise, and neglect, of Trajan, 171; indifference to Tacitus,
173; ridicule of Seneca, 173; view
of Roman history, 157, 204.

Fulgentius, allegorization of *Aeneid*
perhaps known to Dante, 248.

Gagé, J., 144.

Gallus, brother-poet of Virgil, 120;
poet of love, 128.

Galerius: he, not Diocletian, perhaps
ordered the persecution of the
Christians in A.D. 303, 191; 198.

Gallienus, rehabilitation of, 174 f., 180; *alter Augustus, restitutor orbis*, 174; biography by Trebellius Pollio, 175 f.; anecdotes about, 176.

Gelasius, the "Index" not solely his, 188; acclamation of, 231; authorship of "Gelasian" Sacramentary, 244; attitude on Church and State like Dante's, 244, 250.

Gellius, A., quotations from Ennius, 31, 34; respect for Fronto, 148; quoted, 156.

Genseric, 237.

Gerbert of Aurillac, from log cabin to Papacy, 260 f.; an imperial tutor, 260.

Gibbon, E., idea of decline and fall anticipated by Livy, 38; how to read Gibbon, 171; on the five good emperors, 171 f.

Gildersleeve, B. L., sonnet on Ovid in answer to Quintilian, 170.

Gilson, E., on mediaeval humanism, 242; on Dante, 249 f.

Giotto, 218.

Giraudoux, J., Ovidian quality, 137.

Glover, T. R., 7, 19, 52, 186.

Goelzer, H., 160.

Golden Age: in Livy, 49; in Virgil, 61, 121, 124, 163, 198; in Horace, 113, 132, 190; in Seneca, 190; in Tacitus, 163; in the Third Century, 176; in Lactantius, 198; in any black age, 178. *See also* Millennium.

Goliards, companions for Horace, Ovid, and Erasmus, 261.

Government, theories and practice, *see* Aristotle, Plato, Polybius, Thucydides, Cicero, Livy; the three good forms and their perversions, 11 ff.; the best form a combination of the three, 12; tyranny in the First Century, 159; Christian government, 181 f. *See* Christianity; Church and State; Ideal Empire; *Preface*.

Gracchi, Tiberius and Gaius, 37; condemned by Tacitus, 163.

Gracchus, C., studied by Fronto and M. Aurelius, 154 f.

Grandgent, C. H., 247.

Granger, F., 116.

Gray, John Chipman, humanist, 35.

Greek spirit, primarily creative, 4.

Greene, W. C., *Preface*.

Gregory I, the Great, Pope, whose *Pastoral Care* continues the ancient ethical lineage, 268.

Gregory of Nyssa, 221.

Gregory of Nazianzus, 221.

Guarino da Verona, 265.

Gummere, R. M., 166.

Hadrian, Emperor, contempt and benefactions for professors, 147; restores Pompey's tomb, 158; Gibbon's estimate, 171 f.; friend of Epictetus, 185; revival of Empire, 204; Graeco-Roman culture in his day, 212 ff.

Hadrian I, Pope, effect of his temporal power, 243.

Haines, C. R., 148, 156, 158.

Hammond, Mason, interpreter of Augustus, *Preface*, 50, 55, 73, 76, 78, 80, 123.

Hardy, Thomas, *Tess*, 161.

Haroun-al-Rashid, present of elephant to Charlemagne, 224.

Hegel, philosophy of history, 203.

Henderson, L. J., 7.

Hendrickson, G. L., 153, 158.

Henry II, at Canossa, 258.

Heraclius, stops the Persians, 221; tomb of Heraclius and Fabia, 229.

Herodes Atticus, friendly with Fronto, 157.

Herrick, Ovidian qualities, 134.

Highbarger, E. L., 117.

Hirzel, R., 19.

*Historia Augusta*, its historicity, 174 f.; acclamations in, 230.

History, meaning of, according to Santayana, 4; as treated by Plato, 10; literature its full flowering, *Preface*; speeches, 43 ff.; myth that becomes history, 40, (Aeneas) 58; legends in history, 42 f.; legend that becomes history, 47 f., 51; moral reading of, 49, 227; contributions of archaeology and linguistics, 30; pestilence and history, 154; cycles in history, 11;

prognostication of, 11 f.; cerebral cycles, 281; philosophy of, 203 ff., in Florus, 203 f.; *De Civitate Dei* a panorama, not a philosophy of history, 203; in Dante, 204; periods marked by ideals, not failures, 178 f., 181; history *sub specie aeternitatis*, 178. *See* Decline and Fall; Progress; Timelessness; *Preface*.

Hitler, Adolf, agreeing with Livy, 48; compared to Machiavelli, 48; on birth control, 70; ceremony at Coblentz, 230; his variety of Neo-Paganism, 269.

Homer, a model for Virgil, 3; his art of presenting character, 43 f.; *dulcissime vanus* to Augustine, 235; *Iliad* quoted, 88, 145.

Horace: son of a freedman, *ex humili potens*, 184; his independence, 65; tutor to Piso's sons, 8; political views, gradual appreciation of Augustus, 63 f.; a mirror of the prince, 65 ff., 73, 183; religion above the state, 16, 68, 182; Ideal Empire fulfilled, 51; *Carmen Saeculare* its symbol, 68 ff.; Aeneas as Augustus, 71; the *Carmen* and *Ara Pacis*, 71, 216; final expression of all aspects of Ideal Empire in Book IV of Odes, 72 ff.; his poetry, high seriousness, 86 ff.; "grand style," 88; sombre Epicureanism, 89 f.; relation of his Odes to Greek tragedy, 91; dithyrambic poet, 86 ff.; Italian element in his poetry, 102; master of the comic spirit, 102, 112; of banter, 112 f.; laughter at the third person in terms of the first, 113, 128, 131; mythologizes his own experience, 113; sets the Golden Age in the Sabine Farm, 113, 132; laughter a companion for seriousness, 113; light-hearted seriousness in love, 128, 132; satire of romantic lovers, 128 f.; his nymphs, 129 f., no better than they should be, 131; Horace's philosophy, 90 f.; supposed propaganda for vintners, 64; interest in early Republican writers, 155; relation to

Pindar, 86; to Lucretius, 91; intimacy with Virgil, 51; possible collaboration, 63; tribute to Virgil in *Carmen Saeculare*, 71; in Book IV, 74; fondness for younger poets, 133; tribute to Ovid, 133; praised by Ovid, 133; by Fronto, 156; used by Lactantius, 193; by Augustine, 236 f.; companion for the Goliards and Erasmus, 261; his jar of honey appreciated by the church, 268; quoted 13, 16, 131, 183, (over two Harvard gates) 132.

Housman, A. E., relation of his poetry to Horace's *Diffugere nives*, 89 f., to Lucan, 90.

Humanism, Roman, in the Republic, 26 ff.; in the age of Augustus (*see* Virgil, Horace); in Tacitus, 159; its nature (Jaeger), 210; in Terence, 242.

Humanism, Christian, Minucius Felix, 186 f.; Lactantius, 191; Virgilian Christian epic, 200; Constantine VII Porphyrogenitus, 227 f.; a perfect form in Boethius, 241; in John of Salisbury, 261; in Dante, 241 f.; in the "Neo-Paganism" of the Renaissance, 263 f.; core of ancient ethics taken over by the Church, 268.

Humanists, Italian, exaggerated esteem of Cicero, 155; humanistic Popes, Nicholas V and Leo X, 263.

Iconoclasm, lasts over a century, 222 ff.; its significance, 222 f.; outgrowth of Caesaropapism? 223; effect on art, 223.

Ideal Empire, founded on Roman good government, 13 ff.; on political theories of Polybius, Aristotle, and Plato, 10 ff.; of Cicero, 21 ff.; of Livy, 40 f., 48 ff.; on idealization of the legendary past, 40, 51; on religion, 15 f., 25, 27; on humanism, 26 ff., 34 f.; on science, 28 f.; on poetry, 80 (Ennius, 31 ff.; Virgil, 59 ff.; Horace, 62 ff.); on high seriousness and the spirit of laughter, 114; on the achievements of Augustus, and his study of the past, 50; on the counsels of Maecenas, Virgil, and Horace, 50, 74 ff., 77, 79, 80; on the Golden Age, 121; Augustan empire ends in sublimity, 144; Ideal Empire not for Ovid, 126; decline in First Century, 159; return under Nerva and Trajan, 171; mirrored in Plutarch, 212; modern possibilities in the light of the ancients' achievements, 272 ff.; the new society, 274 f.; union all round, 275 f.; defence, 276; unification of the Church militant doubtful, 277 ff.; preservation of the classics, 279 f.; built in the heart as the Kingdom of God, 183. See Catholic Church; City of God; New Rome; Preface.

Ideals, often crystallized in legends, the only solid reality and true index of progress, 178. See Fact.

Irene, Iconophile, cruelty to her son, Constantine VI, 222; not averse to marriage proposal of Charlemagne, 224; purpose of Charlemagne, 243.

Isidore, St., quotes Naevius, 104.

Italian element in Roman literature, 102 ff.

Ivory Gate, various explanations, 115 ff.; symbol of Virgil's doubt, 125; exit for Roman love-poetry (?), 128; not for Horace's, 132; nor Ovid's, 138 f., 142; nor for Augustus, 144; it remains a mystery, 125.

Jaeger, Werner, Paideia, 27, 33, 80, 196, 210 f.

Jerome, St., praise of Fronto, 148; on Arnobius, 188; Chronicles (Eusebius), 204; on the corruptions of the Church in his day, 263.

John of Damascus, St., opponent of Iconoclasm, 223.

John of Salisbury, defends Seneca against Quintilian, 171; genuine bits in the Institutio Traiani ascribed by him to Plutarch (?), 212; agreement with Plutarch in political doctrine, 212; praises the moderns (moderni) much as we (see Cassiodorus), 233; knowledge of Cicero, 247; concordia ordinum, 247; humanistic education, 261.

John the Scot, on Martianus Capella, 199; translation of Dionysius the Areopagite, Celestial Hierarchy, 224; philosophical import of the seven arts, 241.

John the Divine, St., his civitas Dei, 181.

Julia, daughter of Augustus, 123 f.; her sad career, 124; why rebellious, 131; had to marry Tiberius, 159.

Julian, Emperor, anti-Christian measures, 174; praised by the Christian Prudentius, 220, 229; his tomb in the Church of the Holy Apostles at Constantinople, 229.

Justinian I, banishment of philosophers in 529 A.D., 215; mosaic in St. Sophia, 217; as heir of Rome, 221; separation of Greece and Rome, 221; a Janus, 221; attitude toward the Pope of Rome, 221; tombs of Justinian and Theodora, 229.

Justinian II, Rhinotmetos, 222; desire to reconcile East and West, 222.

Juvenal, his sense of humor compared to Dante's, 251.

Juvencus and Christian epic, 200.

Klingner, F., on Boethius, 240.

Koehler, W., 219.

Krumbacher, K., 215, 227, 235.

Labarum, 214 f.

Lactantius, Divinae Institutiones, 191, 202; dedication to Constantine the Great, 192; style, and influence of Arnobius, 192; influence of pagan literature, 192 ff.; of Horace and Terence, 193; of Lucretius, 194; of Cicero, 194 ff.; fragments saved from De Re Publica, 194 ff.; Plato criticized, 195 f.; Carneades criticized, 195; Cicero criticized and admired, 196; unusual quotation from Cicero,

208; quotations from Ennius, 31; as a Christian humanist, 196 ff.; allegorical interpretation of the pagan works, 197 f.; Sibylline verses, 198; tutor to Crispus, 200 f.; perhaps suggested title of Augustus for Constantine, 214; description of the *labarum*, 214; probable author of Constantine's *Oratio ad Sanctos*, 200; one of the great teachers of Emperors, 200.

Ladner, G. B., 223.

Laelius, 153.

Lafaye, G., 135.

La Piana, G., 208.

Last, H., 254.

Latin language, as bond of Catholic Church, 258 f.; of international civilization, 260 f.; a mother-tongue to Pontano and Sannazaro, 263.

La Turbie, Trophy of Augustus at, 217. *See* Frontispiece.

Lednicki, W., 255.

Lesbia, 127, 131.

Liberal arts, fostered by Jesuit Order, 264 f.; lost from education with religion, 266; vital for the present times, 279 f.

Lindsay, W. L., edition of Terence, 193; on Traube's *Regula Benedicti*, 244.

Literature, *see* History.

Liturgy, Catholic Mass, elements of genius in its composition, 259; bits of Greek in it, 259; liturgy an orderly growth, 259 f.

Livia, beloved by Augustus, 132, 144.

Livingstone, R., 266.

Livius Andronicus, ex-slave, 108.

Livy: life, 29; qualities, 38; a liberal conservative, 46; Macaulay's opinion of, 39; *History*, 38 ff.; the lost decades, 39; sources, 41; agreement with Polybius in political theory, 46 f.; *concordia ordinum*, 12; on religion, 15 f.; his reverence for the past, 38; pessimism, 49; moral reading of history, 49; *fatum Romanum*, 42; attitude towards Augustus, 49; on conduct of war, 14 f.; mirror of the prince (Numa), 25, 49; treatment of

myth, 51; tragic treatment of history, 42 f.; speeches, to describe character, 43 f.; to dramatize an actual situation, 44 ff.; influence on Machiavelli, 48.

*Loquela digitorum*, 104.

Lowell, A. L., *Government of England*, 9.

Lowes, J. L., 69.

Loyola, Ignatius, founds the Jesuit Order, 264.

Lucan, *Bellum Civile*, an epic without a hero, 168; his genius, 168; confirms Polybius, 13; used as bait by Dante for Henry VII, 256; relation to Housman, 90; quoted, 270.

Lucilius, on Crassus, 99; member of Scipionic circle, 101.

Lucretius, his genius, 92 ff.; science and poetry, 28; the miracle of common sights, 93 f.; religious awe, 95 f.; Tennyson quoted, 95; nature of his pessimism, 122, 190 f.; praised by Fronto, 156; influence on Arnobius, 187, 190 f.; on Lactantius, 193 f.; on Virgil, 54, 118, 121; on Horace, 91 f.; his unique qualities, 93.

Luther might have waited, 264.

Lutz, Cora, 199.

Lycurgus, as inventor of ideal state, 12 f.; compared to Romulus, 25; commended by Tacitus, 162.

Mabillon, J., 264.

Macaulay, condemnation of Livy, 40; finds him useful for *Lays of Ancient Rome*, 41.

Macedon, 6.

Machiavelli, interpreter of Livy, 48; *Il Principe* of Constantine VII Porphyrogenitus, 227.

Mackail, J. W., *Preface*, 31, 52, 159, 213.

Macrobius, collection of Roman witticisms, 105 ff.; on Virgil, 122 f.; commentary on *Somnium Scipionis* translated into Greek by Maximus Planudes, 235; quoted, 99.

Maecenas, lover of poetry, 79; friend of Virgil and Horace, 53, 63, 65;

counsellor of Augustus, 66, 74, 77; his Gardens occupied by Fronto, 156.

Mai, Cardinal, discovers and edits Bobbio palimpsest of *De Re Publica*, 18 f., 28; Bobbio palimpsest of Fronto, 148.

Manuscripts, palimpsest of Cicero, *De Re Publica*, 18 f.; of Fronto, 148; Byzantine art in manuscripts of the Pierpont Morgan Library, 218 f.; Carolingian script, 245; School of Tours, 246; black-letter script, 246; musical notation, 259; illustrated manuscripts of Jean de Meun's translation of Boethius, *Consolatio*, 243.

Marcellus, 123 f.

Marini, C., 144.

Maritain, J., *Humanisme Intégrale*, 242.

Marius, condemned by Tacitus, 161.

Martial, *basium*, 84; *o tempora, o mores*, 177 f.

Martianus Capella, *Marriage of Mercury and Philology*, 199.

Marvell, Andrew, quoted for the "Grand Style," 89.

Mediaeval life, its lights and shades, high seriousness and jollity, 262; one advantage of knowing no Greek poetry, 262; mediaeval universities, the less learned students, 261; gay Goliards, 261 f.; mediaeval elective system, 261; mediaeval code of love, Ovid's influence of, 138; "mediaeval" a misnomer, not to be applied to the Byzantine period, 233; Μέγα πράγμα, 149.

Melpomene, Muse of Tragedy, rightly invoked by Horace, 91.

Menander, 110 f.

Menenius Agrippa, significance of his fable, 47 f.

Mercati, Giovane, Cardinal, edition of palimpsest of *De Re Publica*, 18 f.

Meredith, George, satire on masculine self-satisfaction, 102; his spirit of comedy, 107 ff.; "the poet's Lesbia," 127; on "the Classic scholar," 280.

Michael III, presents Pseudo-Dionysius to Louis the Pious, 224; 229.

Mierow, C. C., 247.

Millennium, in any age, 178. *See also* Golden Age.

Milton, Horatian sonnet, quoted, 27; his Latin compared with that of Pontano and Sannazaro, 264.

Minucius, Felix, Christian humanism in his *Octavius*, 186; his use of Virgil, 186.

Mirror of the Prince, in the Third Century of our era, 177; in Plutarch and John of Salisbury, 212; excerpts of Constantine VII Porphyrogenitus, 227. *See also* Cicero; Horace; Virgil.

*Modernus*, a term used before our day by John of Salisbury and Cassiodorus, 233.

Molière, Terentian element, *la grande affaire est le plaisir*, 109.

Monastic Orders: Order of St. Benedict, 243, 244 f., 264; Society of Jesus, 264 ff.

Moore, E., 248.

Moore, F. G., *Preface*.

Morison, S., 246.

Murphy, C. T., 63.

Mussolinus, B., 144; Ideal Empire, 269 f.

Mynors, R. A. B., 233.

Naevius, his national drama, 103; fragments of lively comedies, 103 f.

Nature, ancient feeling for, 87 f.; different in pastoral, epic and dithyrambic poetry, 88.

Neo-Attic movement, distinguished from Fronto's programme, 157.

Nero, 182.

Nerva, 171 f.

Neo-paganism, 263 f. *See* Christian Humanism.

New Rome, centred in Constantinople, 209, 233; its strength in Christianity and the East, 214; yet its citizens are called Romans, 'Ρωμαῖοι, 215; the Emperor heir of the divine Augustus and Vicegerent of God (Caesaropapism), 215, 223, 225; duration of the

Byzantine Empire 1000 years, 215; separation of East and West under Justinian I, but special homage to the Pope of Rome, 220; attempt at reconciliation under Justinian II, 222; still a confederate humanity in East and West, 224; Constantinople the seat of the Roman Church? 230; majestic ceremonies, 229 ff.; special homage to the Pope of Rome under Constantine VII Porphyrogenitus, 232; courteous relations with Moslems and other nations, 232; the Paris of the Middle Ages, 232; further rift between East and West (Photius and Nicholas I), 232; separatism in Augustine, 235 f.; no Caesaropapism in him; New Rome and the West under Charlemagne, 243; he an Emperor like Constantine and Theodosius, approved by Augustine, 244; Carolingian Renaissance as part of the New Rome, 224; a kind of Caesaropapism in Gregory VII, 258; none for Dante, Pope and Emperor distinct and both divinely ordained, 249 f.; Dante's New Rome completes the Ideal Empire of Virgil, 252; the "Holy Roman" Empire, 255 f.; development of vernacular literatures, 256 ff.; ancient Rome once more the centre, 257 ff.; efforts in the later Middle Ages to heal the schism of the Churches, 263; luxury and "Neo-paganism" of the Renaissance, 263 f. *See also Urbs Aeterna*; Catholic Church.

Niebuhr, on Cato's *Origines*, 24.

Nock, A. D., *Preface*, 56, 58, 90, 184, 185 f., 214 f., 257.

Norton, Charles Eliot, a light shining in the darkness, 178.

Novius, writer of Atellan plays, 153; studied by Marcus Aurelius, 153.

Numa, Ideal King, 25 ff., 41; prototype of Augustus (so Livy?), 49, 79, of Trajan, 171; law-maker (Tacitus), 162; paired with Lycurgus by Plutarch, 212; a model for Severus Alexander, 177.

Ochlocracy, 11.

Oldfather, W. A., 72.

O'Neill, Eugene, would domesticate Greek Fate in New England, 136.

Oratory, decline in the First Century of our era, 159 f.

Orrery, Pope's, 28.

Otho, Emperor, condemned by Tacitus, 161.

Otto of Freising, influence of Augustine, 247 f.; tendency to absorb the Earthly City in the Heavenly, 250.

Ovid, modern and realistic, 126; Horace's aptest pupil in wit, 132; *Amores* and the mythical world of Corinna, 133; tribute to Horace, 133; appreciated by Herrick, 134; satire on romantic lovers, 134 f.; witty indecencies, 135; serious relief, 135 ff.; French qualities, 135; tragic feeling, the *Medea*, 136; expert analysis of woman in *Heroides* and *Art of Love*, 136 ff.; wit, modernity and perfect art of the *Art of Love*, 137 f.; influence on mediaeval codes of gallantry and politeness, 138; mock *Remedies*, 138; *Metamorphoses*, an epic, 139; philosophy of transformation, 139 ff.; "Divine Comedies," 140; Shakespearian detachment, 140 f.; exile, 139, 141 f.; Getic poem, 141; brave death, 142; first of mediaeval dreamers, 142; unique genius, 143; *Metamorphoses* and *Heroides* translated into Greek by Maximus Planudes, 235.

Palgrave, F. T., his misunderstanding of Ovid, 142.

Panaetius, teacher of Scipio Minor, 17; admirer of Plato, 17, 20; intimate with Polybius, 22 ff.; possible source for *De Re Publica*, 30.

Panda (Pantica), aetiological goddess, 188.

Patch, H. R., on Boethius, 242.

Pater, W., false view of *elocutio novella*, 150 f.; good description of style of Apuleius, 151; date of *Pervigilium Veneris*, 213.

Paul, St., quotes Aratus in sermon to Athenians, 22, 186 f.; supposed correspondence with Seneca, 167; *civitas Dei*, 181; on government, 181 ff.; on slavery, 183 f.; question of the genuineness of his letters, 184.

Peebles, B. M., on St. Peter's burial-place, 258.

Persius, pupil of Cornutus, 8.

*Pervigilium Veneris*, in the spirit of Apuleius, 213.

Peter, St., monarchy honored, 182; the Rock of the Church, 257; martyrdom and burial-place, 257 f.; God no respecter of persons, 278.

Petronius, purpose of his *Satyricon*, 168 f.; Tacitus describes him, 168; on decline of oratory, 160; his varied genius, 168 f.

Phaedrus, ex-slave, fable of the Bat, 100 ff.; social prominence, 184; fable of the Dragon, 270 f.

Philip of Macedon, 5, 7, 14.

Philosophy of History, so-called, simple sort in Florus (Seneca?), 204; acutely criticized by Augustine, 203 f.; Dante repeats Florus, 204. See also History; *Preface*.

Photius, Patriarch and scholar, quarrel with Pope Nicholas, his neglect of Latin literature, 234.

Pierpont Morgan Library, The, Byzantine manuscripts in, 218 f.

Piso, sons of, taught by Horace, 8.

Pius XI, Pope, scholar and librarian, 277.

Planudes Maximus, translation of Latin authors into Greek, 235.

Plato, influence on Roman education, 23, 29; tragedy and comedy in the *Symposium*, 111; in Arnobius, 187 ff.; in Lactantius, 125 f.; poet of philosophy. 202; relation to Augustine, 203; reconciled with Aristotle by Boethius, 239, 242. See also Cicero: Panaetius; Polybius; Virgil.

Plautus, a commoner, 100; witticisms on women, 102; Italian characteristics, 102; renowned as a wit, 105; drama of action, originality, 111; *Aulularia* compared to *Phormio*, 111 f.

Plenkers, H., on *Regula Benedicti*, 244.

Pliny the Younger, 172, 230.

Plutarch, Graeco-Roman, 212; his *Parallel Lives* a mirror of the Ideal Empire, 212 f.; legend of his intimacy with Trajan, 212; political doctrine in *Lives* and *Moralia* is of the Polybian pattern, 212 f.; pairs Numa with Lycurgus, 212.

Poetry, Roman, high seriousness in, 81 f.; Catullus, 82, Virgil, 84, Horace, 86, Lucretius, 92, Cicero (*Somnium Scipionis*), 96; "Grand Style," 88 f.

Pollio, Asinius, a heroic figure for Virgil, 76.

Polybius, tutor of young Scipio and his brother, 7 f.; his *Histories*, 9 ff.; influence of Thucydides, 12; influence of Plato and Aristotle, 10; his scientific researches, 40; dislike of the tragic historians, 42 f.; philosophy of the state, 7, 10 ff.; cycles in government, 11 f.; political prognostication, 12; pro-Roman tendencies, 7, 9; Rome the ideal state, 12 ff.; Roman religion, 15; services to Rome, 16; the *Histories* useful as a background for the fragments of Roman literature in the third and second centuries B.C., 30, 36; his interest in earliest history of Rome, 25, 41; decay of Roman morals described, 132; influence on Cicero, 21 ff.; on Livy, 40 f.; on Augustus, through Cicero, Virgil and Horace, 78 f.; excerpts from his *Histories* made by Constantine VII Porphyrogenitus, 225 ff.; his work a military text-book in France (18th century), 226.

Pompey, Sampsiceramus, 106; condemned by Tacitus, 161, 163.

Ponsard, F., *Horace et Lydie*, 129.

Pontano, G. G., brother-poet of Sannazaro, 263.

Pope, *Dunciad* quoted, 68; his satire

compared to Cicero's, 106; Ivory
Gate, 118.
Porphyry, on laughter, 98.
Posidonius, on progress, 190.
Pride, Catholic doctrine of, in
Phaedrus, 100.
Problem play, modern, a failure in
art, 109.
Progress, idea of, held in ancient
Greece, 72; by Lucretius, 190; by
Cicero, 190; by Livy, 44 ff.; by
Horace, 72; by Arnobius, 190; by
Ambrose, 190; by Prudentius, 190;
not achieved by mechanical inven-
tions (Seneca), 190; only progress
possible that of the individual,
281. *See also* Decline and Fall;
Philosophy of History; Timeless-
ness; *Preface.*
Propertius, German romanticist, 128.
Protestantism, replaces Church by
Bible as authority, 265; individ-
ual interpretations breed dissen-
sion, 256 f. *See* Education, modern.
Prudentius, foremost Christian poet
in adapting Classical models,
200, 220; praises Julian the Apostate, 220, 229.
Punic Wars, 5, 13.
Pydna, battle of, 9, 14, 110.

Quintilian, as literary dictator and
educator, 169 ff.; quotations from
Ennius, 31; relation to Cicero,
170; on the decline of oratory,
160; conception of the orator that
of Cicero and Fronto, 157; finds
criticism less valuable than understanding, 179; estimate of Horace,
86; criticism of Ovid, answered by
Gildersleeve, 170; criticism of
Seneca, answered by John of Salisbury, 170 f.

Racine, quotation applied to Ter-
ence, 111.
Reade, W. H. V., 204.
Reiske, J. J., 228.
Reitzenstein, R., 28.
Renaissance, idea of, *see* Horace,
Virgil; in the Third Century of
our era, 174 ff.; of Greek authors
at Constantinople, end of 9th cen-

tury, 225 ff.; under Charlemagne,
245 ff.; proved by the script of
Tours, 246; and by the Humanistic script of the Italian Renaissance, 246; splendors and dark-
nesses of the Italian Renaissance,
262 ff.
Rendell, G. H., 186.
Ripert, E., 135.
Roads to Rome, *see* Epilogue.
Robinson, D. M., 144.
Robinson, F. N., 129.
Rogers, R. S., 107.
Rogers, Scott and Ward, 144.
Rolfe, J. C., 50, 66, 79.
Rome: a nation of builders, 4 f.;
spirit and genius primarily recep-
tive, 4; Republic, 5 ff.; conquests
in Greece, 5 ff.; in Asia Minor, 7;
*fatum Romanum*, 9, 42; as Polybius's ideal state, 12 ff.; nobility
of Roman character, 13 ff.; Menenius Agrippa and biocracy at,
47 f.; religious aspect of, 15; early
philosophy, 17 ff.; as Cicero's ideal
state, 23 ff.; Roman humanism,
26 ff.; influence of Platonic humanism on, 29 f.; public libraries,
152; Romans good teachers, 8 f.,
200; good business men, 98 ff.;
lack of humor, 99; progress in
the art of laughter, 114; concerted
applause (Nero), 230; acclamations, 230 f.; religion, early Roman, element of metamorphosis,
189; Saliarian feasts, 190; gods for
every time and place, 188 ff.;
nursery gods, 189; Roman married
life, 130 ff.; moral standards, 131;
disintegration of Ideal State, 36 ff.;
originality and high seriousness
in literature, 81 ff.; Roman literature compared with Greek, 210 ff.;
Roman love poets, 126 ff.; Greek
influence on Rome early, 211; Roman consultations of Delphi
(Livy), 211; merging of Greek
and Roman culture in Hadrian's
day, 211 ff. *See* Decline and Fall;
New Rome.
Roman Art, *see* Art, Roman.
*Roman de la Rose*, 287.
Romulus, in Cato, 24; hero-god, 34;

in Livy, 40; divine founder of Rome (Cicero and Augustine), 206.

Rose, H. J., *Preface*, 18, 30, 43, 146 f., 158.

Rostagni, A., 210.

Rostovtzeff, M. I., 171, 177, 180.

Rousseau, anticipated by Horace, 65.

Rutilius Namatianus, farewell to fallen Rome, 253; her immortality, 253 f.

Rutilius Rufus, P., 20 f.

Sacramentaries, Gelasian and Gregorian, 244.

Sage, E. T., 169.

Sallust, studied by Fronto and Marcus Aurelius, 154 ff.

Santayana, his definition of history, 4; better to understand the ancients than to criticize them, 179; value of poetry independent of chronology, 285; Christianity fundamentally new, 180; Church militant and Church triumphant, 279; on his philosophy, 282 f.; a philosopher and poet of timelessness, 283.

Sannazaro, Iacopo, imagination and humanism in his *De Partu Virginis*, 263 f.; banter with Pope Clement VII, 264.

Sarton, G., 143 f., 240, 265.

Satire in beast-fables, 100.

Saturnian verse, 103.

Schurr, V., new light on Boethius, 239.

Science a part of humanism, 28 f.

Scipio Africanus Major, on *otium* and *negotium*, 27; intimacy with Ennius, 34.

Scipio Africanus Minor, pupil of Polybius, 7; and of Panaetius, 17; the Scipionic circle, 18, 26; in Cicero's *De Re Publica*, 18, 20 ff.; respect for Cato, 24 f.; his oratiunculae, 153; moral integrity, 132; humanism, 26 ff.; it includes religion and science, 28; his death, 36; not an incipient tyrant, 37 f.; admired by Augustine, 208.

Sejanus, 100.

Seneca the Younger, quotations from Ennius, 31; career, 165 ff.; tragedies and dialogues, 166; "Silver Latin" style; criticized by Quintilian, 170 ff.; Christian thought in; 166 ff.; supposed correspondence with St. Paul, 167.

Septimius Severus, respected by Tertullian, 186.

Servius, 84, 118, 124; the inexplicable passages in the *Aeneid*, 125.

Servius Tullius, praised by Tacitus, 162.

Severus Alexander, a model for his subjects, like Numa, 177.

Shakespeare, *Lucrece* compared unfavorably with the versions of Livy and Ovid, 42; like Ovid, detached from circumstance, 140 f.

Shapley, H., 28.

Shelley, *Passage of the Apennines*, 88.

Sherwood, M. C., on Hitler and Machiavelli, 48.

Shorey, P., Plato and science, 28.

Showerman, G., *Preface*; 217.

Sibylline verses, in Lactantius, 198.

Sidonius Apollinaris, praises Fronto, 148.

Silk, E. T., Boethius and Augustine, 240; girdle-book of Boethius, 243.

"Silver Age," a misnomer, 172.

Slavery, Christian conception of, 183 f.; in antiquity, 184.

Slaves, Terence, Phaedrus, 100; Livius Andronicus, 108.

Solon, 162.

Spengler, O., 12, 203.

State, *see* Church.

Stewart, H. F., edition of Boethius, 238.

Stilo, L. Aelius, 35.

Strong, Eugénie, 217.

Suetonius, *Lives*, of Augustus, 50, 76, 78, 106, 124, 144; of Caesar, 67; of Nero, 230; of Virgil (in Donatus), 51, 52, 118; of Horace, 66; of Terence, 100, 112; bilingual, 212; imitated in the Third Century, 175.

Suidas, questionable statement about Plutarch, 212; his ignorance of Latin authors, 234.

Sulla, 38; condemned by Tacitus, 161; mildly praised by Tacitus, 163.

Tacitus, criticisms of, 160; *Dialogus de Oratoribus* a genuine work, 159; its true humanism, 159; appreciation of both ancient and modern, 159; views on government essentially those of Polybius, Cicero and Livy, 164; judgement of Tiberius, 159; judgements of Roman history, 161 ff.; a satirical judgement of mankind, 161; not a disgruntled republican, 162; not a "liberal," 164; a monarchist of the Augustan sort, 162, 164 f.; judgement of Petronius, 168; an impartial and final judge, 161, 172 f.; praised by Dryden, 173; quoted, 141.

Taylor, H. O., 188, 246, 247.

Taylor, Lily R., 56, 69, 217.

Tennyson, appreciation of Lucretius and Virgil, 95; on Virgil's doubtings, 122.

Terence, ex-slave, 100; master of high comedy in Meredith's sense, 108 ff.; use of conventional plots, 109; aim of comedy, as for Molière, is *le plaisir*, 109; comic irony, 109; misunderstandings, 109 f.; *Adelphi* and *Tom Jones*, 110; a drama of psychology, 111; *Phormio* compared to *Aulularia*, 111 f.; originality, 110 f.; quoted, 5, 131; quoted by Lactantius, 191.

Tertullian, commends Seneca, 167; homage to Septimius Severus, 186; renunciation of pagan culture, 197; bilingual, 213.

Theoderic, an Ostrogothic Roman, 237; an Arian, 239.

Thomas à Kempis, continues the ancient ethical lineage, 269.

Thomas Aquinas, St., poet and maker of liturgy, 260; dies on the way to the Council of Lyons, 263.

Thucydides, interpreted by Finley, 10; contemporary theories of government, 12; historical prognostication, 11 f.; tragedy and history, 43; speeches, 43 f.

Thuillier, Dom V., and Chevalier de Folard, edition of Polybius, 1727, 226

Tiberius, coolly praised by Horace, 73; Augustus's last resort for a successor, 124; deterioration in his character noted by Tacitus, 159; "wanted to be President and ended as Dictator," 159; had to marry Julia, 159.

Tibullus, a French romanticist, 128; *urbs aeterna*, 254.

Timelessness, an element of high poetry, 82, 84 ff., 87, 97 f.; timelessness of events more important to observe than their *milieu* or causal sequence, 178; an immediate road to Eternal Rome, 281 ff.; in the minds of the Desert Fathers (Waddell), 273, 297; poets of timelessness, Santayana, Eliot, 283. *See* City of God; *Urbs Aeterna*; Decline and Fall; Progress; *Preface*.

Totalitarianism, Constantine VII Porphyrogenitus, an expert in, 228.

Trajan, Ideal Empire returns, 171 f., 204; literature in his reign, 172 f.

Traube, L., on *Regula Benedicti*, 244; *aetas Vergiliana, Horatiana, Ovidiana*, 247.

Trebellius Pollio, 175 f.

Tuck, Edward, *Tropaea Augusti*, 217.

Twelve Tables, Laws of, in Livy, 48; question of Greek influence, 211; praised by Cicero, 155; the language of purists (Seneca), 155; the end of equitable legislation (Tacitus), 162, 164.

*Urbs Aeterna*: Ennius, 35, 57; Polybius, 254; Cicero, 196, 208, 254; Livy, 45, 254; Virgil, 57; Horace (implicit), 66 ff., 69 ff., 72 ff.; Tibullus, 254; Lactantius, 201; Augustine, 255; flights of the City from Rome to Constantinople, to Moscow, 255; shifting centres of the "Holy Roman" Empire in the West — Ravenna, Aix-la-Chapelle, uncertain domiciles in Germany, 255; all the while abiding in Rome, 257 f.; and there in the Renaissance, 262 f.; Eternal Rome of the present, 281; timelessness, 283. *See* City of God, Timelessness.

Van Buren, A. W., *Preface*.
Van Ummersen, H. F., 31.
Varro, quotations from Ennius, 31; on the gods of the nursery, 89.
Vasilieff, A. A., 220 ff., 244, 263.
Vatican, near the place of St. Peter's martyrdom, 258.
Virgil, birthplace, 51; development of his poetry, 51 f.; minor poems attributed to him, 51; *Culex*, 52 ff.; connection with later poems, 53; republican character of its inferno, 54; *Bucolics: Ecl.* IV, 63 f.; as a Christian allegory, Lactantius, 198; in Constantine's *Oratio ad Sanctos*, 200; used by Dante as bait for Henry VII, 256; *Ecl.* VI, 119 ff.; delicate humor, 120; his epic temperament, 52; his heroes, 55; *Georgics:* Golden Age in the happiness of rustic industry, 61, 121; vision of a celestial city, 121; Ivory Gate, 121; *Aeneid:* Homer its model, 3; character of the imitation of Homer, 61; as an allegory of Roman history, 3, 58 f.; development of his conception of the plot, 57 f.; Augustus suggested by Aeneas, 58 f.; a mirror of the Prince for Augustus, 61 f., 79; vision of Ideal Empire, 59 ff.; Ivory Gate, 117; influence of Plato, 117; the poet's instructions to burn the *Aeneid*, 122; Virgil supports Polybius's estimate of Roman character, 14 f.; interest in natural science, 28; intimacy with Horace, 63; high seriousness, 84 ff., 119 ff.; daring satire, 84 f.; Italian characteristics, 102 f.; an Epicurean? 118; his harmonization of incongruities, 120 ff.; his doubtings and sadness, 121 f.; doubts about Augustus (?) 123; Christian Virgilian epic, 200; contributions to Augustine's *City of God*, 236 f.; eclipse of his fame at Constantinople, 234. *See also* Horace; Minucius Felix; Lactantius; Augustine; Dante.
Vitellius, condemned by Tacitus, 161.
Vogt, A., 228.

Waddell, H., interpreter of Goliards and Desert Fathers, 261, 273, 297.
Walsh, G. G., Dante as a humanist, 241 f.
War among the ancients, 13 f.
Webb, C. C. J., 212, 233.
Whittemore, T., discoveries at Saint Sophia, 217.
Wilde, Oscar, on fiction in history, 41 f.
Wilkins, E. H., 249.
William of Tyre, well read in the Latin authors, 234 f.
Wölfflin, E., 84.
Women in France, wise, 102. *See* Cato.
Wordsworth, admiration for Horace, 87.
Wulf, M. de, on Boethius, 242.

Ziegler, A. K., 188, 244.